Born Brilliant

Also by Christopher Stevens

A Real Boy: How autism shattered our lives . . .
and made a family from the pieces (with Nicola Stevens)

Born Brilliant

The Life of Kenneth Williams

CHRISTOPHER STEVENS

JOHN MURRAY

First published in Great Britain in 2010 by John Murray (Publishers)
An Hachette UK Company

1

© Christopher Stevens 2010

A CIP catalogue record for this title is available from the British Library

Hardback ISBN 978-1-84854-195-5
Trade paperback ISBN 978-1-84854-196-2

Typeset in Bembo by Hewer Text UK Ltd, Edinburgh
Printed and bound by Clays Ltd, St Ives plc

John Murray policy is to use papers that are natural, renewable and recyclable products and
made from wood grown in sustainable forests. The logging and manufacturing processes
are expected to conform to the environmental regulations of the country of origin.

John Murray (Publishers)
338 Euston Road
London NW1 3BH

www.johnmurray.co.uk

For Nicky . . .
When I married you, I landed with my arse in the marmalade.

Contents

Camp is a tender feeling.

(Susan Sontag, *Notes on Camp*, 1964)

'I was more pleased than I ever dreamed I would be'

Kenneth Williams was 'brilliant, just brilliant', Bill Kerr said. 'I think he was born brilliant.' The Australian comic, who was Tony Hancock's childlike stooge in *Hancock's Half Hour*, was talking about Williams the entertainer – outstanding in every sphere, as a comic actor in films, in theatre, on radio, as a master raconteur on chat shows, a revue performer, a children's storyteller, a sparkling panellist on parlour games for TV and radio, a mesmerising reader of poetry.

That notion of innate genius, mysterious and unearned, is at the heart of my fascination with Williams. He was brilliant, an apparently limitless talent – but his career was contained within tight boundaries. He never made millions. He did not conquer Hollywood, nor Broadway, nor Vegas. He did not make TV spectaculars or dramas or sitcoms, though he appeared to be a gift for any of them. The greatest playwrights of the age – Orton, Pinter, Bolt – created roles for him, but his theatre work is largely forgotten. He could have straddled the world; instead, he lived all his adult life in a series of apartments along the Euston and Marylebone Road, and all of the buildings can be glimpsed by taking a 205 bus from St Pancras to Paddington station.

I have loved Kenneth Williams since my childhood. The first time I saw him was as the mad scientist in *Carry On Screaming*. The film made such a vivid impact that, when I remember the climactic, lunatic death scene, with Williams grappling an Egyptian mummy in a vat of acid as he shrieks, 'Frying tonight!' I still see it in black and white. To watch the film now on DVD, in colour, is as strange as watching a colourised print of a Chaplin movie. When I was seven, of course, we had a black-and-white telly.

I

Carry On Screaming showcased a marvellous cast, but Williams was the best of them. That much was clear, even to a child. I saw the phenomenon occur again when I discovered *Hancock*, and *Round the Horne*, and *Parkinson*, and even when I watched *Willo the Wisp* or adverts for toilet cleaner. When I acquired a craving for vintage *Just a Minute*, stimulated by an iPod and the internet, I heard it again: Kenneth Williams was king, and the other players acknowledged it and paid homage. At first I wanted to know where that colossal talent came from, and how it had developed. Later I wondered how he had prevented it from sweeping him to international stardom, and why.

There are books that a writer wants to read, and others that he wants to write. I was not sure which this would be, until Nicholas Parsons kindly agreed to be interviewed. His friendship with Williams spanned forty years, from their days together in rep at Bromley, to their long association on *Just a Minute*, and as he analysed Kenneth's career and his personality I started to see how deep his affection ran. At the end of the interview he told me, 'I miss him. I miss him very much,' and his eyes were brimming with tears.

Nothing I had read about Williams, including the extracts from his own letters and diaries, conveyed that sense of heartfelt love. The performances, though, were filled with it. He always looks and sounds like a man who revels in being loved. He demanded attention and created joy.

For all his attention and chat-show celebrity, Williams had a need for privacy, and it became quickly apparent that his closest friends continued to guard this private world after his death. The clearest insight into his personality off stage was provided by the compendium of diary extracts, 800 pages and 400,000 words, which had appeared in 1993. This book, *The Kenneth Williams Diaries*, expertly edited by the broadcaster Russell Davies, constituted between 10 and 15 per cent of the journals that Williams kept from the 1940s to his death in 1988.

The volumes themselves, forty-three of them, had been in storage and unseen for fifteen years: their guardian was a friend and former neighbour of Williams, and the technical director of Sadler's Wells, Paul Richardson. Encouraged by Nicholas Parsons's interview, and feeling that I could not attempt a biography of Williams without permission to quote from the diary extracts, I arranged to interview Paul. After we had talked for an hour, I asked him whether he would ever allow the journals to be read in full by a biographer. Paul answered that he might, if he was convinced that the writer was intent on mapping Kenneth Williams's life from every aspect, without sensationalism, and if he was assured that the privacy of Williams's friends who were still living would be respected.

That remit – to make the most thorough analysis possible, without indulging in spite or cheap headlines – was the best job description in the world. The perks were astonishing – not only the diaries themselves, spilling over with handwriting that was as diverse as his moods, but also a filing cabinet filled with the tightly typed carbons that Williams kept of his own letters; the boxes of correspondence from famous friends – from Burton and Olivier to Babs and Hattie; interviews with dozens of the greatest names in British comedy and theatre. What gave me most pleasure was the enthusiasm Williams's friends showed for the project, by helping in ways I would not have dared ask for. Fenella Fielding, for instance, asked Sandy Wilson to talk to me, and Sandy then arranged interviews with the surviving stars of *The Buccaneer*. Bill Kenwright put me in touch with Trevor Baxter and Michael Parkinson; Stanley Baxter permitted me to print one of his unpublished poems; Ray Galton and Alan Simpson lent me the scripts of all the lost radio episodes of *Hancock's Half Hour*; many others opened their address books, or picked up the phone to persuade friends, or delved into their photograph albums, and at every step I felt this was happening because Kenneth Williams still roused deep springs of affection in his friends.

Two of the closest in every sense, who had never spoken publicly about their fifteen-year friendship with Williams, were identified only as 'Tom' and 'Clive' in the published volumes, both of his diaries and of Joe Orton's. Once they, like Paul, were convinced that my intention was to write a true biography, their assistance was equally generous – not only did they sit for many hours of interviews, sharing their memories with complete frankness, but they made available their unseen archive of letters and photographs.

I cannot claim that I merited any of this help. It has been provided, by so many people, because of the intense regard and love they have for Kenneth Williams. They wanted to remind the world how much he meant to them, and their actions showed it more clearly than anything I could ever write.

During an episode of *Just a Minute* in 1978, Williams was challenged to talk about 'My Biographer'. He began, 'My biographer would need to be something of a genius, not to mention amanuensis, because he never mentions me . . .'

Something of a genius: I'm a long way from that, though I often muttered the words as I struggled to condense three diary extracts, a scurrilous couple of sentences from a letter and a shrewd quote from an interview into one paragraph. Mention him? I've talked of nothing else for two years. This book is the result of it all.

I

'Brushed over with false gaiety'
February 1926–February 1944

Kenneth Williams made an adorable baby, his impish face framed by the frills of a bonnet, with a monocle glinting in his left eye. That climactic shot in *Follow that Camel*, a vintage *Carry On* movie, is a sight gag – the heroine's infant son is the spitting image of Williams, the camp commandant who seduced her. The joke works in every way: predictably bawdy but still unexpected, it exaggerates and mocks the actor's character. The Williams of the *Carry Ons* was pompous, precocious and never more than one shriek away from a tantrum. He always was an overgrown baby, a big mummy's boy, and at the same time it was ridiculous to think he had once been three weeks old.

One portrait exists of the real Kenneth Williams as a baby. He is about one year old, seated on a bench in a photographer's studio, in bootees and a checked smock. His curling hair is golden and tousled. He looks, with his chubby arms and solemn face, like the apple of some doting mother's eye. And he was.

Kenneth Charles Williams was born on a Monday afternoon, at 2.30 p.m. on 22 February 1926, in a two-roomed apartment of a terraced house at 11 Bingfield Street, off the Caledonian Road, north of King's Cross. Two other families shared the house: 'It was a slum all right,' Williams wrote, fifty years later. 'The Calley' between the wars was the heart of London's poorest quarter. It was here, for instance, in 'the vague, brown-coloured slums to the north and east of [. . .] Saint Pancras Station', that George Orwell located *Nineteen Eighty-Four*'s proles. Bingfield Street's terraces have been pulled down, but similar houses survive, around the corner on the main road. Williams's father Charlie was at his birth, because Monday was early closing at the hairdresser's shop where he worked. He and Louisa Williams had been married for ten months, and this was his first child. It was Louisa's second.

Louisa was twenty-four, one of six children born to Henry Morgan and his wife Louisa Alexandra, née Hoare. Henry was a carman, driving a horse-drawn carriage. The Morgans lived in St Pancras at 9 Sandwich Street, in a broad little backstreet with a pub on the corner, the Norfolk Arms, and they were fairly well off: Louisa remembered a front parlour with mahogany furniture, upholstered in red leather. The family was happy when she was a small child. Her brother Sonny was the eldest, followed by sisters Edith, Rose and Alice. Louisa Alexandra was born on 20 December 1901; her sister Daisy was born soon after.

When Louisa was about four years old their mother died, and Henry Morgan turned for help with the children to another woman, Eliza Cod. She was a servant at a house in Bayswater, a strict, bullying woman, and the children hated her. She drank, and was so mean with their father's money that Alice nicknamed her Tin Lizzie. The name stuck. 'Tin was slang for money,' Louisa said, 'and she used to hoard hers.' Instead of butter, she bought the 'eightpenny roll' from the Maypole Dairy, which was half margarine. She made the children do chores – Louisa resented having to carry her stepmother's bag from King's Cross station, and said so: 'I told her I didn't like her and she shoved my head between the iron bars of the bed. I was stuck there till my brother Sonny came and released me.'

Louisa applied for a copy of her birth certificate as a work permit in 1915, which implies she left school at fourteen – a small woman, less than five feet tall, she might have needed proof she was as old as she claimed to be. She took a job washing and pressing clothes at Madame Louise's French laundry in Museum Street, Bloomsbury. Louisa was a natural actress and loved to tell stories, playing all the parts: in one of her favourites she and her friend Gladys had to wheel a wicker trolley of fresh laundry through the streets to the Hyde Park Hotel in Lancaster Gate. That was a long walk, the length of Oxford Street and more, and the girls took it in turns to ride on the trolley. One of the wheels came off while Gladys was aboard – a policeman came gallantly to their rescue, borrowing a hatpin from a flower-girl to fix the wheel back on to the axle.

On another occasion, Louisa was sent to the Oxford Music Hall to deliver laundry for Daisy Dormer who was famous for her version of

'After the Ball'. The star told the laundrymaid, 'How very nicely you pressed this linen, my dear. Would you like to be my dresser?' Louisa turned down the offer and all her life said she regretted it.

At twenty she fell in love with a man called Ted Scarfe, and they became engaged. Among their crowded families it was difficult for a young couple to find any privacy, and sharing a bed before they were married was unthinkable, but one hot July evening Louisa and Ted stole a few minutes together and had sex, standing up in the passage-way of the apartment block where Alice and her husband lived. Their wedding was only a few weeks away. The banns had been posted at Holy Trinity church in Cloudesley Square, Islington, but Ted Scarfe abandoned her when Louisa discovered she was pregnant.

Abortion was illegal, punishable by anything from three years to life imprisonment; in any case, Louisa could not have afforded to pay for a termination. She had no choice but to ask her family to help her. Henry Morgan had died and Louisa turned to her sisters, Edie and Alice. 'In those days, it was a disgrace. You'd get sent away somewhere,' said Alice's daughter, Joan Carlin. 'I can remember Auntie Lou saying to me, "When I told your father, Joanie, he smacked me round the face." My dad wouldn't hurt a fly, but she said, "He was so annoyed with me."'

Louisa's daughter was born in the workhouse infirmary, on 22 April 1923. The address on the birth certificate was given as 129 St John's Road: since the turn of the century it had been the euphemistic practice that workhouse babies were registered at a nondescript address that did not reveal the nature of the infirmary. The father was not named. Louisa's address was given as 38 Thornhill Road, Islington, and at first the child was put up for adoption.

Louisa was sixty-eight before she revealed the full truth about the conception and her broken engagement to her son. Her deepest shame was kept secret all her life: neither of her children ever knew that Alice Patricia was born in the workhouse.

Edie and her husband, a well-off Jewish jeweller called Siegfried Kaufmann, decided to adopt the baby. In the early twenties, this was an informal procedure; Edie's intentions were to minimise the disgrace to the family, and to help her younger sister bring up the child. Louisa was grateful all her life. 'She always said, "Edie was so good to me in my shame,"' remembered Tom Waine, a close friend of Williams and his mother. 'That was the phrase . . . "in my shame". Siegfried and Edie were wealthy, with a house in Vauxhall, which was very ritzy in those days.' Joan Carlin, who was born the previous year, thinks mother and baby lived some of the time with her parents in their flat at 92 Cromer Street.

By 1925 Louisa had been a cigarette packer and a machinist in a pyjama factory, and was now working as a waitress at an Express Dairies restaurant. The pay was poor: she would take home 29 shillings, after deductions of 1s 9d for uniform hire and laundry, and would buy 'three pennorth of stale bread 'cos it was cheaper than the ordinary'. Family myth said she met Charlie Williams, who was living in Liverpool Street in the East End, when he came into the café to order a Welsh rarebit. On the wedding certificate he described himself as a 'hairdresser (journeyman)'. They were married on 7 April 1925 at St Pancras register office, with Edie and Charlie's father as witnesses.

Charles George Williams was born at 82 Sidney Street, Somers Town, on 24 December 1899. He was one of seven children: his brothers were George, Jack and Stanley, his sisters Nell, Ivy and Phyllis, and their mother was Elizabeth Sarah, née Nealon. Their father, Charles John Williams (always known as John), was an engineer's fitter. Sidney Street, behind St Pancras station, was the worst of north London's slums: 'In little dark houses, overrun with rats, infested with vermin, and with rain coming through the roofs, as many as nine people lived and died in one room.' John Williams was a journeyman, taking work where he could. Charles grew up on the cusp of destitution and starvation; he and his brothers and sisters might not eat if their father could not find work. The deepest conviction of Charles's life was that a working man with a trade stood a better chance of survival than an unskilled labourer.

John Williams sometimes worked on the London, Midland and Scottish (LMS) railways, where Charles took his first job, as a van boy. In 1918 he was sent as a conscript into an infantry regiment, the Princess Charlotte of Wales's (Royal Berkshire Regiment), which had suffered such devastating losses at Miraumont and Oppy Wood during the spring of 1917 that it was reduced to just ninety-six men, including two officers, both wounded. By the time Charlie Williams arrived in Flanders, the battalion had fought at Cambrai and been withdrawn to a rearguard position to see out the winter in the trenches.

In late March, the German spring offensive was launched and the Royal Berkshires saw four days of heavy fighting before relief arrived. They were in action again from August, during the German retreat, but by this time Charlie Williams had probably been invalided out: he was not wounded but sent home suffering from trench fever. He returned to the regiment to serve in the Middle East – fifty years later his son pasted a photograph of him into his diary: 'I found this old snapshot taken in Mesopotamia [. . .] of my father Charles. Louie gave it to me just after his death [. . .] This picture was taken when he was a private in the Royal Berks. Regiment. He was very proud of his outfit + the Army + had an enormous portrait of the entire regiment over the fireplace at 57 Marchmont Street.'

Charlie and Louisa, newly wed, took a pair of rooms at 11 Bingfield Street, up the street from Charlie's parents at No. 64. Soon after Kenneth was born they moved to three rooms in Cromer Street, in the building next to Alice and Bill Arthur, at 14 shillings a week. The apartment blocks were put up at the beginning of the century by the East End Dwelling Company, built in brick around an open quadrangle, during the slum clearances. 'Of course there were no bathrooms and of course they weren't spacious, but they provided solid shelter,' Williams remembered. 'People could be neighbourly, could know each other. There was more humanity here than there is in the high-rise block on the modern council estate.'

All the family saw how besotted Louisa was with her new baby. 'Without doubt, Kenny was his mother's favourite,' Joan Carlin, his cousin, said. 'She idolised him and he idolised her. It was always, "My Ken" . . . you could tell he was really the apple of her eye.' Alice Patricia, now called simply 'Pat', became Pat Williams: modern adoption procedures did not begin until 1927 and Charlie was able simply to declare himself her adoptive father. The secret of her illegitimate birth was buried. 'You wouldn't dare mention if somebody was having a baby [out of wedlock], couldn't let anyone know,' Joan said. 'Charlie was a good man. He was a good husband and a good dad.'

Joan grew up on Cromer Street, and her accent is perhaps the clearest evidence of how Kenneth Williams would have spoken without the protection of his polyphonics. During a two-hour interview at her flat in the north London apartment block where she has lived for thirty years, and where Louisa Williams was a regular visitor, Joan's elocution was forceful and clear: a Professor Higgins would have identified her King's Cross accent instantly, more nasal than the cockney, shorn of aspirates but with every consonant sharply in its place. 'Kenny was brought up with the proper way of speaking,' she said, 'like me.'

Kenneth Williams's earliest memory was of his mother, singing as she cleaned the kitchen while he sat on the table. As he grew, he loved to help and copy her. 'Louie was very fussy,' Charlie's sister, Phyllis Gidley, told a television interviewer. 'If there was any mess on the floor, she'd say, "Look at this mess, simply disgusting." Now Kenny would follow round after her with a bit of rag, saying, "Look at this mess! Simply disgusting!"'

Around 1932, Louisa's sister Alice became ill. Joan, who was ten, went to live with her cousins up the street for three months, while her mother was in hospital. She shared a bedroom with Pat – Ken, who was six, had a room of his own. Charlie Williams was a stricter, more heavy-handed father than Bill, a milkman, and Joan found it difficult to adjust to his rules. There was a radio in the house, but it was rarely switched on. At mealtimes, there was little conversation: 'Uncle Charlie never sat down to his lunch without a book in front of him. It'd be a book, a thriller, not a newspaper. Lou would say, "Here's your dinner, Charlie," and he'd be reading a book, propped up, while eating. I used to think at the time, Isn't that rude! Eating your dinner and reading at the same time!'

On Sunday mornings the children would visit their grandmother, Tin Lizzie. If they were well behaved, the old lady would let them play her gramophone. On Sunday afternoons they went to Sunday School: Holy Cross Anglican church stood opposite the Cromer Street apartments but the Williams family were Methodists and they attended the Wesleyan church on Crestfield Street.

The family forebears were from Welsh chapel-going stock, Charlie's side from Port Talbot near Swansea and Louisa's from Pontnewydd in Monmouthshire. Neither Charlie nor Louie worshipped regularly, and they both ignored the strictures on temperance, but Kenneth Williams remembered his father as a God-fearing man, 'sceptical and puritanical . . . a whitewashed-wall Methodist who endlessly told me: "God can see you if nobody else can." ' God was not a personality but a concept, a standard by which man was measured – 'something that was paramount, something that was onerous, something which we didn't know but which we could reach towards'. There were two unbreakable rules: never to tell a lie, and never to keep company with people he would be ashamed to introduce to his parents. The first verses he ever learned to recite were his prayers, and all his life Williams was grateful for the exacting Christianity that was rubbed into the grain of his soul – 'demanding, hard, relentless and endlessly pursuing the conscience, a daily pricker of the conscience, a daily irritant of the conscience'.

Joan and Pat were cynical about their religious education. 'They wanted afternoon kip, that's why they sent us to Sunday school,' Joan said. 'But Charlie was a good father. Tried to bring them up the way they should be.'

Louisa was more frivolous. She loved parties, and though she never could invite a crowd to Charlie Williams's home, there was always the pub. 'Auntie Lou was very much more fun-loving, great fun to be around,' Joan said. 'She'd make everybody laugh. Silly things she used to do, like get little bits of paper and put them on for eyelashes, and start singing. A lot of his mother rubbed off on Kenneth. She was a comedian, definitely.'

'My mother was a great one for impersonating people,' Williams said during a searching television interview in 1974. 'We had a hairdresser's shop and she was always impersonating the customers, giving us impressions of people and often doing a mime with it, going out of the door and coming back in as they would enter. And I always found that very amusing so it rubbed off on me. My father regarded us as a pair of idiots most of the time. A very phlegmatic man, my father, and thoroughly disapproved of theatre. My mother was very volatile, and he had a tremendous passion and temper, and it would pour out, a great rhythm and rodomontade when he was very angry, but that didn't happen very often as opposed to my mother who was never stopping. She was always rushing out and saying, "I've got to do the shopping" – she was round the Norfolk, having a gin and tonic really, with her crony Edie Smith, singing pub songs and things. I learned all my pub songs from my mother.'

Another early source of his love of performance was street theatre. Joan Carlin remembered how excitedly she and her cousins would sit on the kerb when the barrel organ came round, to watch the antics of the actors – often men dressed in drag.

By the time he was six, Kenneth Williams was inventing stories and plays that he acted out with Pat and Joan. The girls were willing to let the younger boy make the rules and be the star. 'He was definitely in charge, he always organised the games,' said Joan. 'Kenny would say, "You can be a princess then, Joanie." He must have had it in him then, to be an actor. This was in the flat, finding old clothes to wear. We'd dress up, and if we couldn't dress up, we'd paint our faces with paints from a box.' They called it Our Game, and it was here that Williams's defining talent first displayed itself, in the ability to create and switch between many characters in one performance. The girls were each given one part to play – young Kenneth would be everybody else. He guided their imaginations, describing what they were doing in vivid detail; if he gave Pat a car to drive, he'd tell her the make and the colour.

The worlds of Our Game went everywhere with him. At school he played it with his friend Wreyford, one week older than he was. Williams liked to cast himself as a Ruritanian king with Wreyford as his treacherous prime minister, in a melodrama of swordplay on castle ramparts and plots hatched by cloaked assassins. His family and Wreyford's would go on holiday together, to Ramsgate and Southend.

It was at school that Williams developed his talent as a mimic. 'I remember the conscious thing of impersonating school teachers as a defence,' he told Mavis Nicholson. 'It was my way of performing. "Do you notice the English master talks in that very pedantic fashion?" and I would do him, and they'd say, "Ooh you've got him off to a tee, ooh that's really good."' He chose a moment of playground mimicry for the opening image of his autobiography: at Manchester Street Junior School, round the corner from Cromer Street, Williams was sending up a schoolmaster when the laughter dried and he turned to see his victim, watching the performance. 'A facetious front may win you popularity,' the teacher warned, 'but you won't be taken seriously when you want to be sincere.'

His school grades reflected his intelligence. He never forgot that one report concluded he was 'quick to grasp the bones of a subject, slow to develop them', but in fact he scored good marks. His best subjects were art and English, where he enjoyed reading aloud and 'caught the infection of romantic poetry which has never left me'. His first memory of performing Shakespeare was in class, standing up to give Antony's speech in *Julius Caesar* that begins, 'Friends, Romans, countrymen . . .' He felt later that he grasped the meaning and the power of it instinctively, without having to analyse. The sensation intoxicated him.

The other pupils sneered and told him he was in love with the sound of his own voice, but the English teacher, Basil Hodges, thought he showed potential and suggested he would do well in the school play. It was 1935, and Williams was nine years old: he made his stage debut as the princess in *The Rose and the Ring*. He nearly did not appear: 'After the dress rehearsal I withdrew from the production because someone was rude to me,' he later told the *Radio Times*. 'I knew I was an enormous asset and should be deferred to.' But the master producing the play visited his father. 'I was threatened with a good hiding unless I returned for the opening night . . . I bawled and stomped around the stage and generally received a lot of attention.'

The *St Pancras Gazette* gave him a good notice: 'Kenneth Williams, with his mincing step and comical demeanour, as Princess Angelica, was a firm favourite with the audience, to whom his snobbishness and pert vivacity made great appeal.' His father was less impressed. 'The stage is for nancies,' he said. He expected his son to grow up and learn a trade, and for that he would need to learn his sums, not lines: 'How do you expect to get on in the world if you can't add up?'

Charlie Williams had taken over as manager at the salon in Marchmont Street, on the northern edge of Bloomsbury. The Marchmont Saloon at No. 57 had been a hairdresser's since 1910; Charlie had worked there since before his son was born, and in the mid-thirties Edie and Siegfried loaned him the money to buy the business. The family moved into rooms over the shop. Louisa worked with her husband, shampooing hair as well as working the till. 'A very hard-working woman,' Joan said. 'She really rolled her sleeves up.' The couple made a double act, with her gossiping and flirting, and his surliness.

Kenneth and Pat did not help out in the shop, but they saw how differently their parents treated the customers. Charlie used paraffin to kill nits; he expected the men to have a short back and sides, and mocked the women who asked to have their hair dyed: 'Henna? Do you want to look like a tart?' On the *Parkinson* show, Williams described his father at work: 'A man I remember once came into the shop . . . "Oh, I'd like a blow wave." And he said, "Blow? You'll get no blow waves from me, I'm not doing no blow waves. What are you, a blooming iron? Iron hoof? [rhyming slang for poof] Iron? I'm not having no irons in my shop, get out!"' When his wife showed off, he would growl, 'This is a hairdresser's shop, not a music hall.'

Williams gained a scholarship to Parliament Hill secondary, a school for academically able pupils. If his parents had let him take it up, he might have gone on to university; instead, they decided the cost of the uniform and books was prohibitive, and sent him to Lyulph Stanley Central School for Boys in Mornington Crescent. Throughout his life Williams tried to compensate for his inadequate education. 'He was very burdened by the fact that like an awful lot of people in this country he had an extremely good mind; there was no questioning his intelligence or sensitivity, but he hadn't had a good education,' the broadcaster Melvyn Bragg remarked. 'If he'd gone to a grammar school, there's little doubt, because he was a sympathetic chap, somebody would have picked him out and tried to get him to go for university. He must have felt that quite keenly. He was interested in ideas, in reading, in thinking. It was all locked up inside himself.'

One of his pleasures, a joy he never lost, was to surround himself with the paraphernalia of letter-writing. 'I always remember being very young – about ten or twelve, and being so happy on top of a bus in Kingsway on a raining afternoon going to Woolworth's in the Strand to buy pens and paper and paper clips . . . Oh! I loved *stationery* and all the accoutrements of *writing*.' One schoolfriend remembered writing the school newspaper with him, and going to Marchmont Street to work on an article.

Young 'Willy' played football with his classmates, though he was conscious he was not an athletic boy and that others thought he was effeminate. When he imagined himself as an adult, it was 'with a gin and tonic and a fag at the bar, in the corner, being rather erudite and elegant', and he was self-aware enough to know that this made him different from his classmates. A teacher told his father that Kenneth was showing off to disguise an inferiority complex: 'My exhibitionism concealed a sense of inadequacy,' he admitted in his autobiography. 'The real self was a vulnerable, quivering thing . . . affectation and play-acting I used like a hedgehog uses his spines.'

He was not bullied – his friendship with the school captain, Reefy, kept him safe. 'Anyone who threatened even remotely to bash me, I'd say, Reefy, Reefy, they're going to bash me, and he always came to the rescue – "Ah get out of it, leave him alone. Touch a hair of his head . . ." And I loved all that. Can't touch me!' The other children were less aware of his differences. Joan Carlin saw him as 'quite a normal child with me and everybody . . . a very likeable boy, very friendly. Any bullies would have had Auntie Lou to answer to. She could stand up for herself. There wasn't two pennorth of her but she could.'

Charlie Williams accepted that his son showed no interest in learning to be a hairdresser, but he insisted Kenneth had to train in some line of work. 'You've got to have a trade, boy, you've *got* to *have* a *trade* – constantly dinned in,' Williams remembered on a *Parkinson* show. A career on the stage was out of the question – actors were effete, pretentious and, worst of all, penniless. 'I've had them in the shop with their la-di-da voices . . . they haven't got two ha'pennies to rub together.' At fourteen, the son was testing his bounds. It was a 'sort of phase I went thro' from about fourteen to at least eighteen. Outwardly it takes the form of cockiness, snobbishness and rudeness – inwardly it is a colossal desire to be loved.'

He defied his father by answering back or not answering at all. When he did talk, he would provoke Charlie into a rage by affecting an upper-class accent. It was a voice he had assumed before he was a teenager, so distinctive that old classmates would recognise it decades later on the radio. 'My father was a cockney; he didn't talk like me at all,' Williams told Russell Harty. 'He hated my kind of talking. He said, "What d'you go round with a plum in your mouth for? Putting it on, giving yourself airs."'

They found, in the end, one point of compromise: Kenneth had some ability at drawing. At first Charlie could see no use for it, unless he started doing cartoons for the newspapers, but the art teacher at Lyulph Stanley suggested the boy could train as a draughtsman. It was a trade, but it also demanded artistic, not practical, skills. There was a school of lithography, Bolt Court, in Fleet Street: after passing the oral exam, Kenneth Williams was enrolled to train as a litho draughtsman. He would learn lettering and perspective, the first step in preparing stone and metal plates for lithographic printing.

This was 1940 – the British Expeditionary Force had retreated at Dunkirk, the Luftwaffe began bombing London nightly and the younger pupils at Bolt Court were evacuated from the city to Bicester, Oxfordshire. The fourteen-year-old Williams, living away from his mother for the first time in his life, was billeted on a family with strict, Anglican beliefs. The selection process was humiliating: the children were lined up in the school playground to be looked over by the foster families. 'I was still there with a few others when darkness fell,' he remembered, 'and the authorities handed us over for the night to the District Nurse. I remember asking her why no one had selected me, and she said, "Because you've got a nasty sneer on your face, that's why."'

Within weeks he asked to move: the proximity of family life among strangers must have been unbearable to an adolescent boy who already guarded his privacy. The Bolt Court pupils were required to help on the allotments, and there he met and was befriended by a retired vet in his seventies, John Chisholm. The elderly man invited Williams to board at the large house where he lived with his housekeeper.

Williams always remembered the house at 19 Sheep Street as 'a magical abode', filled with antique furniture and books. Dim passageways connected rooms lit by candles or oil lamps, the sitting-room was a surgery, the garden was overgrown and a coach-house stood at the back. The young evacuee explored it in fascination.

Chisholm liked to recite poetry, particularly Byron and Shelley, and sing old ballads, loudly, and he enjoyed having an audience. In the evenings when Mrs Woods, the housekeeper, was at Salvation Army meetings, he would perform a repertoire of favourites that he knew by heart, such as 'The Charge of the Light Brigade' and 'The

Yarn of the Loch Achray'; he taught Williams the importance of clear diction and how to use silences to build drama in a poem.

Louisa Williams was anxious to know her son was safe and came to visit, with Edie Smith, her 'crony' from the Norfolk. The two women were horrified: there were mouse droppings in the kitchen, they said, and the mattresses were like ploughed fields, while the sight of Chisholm in his nightshirt with a candle sent them into hysterical giggles. Williams always thought fondly of Bicester, though, and made a short pilgrimage there in the last year of his life; by a pleasing coincidence, he met Chisholm's nephew in the bar of the village pub.

In the spring of 1941, aged fifteen, Williams was sent back to London, to continue his studies at Bolt Court. He also resumed duties as a firewatcher. His sister Pat had joined the Women's Auxiliary Air Force, and cousin Joan, who was about to get married, was working as a lathe operator in a factory. The bombing continued, and because there was no bunker at 57 Marchmont Street the family would take shelter in the kitchen, in a basement under the shop. A skylight opened on to the street beneath a grating: it was glazed with reinforced glass, but in the coal cellar next door the grating was bare. One night, Charlie went to fetch a scuttleful of coal and was spattered by a drunken group of soldiers who were urinating into the hole. 'I've been pissed on!' he roared. 'Pissed on in my own house!' Louisa knew better than to laugh at her husband to his face, but her stepmother, 'Tin Lizzie', was less tactful, or less fearful. In a rage, Charlie sacked her as the cleaner in his shop. The job was added to Louisa's duties.

With Pat and so many others serving away or killed in the war, Christmas that year was a subdued affair – 'almost melancholy, and brushed over with false gaiety', Williams wrote in the first diary entry he ever made. The pocket book, a Collins Emerald diary, was probably a Christmas present. He carefully filled in the page of 'personal memoranda' – weight, seven stone two; height, five feet, three inches; collar size, fourteen; hat, seven; gloves, seven; boots, six and a half; plus his phone number, bicycle number and ID card number. The entries were clipped and brief ('Have smashing overcoat. Went to the Dominion . . . those stairs!') but he tried to record something every day.

At Bolt Court he was learning to etch on metal, and to make prints with carbon tissue and with zinc ('It seems rather dashed hard'). He learned about photography, and lantern slides, and had to sketch a pair of wings, which he copied from a greetings card. In the evenings, he went to the cinema when he could. He was also reading widely – *Jew Süss* by Lion Feuchtwanger was 'very good', Sir H. Rider Haggard's *She* was 'balderdash! tripe! eyewash! blah!'

His pastimes were not all intellectual: he enjoyed billiards and bike rides. His chief hobby was stamp collecting, which could keep him occupied for hours at a time, sending off to Gibbons and other firms for packets of used stamps, and arranging them in his album, which had cost him 17s 6d. Family incidents did not often merit comment, though he tried some cooking one Sunday, making bread rolls, and played Monopoly with Edie's daughter Joy. Pat's arrival home on leave in November caused excitement – she had hitched home from Lancashire on a lorry. He referred to his parents as 'Mum' and 'Dad', not 'Louie' and 'Charlie', as he began to call them after the war.

There was little evidence of sexual feelings. Williams certainly knew his inclinations were homosexual, and in his autobiography he suggested his first experiences had been with boys at school – 'all clumsy, furtive fumblings and really very innocent'. He remembered in his diary how he had been infatuated with, and frightened of, a boyfriend of his sister's, called James. It was before the war, and Williams was thirteen or perhaps younger; they were on Tonbridge Street, walking to the Regent cinema, when James offered an alliance: 'With my brawn and your brains we're a marvellous combination.' Williams refused. He couldn't even offer a compliment in return. Long afterwards, he wished he could see James again – not to try to resume their pubescent friendship, but just to look at him.

During the summer of 1942 he met a 'nice fellow' called Alan Knight, and they spent several days together, including a day-trip to the Empress Eugenie's house at Chislehurst. On another Sunday, he 'went to Alan's. Glad wasn't with M. and D. Am to see him on Monday night.' This reticence about his longings and emotions was probably demanded by his fear of discovery, especially by his parents – 'keeping a diary is a fine idea, so long as it is in such a place that access to it is only possible by the right people'.

Williams at fifteen barely took notice of the events shaking the world. He had no interest in analysing the strategies and politics of the war, and made only cursory mention of pivotal events. 'Capture of Bali by Japs', he noted on his birthday, between a list of the aunts who had given him money (it came to £1) and a promise to himself that he would get an attaché case. A Bolt Court teacher who lectured the pupils on the war was a 'patriotic windbag'.

He was engaged only when it affected him directly: in late July 1942 he attended two Sea Cadet Corps meetings in Paddington Street with a cousin, Ronnie Hayden, and learned about torpedoes, signals and mines. He enjoyed it enough to apply for membership, though it was the uniform that he wanted most – he fretted for two months that he was still in civilian clothes, until he passed the medical on 30 September and was kitted out. The hat was too small, the tunic too big, the belt arrived ten days late and he had to pay a tailor 5 shillings to adjust it all, but it was worth the frustration. His friends were 'jealous as hell!!'

When Pat came home, they were photographed in uniform together. With the Sea Cadets, he visited the War Cabinet offices, learned to take a compass reading and to sound the depth of water, practised his knots – 'terrible!!! almost makes one feel ashamed' – and drilled on parade.

His skills as a draughtsman were developing more quickly. In March he had applied for three jobs and was invited for interview at Edward Stanford's, a map-making firm in Long Acre. The opportunity filled him with apprehension. 'Do hope I will be successful. Please God, I shall be!!' he wrote the night before the interview. He got the apprenticeship, and for the first few weeks his diary was full of anxious prayers. His first fortnight's wages, paid on 10 April, were 18s 6d. His lettering became more confident, as he discovered that left-handedness was an advantage when he was writing in reverse on stones for flat-bed printing.

An eager correspondent even at sixteen, he often wrote letters to friends and was continually expecting replies. His first surviving letter was to Alice and Bill, whose son Albert, a signalman in the Royal Navy, had been killed on active service. In the back of his diary, he struggled to compose a note of condolence: 'It seems there is very little to write that can express our sympathy enough, but believe it, our hearts go out to you in your trial, and you are constantly in our thoughts. But even the worst news can't desist us from hoping [. . .] you understand, it is impossible to write a long letter, news does not somehow seem to fit into this sort of letter [. . .] It is gratifying to know that you yourself are well bodily [. . .] Therefore I shall finish by echoing all our wishes for your future well-being and all our Love.'

At Stanford's he was again befriended by an older man, an Ordnance Survey cartographer named Valentine Orford, then thirty-six, who encouraged his reading and gave him his first proper introduction to the theatre. They saw Wilde's *The Importance of Being Earnest*, and *The Doctor's Dilemma* by George Bernard Shaw at the Haymarket: 'I was entranced and fascinated. Never before had I heard such lively argument and such irreverent wit . . . this was the sort of part I wanted to play – these were the aesthetics I wanted to proclaim.'

Convinced he had talent as an actor, he joined the Tavistock Players' Little Theatre, which rehearsed at the Mary Ward Settlement in Tavistock Place, round the corner from Marchmont Street. This amateur dramatics society welcomed him: they were short of male actors, and his first role was an older man's part, as Gaston in *Villa for Sale* by Sacha Guitry. The ladies of the group tried to teach him how to apply his make-up and to project his voice on stage. His natural gift was for ad libs and, when half of his false moustache fell off, he got a laugh by turning away and bending over as he stuck it back on. During the post-war years, when he was regularly petitioning BBC producers and rep directors for work, he liked to emphasise his background in am-dram and felt it showed the strength of his actor's vocation.

Conscription was looming. 'Where will I be 2 years hence?' he wondered. He hoped his involvement with the Sea Cadets would lead to a naval posting: the older draughtsmen at Stanford's suggested he could be a hydrographer on a survey ship, working on navigation charts. Williams liked the idea of a full seaman's uniform. When his call-up came in February 1944, however, he was handed a rifle, a bayonet and infantry fatigues.

2

'Happy days, what a laugh! Oh! Life!!'

February 1944–December 1947

Within days of his eighteenth birthday, in February 1944, Williams received the summons that marked the first stage of his call-up, to attend a medical examination at the drill hall in Dukes Road, Euston. Throughout his life he loved to tell stories of his military service; he was also fascinated by medical procedures, and so this anecdote became a favourite: 'I won't bore you with the tedious account of the examinations I underwent for proof of military fitness: suffice it to say that *four* medical boards shook their heads in disbelief over my nudity, and packed me off to a gentleman in Harley Street who looked like Bela Lugosi and had vampirish tendencies. I left there with a pint less blood, a verdict of anaemia, and a card bearing the grading B2. This meant I was not considered infantry material.'

In fact, his initial grading was B1, according to his Soldier's Service and Pay Book, and the board must have felt he possessed at least the potential for 'infantry material', for within weeks he received his full call-up. Williams preserved his enlistment notice, which was dated 11 April and required him to present himself on the morning of Thursday 20 April at No. 68 Primary Training Wing of the General Service Corps, Carlisle Castle. A postal order for 4 shillings was enclosed in advance of service pay.

He was assigned the army number 14747886; his trade was listed in his pay book as litho artist, and his religion Church of England. At five feet six and a quarter inches, he had a chest measurement of 31.5 inches and weighed 111.5 pounds, just eight ounces under eight stone, which was regarded as underweight. His complexion was described as very pale, his eyes blue, his hair fair and his only 'distinctive marks and minor defects' were scars on his forehead. His parents and sister were listed as next of kin (though he recorded his mother's name as Louise Alexandrina) and the four pages of forms for his will were left unfilled.

Williams's war service was not perilous. Though technically eligible for action, he missed the horrors of the Allied advance across Europe and the Burma campaign. During his stints as a firewatcher he had been exposed to more risk than he ever was as a soldier. To him, though, it was the greatest adventure of his life. In his autobiography, written during his fifties and published just three years before his death, he spent almost twenty pages on the two and a half years between conscription and transfer to the entertainment corps: it was the most lucid and flowing section of the book, full of earnest detail. Several of the anecdotes were ideal for television: 'I'd always had my own room, even when we were evacuated,' he told Terry Wogan. 'And suddenly in this barrack room I had to [undress] . . . I used to take the trousers down and put the pyjama bottoms on and then do the rest. And they rumbled it, they rumbled it in the barrack room, and said, "Hoi, you frightened of showing us your willy?" I became quite uninhibited after that.'

When he was scared and homesick, the chaplain encouraged him – 'my first real mentor [. . .] he let me pour it all out to him'. But within days of joining up, Williams had discovered he enjoyed the masculinity of army life. His comrades gave him a nickname, Casey, because his initials were K.C. He liked sleeping in a dorm with a squad of other young men, and his self-confidence grew as he found he could get their attention by clowning and telling stories. Just as he had at school, he cultivated friends to be his protectors. With his elegant calligraphy, he would inscribe each man's name on his kit – an amiable act of ingratiation. He threw himself into training and sports, and during a football game he took a blow in the face that fractured his nose (he usually said this was a kick, though once he claimed on *Just a Minute* that he was punched while doing an impression of Churchill). The injury, when it healed, gave his right nostril its distinctive, crooked flare.

Shortly after his arrival in Carlisle in April 1944, Williams was sent 'with a pathetic group of pale and skinny conscripts' on a six-week course at No. 1 Physical Development Centre in Hereford: 'You scrawny horrible creatures come in here looking like something out of the workhouse,' the sergeant told them, 'but after we've finished with you, you go out looking like athletes!' Fattened up on meat, butter and fish, and helped around the final assault course by the sergeant on the crossbar of his bicycle, Williams was regraded as A1, and returned to train with the Border Regiment in Cumberland. Primary training was completed on 9 August; his squad took the prize for best recruits.

His draughtsman's skills saved him from being posted to a combat regiment. Ordered to report to the Royal Engineers' Survey Training Centre in Ruabon, Denbighshire, Sapper Williams joined the Map Reproduction Section (MRS). He was transferred to south-east England, stationed at Northolt in west London and also Ruislip in Middlesex; here, army discipline was easygoing ('even brass buttons no longer required polishing since we were issued with plastic substitutes') and he had frequent leave – nine days in October 1944, nine more in January 1945. He kept his last pass: stamped February 1945, it bestowed permission to travel into the city daily, allowing him to leave camp when his duty ended and return no later than a minute to midnight. Whenever possible, he hitched home to Marchmont Street.

Williams kept no diary in 1943 or 1944. Decades later, he regretted this: 'Pity I didn't keep a record from the period of enlistment.' The first full diary to survive in the unbroken series extending to his death in 1988 was the 1947 volume. There is evidence, however, that he did begin keeping a journal from early 1945. Tucked inside the flap of 1947's diary are three pages, apparently torn from a daybook similar to Williams's 1942 Collins Emerald – the last sheet has the same distinctive marbling on the back. These pages appear to be a summary of his diaries for 1945 and 1946. In pencil, and then faded ink, he noted the stages of a journey that took him to India, Ceylon and at last Singapore.

His posting overseas came as a shock. The end of the war in Europe seemed near, but Williams was fearful of being caught up in the Pacific atrocities and, when his order papers came through, they contained no clue to his destination. The three small sheets of notes folded under the leather cover of the 1947 diary show that his detachment of Royal Engineers travelled through the night from

Longmoor camp in Hampshire, to Greenock, on the south banks of the Clyde near Glasgow, where they boarded a troopship on 12 April 1945. Five days later, as part of a convoy escorted by destroyers, they set sail.

On 23 April, they rounded Gibraltar: 'Up to now going has been steadily calm, no sea sickness, and apart from accommodation trip proves quite enjoyable.' There were not enough hammocks to go round, and many of the troops were forced to sleep on tables or the deck. By Saturday 28 April, they were anchored at Port Said, and the following day entered the Suez Canal, reaching the Red Sea that evening. 'Jelly fishes and porpoises – numerous, also a Suez bird with a face like a frog – amazing.' A second week's sailing took them to Bombay, where they disembarked on 7 May; the next day they travelled for two hours by lorry to the transit camp at Kalyan: 'Arrived in darkness under utter confusion.'

There was no mention in the crabbed notes that the Germans had surrendered or that Tuesday 8 May was VE Day. Other notable events also went unremarked – the swearing-in of Harry Truman as US President on 12 April, following the death of Franklin D. Roosevelt, and the suicide of Adolf Hitler on 30 April. The lack of significance Williams attached to world headlines, a tendency he had revealed in his first diary, was a trait that would endure for decades: all his life he listened to news bulletins on the radio, but he did not chart his personal story by any outside events, however momentous. It was not until the seventies that he would develop into an attentive chronicler of current affairs.

Bombay was at its hottest in early May, typically around 35°C, and Williams loathed the heat and the mosquitoes. The sappers tried to ward off the insects with tobacco smoke but, within days of arriving, Williams was caught with a cigarette while on sentry duty at Kalyan's armoury and placed on a charge. After a night in the guardhouse, he was brought before the commanding officer and accused of dereliction of duty; 6,000 miles from home, in a strange climate, terrified at the prospect of military prison, he burst into tears and pleaded nervous exhaustion. The charge was dismissed. He spent the next night in the infirmary.

On 15 May he embarked on a gruelling, three-day journey by train to Dehra Dun, in the Himalayan foothills. The carriages were so packed with men that Williams had to struggle into a luggage rack to sleep. From the windows of the train, though, he experienced India's spectacular beauty for the first time: 'The clouds hung like great golden peaches,' he wrote to his colleague at Stanford's, Val Orford – 'each within itself, burnished and glowing in the fading light from gold to silver to grey – to nothingness. And then – a thousand stars to light the way.'

In Dehra Dun, working as a 'photo writer' with the offset litho presses in map reproduction, he was stationed for nearly four months; the air was cooler and, though he was still plagued by heat rash, he thought it 'quite a pleasant sort of hole'. The Japanese surrender meant the disbanding of his section, and on Monday 3 September he was sent to Delhi, arriving (as his notes record precisely) at 3.15 p.m. From there he was sent to Madras in the south ('6 Sept '45, Thurs 7.20 evening, arrived there on Saturday 8th, midnight'). Then, and for the rest of his life, he noted the exact times of his departures and arrivals – a matter of five or fifteen minutes in a journey seemed too significant to be ignored.

After two days at a rest camp in Madras, Williams embarked for Ceylon, spending a day in the capital, Colombo, before joining 62 MRS at Kurunegala, arriving on 13 September. He would stay in Ceylon for almost a year.

At nineteen, Kenneth Williams was still sexually naive. Aware since his early teens, at least, that he was attracted to other men, he did not hide his homosexuality from his comrades, though there was a gulf between inclination and action. In Ceylon he experienced an infatuation with another sapper, a Londoner called Ted, with 'dark curly hair and deliberate speech. I was extraordinarily fond of him.' When he tried to renew the acquaintance later, in Singapore, he was brushed off: 'I didn't need a house of bricks to fall on me. It was obvious that he didn't want to know me.' The idea of a sexual approach by a complete stranger, one who was not British, was less intimidating; in a coconut grove outside Camp 320, he made a tentative experiment in masturbation with a young Sikh from the billets of the IOR – Indian Other Ranks. The encounter excited Williams, but he did not attempt to repeat it.

In Kurunegala, in huts built from matted rushes, his duties were cursory – 'I spent a lot of time in the office . . . I used to type and do odd clerical jobs.' He corresponded constantly with Val Orford and was visited by his sister, Pat, who had married and was on her way to join her husband in Australia. Dramatic incidents were rare. One afternoon, while typing at a desk in a bungalow hut, he heard a swishing sound and, looking down, saw a snake. Unsure whether it was poisonous, he shouted for help – his commanding officer, Captain Hardman, ran in and shot it with a revolver.

By May 1946, Williams had been appointed a lance corporal and took his turn as duty NCO. The promotion led to a confrontation with the Indian soldiers, an incident that made a profound impression on him. Left in charge of the camp one afternoon, while the other men went swimming, Williams went to investigate the noise of a radio in the mess hut and discovered the whole contingent of Indian troops crowded around the wireless set. He pushed through, switched off the broadcast and, accusing them of trespassing in British quarters, ordered them out. When Hardman returned, Williams discovered he had caused real offence: not only had he shut off a news bulletin about plans for Indian independence, but he had behaved disrespect- fully to the subadar, the Indian officer.

Hardman expected his lance-corporal to make a full apology on the parade ground, and Williams made a performance of it, deliver- ing a speech in front of all the IORs: 'Subadar Sahib, I behaved in a stupid and discourteous manner. I acted on the spur of the moment without realising the gravity of the occasion. I hope you will over- look this unhappy business and accept my sincere apologies.' The officer embraced him, the soldiers cheered him, and he was invited to eat with them. When Williams expressed astonishment, the suba- dar quoted the Lord's Prayer at him: 'Isn't it written in your book – "Forgive us our trespasses as we forgive them that trespass against us"?'

That series of events – offence, humiliation, apology, absolution – became a sequence that Williams sought to repeat throughout his life. When he had recited his prayers in the Methodist pews of his childhood, their meanings had not touched him, but this experi- ence of forgiveness was a spiritual revelation. The drama had to be enacted in many different ways over the years before he fully understood its effect: he needed to behave in a way that provoked outrage, and to feel belated disgust at himself, so that he could make a formal and self-abasing declaration of his sins and hope to feel purified. He felt the presence of God mostly strongly when he expressed regret and meant it, and when he was washed clean he felt the divinity of God. At the age of twenty, after a nonconformist upbringing by a father who did not live by all the truths he insisted his son should believe, Kenneth Williams had begun to discover meaning in his religion.

He made tentative efforts to express his emotions in poetry, with titles such as 'Dejection', and 'Regrets', and 'Obbligato Nostalgia'. Five final drafts were typed up and survive in his archive. The most revealing is called 'Catastrophic Man', and describes his decision to repress emotion beneath façades and inhibition:

> Lying alone in the top-frozen puddles
> Gaping for breath
> Fighting for life [. . .]
> Living and dying in the measured minute.
> Dying to live, living to choose
> And in the choice remembering
> The outward calm of pregnant women,
> Or the flat sea in its windlessness.
> Do not search beneath.

The metaphors were inside out, the reverse of his reality. Williams never was top-frozen, nor outwardly calm, to say nothing of wind-less. His cooler emotions were able to surface, 'gaping for breath', only when he was alone, writing poetry, letters and diary entries. The presence of other people produced a chemical reaction in his personality: it exploded noisily, more like a flashbulb than a façade.

'When I was in the Army,' he said, 'I had no real confidence and I found that when you got laughs you got authority. I was terrible as an NCO at first. I could never give orders properly but after I got lots of laughs in the NAAFI I found I had no fears about being an NCO. Authority is all a façade, really.'

He began to develop his instinct for comedy, and during the heavy days and humid evenings he worked up impressions, of Bette Davis, Nellie Wallace and Winston Churchill. He sang pub songs and sent up officers and, after helping to write and produce a NAAFI show, he was urged by his quartermaster sergeant to apply for the Combined Services Entertainments unit, based in Singapore.

When the Map Reproduction Section was disbanded, Williams asked Hardman to recommend him to CSE. 'He did. [The commendation] said, "I think that L/Corporal Williams will be of more use to CSE Singapore than he has ever been at 62 MRS Kurunegala." Really quite acid. I was very offended. I went up to his hut. He was in the shower. I shouted my complaints. He laughed and shouted, "The real letter is in the In Tray," and I went back to the office and found it. He'd written a charming letter saying how good I'd been in the impromptu cabaret things we'd organised in the mess.'

The folded packet of notes, tucked under the clasped leather cover of his diary, records that the map section disbanded on 27 June 1946. Williams spent three weeks with 'pack up squad No. 66, at Raudy (B2 Camp)' before quartering with the Map Reproduction Unit at Kelaniya for a week and then departing for Colombo. He passed a month at Victoria Park in the city and boarded the SS *Cameronia* on 24 August, landing at Singapore on the 31st. A car was waiting for him at the dockside: its driver was a Captain Olm, a big man with a broad face and small eyes. 'He said, "What do you do?" and I said, "Impersonations," and he said, very tiredly, "They'll be getting performing seals next."'

Post-war Singapore had a lurid, hysterical air. Occupied by the Japanese ('the worst disaster and largest capitulation in British history', as Winston Churchill described it) from February 1942 until its liberation in August 1945, the city had suffered desperate food shortages while the harbour blockade of sunken ships and underwater explosives was cleared. For six months a British military administration struggled to deal with unrest and financial collapse. Looting and vengeance killings were rife. By the time Williams arrived, the worst problems were over: in April 1946 civil government had been restored and the city was now a Crown colony, under its governor, Sir Franklin Gimson. The Malay population no longer trusted the

British, though, and a Communist insurgency was building, which would erupt a year later in the Malayan Emergency.

Combined Services Entertainments was based in No. 1 British Transit Camp, Nee Soon, fifteen miles to the north of the city. The artistes lived in an off-white block on a hillside that sloped down to a ravine, with a marquee for a mess hall, and tennis tables, an upright piano and recliners under striped awnings, and coloured paper lanterns in the trees. Sprawled around this Production Centre were the parade grounds and barracks of the transit camp.

Auditions were held at the garrison theatre, the Gaiety, and when Williams arrived he joined a queue of hopeful performers – 'conjurors, tap dancers, singers, acrobats, musicians and heaven knows what else'. A sergeant with a clipboard ticked off his name, told Williams to call him 'Terry' and explained that most of the acts would be dismissed with the order RTU: Return to Unit. One by one, they tried and failed, and when Williams walked on to the stage his confidence was slipping. As he launched into his impersonations, a languid voice in the stalls complained, 'Oh dear, oh dear.'

When he limped off stage with his RTU, he felt defeated and humiliated. He had come 1,700 miles to fulfil his promise to the Royal Engineers that he would become an entertainer: they had cheered him when he set off, and now he had failed the audition. Terry the sergeant took pity and asked him what other talents he had. He was a draughtsman, Williams said. 'Hang on till the break, dear,' Terry reassured him. 'I'll tell the Old Man you can do posters for the shows.'

Not long after this, Local Acting Unpaid Sergeant Williams was dispatched with a pad and a pencil to the Victoria Theatre, over the Pedang river in the south of Singapore, where CSE was rehearsing 'a melodramatic farce' with the title *Seven Keys to Baldpate*. The producer, Flight Lieutenant Albert Arlen, greeted him with anxious enthusiasm – one of the cast was in the hospital bay with malaria, and Arlen needed someone to read his part. Williams was handed a marked script. A few days later, the show opened with Williams in the first professional role of his life, as 'Jigs Kennedy, a police inspector'. A posed photograph survives of Williams as the detective, in a fedora and a fake moustache, grimacing as he slaps the handcuffs on a cringing Jimmy Viccars. The scene was also immortalised in his repertoire of chat-show stories – one night, he claimed, he left the key to the cuffs in his dormitory and Viccars had to ride back to the barracks in manacles.

During the play's two-week run, at the end of 1946, a Sunderland Flying Boat landed in Singapore harbour. A twenty-year-old Scottish actor came ashore, looking for a ride to CSE's production centre in Nee Soon. His name was Stanley Baxter, and after the bombed-out darkness of Rangoon the young man from Glasgow was immediately at home in the noisy, colourful streets of Singapore. Dumping his kitbag at the Raffles Hotel, he set out to find a place to eat: 'If in doubt you always go to a café with a name like the Lucky Café, so I went in, sat down to steak, eggs and chips, then asked some servicemen at another table, "Do you know how I could get to Nee Soon?"'

Stanley Baxter at first felt too protective of Kenneth Williams to discuss their forty-year friendship for this book. Having made it plain he remained fiercely defensive of Williams's fragility, he staged every scene he described, as he had in his spectacular television sketches, playing all the parts, with the dialogue tumbling out in a vivid stream of voices and mannerisms. He didn't just imitate Kenneth Williams – he seemed to channel him.

The essential difference between their personalities was defined by their first reactions to Singapore: where Baxter was confident, practical and curious, Williams was lost and vulnerable. Baxter was not afraid to ask for help, but Williams was wary of accepting it. Once he did begin to feel at home, though, Kenneth Williams buried his insecurity under layers of bravado and exuberance. As soon as he found his feet in the *Baldpate* cast, he dominated it.

Sent over from the Lucky Café to the Victoria Theatre, Stanley Baxter found the stage door. 'Everybody was in civvies, because once you were taken on with CSE, you never wore uniform at all. I approached one of them and asked if they were going back to Nee Soon. "Yes." Any chance of a lift? "No, mate, we've got ourselves, we've got a girlfriend, we've got no room for any more." Suddenly this incredible figure came through them all. His hair had been whitened – he looked a boy of fifteen who had been made to look old, with grey temples, but the face of a child. And he said, "*What is this?*"

I started to explain and he cut in, "What do you mean, they can't take you?" I said I just wanted a lift to Nee Soon . . . "*Of course we can take him!* Yessss, he can go out front, see the show, it's pretty bad, but still it'll be nice to have one more in the audience, it's been half empty all week. Yes, come back, we'll take you."'

A backstage hand nervously attempted to defy this regal fury: 'But, Ken, we don't know if there's room . . .'

'*Yesss*, course there's room, we don't want all that *rubbish*, all you and your fucking *girlfriends*.'

At the barracks, Baxter hung back. In CSE, the lowest rank was sergeant, and only officers were allowed to write and direct shows; Baxter was still a corporal and felt uneasy about taking a billet. 'I said, "I'll have to go into the general camp until I'm accepted."

'"Rubbish! That doesn't make any difference, dear. Don't you worry! It's lovely. You've got a bearer – does your shoes!" So, illegally, I moved into a room for two. I was the only person in there.'

In uniform, Kenneth Williams's worst misdemeanour had been smoking on guard duty. In CSE, he had learned that his innate respect for hierarchies could be set aside. Talent mattered; rank mattered less. He was thrilled by the open talk of liaisons between men of all ranks. Arlen had written a classical rhapsody, the Alamein Concerto, which, Williams insisted, was a hymn to a lover, killed in North Africa. The brass were the tanks, the timpani were the artillery, and the piano theme was 'her bit of rough! Yerss! [. . .] Scots guard, very butch. Got killed [. . .] so she wrote the concerto to immortalise their love. Don't say a word against it, if you don't want to be RTU'd. She thinks it's better than the Rachmaninoff.'

By Christmas 1946, Williams and Baxter, after small roles in a musical revue called *Cabaret-Cabaret*, were featuring in a similar show, *Going Gay*. Both men were writing poetry, and Williams provided the lyrics for one song in the show, 'The Stranger'. On Christmas Day, they staged a send-up of *Baldpate*, titled *Seven Stops to Aldgate*, in the green room at the barracks. That night, Williams made his first entries in a small journal with a stippled cover. The word 'Diary' was embossed in gilt on the front, though it provided only six thin lines for each day; that year he filled them all with a meticulous script, barely sparing a scrap of space. If he had any ambition to compile the broadest and most scabrous diary ever written, and to sustain it for the rest of his life, he gave no hint – though the first entry does end with an unconscious echo of Pepys: 'Bed very late this night!'

On New Year's Day, 1947, Stanley Baxter was moved into Williams's two-man dorm. 'Kenneth fascinated me,' he said. 'He was such an incredible character. I realised he was going places. Whether to jail or to fame, I couldn't predict, but he was certainly way out on a limb, unlike anybody I'd ever met before. So of course we stayed friends, and we'd blow all our money on a Saturday night by living it up and going down for a gin and tonic, and a nice meal in Singapore, but on our wages it'd be the sergeants' mess for the rest of the week.'

When they went into the city, they generally travelled by gharrie, drinking at bars called Pegasus, the Magnolia and the Shackles Club. At the camp, Williams would sunbathe or laze on a charpoy while he picked books from the parcels Val Orford was sending – mostly poetry and fiction, including T.S. Eliot, H.G. Wells, de Maupassant and Forster. He adopted CSE's slang, picking up phrases that he would use for the rest of his life: 'It's the end! It's *Death*! I was sent up – through the roof!' The diary reflected this idiom, which consisted mostly of private jokes and catchphrases.

In London's gay circles, the coded parlance of Polari was gaining vogue, but in CSE it appears Williams was not yet using this convoluted, camp Esperanto. Instead, he was coining his own euphemisms: 'Traditional worries' hinted at masturbation; 'Solitary coffees predominant' suggested servicemen sitting alone in cafés, hoping for a pick-up; 'Shocking American type [. . .] dropping tiaras' conjured up an excruciating queen. He was already passing judgment on everyone around him: 'Tandy extremely rude and insulting. Stan and I to ostracise him.'

Between these rushes of social excitement, the performers were rehearsing a new revue called *High and Low*, 'a bright new musical [. . .] devised and produced by Albert Arlen', starring Babette O'Deal and featuring Kenneth Williams as a comic brigadier, with a 'full supporting services cast'. The preview night was to be staged at the barracks, in front of an invited audience of officers and Singapore society, and the cast was in a panic for three days beforehand: a generator broke down, which meant the cancellation of a lighting rehearsal, and then Arlen attempted, in two marathon sessions, to pull the show together.

The following night's preview was a triumph ('Terrific reception – wonderful applause') but the show's first performance at the Victoria on the 27th was a disaster: one actor was too drunk to go on, most of the cast ('nitwits') were paralysed with fear of being RTU'd and 'half the audience walked out during the interval'. After that, it got better. 'Special mention should be made of Peter Stretton and Kenneth Williams for their first rate characterisations,' reported one newspaper critic.

He was living on about $45 (Singapore dollars) a week, supplemented by occasional gifts from home that came via registered mail. About a third of his pay went on drinks and cinema tickets but his other luxury was his letter-writing: in February he spent $10 on a Swan fountain pen and stationery. He docketed every letter to and from Orford – by the end of March 1947 his friend had sent 136, and Williams had replied nineteen times that year alone.

High and Low ran for ten days, before the cast were told they were taking the show to Burma. The commanding officer, Major Woodings, called it the toughest assignment in south-east Asia – 'not only because of the nature of the country, but because ENSA had been *free* but now, CSE was charging fourpence a show and the troops resented it'. With his usual precision and an undercurrent of apprehension, Williams recorded that they sailed on the SS *Empire Pride* from Singapore docks at 4.15 p.m., and landed four days later at lunchtime in Rangoon. On the way they stopped at Port Swettenham, south-west of Kuala Lumpur, to take 300 Indian troops on board. Williams, who detested sleeping in a hammock and had little to do but watch flying fish and sharks from the deck, was filled with a nasty, Blimpish resentment: 'These wogs are a filthy lot of swine'; 'This ship is bloody awful [. . .] of course the accommodation stinks to high heaven'. On the day they reached Rangoon, he made no reference to his twenty-first birthday – he noted only that the day was 'lousy. Frank B. reported 5 of us for being late out of the canteen.'

They were billeted at Burma Command HQ before moving to a CSE hostel. When the scenery arrived, it was damaged, but *High and Low* opened at the Garrison Theatre to a good reception and Williams began to settle again. Their tour began with a visit to the RAF station at Mingaladon on 11 March; on the 17th they went by train to Toungou station, stayed overnight, and went on to Meiktila and Mandalay. On the 21st they were in Maymyo, staying at Croxton Lodge.

By now Williams was revelling in his adventures – he and a friend invited two local girls out for dinner and found themselves in a brothel, after mistaking it for an 'awfully tatty restaurant'. They fell about laughing: 'Happy days, what a laugh! oh! life!!' Returning via Mandalay, they went by train through Thayi to Rangoon on the 28th, where Flight Lieutenant Arlen made a surprise visit. He arrived by flying boat and railed at the cast for disobeying orders: in the opening chorus they were supposed to have forage caps but 'we had left them all off, cos we hated wearing the bloody things'.

During the tour Williams added more impersonations to his act, including comedian Suzette Tarri, and the actors Leslie Hutchinson and Felix Aylmer. He made tentative efforts to write extra material of his own; his act now ran to about eight minutes.

Back in Rangoon, he made his first radio appearance, doing impersonations on Radio Burma – 'good experience!' – and making the announcements on *Blighty Calling* for Forces Network of Radio Rangoon two days later.

By now, after three years in the army, Williams was beginning to think of a career on stage. His friends were dubious: one told him it was impossible without an independent income, but the success of his impersonations, the applause out front and the praise backstage were all thrilling to him. Though there were days when he longed for demob, eight months had passed since he had left the map section and he realised that he was no longer looking forward to returning to Stanford's as a litho artist.

On 25 April, his unit boarded the *Empire Pride* and sailed down the western coastline of the peninsula for four days, even putting on a show on the troopdeck. After docking at Singapore on the 28th, they spent a final night on board, with Williams sleeping on a chair in the open. Back at Nee Soon they found new faces: 'Met John Schlesinger

– charming fellow'. Another, less outgoing, was Peter Nichols who found Williams frightening but impressive: 'the impeccable diction, nasal resonance, flared nostril, upturned chin, and the whinnying laugh like a horse played slow. His virtuosity was complete, owing nothing to anyone.'

Arlen saw it too: he cast Williams as the narrator in a dramatic reading, for just one night at the Gaiety, of *Hiroshima* by John Hersey, which was based on the testimonies of eyewitnesses. Arlen had also started rehearsals for a farce called *Not So Much the Heat*, but a dispute over performance rights meant the show was abandoned in mid-May. Williams was drafted into an existing production, *Over to You*, to do impersonations, while another revue was assembled. He moved into the Union Jack club with the cast as they took the show round Singapore.

Rehearsals for Arlen's new show began the following Monday. This time, Kenneth Williams and Stanley Baxter headed the bill. It opened with the title number, 'At Your Service', which inspired another favourite chat-show story: 'There was all this anger about any kind of effeminacy. Our opening number was, "We're boys of the service, We're at your service, entertaining *you*!" And [Major Woodings] watched this and he said, "Dreadful, dreadful, it's too effeminate. And all those sibilants – boys of the service, terrible. No, let's make it *men* . . . men of the service. Now go back off and come on again, and sing *men*." So we all came back [fey and mincing], "We're *men* of the service . . ." He said, "Ah, yes, that's more like it. Show 'em you're fellow men."'

The flavour of limp cabaret was made worse by their costumes: 'Flight Lieutenant Albert Arlen, with a face like a St Bernard, had decided that the line-up should be in military uniform – not khaki, but sky-blue trousers and the military jacket in yellow with your three tapes up,' Stanley Baxter remembered. 'I said, "That's making us like camp sergeants." He said, "It's not camp, and you are sergeants." I thought, Oh the boys are going to love this.'

Every night the opening chorus would stir up the hecklers, and the sergeants in yellow-and-blue would come smartly to attention, wheel left and march off to catcalls and raspberries. That left the opening act with a performer's nightmare, a hostile audience at the outset of a show – and Williams had the first solo spot, with a parade of impressions billed as 'Famous People'.

'Ken engineered himself to the end of the line,' said Baxter, 'so as we all marched off, he'd turn when he got near the wings and say, "Yesss! I'm not with that lot! Don't worry!" And of course they'd fall about laughing, so he'd got them back. And he could do that with any audience. He'd have been a wonderful vaudevillian, because no audience would have frightened him.'

The impressions were done at full pelt: 'lightning flashes', Peter Nichols called them. Williams capped the act with a burst of music-hall innuendo, kicking up his legs to Harry Champion's 'Any Old Iron' – 'iron' could be an abbreviation of 'iron hoof', which was rhyming slang. In a second solo slot, he performed 'I Wonder What Happened To Him', the first in a lifetime of Noël Coward numbers. Anxious about forgetting the lyric, he inscribed key words on one of the props, a fake cigar. The show also featured Williams in drag, as Princess Mah-Mee in *Aladdin*, a 'potted pantomime' written by Baxter – the author played Fairy Watermelon Seed, with Rae Hammond as Gin-Sling, the Slave of the Lamp. The whole cast came on to sing 'Pedro the Fisherman', a romantic number that required ensemble whistling. Williams would dart between the two rows of men, goosing them, so that they could not whistle for laughing.

During these weeks, while they toured *At Your Service* around Singapore, with occasional revivals of *Over to You*, two events occurred that became the defining legends of CSE's saga.

Company Sergeant-Major Hank Marriott committed suicide by swallowing cyanide: Rae Hammond had watched him pouring the powder into a glass decorated with enamelled flowers and assumed he was mixing up a dose of liver salts. The CSM was on $6,000 bail for charges of theft and extortion, and had already served six months for firearms offences; he had been trying to collect fake invoices and receipts, evidence of fraud with which he hoped to incriminate his commanding officer. Instead, his American wife kicked him out of their house near the Cathay cinema in Orchard Road and the CO, Woodings, moved in. A few days later Marriott's dossier of black-mail scraps disappeared from their hiding place in the sergeants' mess. Marriott sat down in a billet, swallowed the poison and died before

Hammond and his friends could carry him to the medical quarters next door.

Williams relished everything about the scandal – the sexual triangle, the corruption, the suicide and especially the funeral. With every retelling he embellished and distorted it, until he had the pallbearers sliding and tumbling into an open grave as the monsoon drenched the cemetery.

The other event was the arrival of a civilian show from England, starring a dancer called Barri Chatt who 'had the most extraordinary effect on the military when he arrived. Outside the HQ were several generals and brigadiers with rolled-up maps and field-glasses, and this dancer Barri did a pirouette about six times very fast indeed and then tapped this brigadier on the shoulder and said, "Tell your mother we're here, dear, and put the kettle on."' Thirty years later Peter Nichols would use Chatt, with a measure of Williams's acerbity stirred in, as the model for Terri Dennis, who was the central figure in his musical play based on CSE life, *Privates on Parade*. Barri Chatt delighted Williams, who would mimic his catchphrase and his Durham accent: 'Let's face it, dooky, it's *life*! It's the *theatre*!' But he was also disturbed by Chatt's promiscuity, which made him a caricature of the theatrical queen.

In *At Your Service*, Williams was still experimenting with new material, which had to be approved by Arlen. He dropped the Bette Davis impression, for instance, replacing it with Arthur Marshall, who was famous for his female impersonation, Nurse Dugdale, on radio. For two nights the skit was 'amazingly successful', and then at Black Amati on 11 July 'it died a natural death!!!!' The following week they did a show aboard HMS *Terror*, with performances at RAF units and regimental camps almost every night. Another tour was threatened, either of Burma or of Malaya, and Williams, filled with anxiety again, decided he had to return to England. On 20 June he had signed up to stay with CSE, but at the end of July he applied for his discharge papers. The request was granted: on his return from the tour, he would be released.

On 3 August, the cast of *At Your Service* set off on the first stage of their Malayan tour in taxis: the lorry to take them to the station had not turned up. A journey through the night brought them to Kuala

Lumpur, where they were billeted at 64 Reception Camp. Williams saw Carol Reed's *Odd Man Out* – 'wonderful film' – and the following day they went by road into the Cameron Highlands, to a hill station above a tea plantation. Williams set to work as a stagehand, enjoying the chaotic rush before the evening's show.

The next day took them to Taiping, where barely two dozen people paid their 4d to sit in the theatre at the Chinese Girls' School: 'Really disheartening. Rained all the time'. In Penang the next day they were billeted with the West Yorkshires, for a short and disastrous stay. By the end of the week they were back in Kuala Lumpur, after an impromptu cabaret at a NAAFI canteen in Ipoh had been cancelled because just ten people had come to see it.

Away from Arlen and Woodings, and with their time free for most of each day, CSE's 'men of the service' felt at ease, and it showed, which irked the staff officers at 64 Reception Camp. When some of the artistes were overheard complaining about conditions in the barracks, the whole cast was ordered to parade in uniform. This humiliation was averted with an apology. After a thirty-minute broadcast on Radio Malaya and a show at the officers' club in Seremban, their final date was the barracks theatre in Tampin. A few friends, including Nichols, treated Williams to a farewell meal at the Betty Café; while they ate jam pancakes, a heavily painted prostitute danced around their table, trying to entice them to the Betty Lodging-House upstairs. The young men threw food at her.

They arrived in Singapore on 29 August. Four days later Williams collected his demob papers from Woodings: he was to travel to Hong Kong with the rest of the company and board a troopship for home, though he was warned his documents could be rejected and he might have to return to Singapore. By now he was fed up with army muddling and barrack-room life: 'Tandy became quite drunk and threw beer over me! He and Hargreaves made thorough nuisance of themselves! – behaved like the swine they obviously are.'

On 5 September they sailed on the SS *Empress of Scotland*. The passage across the South China Sea was calm – Williams sunbathed till he burned, read G.K. Chesterton and helped put on a show, *All at Sea*, in the lounge. By 8 September they were in Hong Kong, and Williams spent the week wading through bureaucracy, presenting his papers to the garrison adjutant, drawing his civilian clothes and having his final medical.

Then the tour started. They took *At Your Service* to Fort Stanley and on to the Chinese mainland with a show and a cabaret for the Devonshire regiment. Back in Kowloon he went shopping for presents, spending his $60 fortnightly pay and most of his savings. It was a spree but every purchase was entered on the cash account pages at the back of his journal: dress material, nylons, jewellery and crêpe de Chine for his mother, three shirts for his father, and shoes, a watch, and a shirt and tie for himself. The total came to $279, a sum so extravagant that he had to write it out in words as well and initial it.

Williams loved Hong Kong. Twenty years later, he noted: 'How curious it is, that certain events stay in the mind. I shall always remember lying on that top bunk at the Fleet Club, with the magnificent view of the bay + Kowloon and going to sleep – aware of the sounds and the breeze and the smell of the sea – it has become idyllic in my mind.' He went midnight swimming after the shows, three nights in a row, larking about in the water and chatting with sailors: 'So gay it wasn't true.' On Saturday 4 October, *At Your Service* was performed for the last time, at the fleet theatre: 'Huge success all round, very enthusiastic audience. Hope this is the last time I work the show though for I'm heartily sick of it – and the company!' The *China Mail* loved him: 'Making his first appearance in Hong Kong, Ken Williams' impersonations were cleverly done and kept the audience in roars of laughter throughout.'

They had to do the shows without Nichols, who was confined to a hospital bed with amoebic dysentery, and could only listen as an excited Williams and Baxter visited to tell him of their starring roles in a radio production of *The Death of Nelson*, for a broadcast on Trafalgar Day, 21 October.

During his last few days in Hong Kong, Williams struck up a brief friendship with David Whitfield, a leading signalman on HMS *Black Swan*, who had a fine singing voice. On Saturday 25 October the CSE troupe boarded the SS *Devonshire*. Williams appears to have pushed his ambitions of a theatre career to the back of his mind, and a few days before departure had written to a man named Thornton about a job with the Metropolitan Water Board – 'interesting opportunity?'

Once again, they put on a show mid-ocean. Nichols wrote a parody of a Western Brothers number – he and Williams called themselves the Far Eastern Brothers. Williams also starred in skits called 'Radio Pirates' and 'Big Girl Now', and threw all his energy into his last CSE production, pouring out ideas to the director, Geoff Deakin. On the last day of October the *Devonshire* sailed out of Singapore, leaving the entertainers ashore as Williams, suddenly lonely, began his journey home. He immediately signed up for the ship's concert party, rehearsing for two hours each day.

There was a day's shore leave in Ceylon, though he was more concerned with devising and rehearsing routines: having disentangled himself from the entertainments corps, Williams felt less cynical about a show than he had ever been. He called it *Arts and Farces*, and revived a Three Caballeros routine from a Arlen revue, switching it about so that two of the trio were in drag. Although there were no backdrops to be had, and several sketches had to be dropped at the last moment, which made for a chaotic dress rehearsal, the show itself was a storming success. They opened on the promenade deck on Tuesday 11 November, and by the third night, as they sailed out of Aden in Yemen, the exhilaration was too much. The whole cast got drunk after the show, Williams was sick in his hammock and, when he woke, the gold watch he'd bought for $60 in Hong Kong was gone (it turned up, 'rather the worse for wear', ten days later).

His favourite co-star was the tumbler Ted Durante, who had worked as a clown with Bertram Mills Circus. His physical routines delighted Williams, who was beginning to realise that he could barely hold a teacup himself when he was acting. His own impersonations were all about the face and the voice, which were so mobile that the audience seemed not to notice that Williams found it hard to move and deliver lines at the same time.

At the entrance to the Suez Canal, the *Devonshire* hit a bridge and there was a two-day delay before they could proceed. Along its whole length, the troops were subjected to whistles and catcalls from locals on the canal's banks. All the men, even in the concert party, had to wear battle dress. They reached Port Said late on the 19th; the following day, the troops were crowded around radios, listening in silence to commentary from St Paul's on the wedding of Princess

Elizabeth. After the Indian Ocean, the Mediterranean was bitter and choppy: in the shows, Williams recalled, 'you could hardly hear any clapping because they were so cold, the troops, they wore gloves and it was all terribly muffled.'

On 27 November they rounded Gibraltar, and the weather got colder and rougher. Williams, miserable in battledress and sick of 'this filthy ship', was counting the hours till they would dock in Liverpool.

They pulled into dock at 9.30 a.m. on Tuesday 2 December, and he immediately wired his parents at 57 Marchmont Street. For the next forty-eight hours, Williams recorded his itinerary with excited precision: at 7.45 a.m. on the 3rd he disembarked, was pushed on to a train to Farnborough at 9.45 a.m., arriving at 5 p.m.; reached Aldershot barracks at 5.30 p.m.; was in bed by 10.30 p.m., and was demobbed on the morning of the 4th. At 2.30 p.m. he arrived home. With his mother, father and their friends he got drunk in their locals, Henneky's and the Holborn Bar. 'Walked back – pouring rain. Lovely to be home again.'

3

'The dream from which there is no awakening'

December 1947–February 1950

A s Kenneth Williams arrived back at the hairdresser's shop in
Bloomsbury, a young RAF officer named Robert Hardy was
returning to Magdalen College, Oxford, to complete his English
degree. 'Oxford,' he remarked, 'was actually a clever move because
it got me my first job just like that.' As the war had emptied the stage
of juvenile male leads, 'there was a mass of people who were actually
six years older, or dead. And therefore thousands of places to fill. It
was terribly easy. I took my finals in November 1948, and in January
1949 I was rehearsing at Stratford-upon-Avon.'

Hardy was four months older than Williams. He had been educated
at Rugby and his father was headmaster of Cheltenham College. He
was confident of his talent and the theatre embraced him.

Williams had no confidence that he belonged on stage. As a working-class NCO in the entertainments corps, he had made no useful
contacts in theatre: he knew no one at the BBC, for instance. Unlike
Hardy he had no inherent expectations. Though he pretended an
arrogance about his talents, he did not in fact feel entitled to his
ambitions. To hope for a career was too much; his father insisted
he should have a trade, but Williams was almost ready to settle for
a mere job, just to get the security of a wage – even a clerk's wage.
He had his interview with Mr Thornton of the Metropolitan Water
Board, before Christmas, and he talked to Val Orford about resuming
his litho apprenticeship, but he could not make up his mind.

The new diary was an A5 Letts with a hardboard cover and thirty
lines for every day. Williams's handwriting suddenly became flowing
and easy, and much more legible than the cramped abbreviations of
the previous year. Most of the entries were written in a single session,
so that the style of lettering on any given page remained consistent.

(In later years, the handwriting and the ink could change half a dozen times on a page, as he returned to the entry throughout the day.) The bigger format suited him – for a few weeks at the start of 1948, even when nothing significant was happening, he was cramming every page. On occasion he pasted in an extra sheet or added a piece of notepaper with a stapler to give himself more room. All his talk was of going out with friends to cafés and pubs, trips to the theatre and the cinema, lunches with Orford and letters from CSE colleagues.

He made sure his parents saw him with female friends as well as men. Two young women, Toni Marks and Nicky (or Vicki), who had been in Singapore with *Stars in Battledress*, liked to call round late at Marchmont Street, once even waking Williams after he'd gone to bed. They would stay for hours, and Charlie and Louie would sometimes join them, talking and drinking. Toni tried to persuade Williams to rehearse a comedy double act with her, and he was happy to let his parents wonder whether the banter ('conversation was light, but outrageously suggestive') hid an attraction between them. He admitted to himself that it didn't – 'I'm C.C.L.,' he noted, code for 'couldn't care less', and he scoffed at 'this Hetero Goldwyn Mayer stuff'. But he was not able to accept that he would never find any woman desirable, especially as he also shied away from any kind of physical intimacy with men.

When he had told Stanley Baxter about his inhibitions, in an earnest confession as they stood on the Anderson Bridge over the Singapore river, his friend advised him to talk to an army psychiatrist. Now, he made an older woman his confidante – another Singapore acquaintance, Marie Earley, who had a son almost the same age as Williams. Marie assured him he would fall in love, and that when it happened he wouldn't be able to mistake the symptoms.

'I came out of the cinema and standing there, on the steps, confronting that ugly hulk of St Pancras station, suddenly seemed to feel the realisation of a great truth. The necessity for "belief" – faith, if you will, in this life of ours. I suddenly felt completely awed by the absolutely temporal nature of everything [. . .] I have a horrible feeling tonight that I just can't cope with the future – it all seems so dreadful in prospect! Will I ever meet that "real love" in another which Marie spoke of at our last meeting? – although I feel it hopeless

– yet I shall go on hoping and looking for it.' This dual longing, the romantic need bound to the spiritual, would haunt him all his life.

He had turned down the Water Board and decided to resume his training as a draughtsman. Stanford's, which had been taken over by George Philip's, a map-maker based in North Acton, offered to start him at £6 8s 6d a week. Williams was aghast at the munificence of it and worried that his employers would be made to look stupid if he didn't deserve the salary. He immediately treated himself to a second-hand typewriter, for £6, and began to fret: 'I feel somehow nervous, and not very confident about my capabilities as a litho-draughtsman. I prefer paperwork really [. . .] Oh! how I wish my employment were with theatre work of some sort.'

By the end of the first week his supervisor was assuring him that his work was good and he was worth his pay, and Williams was pleased to discover he had not lost the lettering skills learned before the war. But the grinding routine of the job, and the grim conditions, horrified him – it was 'tedious and misery-making'. His workmates were foul-mouthed, which didn't bother him, but unimaginative, coarse and homophobic with it, which he detested. Within a fortnight he knew he would not be able to stand the atmosphere for long. He still didn't dare try for theatre work; instead, he wondered whether he should become a hairdresser, like his father.

News came from his CSE comrade Geoffrey Deakin: 'He is home again in England – mar dear! the scandal – can't wait to meet him again (me beads!)' On Deakin's first day back in London, Williams took him back to Marchmont Street and they slept in his parents' double bed (Charlie was in the Homeopathic Hospital for a hernia operation). The relationship might not have been sexual – Williams never suggests that it was, though it was clear he was thrilled by the friendship: 'He makes me feel curiously elated, in this other-wise "dual" environment.' They talked of taking a flat together, but Deakin had the chance of an acting job with Luton rep and he stayed in London only five days.

Two abject days at Philip's, shivering in his overcoat without any heating, convinced him he could stand it no longer: 'I nearly died of cold, and wish I had in a way, because at least it would have put Philip's a little out of routine for once.' His instinct for obedience held him back, so he wrote to the labour exchange, asking whether a working man could legally change his occupation, and trudged through heavy snow on a Saturday morning to be told, to his surprise, that he could. He handed in his week's notice the following Monday.

By the time he dared to broach the topic with his father, he already had doubts about retraining as a hairdresser. Charlie would not hear of his studying at college and insisted he would learn his trade faster at the shop. As the discussion became an argument, Williams realised they could never work together. It was Sunday 29 February – Leap Day – and two other events coincided to give him the courage to make his own leap. Stanley Baxter wrote, with news that he was to audition for the Old Vic, forcing Williams to face the truth that he could never be happy doing anything but acting. And at midnight, a phone call came with the news that Louie's stepmother, 'Tin Lizzie', had died.

The rush of family activity and emotion seemed to give him conviction. His cousin Joan remembered how buoyant he was as they stood together cutting sandwiches in the basement kitchen in Marchmont Street: 'The day of her funeral, Ken and I were staying behind, and he said, "Come on, Joanie, we'd better get these sandwiches made before they come back." He was buttering them and I was filling them, and we were laughing – he said, "We mustn't really laugh, but never mind, she's gone to a better place."'

The funeral was full of traditional cockney ceremony, with the hearse standing for several minutes outside Eliza Morgan's old home in Sandwich Street so that neighbours could bring out wreaths of lilies and tulips, and pay their respects. While Louie and her sisters were making the arrangements, Williams was hammering out letters to influential theatre figures such as Alan Dent, Basil Dean and Peter Cotes. He was burning with uncharacteristic optimism: these were 'long shots, but they might strike – one never knows! [. . .] retire to bed, full of hope'. The long shots clipped their targets: he got an invitation to phone Dent and the chance to audition for Dean's British Theatre Group. Dent liked his voice and his attitude, and offered to help him find repertory work if the audition for Dean failed.

His first real chance was for a revue in Manchester – 'so I packs me bag and goes traipsing off [. . .] nothing ventured, nothing gained and all that'. The rail ticket cost him £2 10s; he knew the investment was wasted when he saw the show. *We're After Laughter* was 'quite bloody [. . .] I was pained at the sight and sound of the whole thing'. The producer, Hugh Bernard, offered him a singing part and gave him an introduction to London impresario Roy Limbert. Arriving back at Marchmont Street at dawn the next day, Williams walked down to Haymarket to meet Limbert: 'a massive, fat Jew – cigar, a dozen phones and all. The outcome? – nowt!' Another phone call kept his hopes alive, for an audition with Wycombe rep: 'I am madly hoping and praying for success.' All he got from the producer, Anthony Stuart, was a lecture. 'This is no calling for the faint-hearted,' he warned. 'There are so many pitfalls, disappointments and setbacks. One must simply go on bashing one's head, however obdurate the brick wall – it's hell, but it's the theatre.'

The only reply to his advert in *The Stage* invited him to purchase an apprenticeship, for 150 guineas, as an unpaid stage manager with 'the "Q" theatre'. By now Williams was miserable, brooding on depression, failure and thoughts of suicide. His journal entries fore-shadowed the tone of his diary in the days before his death, exactly forty years later. 'Oh! what the hell, what's the good?' he concluded on 3 April. 'What's the bloody use of it all?' In desperation, he looked for encouragement to his horoscope: 'According to the stars (mine – "Pisces") Tuesday will see the reward of much hard work. I am to expect fortunate news!' The stars were improbably right. Tuesday brought enquiries from reps in Newquay and Felixstowe, with another from Malvern the next day. By the time he accepted the job in Cornwall, three more offers had come.

To raise some capital, he sold his stamp collection for £6 10s and caught the Riviera Express from Paddington on 29 April, to join the Newquay Repertory Players at £4 a week. The troupe was run by a feuding trio that called itself the Company of Three: the director Anne Keble, the actor/stage manager John Field, and the leading lady Linda Hayward. Williams was instantly in his element. He arrived in time to catch a performance of Emlyn Williams's *The Light of Heart* at the Newquay theatre, and to meet the cast. The following evening after the show, a party at the Penolver Hotel gave him the chance to size them up. Keble, with her brisk manner and penetrating questions, made him bristle, and he was inclined to side with Hayward, whose acting impressed him.

The party stretched on till 3 a.m., and to his alarm Williams realised there would be another the next night. Already rehearsing for his first production, and with his lines to learn (as Ninian, in St John Ervine's *The First Mrs Fraser*), Williams pleaded a headache. As he had discovered in Singapore, he lacked the stamina for regular nights of heavy drinking. At rehearsals he was nervous, fluffing his lines, but his eidetic memory made him word-perfect well before the dress rehearsals. He could hear a speech or a poem once, and recall it accurately weeks or years later. This talent had not been evident at school and must have developed from his love of literature as a teenager, probably fostered by the old vet Chisholm, who was his guardian as a wartime evacuee and whose grandstanding poetry recitals Williams never forgot.

Between rehearsals, the cast helped to build and paint the scenery. The first night was Thursday 6 May – the local paper's critic spotted his performance and praised him as 'well cast', 'the right type' and 'worth watching'. Williams felt pleased with himself after the show as he collected the script for his next role, as Dr Harvester in Somerset Maugham's *The Sacred Flame*: 'I think I shall use the [Ronald] Colman voice for this.' His attitude to acting was revealed in that comment. Technique mattered more than truth, and ridicule was the better part of humour. Beneath this lay a selfishness, and within that an uncertainty. Williams needed to stand out, to lay claim to the biggest laughs and, though he was already too subtle to show-boat or scene-steal, he could be indifferent to his effect on the rest of the play. The immediate danger was to the producer, who could hardly criticise Williams for being better than everybody else; in the long term, though, it was Williams's own career on the stage that would be damaged.

Various employers would handle this problem of uniqueness in different ways: egotists like Orson Welles and Tony Hancock slapped him down; impresarios such as Michael Codron and Bill Kenwright sometimes despaired of him; and the *Carry On* producer Peter Rogers manipulated him with charm. Anne Keble, tolerating no nonsense, gave him a ticking-off when he failed to turn up for an afternoon setting up the scenery. Williams was livid: 'Told her I'd a part to learn! – and that I considered it more important! Couldn't care less about her anyway. She's just a silly "elocutory" old bitch with sibilant "S"s as far as I'm concerned!'

He hated to be criticised, and flashes of that filthy mood were recurrent during the next few, exhausting weeks. Presenting one role as he learned and rehearsed another, Williams discovered how gruelling rep work could be. He played the Lord Chief Justice in another Emlyn Williams drama, *Night Must Fall*; and the part of Dudley in a Gerald Savory drama titled *George and Margaret*: 'in the person of Kenneth Williams, youth "stole the show". He got every laugh the author intended and many more besides,' the local critic reported. In his first three months in theatre, he worked on thirteen productions.

His diary traced the convoluted backstage politics of the Company of Three, who brought in an experienced rep director, Richard West, from the beginning of June, in an effort to quell the infighting. West immediately impressed Williams: he was energetic, visionary, dramatic and ambitious. He was a decisive director too, but ill suited for the pettiness and factions of the company. Williams revelled in the intrigues and walk-outs, and when West left in July there was a mass resignation: 'All our notices have been handed in. Now, we've either pushed the lifeboat out or burned our boats.' Anne Keble simply ignored it.

Amid all this, he made the most earnest attempt of his life to fall in love with a girl. Her name was Sonia Moray, the assistant stage manager and a novice actress with the company, and she shared his lodging-house. They met two days after Williams arrived, and he thought her 'very charming. Lovely features and voice'. The next day they rehearsed together, 'and talked and laughed a hell of a lot'.

He had a powerful motive. Geoffrey Deakin had written with horrible news: his mother had read his letters and diary, and discovered her son was homosexual. Deakin was so mortified that he abandoned the theatre and threw himself into Salvation Army work.

Charlie Williams already harboured a homophobic disgust for the theatre. If he became convinced his son was gay, he might order him to quit the stage or disown him – or, worse, make Louie disown him. That thought was unbearable. For all his aloofness and quirks,

Williams was strongly conventional. He believed promiscuous sex, homosexual or not, was sinful. Marriage was natural and right, and only love could fulfil life's spiritual meaning. He wanted his parents to see that he was leading a good and moral life, which meant that he needed to emulate them.

Sonia was several years his junior, and her lack of confidence was part of her charm. She laughed, and she listened, and she was boyishly pretty. For a few weeks they appeared to be courting – walking together morning and afternoon, on hikes to the villages and across the headlands, going to the cinema, eating in cafés, and learning their lines together. Sonia struggled with her acting: she needed elocution lessons, which Williams regarded as 'a complete waste of time as far as she is concerned'. There was no sexual spark between them; Williams was too honest to have pretended otherwise. And he soon tired of playing the masculine role: 'Went out for supper, with Sonia, in the evening, expensive but just *had* to! (She hasn't paid yet, and doesn't look as if she's likely to offer – to hell with bloody girls!)'

When Richard West arrived and took an immediate interest in the shy ASM, Williams side-slipped into a sexually neutral role, as the third person in a couple. He could flirt without risk and dominate without having to take the lead. It was a pattern that he repeated two decades later in the most successful relationship of his life, and arguably it was the androgynous role he played in his most successful radio and film series.

Sonia must still have hoped that Williams's sexual anxieties would evaporate, but by August, with her twin disappointments as a lover and an actress, she decided to leave Newquay. She broke the news to Williams, who responded with polite regret and pasted two photos of her into his journal: 'Shall be sorry to see her go, though, for I have become very attached to this charmingly fresh ingenue!! We've had some good times together.' He waved Sonia goodbye from Newquay station on 15 August and wrote in his diary: 'The poor lamb was in tears as the thing steamed out! I'm going to miss this sweet child of whom I have grown so fond, during the past few months. She has always been *such* a companion – so placid and tolerant with me.'

The Newquay Players continued to stage a new production every week, even as the controlling Company of Three fell apart. John

Field left and invited Williams to go with him; instead, he accepted Anne Keble's offer of £5 a week to stay, though he loathed them both. 'God! This woman continually talks down to me – Grandma to the adolescent! Christ! I shall be glad to leave the whole bloody shoot of 'em!'

Had he really wanted to go, it would have been easy, for Stanley Baxter was urging him to visit Scotland. He stayed in Cornwall, addicted to the intrigues, and was rewarded by a dramatic telegram from Richard West in London – 'RETURNED ITALY TODAY RING ME TONIGHT HOWEVER LATE REVERSING CHARGES MOST URGENTLY.' West swept back into Newquay and on to the board of directors, and after one final production the troupe took a break before re-forming as the Dolphin Players. West wanted to introduce more challenging plays, by Ibsen and Chekhov; he opened with Shaw's *Candida*, and followed it with *Tobias and the Angel* by James Bridie and J.B. Priestley's *An Inspector Calls*. Williams was exhausted by learning the Bridie: he played Tobias, and was determined to be word perfect in the long and demanding speeches. The production was easily the most complex he had worked on, and as he helped West to fit music to the scenes – choosing Ravel, Mussorgsky and Liszt – he began to see how ambitious theatre could be.

It was, in fact, too ambitious; the company's finances buckled and despite frantic talk of a tour and a panto, Williams returned to London, with no job and £24 in the bank, at the end of November 1948. Sonia Moray joined him, staying at his Aunt Alice's pub in Islington. For a few days he showed her the city, staying out so late that his family started to talk. But he tired of it within a fortnight: 'Sonia rang up, and we had a fruitless conversation about generalities. I think she's probably very lonely in London now – but I'm afraid I've neither money or time to spend on her these days. I am so occupied with my own affairs, and for the rest – well, it's lovely just to laze.' And then he had a taste of real infatuation. At a Christmas party, Williams met scenery designer Oliver Ford, and for an exhilarating few days allowed his emotions to sweep him along.

Arriving back in Marchmont Street at 5.30 a.m., he tried to set down in his diary how thrilled he was – 'tight, tired, but elated. Life has taken on a wonderful design. I need never be morbid any more. A motive for working has been supplied. I feel NEW, and clean again.' He was falling in love, something he wanted so desperately to happen. They met the next day, and the next, and went on meeting until, on Christmas Eve, Ford moved into No. 57. It is unlikely that Charlie Williams would have agreed to let the young men share a room, especially as Pat's bedroom was empty, but Kenneth and Oliver certainly slept together. And then, abruptly, it ended. The last mention of Ford in Williams's diary is 29 December: 'This boy is the personification of indecision. Just doesn't know what he wants to do with himself.'

Williams expanded on that hint when they met again, long after, in 1971. 'Suddenly I looked across the dance floor [at the Dorchester Hotel] and there was OLIVER!! dancing with a sequined lady . . . looking just the same and careering round the floor at a pace I couldn't possibly manage! He was at Peter Rogers' table: he saw me, and eventually came over and talked . . . He said, "Why have we wasted all these years?" and told me, "I am still in love with you, you know . . . I never fell out of love . . ." I said, "You were never dominant enough. You should've taken over," and he said, "No . . . you would have hated me afterwards . . ." '

The regrets lingered for the rest of Williams's life. The end of their brief affair inspired a poem, a year before he died:

> We said goodbye at the bus stop
> The friendship was hardly a ride
> Actors in front of a backdrop
> With words which the action belied
> Actions had made for the tension
> The rest could be taken as read
> I knew that I never could mention
> The bodily smell in the bed
> Odd that repugnance should reach us
> When we're told something else by the heart
> Without body odour they teach us
> Our dogs couldn't tell us apart
> But the physical spell had been broken

And ruling returned to the head
The real reason just stayed unspoken
We talked of the weather instead
Just at the point of departure
When I had practically turned
You said 'I just hope that one day
You'll find your affection is spurned'
The spite seemed akin to madness
I hardly believed what I'd heard
All I could feel was sadness
There wasn't another word.

Williams began to pick up work again at the start of 1949, including his first BBC recordings, minor parts in two episodes of a courtroom serial, *Gordon Grantley KC*. He appeared as the bellhop, with just half a dozen lines, in Garson Kanin's *Born Yesterday* at the Intimate Theatre in Palmers Green, and Richard West, now directing in rep at the Theatre Royal, Stratford, hired him for *Fly Away Peter* and *Ten Little Niggers*.

The first night at the Theatre Royal earned him a mention in three local papers – 'excellent', 'pleasantly droll' and 'a clever foil'. He snipped out the reviews and pasted them in his scrapbook. Agents were taking an interest too, and one, Mary Woolrige of Harbord's, recommended him to Ronnie Kerr, at the New Theatre in Bromley, Kent. Kerr had a reputation for brilliance and enterprise, and the salary was £9 a week. Williams agreed without hesitation.

One of the actors under contract at Bromley was Nicholas Parsons, who would remain a friend for forty years. 'He was difficult to cast as a young man. He wasn't a leading actor; his natural casting was as a character actor. And when you're young and you're a character actor, the parts are limited. Also his diminutiveness was against him.'

Williams's first role at Bromley was Snake, a minor part in Sheridan's *School for Scandal*, which required him to learn the gavotte – 'It was absolutely bloody. I hate dancing.' He did enough to impress Kerr: 'Obviously clever – brilliant imaginative type. Cruel wit – something of a sadist. Very charming. Rather like him.' A week later the director invited him to play a blackmailer in Edward Percy's *The Shop at*

Sly Corner. Williams was delighted: 'The part is very good and absolutely "me".'

It is not hard to see how Percy's description of the venal young man, a jeweller's assistant, appealed to Williams. Fellowes 'is a good-looking boy of twenty or twenty-one erring on the side of effeminacy. He has a pale face and thin red lips. His eyes have a way of looking out of their corners [. . .] His manner is superior, but there is an attitude of indefinable insolence about him.'

Nicholas Parsons, who played the detective in *Sly Corner*, thought the performance unforgettable. 'There was a character who was evil, young and sly, very sinister, and a young Kenneth Williams came down to play it. And he was a bit of a character even then. We got on very well. I think he had a natural theatricality. Some of the other regulars who were more staid thought he was a bit too much of a character, though they respected his ability. I remember once we were rehearsing the scene where he dies, and he did it very well – he was saying, "Oooh, weren't I wonderful, it was soooo dramatic, there was some real theatre there!" It was a role made for Kenny, a nasty little character, and he really gave it his all. You remember it, almost sixty years later.'

The local papers were also impressed. 'His is an odious part,' wrote one reviewer, 'played with a sneer that seems to come from the heart – as neat a piece of acting as the company has ever given us'. Another noted that Williams 'played the aggressive young blackmailer so well that a sigh of relief went up from the house when he was strangled'.

Richard West contacted him during rehearsals, to offer a job with the revived repertory company in Newquay at £10 a week. After appearing in Noël Coward's *We Proudly Present*, at Bromley, Williams had walk-ons in two BBC features and joined West for a short run of *An Inspector Calls* at Stratford before starting to learn his parts for the double bill that would relaunch the Newquay Players – Chekhov's *The Proposal* and Shaw's *The Man of Destiny*. On the flyers, Williams took top billing.

With most of the Newquay company, he caught the Cornish Express from Paddington on 16 May, and detested his lodgings in Crantock Street immediately: 'These digs [. . .] are terrible!! I shall go raving mad if I stay here long. Madly working class'ish. Quite the end.' He moved to Tower Road and liked it no better: 'A ghastly day – especially with the Merrifields. I feel absolute saturation in this household. Never have such a collection of basically good people been so utterly horrible. They're the typical paradoxical English family AT HOME! in their revolting barbaric way.' After the double bill, Williams had no role in *The Sulky Fire* by Jean Jacques Bernard ('Annette Kerr simply superb. I sat in the stalls. Everyone recognised me, and whispered') and the rest of the season's plays occupied him without stretching him.

Whenever he could, he would swim in the bays and walk on the cliff paths. Otherwise, he was bored: 'Rehearsals – bloody. Val came from Torquay – bloody. Performance in evening – bloody.' Like a disruptive child, he started to entertain himself by stirring up trouble, spreading rumours, passing on snide remarks, goosing people as they went on stage, provoking others into giggling fits, and then protesting his innocence. This malicious sense of fun damaged his friendships, with West as well as with the actors he liked best, such as James Naylin and Joan Dale.

'Naylin spends the entire day sulking,' he noted smugly during a week-long run of *The Letterbox Rattles*. 'R. [Richard West] had fit of giggles [. . .] He tried to blame me for his own lack of self-control in the afternoon, simply to save his own face. Very naughty of him actually.' 'Pinched Joan Dale's bot as she was going on! She sulked about it rest of evening.' 'R. didn't speak to me at all in the dressing room. If he thinks he's going to start a sulk with me – his most loyal friend – he's bloody well mistaken.' Behind it all was a sense that he had outgrown provincial theatre and felt trapped in the cycle of play and rehearsal.

'I must get out of this weekly rep,' he wrote. 'More and more I am beginning to be frightened of its spider web ramifications – its insidious trick device. Misery making. Both R. and Algernon [West] expect you to have NO tricks AND do a part a week as near w/e [West End] standard as possible [. . .] It's just impossible, and unutterably stupid of them (as well as selfish).' 'A tat town of the West Country appeals neither to my sense of comfort or humour. I did 18 months of this in Seac [South East Asia Command], and don't fancy doing it any more.' When the curtain came down on the company, at the end of September, they threw a party on the stage. Williams read out an ode, rigid with in-jokes and innuendo.

Within a day of arriving home at Marchmont Street, he was writing to agents and producers, and within a week had hopes of work in Richmond, High Wycombe and York. Donald O'Malley at Wycombe rep offered him £8 a week, starting in October, and Williams wrote at once to accept; when confirmation did not come quickly enough, he wrote again. For all his complaints about weekly rep, he hated unemployment more.

Travelling between Buckinghamshire and King's Cross every day was more wearing than he'd expected. So were the productions: O'Malley wanted overt acting, and he wasn't satisfied until Williams turned in a sarcastic performance of sheer ham. A friend from Norway, Annette Kerr joined the company in the second week, which raised his spirits, and (playing Lachlen in *The Hasty Heart*) he wrote: 'I am so happy playing "Lachie" – I don't think I've ever enjoyed a role *so* much in my life before. The company are so charming too. Life is very good.' O'Malley liked Williams better when he was miserable, though, accusing him of lacking sincerity in his roles and of substituting technique for conviction. That pricked the bubble and the producer regained his unhappy actor.

Williams would not walk out without another promise of work, but with Annette Kerr he planned his escape, auditioning for rep at Eastbourne. They gave notice before Christmas, but were contracted to two more productions. The first was *Treasure Island*: O'Malley tore into the cast after three shows, berating them for bad timing, missed cues and not knowing their lines. 'Petty-farting little notes,' sneered Williams, 'but one of them hit at the real trouble with this production [. . .] his own shocking performance which can only be described as obscene.'

He was rarely alone and saw friends from provincial rep almost every day. Richard West, Sonia Moray, Nicholas Parsons and Rae Hammond were all in London, and he kept a record of others as he was introduced to them. A short engagement in early 1950 at the New in Bromley, playing Read in *The Guinea Pig,* ended badly: 'Ghastly contretemps [. . .] with a pansy s/director. Complained to [producer] Jean Shepherd who's just as barmy. Never again!' His life had lost direction. Looking for a purpose, and finding nothing in London, he decided to visit Stanley Baxter in Glasgow.

The train journey took eleven hours. Struggling on to the platform at Glasgow with his case, he missed his friend and had to take a taxi to his lodgings on Wilton Street. When Baxter returned he was with a friend, Laurie Sellstrom, and Williams was smitten. He felt suddenly certain that this was the purpose his life lacked, in the shape of a handsome, confident, articulate young man. Baxter introduced his girlfriend, Moira, who was to become his wife of more than forty years. Williams barely registered her, noticing only that she was 'sweet' and that she and Stanley were 'having a vague sort of thing'. Sellstrom filled his mind. After a snowy night, they drove out through the white-quilted Lowlands, and Williams felt elated: 'This is the dream from which there is no awakening. At last – no more worries now. Everything about it is honest + sincere.'

Three days later, with his impending return to London, the joy started to fade, but when Sellstrom phoned to offer him a lift to the station, the call came 'like a rainbow!' Their newborn love would endure, he swore. It expired, inevitably, after a short correspondence: a letter from Sellstrom, on 9 March, 'read like an advt. for Frigidaire. Of course to read between the lines is to read finis.' This affair, brief as a flicker, set a trend, and for years Williams would feel safest with infatuations at a distance, with young men he met on holiday, or visitors to England, or penfriends. He would not run the risk of seeing anyone day after night after day, as he had with Oliver Ford, where the relationship would have to develop, or be destroyed.

4

'What is right in this haphazard career?'

February 1950–October 1954

Rehearsals began in Eastbourne on the Tuesday after he left Glasgow. Williams was reunited with Annette Kerr and also introduced to John Hussey, whom he liked immediately. His capacity for lasting friendship was as deep as his love affairs were shallow: he warmed to Hussey's wit, charm and musical taste, and discovered a shared enjoyment in philosophical conversations.

Their rapport was so relaxed that they considered renting a place together in London, and in fact, for a few weeks at the end of the fifties, Hussey would have the unique distinction of sharing a flat with Williams, who was then between lodgings. For a quarter of a century, the friendship survived widening disparities between the fame of one and the disappointments of the other; it also weathered several coolings over borrowed money, and even outlasted Hussey's emigration to South Africa, until finally it petered out through lack of correspondence. Laziness in replying to letters was, as Williams often warned, a cardinal sin.

The first production at Eastbourne's Devonshire Park Theatre was the thriller *Night Must Fall*, one of three plays by his namesake Emlyn that Williams had tackled previously. This time he was the central character, Dan, a 'sadistic, Bible-reading pageboy with a twisted mind', whose introverted hatred for the ruling classes boils over into murder – 'a superb and fascinating performance', reported the *Eastbourne Gazette*.

The following week he had a small role in St John Ervine's play, *Robert's Wife*, and also rehearsed *The Letter* by Somerset Maugham: both shows would be presented at the Margate Hippodrome in Kent as well as at the Park. They took a coach across the southern counties, through Hastings, Winchelsea and Canterbury, to arrive in a seaside town that was 'freezing cold and miserable. The theatre is like an ice box and vulgar and horrid.' As the union deputy, Williams presided over the cast's Equity meeting that week; the company, run by the producer Jennifer Sounes for Bell and Winwood Theatres, was struggling, and within days three actors were dismissed.

In mid-March the company returned to Eastbourne and started rehearsals on *No Time for Comedy* by S.N. Behrmann: Williams took the lead once more, as the philandering New York playwright Gaylord Easterbrook, putting 'a great deal of action into a clever impersonation'. He itched to get away from artificial rep comedies, to play challenging roles in serious plays, and kept hoping that Richard West would put together a new company.

Typically dramatic, West did send a telegram, urging Williams to walk out and join him at High Wycombe, but this only promised more rep and a reduced salary of £8 a week. Instead, he took the coach back to Margate with another frivolous comedy, playing a man who must forfeit £1,000 if he tells a lie, in *Nothing But the Truth* by James Montgomery. Both this and *The Girl Who Couldn't Quite*, by Leo Marks, were produced by Donald Morley, a friend and regular caller at 57 Marchmont Street, whom Williams found rude and condescending as a director. Jennifer Sounes was working her notice during the next production, *Fools Rush in*, and neither Williams nor Kerr was surprised to be dismissed in the middle of May.

'I love the theatre more than anything else in the world,' he told the *Margate Chronicle*, 'but I can never quite make out why. Probably because I am a complete exhibitionist.' As he collected his pay-off, an extra two weeks' salary plus his fare back to London, it was difficult for him to think of any better reason, or of another career that could offer such fleeting rewards for such constant commitment.

He spent the following few weeks looking for work, writing speculative letters to producers, agents and the BBC. What rescued him, bizarrely, was his name. The Arts Council of Wales had commissioned the producer Clifford Evans to put together a Welsh company for a season at Swansea's Grand Theatre, with Richard West as his assistant director. For the first time, Williams was part of a cast that was rich with talent, including Rachel Roberts and Wilfrid Brambell. It was soon bolstered by Richard Burton, with his wife, Sybil: 'The Welsh were trying to start a national theatre in Swansea,' she explained. 'And Kenneth was there, because his name was Williams, as was mine. I was enchanted by him. He made me laugh so much. I loved him to bits straight away.'

The force of Evans's directing made a vivid impression on Williams, who recalled in his autobiography how a single word of instruction to one actor – 'Walk!' – transformed a shambolic, crowded scene into a dramatic stage entrance. The first production was *Family Portrait* and Williams struggled for days in rehearsal, fearing he would be sacked, before Evans took him to one side and talked to him. 'At last I seem to be getting somewhere with this part,' Williams exulted. They opened on 1 August to 'great, great success. Most exciting reception. We took 12 curtains. Thrilling.'

After a two-week run of Noel Langley's *Little Lambs Eat Ivy*, Burton arrived, to play Trigorin in *The Seagull*. Williams was appointed his understudy, with the promise of a leading role in *Saint Joan* next. He thought himself honoured to fetch drinks between acts for Burton, who was fresh from co-starring with John Gielgud in the West End. The first night was a triumph; the third was nearly a disaster as Burton, either drunk or (as he claimed) ill with food poisoning, declared he could not go on. Williams, the understudy, confessed that he couldn't either: he had not learned the part. 'Awful shock [. . .] Nearly died thinking I might have to go on!' That night became in the retellings a Williams legend, Burton fortifying himself with pints between scenes, belching and bellowing songs in the wings.

After the Chekhov came the Shaw, despite audience complaints to the Arts Council that the Grand was staging too many serious plays. Williams was the Dauphin, a role that would supply his first major success – but that success would not come for another four years, with a London version. This time, St Joan was played by Hermione Hannen, Clifford Evans's wife, with a valleys accent. The production did earn a national newspaper review: 'The Dauphin of Kenneth Williams is a delightful portrait of petulant archness,' reported the *Daily Herald*. 'The time has now come for us to feel proud of our Theatre,' declared the *South Wales Evening Post*.

Williams shared his digs in the Mumbles with John Hussey and Annette Kerr, who knew his passion for late-night analysis of theatre and philosophy, and could cope with his moods. A jaunt to Rhossili ended when he lost his temper with Kerr and Richard West, and stomped home alone. The incident didn't mar their friendship. One massive argument, on the other hand, was enough to kill off a flirtation with Rachel Roberts. In mid-November, Williams was both amused and aroused to realise she had developed a crush on him. Her conversation backstage and over late-night coffees was 'madly sexually analytical' as she made advances and he 'tried to make her see the futility of it all'. The illusion of romance was blown away by a row, a few days later, and never returned.

After *Saint Joan* came a lightweight double bill and then Jean-Paul Sartre's *Crime Passionel*, with one local reviewer hailing 'the amazing performances of two young geniuses – Kenneth Williams as Hugo, the assassin, and Rachel Roberts as Olga'. But the houses were more than half empty, and it was clear the Arts Council could not sustain the company. The cast's final production was *Twelfth Night*, with Williams as Feste, at Burton's suggestion. 'Richard was very good at that, spotting something that no one else saw – no one else would think that someone as comical as Kenneth could actually play Feste,' Sybil Burton Christopher said. 'Richard felt that Ken could do anything – he was just a wonderful actor.'

Burton wrote to Williams from New York: 'A great pity that the place is closing down, but we all knew, didn't we? that it was inevitable [. . .] We'll act together one day, I'm sure, and we'll make *bloody* sure we have a lot to say [. . .] If you don't do something in the West End within one year from now, something is rotten in the State of England.'

The prediction failed. It would be two years before Williams appeared on a major London stage, and then only with a minor part, in pantomime. Before that would come months of unemployment and financial worry, punctuated by spells of repertory work in dated and irrelevant comedies, and these accreted frustrations wore down his confidence. The decision in 1947 to ignore his father's mantra on the need to learn a working man's trade had demanded all his courage, and that was drawn entirely on his faith in his own talent as an actor. His faith remained, but by 1951 he no longer trusted the theatre to recognise his gifts. So many second-rate plays, so many blind egos in the company and boors in the audience: the futility of it made him desperate.

On bad days, he could not leave his parents' house: 'No news of any work. I get to feeling absolutely awful. Stayed in, in evening, and heard TERRIBLE broadcast. HELL.' Rallying, he forced himself to go to auditions and agents' offices and actors' parties, but the bitterness he hid was eating him alive: 'Each week drags itself by, and the depressions spread thro' my being like an evil cancer. Inside I am screaming and shouting. Inside. Outside everything is studied normality.' Other pages, sometimes days at a time, were left blank.

The misery was made worse by the hints in Swansea that theatre could have meaning, that art could thrive. It was true they had played to houses of fewer than a hundred, while cinema queues stretched round the block, but Williams knew he had excelled in Sartre and Shaw. He wanted to subscribe to Richard West's vision of the uncompromising company, a theatre band devoted to serious new work. Kerr, Hussey and Joan Dale would share in it. Michael Harald, whom he'd known in Newquay, would both write and direct. But they had been talking about this for years, and every time the fuse was lit, it sputtered out.

In a long entry, across six pages in February 1951, Williams analysed his ambitions. He knew that the theatre he deserved – a working-class meritocracy, high-minded, didactic, noble, philosophical – did not exist. He was twenty-five years old and no longer young enough to sustain naive dreams.

I become increasingly obsessed, with the feeling that I shall never be able to CREATE my own background – give myself some kind of meaning in the world. Surely my existence cannot be so purposeless? In the past, it was always just enough to say that I felt I belonged to the world of theatre. Certainly this still applies, for I can think of no other sphere into which I can fit ideally. But *is* it enough? It seems that my work in the profession is not HARNESSED to anything. The first reason was pure vanity – and one can't build an existence on just that. There must be something more. The answer seems to be a theatre group of some kind, with a definite motive for presenting plays, but MUST the 'theatre' (as such) HAVE MOTIVE? Isn't it enough that it ENTERTAINS? I *don't* believe so.

Williams had appeared in several of West's productions at the Theatre Royal in Stratford, in the East End. It was this stage that the group of friends hoped to seize as their base for a 'commonwealth company', sharing profits on socialist principles. The dream came to a cringing end: with the Royal scheduled for demolition unless investors could be found, one of the group, Susan Sylvester, approached Noël Coward and begged him to phone West. Coward took umbrage. He called, demanding to know whether this was a practical joke. West's stuttered explanations made the enterprise sound half baked and, with a stroke that killed both the call and the fantasies, Coward cut him off.

Williams could be obstinate, but not for ever. He abandoned the idea. Had he clung to it for one more year, he might have been involved when Joan Littlewood established Theatre Workshop at the Royal: leftist and ablaze with ideals, the group staged Behan, Brecht, Delaney and others, attracting working-class firebrands from Harry H. Corbett and Barbara Windsor to Lionel Bart and Richard Harris.

Instead, Williams scraped along, in Worthing rep for *Mrs Inspector Jones* and, after failing an audition for Alec Guinness, played at Guildford as Harrison in *Random Harvest*. On the night the play opened, he returned to Marchmont Street, where his sister, Pat, was staying on a visit from Australia. Pat's marriage was in trouble, and the mood in the basement kitchen was volatile. Charles was growling about 'poofs and whores' in the theatre. Williams made a retort that rattled all the family skeletons – something along the lines that his work was legitimate at least, which was more than anyone could say about Pat. In the row that ensued, Williams admitted his homosexuality: 'Awful truth comes out. Ridiculous to make such a thing about it. Just to be accepted – that's all.'

The following day, sucking penicillin lozenges for a throat infection, he called on an agent named Peter Eade, whom he had met a few weeks earlier at West's suggestion. Eade had been laid off from the casting department of Denham Studios and had set up an agency in Cork Street. His first office, before he moved to premises across the road, was a cubbyhole with barely room for his desk and his secretary, Elsie Weedon. Eade, a bachelor, lived in a small flat with shelves and stacks of books around him; he was a ceaseless reader, who would not offer a script to an actor unless he had first read it himself.

The writer Norman Hudis, a former Denham's publicist, was one of his first clients. 'Peter quickly became very respected,' he said, 'because he was an extremely honest man of great probity and charm and reliability.' Eade offered Williams a contract for a BBC radio broadcast, *The Immortal Lady*, which he took, but the transmission was three weeks away, and the Guildford run was a short one. For the first time, Williams was forced to sign on at the labour exchange, collecting benefits of 20 shillings. Four plays at Guildford followed, 'tat of the most menacing order. The Festival of Britain season started with Coward's *Tonight at 8.30*; Williams hated it so much that he agreed to join Richard West at his latest rep, in York, the following month. 'I have a terrible feeling that it's quite the wrong thing – but then, what is RIGHT in this haphazard career? I am an actor because it is literally – the only thing I can do well.'

In the meantime there was *Two Dozen Red Roses*, Gordon Daviot's *Richard of Bordeaux* ('a touching study in devotion by Kenneth Williams', wrote the critic Penny Plain) and *Venus Observed* by Christopher Fry. By now, Williams was so fragmented that on one night he could write to Stanley Baxter of the 'wonderful magic', the 'electric excitement', and the 'handclapping and floor-banging'; on another, he broke down and cried backstage. Sexual frustration made it worse: 'Like a skin rash, sex still breaks out with renewed emphasis, every so often,' he wrote to Annette Kerr, 'and my mental pictures become more and more elaborately perverted. Nonetheless, I remain controlled enough not to share them with anyone else in the physical sense, and consequently become taut and screaming inside so that I am often quite unbearable to the nicest examples of utter mediocrity.'

The diaries during these months contain only jottings. Unlike in previous years, Williams was not filling every page, or even half of it. But the morsels he kept were rarely bland: 'Breakfast at 6.30 for no reason whatsoever. Mad hangover effects send me careering around the landings like a rubber doll on casters.'

He put off the switch to York when Clifford Evans invited him to return for the Welsh Festival pageant play, *Land of My Fathers*, at the Sophia Gardens Pavilion in Cardiff. Rehearsals for the pageant lasted six weeks ('It will at least be a break from the sausage machine,' he told Baxter). York could be postponed no longer when he returned to London, and though he felt no enthusiasm for the first production, a school drama by Peter Watling called *Wilderness of Monkeys*, he started to learn his role even before he caught his train. The slipshod attitude of other actors irritated him: 'The show is in a shocking state considering it's the second week, everyone with the usual excuse about rep. tiredness. I can't recall rep. tiredness ever stopping me from turning up at rehearsal KNOWING my lines.'

The season wore on, with a cruel disappointment in November when Peter Eade arranged an audition with the Royal Shakespeare Theatre. For the first time in years, Williams was praying for success, as earnestly as he had done as a schoolboy before he began his indentures. The audition was a failure, and Williams returned heartsick to York, nursing one of the cruellest wounds of his career, and one which intensified his doubts and barred his way in serious theatre. If he could have joined the RSC in 1952, he would have been directed by Anthony Quayle, learning from Ralph Richardson and Michael Hordern in *The Tempest*, *Macbeth*, and *Volpone* by Ben Jonson. Instead, he returned to jeers from the gallery. Seeing him desolate, Annette Kerr took him to the cinema and then 'wrote me a beautiful autumnal nocturne. She is a darling.'

Back in London, he began rehearsals with Donald Wolfit ('so unutterably common. Terrible man. Such a vulgarian') in *King John*, for television, but quit the same day when he was offered the lead in another TV play, produced by Douglas Allen, as the angel in H.G. Wells's *The Wonderful Visit*. Full of hope, he threw a party for about twenty friends at Marchmont Street, which went on into the small hours: 'I hardly sat down once during the entire evening – crawled into bed at 3.30 feeling utterly exhausted.' Charles and Louie threw themselves into the occasion, generous and welcoming to everyone, and Williams felt a rush of love for them: 'a success entirely due to their own particular brilliance as hosts. Everyone loves them. I know they are a wonderful couple of terribly human + lovable people.'

The Wonderful Visit was broadcast live on Sunday 3 February 1952, with Williams as the angel whose luxuriant wings dwindle to a scrag-end of duck feathers as he becomes worldly. Television plays were always live and never recorded in the early fifties, but a repeat performance was scheduled for the following Thursday; it was cancelled when the BBC shut down its broadcasts as a mark of respect for King George VI, who had died during the night of 5 February.

Michael Harald invited Williams to play the lead at the Chepstow Theatre in Notting Hill Gate, in a play by the Polish author Zygmunt Jablonski titled *Before You Die*. John Hussey and another of the circle, Michael Hitchman, had supporting roles. Williams began rehearsals in a downcast mood: a day earlier, he had been turned down for a film role by the producer Herbert Wilcox, because he looked too young. The Chepstow was an unfashionable theatre, and the Jablonski was grim, 'a terrible play – though a good dramatic idea – written in the most deplorable English. Really reely awful. The Chepstow was terrible. Cold and horrid little place.'

The opening night audience was sparse, and by the Saturday, despite a review in *The Times* that praised Williams's 'explosive emotion, rendered with sensibility and remarkable control', the auditorium was so empty that the performance was cancelled. The actors wiped off their make-up and went home. But the following week was suddenly hectic. Wilcox had rewritten the part of an old gardener who discovers a corpse, so that Williams could play it as a naive and garrulous youngster, in *Trent's Last Case*. Filming began at Shepperton on 3 March, during the last week of *Before You Die*.

Unemployment followed. Unable to bear inactivity, he threw himself into redecorating 57 Marchmont Street. The previous autumn, he had painted 'the downstairs lav [. . .] The walls in a sort of erotic dirty yellow, and the woodwork in a completely negative, but very clean-making cream.' Now he launched himself at his mother's bedroom and the staircase, laying twenty-five yards of stair carpet, pasting up pink wallpaper and painting the woodwork. Though he hated signing on, he was forced back to the labour exchange and, for the only time in his life, channelled the experience into a short story.

Williams had been convinced of his destiny as an actor for years. His friends constantly encouraged his self-belief: 'Beloved,' John

Hussey had written to him eighteen months earlier, during the Swansea season, on crisp blue tissue, 'Do you like this paper? I can imagine it rustling as your biographer turns the pages of your ancient and dusty files.' He preserved his correspondence and kept his diary, because his life would have public significance. He knew it. But he also doubted it, and the doubts were overwhelming him.

He turned down an audition which Peter Eade had arranged at the Old Vic: 'Really see no point in going. Just the old old story.' That 'old old story' was audition followed by rejection.

Another round of rep, another stint as the valet, Bastien, in *By Candle Light*: Williams accepted it with a shrug. 'Bet the actress I have to play with, has bad breath!' he grumbled. This time it was Salisbury, and all the company, apart from his friend Hitchman, were 'a negligible lot of creatures who obviously over-eat and over-rate themselves highly'. Sharing digs with strangers was still worse, and Williams kept to a cold bedroom rather than try to learn his lines in the living-room 'with this awful Scot [. . .] who will keep whistling through his teeth and tapping the table with his fingertips and making the chair creak ominously every time he fidgets which is every other second'.

By Candle Light opened on a short tour while the company rehearsed *School for Scandal* in the afternoons; Williams was livid to be scolded, in front of the cast, for his starry performance in the first play by the producer of the second, Guy Verney. The local paper loved him, though, and headlined its review 'Kenneth Williams' Success': 'Bastien popped and bubbled. Looking, at times, extraordinarily like an abridged Danny Kaye, he signalled everything from danger and distress to pique and a disarming devilment with a mere twitch of the face, a gurgle or a sulk'. In *School for Scandal* he was 'grimy, slimy, nasal-toned [. . .] superb'.

Throughout the summer he was offered almost nothing – a television walk-on, which he turned down, and an audition for a French farce, which he also sidestepped. He did accept a small role, as Curio, in *Twelfth Night* for radio, and secured an interview through an imploring letter to a BBC features commissioner, Terence Tiller: 'You must believe that I am a young man of unusual talent & belong in the theatre [. . .] I assure you I shall not be wasting your time if you see me – and you'll hurt me terribly if you don't.' Tiller saw him a month later, and Williams summed up the encounter in two initials: 'N.G.'

By the end of August he was 'unspeakably depressed and melancholy. Long to be doing some work of real importance', and even added a listless doodle in one corner of the page – something almost unique in all the diaries. At the start of September he wrote for work as a teacher; that was unrealistic, since he had neither degree nor qualifications, and the next day he resolved 'to seek work in snack bar and typing etc'. He had a day's work in the middle of the month at Elstree studios, playing a window dresser in *Innocents in Paris*, but the drought did not really break until an audition for Peter Brook and Laurence Olivier at Shepperton studios, where they were making *The Beggar's Opera*. Williams was cast as Jack the pot boy, though Brook and Olivier had doubts about his cockney: they thought the accent did not sound authentic. Williams protested that he'd been born 'up the Calley'; he was humiliated to discover later his voice had been overdubbed.

By now, though he was always eager for a discussion about religion or philosophy with friends around his parents' kitchen table, Williams had despaired of staging radical, left-wing theatre. When he talked with Richard West, their old ambitions for revolution seemed unreal and pathetic. He hoped for a breakthrough in films or television, but he accepted what he was offered. For Christmas 1952 it was pantomime, as Slightly in *Peter Pan* at the Scala in Charlotte Street, his first appearance in the West End. The producer was Cecil King, who had known the playwright J.M. Barrie and believed he had a mission to present the play as it always had been, without any changes; this was his thirtieth reprise.

'I tried to make some kind of a stand,' Williams told Annette Kerr, 'about ribbons in my hair. "I just don't feel it's in my character," and all that old stuff, but it didn't work. "My dear! All the Slightlys play it with ribbons, it's the traditional biz" – and you either have hysterics or give in to utter defeat.' The thoughts he confided to his diary, as usual, were darker: 'I feel perfectly bloody and am full of awful forebodings. Can't help feeling the whole thing is a chronic waste of acting time. All the kids in it are frightful little bastards up to all kinds of larks. Hateful. Oh dear oh dear.' The cynicism did not reach the core, though, for he invested his first week's pay in a tape recorder, to help him learn his script. He used tapes for the rest of his career, laying down the other actors' lines with silences for his own.

Peter Pan consumed the next four months. The critic in *The Stage* saw how he was constricted: 'Kenneth Williams is an excellent Slightly, whom, one imagines, would do even better if allowed a little licence.' Williams felt a disembodied helplessness about the show: 'I suppose I must have written the entry on Page 8 last night,' he noted on 7 January 1953, 'but I can't for the life of me recall doing so. 6th Jan seems an eternity ago. Ever since this ghastly show began, everything has seemed incredibly unreal. As though I were viewing myself from another body and not recognising myself. Wondering and bemused, not quite believing events could turn out so.'

Stifled on stage, he began to develop as a writer. As well as his poetry and the labour exchange vignette, he had tried in a one-act playlet to recreate the atmosphere of post-war bickering at his parents' home. The script was full of his father's cursing and his mother's pet phrases ('LOUIE: I don't like that Mrs Houth, I think she's a dirty bitch [. . .] you could spit in her eye and it wouldn't choke her'). The scene had no storyline but the voices were recreated with mechanical precision. In his mimicry, Kenneth Williams was as accurate with a pen as he was at a microphone.

He started to experiment with this while touring with *Peter Pan*, noting observations of strangers such as the couple who ran his boarding-house in Stoke, and also tried his hand at writing to the newspapers, about the Craig and Bentley murder trial; he was furious when the *Observer* did not print his letter.

Though he was relieved to escape from panto when the tour ended, Williams quickly tired of Marchmont Street, where his mother was confined to bed with sciatica. One year after he had turned down the Old Vic, another offer came to audition, in May 1953, and he endured six weeks of churning anxiety as he rehearsed his showcase speeches: one was as Ferdinand in *The Tempest*, another was from *Henry VI*, and he could not settle on a third. 'Can't relax at all,' he fretted. 'Jumpy feeling the whole time.'

John Hussey cabled from South Africa, suggesting Williams should apply for juvenile roles at Durban's theatre. The proposal might have tempted him, but he had agreed to a short season at Birmingham rep, where the director Douglas Seale was staging Shakespeare's *Henry VI* trilogy, the first time for decades that all three parts would be played in sequence. Williams arrived in a dire mood, knowing almost no one and afraid that his colleagues would dislike him. His instinct was to curl up into a prickly ball.

'Birmingham is a filthy town,' he wrote on his first night in digs. 'Full of the most awful people: shall be terribly glad to leave. Dirt everywhere. O! horror.' Other actors revolted him: 'Norman Pitt is a great bulbous creature, ungainly and incapable. All his lines are dirty, and lack point. He is obviously BAD in every way and should leave the theatre entirely. All in addition to what – he is a vicious bitcher to boot.' In calmer moments, he understood that he was lashing out before he could be attacked, and that the people, the production and the city were not as awful as he pretended. Knowing this, though, did not make him less defensive.

The run transferred to the Old Vic in London, where Williams was welcomed by Sybil and Richard Burton, with a celebratory supper at their house in Hampstead. Burton and Claire Bloom were headlining the Old Vic's season, with Rachel Roberts also in the company, and within days Williams had joined them. His audition in May had gone well, and the artistic director, Michael Benthall, had admired him in *Henry VI* as Rutland, the boy who is murdered in Part Three, but probably the invitation hinged on Burton's urging: his influence in the company was supreme, and he had already shown that he believed his protégé could excel in Shakespeare. Williams began rehearsals as Prince Henry in *King John* immediately, with a minor role in *Hamlet*. Finally he was part of a company of great actors. Here was the opportunity that would free him from drudgery in rep, where a discerning public, including the leading critics and impresarios, would have twelve months to absorb and admire the breadth of his talents. This was luck at last, but he had worked all his adult life to achieve it.

One week later he told Benthall that he didn't want to be tied down to minor parts for a year, and walked out.

Williams never expressed regret at his decision, nor tried to explain it. The closest he came was a letter to Rae Hammond: '[Benthall] stood on the stairs of the Vic, shaking his head and saying I was being very unwise and that this was the "Burton–Bloom season at the Old Vic" and would be very fashionable. He said to me, "Go and have a good lunch and think about it, then tell me what you want to do." There is nowhere in the Waterloo Road that you can have a good lunch, so I think he imagined the combination of hunger & guilt would make me retract. It didn't.'

The diary entries from July 1953 are terse and note only that Peter Eade was dismayed at the thought of upsetting Benthall. Williams cannot honestly have felt he was too good for supporting Richard Burton in *Hamlet* – three years earlier he had been happy to fetch the star his beers backstage at Swansea. And after months in panto or on the dole, what better work could he count on? In the event, none: he spent six of the next eight months out of work.

Robert Hardy, who was also in the company, believed Williams lacked the confidence to compete as a bit-part player among such charismatic, overbearing stars. 'Richard Burton could be absolutely wicked,' he said. 'For the scene in *King John* of the siege of Moulon, with the Bastard of Falconbridge played by Burton, there were twenty or thirty of us lined along the stage facing the audience, looking out over the audience at the walls of this fortress. And Richard came down across us to do his speech, walked all the length of us, and was behaving with extreme subtlety and wickedness, and the whole lot of us were in such fits of laughter, we all had to turn our backs on the audience. It was one of the most disgraceful exhibitions by a company of actors that I ever took part in.'

Melvyn Bragg suggested that a lack of formal education contributed to this crisis of self-confidence at the Old Vic. 'That company was a very intimidating bunch of people by all accounts. He might just have felt frightened and friendless, and not have had the training to stick it out. In this bunch of very, very confident, particularly macho actors, I think he might have felt intimidated, and thought, I'm never going to be like them, so I'd better go now. And then because he was a clever man he would have found justifications for leaving. He obviously had a seriously good mind. I think he was at ease with people who had also left school early and lived on their wits. But when he came up against people who'd had a formal education, it was like having a different accent. It is a different world. I think he pulled back out a mixture of envy, regret and fearfulness that he was going to make a fool of himself.'

By the time he found more work, with a small film part at Pinewood, Williams's confidence had guttered so low that, between takes, he retreated to a corner and read the newspaper. He was convinced the director, Ken Annakin, nurtured an intense dislike for him, and that the star, Jack Hawkins, shared it. Unable to make friends on the set, he suffered through repeated retakes until the part – the orphaned youth Wishart in *The Seekers*, 'a sort of psycho neurotic coward on the brink of adulthood' – made no dramatic sense to him. The first shots were done at night, in a muddy trench, sluiced by fire-hoses to create a rainstorm. He did not return home until 7 a.m., spent the day asleep and woke with a bitter loathing for every kind of technology that interfered with acting: in television, films and radio there were machines, and people operating them, to thwart his genius. It was 'deplorable', 'utterly mediocre', 'shocking' and 'meretricious'; if he was to act well, he had to work in the theatre. He seemed honestly unaware that he had recently turned his back on a year's stage work with the best company in England.

Another night at Pinewood made him sure he was coming down with flu, or bronchitis. He was not yet the hypochondriac who talked obsessively to friends and strangers of his health, but he was becoming preoccupied with symptoms and medicines. On the back of a letter he jotted a diet sheet: one pint of milk per day, two yogurts, brown bread and wheatgerm from Wigmore Street Health centre, two tablespoons of blackstrap molasses daily, combined with halibut liver oil pills after breakfast, Vitamin C tablets and brewers yeast.

A brief optimism seized him after the film was over. He became animated, boisterous and impulsive, dashing down to Bournemouth by train to see Annette Kerr, only to leave her two days later, 'because I suddenly felt very bored with all this walking about and breathing fresh air'. The winter had been achingly cold, and after one bitter frost he had to climb on to the roof at No. 57 to unfreeze the water pipes with a blowlamp. The heavy snows of January 1954 cost him a job too, when he was invited to play Cupid at Bromley: 'decided not to do so, in view of the nakedness of the role and the inclement weather'. This was not the only work he lost: Peter Brook auditioned and rejected him at the Aldwych; he was turned down at the Globe because he looked wrong for the part, and by the BBC producer John Warrington after an audition for a TV play that had entailed a wait of two and a half hours at the Lime Grove studios.

By now his optimism was fraying: 'I think John Warrington is pure crap. He is said, however, to have a "heart of gold". Therefore, I am probably just bitter cos he didn't give me a job, and saying nasty things. Nonetheless I thought he was crap when I met him in '48. And it's '54 now. I still think he is crap.' Williams was urging Eade to try anything, from television and films to repertory work at Hornchurch. Another chance came up at the Globe, in Thornton Wilder's *The Matchmakers*, but the producer, Tyrone Guthrie, was unimpressed: 'He was very kind and I was very bad and nothing will accrue from it [. . .] I don't see how any sensitive actor can possibly get through an audition. Everything is against him being a success and he KNOWS this. So he is horribly weighted down, from the very start.'

A seething, bilious resentment swept over him when he saw others getting work: 'As an actor, poor Alfred [Burke] hasn't the panache necessary for the single "personality" performance, so there is only one thing left for him in legit. That, of course, is character acting. Sadly, he possesses no talent for mimicry, no vocal flexibility, no good looks, and no charm whatsoever. What hope therefore remains to Alfred? Obviously he should establish himself in the British film industry, where there are hundreds of people like him who are called actors too.'

When John Hussey renewed his invitation to try rep in South Africa, Williams dismissed Eade's objections and drew up a list of reasons to accept: he was sick of his home, of Bloomsbury and of London; he could regain his independence from his parents on the other side of the world; he would be in work, and with an old friend; and 'the boat trip would be exciting'. This was an escapist fantasy, he knew, but anything would be better than continual rejection. After a month of arguing, Eade conceded that six months in South Africa might do his client some good, and arranged a meeting with a man named McNeile from the Durban repertory company. Offered £15 a week and the prospect of a season in plays by 'Agatha Christie and that tribe', Williams realised he liked the idea less than he had pretended.

Peter Ashby-Bailey, his colleague from Newquay rep, supplied the first work Williams had had since Christmas, with four weeks in Bridgwater. The plays were a grim prospect, 'the usual sort of well-bred, drawing-room nitwit stuff', but the weekly accounts in the back of his diary showed how badly he needed work: his bank balance had dwindled from £207 17s 6d at New Year to £52 11s 1d. Bridgwater would pay £8 a week, though half of that went on his lodgings. When he opened, as Tom in *Traveller's Joy*, it was his first appearance on a stage for ten months. His biography in the programme noted, 'Kenneth loves lying in bed all the time reading books: he thinks mass communication has supplanted education and deplores the mammon-worshipping tendency of the present day.'

The discipline of learning and performing six roles, after so much inactivity, had a galvanising effect. Williams returned to London with no work in prospect but determined to achieve control over his life. He spent a day clearing out his room and resolved to impose order on his files; then, as though he intended to purify himself of the past, he made a bonfire of his old letters and burned hundreds of them. All the numbered dispatches from Orford and Kerr were destroyed, together with many carbons of his own letters; only a handful were preserved, such as Richard Burton's letter from the Royale in New York. It was not the only time he would destroy his correspondence, but it did the most damage.

The Seekers was released, to good reviews, and Williams was relieved to know that his voice had not been dubbed. He was writing hopeful applications to BBC producers again, but it was probably success of the film, rather than a letter, that reminded Douglas Allen how good he had been in *The Wonderful Visit*. Allen was staging a broadcast of Shaw's *Misalliance*, and offered him the role of Bentley Summerhays.

Misalliance was transmitted live on Tuesday 27 July 1954. Two years earlier, critics had been in raptures over Williams in *The Wonderful Visit* and it had brought him nothing; the notices for *Misalliance* were unexceptional, but this broadcast was the catalyst that altered the chemistry of his career. On the morning after *Misalliance*, Williams was invited to audition for John Fernald, who was producing another play by George Bernard Shaw, *Saint Joan*, at the Arts Theatre. Fernald asked him to play the Dauphin. Williams grabbed the chance.

He had acted the Dauphin four years earlier, in Swansea, but the preparations for a West End production could not be compared with a week in rep. Rehearsals lasted a month, before try-outs at Cambridge. Fernald impressed him: 'I am amazed to find such a good person in the position of producer [. . .] I notice a number of actors – and the "star" – smoking while rehearsing, actually speaking and moving with cigarettes in their hands. I think it is very liberal of John Fernald to allow this, but I think the actors are paying him a poor compliment by behaving in this slipshod fashion.' The star with a cigarette constantly in her hand was Siobhán McKenna, whose Joan would be acclaimed as among the greatest in the play's history.

Fernald had already won Williams's trust with praise on the second day of rehearsals. 'I think you're going to be *very* good – it's an original interpretation,' the director commented, to Williams's delight and embarrassment: 'I was horrified at being complimented at such an early stage: *so* I changed the subject quickly by talking about GBS. Nonetheless, my heart warmed to Fernald for this praise. No other producer has ever complimented me at such a stage, (and the initial reading stage can be a fearful one for the sensitive, apprehensive actor) and it made me feel terribly grateful.' His confidence was so much bolstered that he regarded all the cast with benevolence, finding them pleasant, sensible and reasonable.

It is not difficult to see how Fernald, as he watched *Misalliance* on television, had spotted his Dauphin in Kenneth Williams. Shaw describes the French prince, who appears in only two scenes and the epilogue, as 'a poor creature physically [. . .] little, narrow eyes, near together, a long pendulous nose [. . .] the expression of a young dog accustomed to be kicked, yet incorrigible and irrepressible [. . .] neither vulgar nor stupid'. Williams knew his physical suitability would not be enough to carry the role; he would have to create a personality. 'The part is not madly easy,' he mused. 'The thing is a question of technique. The deliberate assumption of unsophisticated and apparently involuntary wistfulness. I'll get it somehow. I'll think.' The scene that placed the greatest demand on technique was the epilogue, like the denouement of a detective story, in which all the characters assemble in his dreams, twenty-five years after the Dauphin has been crowned king. He is no longer a youth, petulant and sly, but a mature monarch, with battle scars and duller wits. The audience must believe that, during the minute that has elapsed since they saw Joan dragged off the stage to be burned, King Charles has lived his whole adult life.

When the play opened at the Arts on 29 September, Williams portrayed this transition with a conviction that would never be forgotten by many who saw it. Norman Hudis, his colleague at Eade's agency, said: 'Of all the shows I must have seen in my time, that's as clear to me, sitting here in California, as it was that night at the Arts Theatre in London. Quite stunning. Ken was unique. Like all really great people, there was something about him that was not reproducible elsewhere.'

Nicholas Parsons, among others, recognised how Williams could convey the disturbed undercurrents of a personality, just as he had as the vicious spiv in *Sly Corner*: 'The Dauphin is written as a very strange, ineffectual young man without much charisma [. . .] I remember Kenny [in the part], not because I knew him, but because his performance was just amazing. He's got an unusual personality, offbeat, and when he plays a character role he brings this individual, unique quality that he has, imbuing the part with something different. It was memorable.'

Throughout rehearsals, Williams filled his diary with analysis: of Fernald's direction, of the other performances, of the changing moods in the cast, and of his own role. After the opening night, when the critics had been admiring, and cartoon caricatures of Joan and the Dauphin had appeared in *Tatler* and *Punch*, the commentary ceased. For the only time in his career, Williams was content to appear nightly without fretting over changes between the performances or responses from the house.

The spiritual subtext of *Saint Joan* did continue to affect him. His Methodist upbringing responded to Shaw's insistence, in the play's preface, that Joan was killed because the Catholic Church could not permit other religious figureheads to claim a direct line of communication to God. Williams acknowledged the existence, if not of a divinely human God, of a deity. It was, he believed, as obvious as oxygen. But he was not a churchgoer, and he resented any institution that tried to impose a framework on his beliefs.

He wrote to Annette Kerr, lecturing her on the atmosphere he had perceived at Norwich, her home city – it reeked with the 'business of religion', which was proud and bogus and snobbish. Those sins were as bad on a stage as they were in a church. Like Joan of Arc, Williams believed that an individual who was fearlessly true to his calling would be favoured by God. And after seven years of testing in a repertory wilderness, he came to his rewards.

5

'Too popular. Quite so. Reely. I don't mind'

September 1954–June 1959

The versatility Williams displayed in his transition from young Dauphin to elderly monarch made an impact beyond the theatre. It brought him the chance of national stardom on *Hancock's Half Hour*, a show so popular at its height that publicans and taxi drivers complained their businesses were suffering. And it began a deep friendship that decayed into the most profound enmity of Williams's life.

Days after *Saint Joan* was 'rapturously received', the BBC producer Dennis Main Wilson visited the Arts Theatre, intending to meet Williams backstage and offer him radio work, if the young actor was as accomplished as the critics said. Main Wilson was the trailblazer of British radio comedy. He had talent-spotted Peter Sellers, Bob Monkhouse and Tony Hancock in the late forties, when they were all unknowns peddling comedy routines at the Windmill Theatre and other, even less prestigious venues. A regular at the Grafton Arms, where Sellers, Spike Milligan, Harry Secombe and an assortment of friends were improvising cascades of surreal jokes, Main Wilson was a former wartime propaganda-maker who had first joined the BBC in 1941, aged seventeen. When he became a producer for the corporation's Variety Department ten years later, almost his first act was to launch a series called *Crazy People*; within months, it had been renamed *The Goon Show*.

Ray Galton and Alan Simpson were junior scriptwriters on a faltering fortnightly show called *Happy-Go-Lucky*, starring Derek Roy, when Main Wilson was drafted in as a replacement for the previous producer, Roy Speer, who had suffered a breakdown. At an emergency meeting of the cast in Derek Roy's flat, close to Marble Arch, Galton and Simpson were promoted from one-line-gag merchants, earning 2s 6d for every joke the comic used, to the show's chief writers, responsible for producing almost all the material for the last three hour-long broadcasts. Both men had only recently been discharged from the tuberculosis sanatorium where they had met: they were supposed to be recuperating, but with Main Wilson's encouragement they threw themselves into eighteen-hour writing sessions in the sitting-room of Simpson's mother's home.

'Dennis used to bring us food – fish and chips, after closing time,' Galton said. 'Then he'd sit there with us, to give us encouragement.'

'He didn't contribute many lines, though,' Simpson commented. 'Used to fall asleep, mostly.'

Two years later, the young writers were developing plans for a radio series with Tony Hancock that would abandon the variety template of gags and musical interludes, and replace it with recognisable situations and credible dialogue. It was natural they should take the concept to Dennis Main Wilson, who embraced it. Even before Hancock's signature had been obtained, Main Wilson was enthusing in a memo to the BBC's Assistant Head of Variety: 'The comedy style will be purely situation in which we shall try to build Tony as a real life character in real life surroundings. There will be no "goon" or contrived comedy approaches at all.'

A cast was assembled around Hancock, including Bill Kerr, an Australian comic who was another Grafton Arms regular, and Moira Lister, a South African-born film actress. Sid James was drafted in after Galton and Simpson saw him in the Ealing comedy *The Lavender Hill Mob*. All four played fixed roles: Hancock was the pompous, gullible, bullying, vulnerable hero of the stories; Kerr the put-upon friend; James the sly conman whose schemes lured Hancock into weekly catastrophes; and Lister the arch, despairing girlfriend. The composer Wally Stott wrote a blustering theme tune for tuba and piccolo after Main Wilson acted out an exaggerated version of the Hancock character for him. All the producer needed to complete preparations was an adaptable actor to supply bit-part voices, someone who could portray policemen and henchmen, navvies and High Court judges, without resorting to what Galton scathingly called 'funny voices'.

Main Wilson wrote to several theatrical agents, explaining what was required. One of them, Peter Eade, phoned him with the suggestion he should take a look at Kenneth Williams in *Saint Joan*. The producer went to Great Newport Street and was impressed: he saw Williams as 'tremendously dramatic, but funny'. Backstage, however, he found the actor was too busy to see him, so he left a message that he would be waiting around the corner, in a public bar. After a delay, 'this elegant, Irving-Garrick-type actor laddie comes in, and booms at me, "Well? What do you want?" When Main Wilson explained who he was, Williams retorted, 'I don't like the wireless,' but he accepted a drink – a pint of light ale – and listened offhandedly as Main Wilson tried to convey how original and hilarious the Hancock show could be. 'We were halfway through this,' he said, 'and Ken Williams collapsed into a fit of giggles, and said, "I don't care, I'll do it!" He took me in for about half an hour.'

Alan Simpson said, 'Dennis came to us and said, "I've found the perfect actor to do the voices. He's never played comedy before but he'll be very good." Ken turned up at rehearsal, and that was the first we'd ever seen of him. We'd never seen him in theatre.'

On Tuesday 19 October 1954, Williams visited Main Wilson's office at Broadcasting House to discuss the offer. His weekly fee was 12 guineas, with residuals of 6 guineas for repeat broadcasts, and his first role was as an outraged peer who returns to his London mansion to discover it is the scene of the Hancock show's first-night party. Drunken radio critics and BBC executives have smashed the windows, slashed the furniture and built a bonfire on the dining table. Williams scanned his half-dozen lines at the tail-end of the script, spotting his best chance for getting a laugh: 'Tell me, who threw jelly over the Rembrandt?'

'I knew I could make this funny,' he recalled. And he did, affecting just a hint of reprimand with the word 'jelly' and speaking the painter's name with more sadness than outrage. Even before delivering that line, Williams had already made a mark – his upper-class accent is no caricature, and no one listening could have guessed the actor was only twenty-eight. 'Hello, we're a bit posh, aren't we?' Hancock told him, with a touch of what sounds like genuine admiration.

Hancock's own characterisation was far from finished: he sounded affected rather than pompous, and less guileless than plain slow-witted. Bill Kerr, whose stage act was based on a doleful, trudging voice, was flipping between idiocy and intelligence, and Moira Lister sounded far too sensible to have anything to do with the pair of them. Only Sid James slipped straight into his role, delivering his patter just as he would be doing five years and thirteen TV and radio series later: menacing and cynical, a conman oozing confidence. When he ran through his haul after the party, his rhythm was perfect: 'With the pudding still to come we got sixty-five wallets, twenty-three watches, fifteen cigarette cases, three dozen tie pins, two pairs of socks and a vest.'

The first recording was made at the Camden Theatre, and Williams evidently felt satisfied with the performance, commenting in his diary that it 'went very well really'. The following week he was more critical, noting that he'd played a judge and a policeman, 'both badly'. The writers had no complaints: Williams's acting was exactly what they wanted. 'He took to it like a wasp to honey,' Galton commented.

Most of the voices began as impersonations, of actors such as the president of Equity, Felix Aylmer, or of the London voices he had grown up with in Marchmont Street. 'Ken would get his chosen voice straight away, he didn't experiment,' Simpson said. 'If he was doing judges, anybody very imposing, an MP or a doctor, he would either use the old Aylmer, very wavery, or for professional men he had this clipped, Patrick Cargill-type voice.'

'Terribly well spoken,' Galton agreed. 'He'd also do cockneys. He had two or three old men voices, a different voice for each part. None of his characters had a name.'

Peter Sellers, the mimic of the Goon shows, replaced him for a single episode, but Williams was hired for virtually every other programme of the first series. Galton and Simpson began to give him more than one laugh-line for each walk-on part, though the gags usually focused on Hancock's antics.

The writers were aware that Williams's elastic voices hid his personality more than they revealed it. Alan Simpson felt the actor had no voice of his own, but changed it to reflect the company and the conversation. 'If Ken was talking to you as himself it would vary, depending upon the subject matter and depending on the voice he used. It was almost as if he couldn't be himself, as if he didn't know what "himself" was. Ken would be telling you a story about himself, and about his mother and his father, and his personality would go from one to another, like a chameleon. So it was very difficult to tell who he was. I doubt whether he knew himself.'

It was his face that provided the best clues. 'He had big eyes, I'll always remember the eyes,' Galton said. 'He was winking at you in that quizzical way when he was telling you something. Everything showed on his face. It was a theatrical flair . . . the eyes and the nostrils. But he used to really look at you – his head would turn around and look at you with his great eyes, almost like an illustration from a fairytale book.'

At the last recording session of 1954, taping two Christmas episodes, technical faults held up recording for twenty minutes. The cast had to keep the studio audience entertained, and Williams performed an impromptu music-hall act: 'I sang old cockney songs and went down very well. They were all very pleased with me.' Bill Kerr said that in the pub after recordings, 'Ken would love to sing all those . . . coster songs from the great period of variety in the 1860s and 1880s. A few times when we let our hair down after the show, I'd sing some Australian bush songs and he'd do his cockney songs, and it was brilliant. "Knees Up Mother Brown", "'Enery the Eighth", exactly that sort of thing.'

Impressed by Williams's versatility, Hancock advised him to make his career as an entertainer, in variety. The advice echoed what Stanley Baxter had been urging him, and Williams was beginning to think of Hancock as a mentor as well as a colleague and friend. He was less than two years younger than Hancock, but the older man had been working regularly since the war in light entertainment shows such as *Variety Bandbox* and *Educating Archie*. After watching Hancock's performance in *Talk of the Town* at the Adelphi, he noted the star was 'v. good but the rest was rather tatty'.

Moira Lister left the show, the experience soured by a stand-up row with Hancock, who was furious when she announced she would be missing one episode to attend a film festival in South America. Lister did stay till the end of the series but, since she was expecting her first child, it was arranged that she would not return for the second run: she was replaced by Andrée Melly, the sister of jazz musician George Melly. When recording started, Melly was not the only new face: Harry Secombe was standing in for Tony Hancock, who had broken down under the strain of nightly stage performances.

Dennis Main Wilson had gone to see Hancock backstage at the Adelphi, to be told the star had stopped in the middle of his act and walked out of the theatre, shaking and mumbling that the stage was 'too steep'. With Jimmy Edwards, the co-star, Main Wilson searched Soho's nightclubs and drinking dens without success, before returning home to receive a phone call from a friend in Scotland Yard's Special Branch, Chief Superintendant 'Ginger' Rose. Rose had two complimentary tickets to the recording of *Hancock's Half Hour* the following day: was it worth his while even to turn up at the studio, since the star had just been seen boarding a flight for Rome? The policeman offered to have him followed and reported the next day that Hancock had hired a car to Positano in southern Italy, after spending the night in a Rome hotel.

Main Wilson asked Galton and Simpson, without telling them where Hancock had gone, to adjust the show for Secombe. The BBC in the mid-fifties was in thrall to its hierarchies: before asking Secombe if he'd be prepared to take over Hancock's role, Main Wilson had to persuade first the Goons' producer, Peter Eton, and then Secombe's agent, Jimmy Grafton. 'We were always under the illusion until quite recently that the BBC, along with the rest of us, didn't know where Hancock was,' said Galton. 'But what an amazing thing for Harry to do. It could have led to anything, that series.'

Williams was equally impressed: Secombe, he noted, was a comic in 'the true "lunatic grotesque" tradition', who exaggerated every nuance until it became hilarious. The pace and bravado of Secombe's performance, piling up laughs with lines that had been written for a completely different personality, exhilarated Williams. His own performance became bolder and more assertive. Before Hancock could return from Italy to claim his show back, another character appeared who would threaten to take over, and he announced himself with a simple 'Good evenin'. . .'

'We wanted to get the show with no jokes as such, no catch-phrases, no interruptions and no funny voices,' Galton said. When he and Simpson wrote a jockey into the third of the Secombe episodes,

The Racehorse, they gave Williams a hint of how to play it: the word 'Snide' was jotted beside his lines.

Taking his cue from the exuberant new hero, Williams unleashed all his own grotesquery for the snide jockey. He made the voice whine, sneer, leer and drawl, from the back of his palate and out of his nose. It sounded as if he was laughing at the other characters and mistaking the audience's roars for their complicity in the joke. All four Secombe broadcasts have been lost, but an early version of 'Snide' can be heard on *The Rail Strike*, recorded on 6 June 1955, as a salesman who tries to flirt with Andrée Melly: ''Ere, I'm a commercial traveller. I travel in suitcases . . . saves me renting a room, see?'

'It brought the house down,' Galton said. 'We just looked at each other and said, "Well, so much for funny voices and catchphrases." The other lines we used to put in weren't intended to be catchphrases.' One of those was 'Stop messin' about', which could as easily have been 'Stop playin' about' or 'Stop foolin' around'. Williams's delivery transformed it: 'He did, "Nahoowwww . . . stop messin' abowhht!' And the other one was, "No, don't be like that," when he was getting annoyed.'

The scale of the laughs from the studio audience was mirrored by the listening figures: the ratings rose from 4.14 million for the first show of the series, to 5.64 million for the ninth. By now Hancock had returned – 'like a little dog with his tail between his legs', Main Wilson remarked. The tensions were back too: a suggestion arose that Williams was being given too much to do and that another character actor should be drafted in. Williams made no complaint during rehearsals, but in his diary noted the idea was 'really absurd'. It came to nothing, probably because of budget constraints.

Episode 9, *The Television Set*, was the first show that 'Snide' completely annexed. Entering at twenty-one minutes, he played Hancock's importunate neighbour, calling round to beg some milk and a bit of fish for his cat: 'Any old bits'll do, he's not fussy . . . cod fillet, bit of plaice, nice cat, he is.' ('Nice cat?' Hancock bellows. 'Yeah, I've seen him, digging up me rhubarb!') 'Snide' invites himself in to watch his host's new television and proceeds to 'adjust' it, finally burning the house down. ('Well, I don't think I can be of any further assistance, gentlemen, so I'll say goodnight,' and 'Snide' exits to a round of applause.)

Freddie Hancock, who was Tony's publicist and later became his second wife, believed the writers were subconsciously exaggerating characteristics they saw in Williams himself. 'He was that kind of a mischievous character,' she said in a telephone interview from her home in New York. 'He was also pretty nasty to certain people. He wasn't the nicest human being. I can remember him being catty, or mean . . . Stop messing about, don't be like that – it was very much a sort of a spoiled child. That was an extension of his natural idiom.'

Andrée Melly saw the effect that the popularity of 'Snide' had on the show's insecure star. She explained: 'Hancock felt slightly threatened by Kenneth Williams. During the two series I did, Ken's confidence increased a lot. I got the feeling that probably Hancock was wanting him written down a bit, because Galton and Simpson were giving him more to do . . . because he was very successful in it, very extreme and very funny. But Hancock was the funny one, we were all meant to be feeding him. There was rivalry there.

'[Williams] seemed to have profound confidence as a performer because he dared. He admired anyone who dared – he admired nerve and not losing your nerve. As a performer he had a kind of confidence that didn't really need approval. He gave it to himself, it seemed to me. I remember him talking once about Sophie Tucker: he adored her, [perhaps] because she couldn't sing, she was really quite ugly and she had a very limited talent, but she had enormous nerve and daring and confidence. And he thought that was wonderful. Sophie Tucker wasn't a gay icon, so it wasn't like a Judy Garland thing – he just admired that nerve. And this is what he was doing in the Hancock show, just daring. Hancock was a bit unnerved by it, it always seemed to me.'

Bill Kerr experienced the same effect: 'When you were on with Kenneth, not only did Tony have to raise his game but so did everybody else in the show. Me included, Sid included, and Hattie [Jacques]. It wasn't competition, it was almost self-preservation. You knew that you had to be good because you were working with the best . . . I thought he was brilliant, just brilliant. I think he was born brilliant. He was a complete one-off.'

Most of the shows were recorded on Sundays, to allow Williams and others in the cast to fulfil obligations in theatre. They would be broadcast later that week, usually, and sometimes on the following day, after editing ('Waiting for the negative to dry,' as Galton put it). Rehearsals started at 10.30 a.m., when the actors saw the scripts for the first time. First read-throughs could be uproarious.

'They used to make each other laugh,' Galton said. 'Hancock would read a line and do it perfectly. It was a skill he had, uncanny. Sid was very good, Ken was very good at first sight, but Bill used to stumble a bit – he'd be head down, and you'd think, Oh Bill, and suddenly he'd look up laughing, and it would be uncontrollable laughter. Quite amazing. All four of them, the male members of the cast, were enormous guffawers. Hancock used to roll about on the floor almost. Sid was a guffawer, Bill was very loud and Ken had his braying, so if something appealed to them all four of them would be roaring with laughter.'

'We didn't need a public audience,' Simpson admitted. 'We just needed those four.'

Fenella Fielding, who was to co-star with Williams in revue in 1959, first encountered him as the Dauphin, and was so impressed that she returned to see *Saint Joan* a second time. When she was interviewed, she offered up a stream of stories and remembered details, describing Williams as 'fabuous, terribly fun', in the *Hancock* shows: 'I used to go to the recordings, in the audience, because I was doing another radio series with the same producer, Dennis Main Wilson. So we were all entitled to go if we wanted. People would vie to go with me, because it was such a popular show.'

The presence of an audience pushed Williams to fresh levels of invention. Galton and Simpson saw him introduce a visual element to enhance the comedy – 'he would use his face like it'd be television' – projecting surprise, outrage, delight or hilarity: 'It was all acting, of course, but he would use it to great effect on the audience.'

'That was such a contrast,' Fielding explained, 'with having seen Kenneth in *Saint Joan*. He physically acted the part but most radio people do. You can't imagine they're going to just stand there, and somehow this extraordinary, other voice comes out of this calm, cool-as-a-cucumber exterior. You're confined to a spot because of the acoustic, but it's terribly difficult to actually get all the feeling for what you're doing without making some kind of movement. And an audience respond to how you are, what you look like, as well as what you sound like. If you listen, there's a laugh when somebody says a line, and then they laugh again. It's usually because somebody's raised an eyebrow. Anything vocal is very physical.'

Andrée Melly, standing beside Williams at the microphones, saw this differently: 'He didn't act, his body didn't change in any way. He had this enormous talent for mimicry, with this rather large mouth, and he'd sort of mouth things. He might pull faces but there was no Stanislavsky going on.'

Louie Williams was a regular in the audience, as were Lil Simpson and Bill Kerr's mother, Ann. Lil and Louie became friends: both Londoners from similar backgrounds, they would visit each other's homes, and Alan Simpson remembers dropping in regularly to the barber's shop in Marchmont Street to give his mother a lift home. Williams still lived with his parents. 'His mother used to come to every single radio show,' Melly said.

When the recordings were over, the cast would decamp to a nearby pub – the Captain's Cabin, when they were playing the underground Paris Cinema studio in Lower Regent Street – before drifting away in ones and twos. The pub was an essential part of the ritual, Freddie Hancock said: 'It was like the end of term after the exams. And if you thought you'd done a lousy show, if you had stepped on somebody's line or fluffed something, everybody would try and persuade you otherwise and say, "It really doesn't matter, nobody noticed." That part of it was cameraderie. But Tony might not forgive them in his heart of hearts. Often he couldn't even talk to them.'

Afterwards Hancock, Sid James and their wives would usually go to a restaurant together; Galton and Simpson liked to take their part-ners for a Chinese meal, but Williams never joined any of the *Hancock* team. Andrée Melly agreed: 'He just didn't socialise. We'd go to the pub after the show, and Kenny used to talk to Hancock a bit but never much – he just wasn't very communicative in that kind of way. So you never got to know him personally at all.'

Williams's reluctance to stay out late on Sunday nights was due in part to tiredness: during the five years he spent with Hancock, he starred in seven West End runs as well as launching his movie career. He certainly felt ill at ease with the coarse, heterosexual banter typical of Sid James and others in the cast. 'There is simply no point of contact – their world is totally alien to mine,' he wrote. Ray Galton noticed that Williams seemed to be out of his element: 'a very theatrical person, far more than a radio or television person'.

The BBC world was as straight as it was square, but there was little homophobia. 'In my time, if you were gay you knew you were perfectly safe within the bosom of showbusiness,' Bill Kerr said. 'I don't think there was any mention that Ken was gay. Never a word about that, not one dicky-bird. He was just treated as a very highly talented man.'

'He was very obviously camp, but over-camp, because in those days it was not politically correct to talk about gayness or homosexuality,' Freddie Hancock said. 'He was always dressed very nicely. He wore light grey or pale blue suits, and he wore a tie. He always looked well groomed . . . the accent on detail.'

When he did stay to talk in the pub, Williams was most likely to sit with Hancock and Freddie – or with Hancock and his wife at that time, Cicely. Both men enjoyed philosophical conversations, but it was impossible to sustain an intense, earnest exchange in the Captain's Cabin. If they adjourned to Hancock's apartment or to a friend's flat, the talk could continue all night. On at least two occasions in October 1956, as Britain watched the situation in Suez build to a crisis, Williams and Hancock stayed up talking through the small hours.

Williams may have misread the depth of their friendship. 'Tony and Ken were mates,' explained Freddie Hancock. 'Tony had mates, he didn't have friends. A mate is someone you can put your arm around, but a friend is someone you tell all your soul to.'

They had first discovered an intellectual affinity after the star checked himself into the London Clinic in an effort to lose two stone. Williams visited, three days after the treatment began, on 3 January 1956, and saw H.G. Wells's *Outline of History* lying on the bed. 'We talked at length about theories of historical inevitability, the Malthusian doctrine and the decline of great civilisations,' he wrote in *Just Williams*. The diary adds that the conversation was cut short by Cicely's arrival, but they continued it a few days later with a debate about anarchy. Williams suggested his friend should pay for private tuition from a university don, but the idea was dismissed – both men were self-taught, and neither was suited to the structured discipline of academic study.

Alan Simpson, also self-taught and, like his writing partner, an omnivorous reader, recognised that Williams needed serious conversation after a day of comedy. 'He wasn't always laughing – he used to discuss politics, he used to tell us stories about the army, and he was very well read,' Simpson said. 'It certainly didn't come from his mother and father. I should think [the catalyst] was when he went in the army at eighteen and then he invented himself, he made himself into what he wanted. Acting is an ideal profession for that sort of mentality.'

The debates gave Williams one of his favourite anecdotes about Hancock, which he retold on television in various versions: ' "What's life about, Kenny?" he asked me. "I mean, what if it's all just a joke?" And I said, "Well, if it is, better make it a good one." But that didn't satisfy him.'

Glib retorts didn't satisfy Williams's longing for understanding either, even if he did relish the bleakness of his own wit. At the Hancocks' flat on the fifth floor at Queens Gate Terrace, South Kensington, the fastidious actor and the slovenly comedian drank wine and smoked cigarettes as they argued over the necessity of faith and the meanings of Nietzsche's *Thus Spake Zarathustra*. 'Went back with Tony Hancock and Cicely to their flat for supper,' he wrote. 'Also there was Syd James and Val. I talked with Tony till about 3'ish – got home about four this morning.' For Williams to endure the squalor of Hancock's home, he must have been gripped by their conversations.

The relationship with Hancock supplied an anecdote that Williams retold all his life, including it in his triumphant TV special *An Audience With* nearly thirty years later. Filling in during a technical hitch in recording, the team performed 'crossover gags' – a music-hall tradition where the stand-up attempts to deliver a monologue from centre-stage and his stooges run on with interruptions and lame jokes from the wings. Bill Kerr drew groans with an 'I-say-I-say' about the meat he'd bought from the market for a shilling ('Was it mutton?' 'No, rotten!') and Williams danced across the stage, flinging his arms around as if he was scattering flowers. 'I had to come on and say, "I am sprinkling dust! I am sprinkling woofle dust to kill the wild elephants." And Hancock was to say, "There are no wild elephants around here," and then I was to say, "Well, this isn't real woofle dust . . ." That was the gag. I know it sounds awful but they used to go quite well. But he was supposed to say, "What are you doing?" while I was doing all this. It was the whole point of the gag. He didn't do anything, so I said, "Ask me! Ask me! Ask me what I am!" He said, "We all know what you are!" It got a much bigger laugh.'

Their friendship was strong enough to survive the jibe. By contrast, a similar incident several years later almost brought a West End production to a halt, and drove Williams's co-star to the brink of a breakdown.

Despite this bond, Hancock did not want Williams in his first series of the *Half Hour* on television. Galton and Simpson, adapting their style to a new medium, agreed with him: 'If we kept the whole cast in there it would have become crowded,' Ray Galton said. Used to the surreal landscapes of radio, where they could tip houses over cliffs, race to Monte Carlo in Edwardian jalopies, tow prams behind Stephenson's *Rocket* or build a flyover above a prize marrow, the writers were dismayed to realise that live television was more restricting. 'The cast had to be hiding round the corners, off the screen, waiting to come on, and we thought, This is terrible! We can't bring in everyone all the time.'

There was another reason: Hancock's jealousy of Williams's popularity had been growing. 'Tony thought the balance of the show was going a little too much towards Kenneth,' said Bill Kerr, who was also left out of the TV shows. 'I think it was a bit of a strain for him to know he had to keep up. He felt the pressure.'

Galton and Simpson, torn between Snide's popularity and their original vision of a situation comedy without catchphrases or funny voices, tried to find a compromise. 'Hancock was getting fed up with it,' Simpson said. 'Tony didn't mind people getting laughs – the problem was that the whole show stopped and the story stopped while he did his Snide bit. His bits were becoming the highlight of the show, what everyone was waiting for.'

'A round of applause when he came in, a round of applause when he went off, which wasn't what we were trying to do,' Galton said. 'Everybody thought Snide was too much of a caricature for what we were trying to achieve. Which was reality.'

'They're cutting down on the snide character,' Williams noted in his diary during the third radio series at the start of 1956. 'Too popular. Quite so. Reely. I don't mind.'

The compromise was to exclude Snide from the television scripts, while keeping him in the radio shows. Dennis Main Wilson helped to persuade the star. 'Dennis was slightly sycophantic to Hancock,' commented Andrée Melly. 'Maybe sycophantic is unkind – he was obviously cosying Hancock along.'

At the end of 1956, Galton and Simpson were placing Snide at the centre of their plots. When Hancock and Bill Kerr came home from their holidays, they found Snide and his cats had taken over their home; when they were arrested for queue-jumping to see the Bolshoi ballet, Snide was the policeman with his helmet down over his ears; when Sid James wanted to marry Hattie Jacques, Snide was the registrar who accidentally married himself to Hancock; and in his most famous appearance, Snide was the RAF mechanic who perched on the lap of test pilot Hancock as he flew a supersonic fighter jet ('What's this button? Oooh, it's the ejector seat! Come back, where are you?').

In the penultimate episode of the fourth series, the writers appeared to kill off Snide, making him the incompetent pilot of a jumbo jet that was running out of fuel. Hancock and Bill Kerr's characters were killed off too, so the incident seemed to be no more disastrous than the riots, crashes and explosions that ended many *Half Hours*. At the following week's recording, however, Williams found he had 'hardly any part at all . . . Couldn't bloody care less,' he wrote.

He was invited to appear in the second television series the following month, even playing Snide in the first show. A six-minute scene is all that survives of the half-dozen live broadcasts: Hancock and Williams, fighting over the single bed in an Alpine chalet, are wearing Tyrolean short trousers. He enjoyed being fitted for the costume: 'I've got the legs for it, let's face it.' The routine infuriated Hancock, who claimed later that two men sharing a room with one bed was 'poofy'. By June 1957, Williams knew he would not be asked to do more television. '[Hancock] thinks that set characters make a rut in story routine . . . so much for the obligations of loyalty. Tonight's show was rather dull, I thought. I didn't have a drink with them after – just got on the bus and came home, feeling rather sad about it all.'

The following year, with the fifth radio series under way, Williams collected his script at the start of rehearsals in the Paris Cinema and discovered Snide was back, as a vet who treats Hancock's broken bones after he is crushed by a python. 'When Tony arrived . . . he was angry about it . . . he really believes it is "cartoon" and etc. etc. He has certainly gone down in my estimation. Every time he asks me if I mind, I have to say *no* because after all this fuss I'd feel *awful* doing the damned voice! And every single time, he says, in front of everyone, *and me!* – "It's no good – it's a gimmick voice, and untrue to life . . ." It's a bad argument. O well – I suppose it's a compliment in a way.' Another compromise was reached: the part was kept, but the catchphrases were cut and Williams dropped the voice, instead playing the vet as a camp, ex-public-school boy.

The episodes that followed – including *Hancock's Car*, *Sunday Afternoon at Home*, *The Junk Man* and *Hancock's War* – are widely regarded as the greatest in the Hancock canon. With Galton and Simpson's invention at its height, and the cast an intuitive team who shared sublime, almost telepathic timing, the show was at its zenith. By now, however, a desperately hurt Williams hated it and all his colleagues. He still delivered scene-stealing performances, showcasing a new voice every week. His turn in *The Prize Money* was a pitch-perfect parody of a smarmy quiz-show host, unexpectedly revealing one more talent that was never developed. Williams might have been wonderful, two decades later, as the presenter of *The Golden Shot* or *The Generation Game*.

If Hancock was aware of how deeply his former 'mate' had been wounded, he dismissed it. 'Tony thought Kenneth was very talented and his timing was brilliant,' Freddie Hancock said. 'But he felt showbusiness was the most demanding and selfish career you could have, and there wasn't room for compassion. That totally extended to his relationships.'

Williams's diary entries seethe about his last few *Half Hours*: 'Did the Hancock show. It went very badly. The scripts seem to get worse and worse. There was a time when Tony would have complained. He seems quite happy with them. They are terrible. This one was a load of inconsequential rubbish about rubbish. Hardly a joke anywhere.' 'Did the Hancock show from the Piccadilly. It was a general disaster. Really terrible. This team is so dreary to me now . . . this crowd, esp. James and Hancock, are so listless and disinterested and their conversation is real pleb stuff. I don't care for any of them at all.'

When these comments were published in 1993 in *The Kenneth Williams Diaries*, the depth of Williams's disgust for the show shocked many. 'Some of the bits were hilarious, but then again some were so vitriolic,' Bill Kerr said. 'The terrible thing was, the people he wrote about thought that he loved them. And when they read this they realised that he didn't like them very much.' Galton and Simpson, whose work took the brunt of the hatred that Williams clearly intended for Hancock himself, were astounded. 'It came as a complete revelation,' Ray Galton said. 'I didn't know he was like that.'

'It was totally the opposite of what we knew about him,' Alan Simpson agreed. 'So it was Jekyll and Hyde. When he was at the show, rehearsal started at ten o'clock in the morning and we'd go through to about ten o'clock at night in the pub, and he was wonderful company – funny, laughed at everything, laughed at stories that Sid was telling . . . when we were sitting around doing nothing, guffawing at things Hancock said.'

'And then going home and saying what a boring man Sid James was and what an awful actor, and Tony Hancock's so overrated,' Galton added, 'and if you'd been there during the day you'd think he was with his best friends. And then the next week going through the exact same charade. And he gave no indication of resenting anybody or resenting Hancock . . . I can't even remember saying, "Oh, he's a bit moody".'

The writers were so confident that Williams shared the team spirit that, six weeks after Snide was banished, they were pulling his leg on air. Hancock, playing an actor-manager in the East Cheam Drama Festival, announced: 'Mr Kenneth Williams, the celebrated character actor, will be seen in a multitude of parts, a multitude! All of which he has pinched from other celebrated character actors.'

When Williams saw this in the script, he shrugged it off. 'Ken said, "You bastards!"' recalled Galton. During the broadcast, his braying laughter almost drowned Hancock's punchline.

'If he did hate everything about it, he never let his guard down,' Simpson said. 'He never once even minutely lost his temper with Hancock or Sid. Very controlled, without us even being aware that it was controlled. It just seemed that he was having a bloody good time and enjoying it. It's bewildering, incredible in the real sense of the word – unbelievable. Almost as if the diary was written by somebody else.'

At the beginning of the sixth series, Williams decided he could bear it no longer: 'I think that I am quite superfluous now, and will telephone Peter [Eade] tomorrow to get me out of the rest of the series.' The following day, Eade 'rang Tom Ronald [Hancock's producer] who was delighted for me to withdraw: so I'm well out of that entire set-up'. By now he was part of the regular cast on *Beyond Our Ken*, another BBC radio comedy: 'Lovely to work with this team – so refreshing after the stagnance of HHH.'

He rarely saw Hancock again, and when he did the feelings of anger, hurt and rejection were always close to the surface. Even listening to one of the *Half Hours* was enough to put him in a foul temper. Eight years after he left the show, he played an LP of excerpts and sat down to write a lacerating critique: 'Hancock doing his pompous bit in too slow a tempo. I think this was the great defect with H.: the absence of real professional expertise and technical cleverness. The sort of rough ability he did have was sufficient for a duo of the Morecambe and Wise type of act, but not for the more advanced kind of comedy which he really admired (Benny, Tati, etc.) It's really the difference between a comic and a comedian. H. never properly decided on either.'

An even more telling comment was to come. When Williams was invited to compile his entry for *Who's Who* in 1979, he listed all his stage successes and many of the more minor achievements, such as voiceovers for children's cartoons. He also cited his role in *Hancock's Half Hour* on television. But the five series on radio passed without mention.

6

'I could no more share a flat with Anyone than I could fly'

November 1954–June 1957

Williams placed little more significance on those radio and tele-vision performances than he did on the films he saw at the cinema. His real life was the theatre.

In its first incarnation, *Saint Joan* ran at the Arts for a month, until the end of October 1954. That brief success launched Williams on the most varied and prestigious series of roles he ever enjoyed, as well as bestowing a social cachet that he loved. There were parties: 'Invited to Geoffrey Sharp's party, 9 o/c'ish. This was riotous, with everyone there! Never seen so many fabulous people. Kenneth Tynan gangling over the heads, smelling out the interest like an overbred reindeer.' There were congenial BBC producers, unbidden, who wanted to cast him, and he had money for new clothes. In January 1955 *Saint Joan* was revived, this time at a leading West End theatre, St Martin's; Williams felt bold enough to reject the offer of £15 a week and hold out for more. John Fernald would be stage director, but the producer now was Henry Sherek, which raised expectations of a transfer to Broadway.

Williams had all he needed for contentment – work, and plenty of it; old friends and his family, especially his parents and their gener-ation; more theatres, cinemas and cafés within walking distance of the barber's shop in Bloomsbury than could be crammed into any other square mile on earth. The idea of transporting his Dauphin to New York was unappealing. He would rather luxuriate in London. One afternoon, for instance, he had tea with his mother at Lyons Corner House, Marble Arch, before joining Peter Nichols to see Beatrice Lillie: 'As I suspected, greatly over-rated. First half consists of old sketches refurbished [. . .] vague, woolly and vacuous.'

He was generous to acquaintances, and gave away a brand-new blue serge suit to an unemployed actor. His mood was soured when he learned that three characters were to be recast, including Tremoille, originally played by Bill Abney, who had become a friend. A string of tirades filled the diary. Abney's replacement was 'a creature called Grey, who is the full querulous queenly cup – black shirt, white tie, and thoroughly perverse'. The gallant commander Dunois was now played by Robert Cartland, 'a coarse featured actor [. . .] singularly graceless [. . .] He seems vulgar too. At the first rehearsal at the Duchess he sat in the stalls, watching rehearsals with his feet up on the next rows of seats.' The man who had hired these substitutes – 'wretched creatures with little or no dramatic qualities' – was Fernald, now the target of acid bile: 'The same old Fernald methods are at work. Lines are being repeated ad infinitum ad nauseam, and original purpose + meanings are muddied and lost [. . .] It is sad to realise how utterly bogus Fernald is.'

By the time the play opened, Williams could not hide his contempt for the production, though he did respect McKenna's rich performance. In deference to her, he curbed his urge to disrupt the speeches, and when he did misbehave or giggle, he was contrite later. But he did not forgive Fernald and continued to boil over in the diary:

> There are two main tasks in the presentation of a dramatist's work. These are – 1) the practical business of stage setting and curtain pulling, etc. 2) The direction of acting: in the sense that a conductor controls a set of instruments. This last task presupposes a man who not only understands his score, his instruments AND how to get the best out of them, but ALSO a man who understands ACTORS. All the rest is embellishment, and is of minor importance. I have never met a man with the qualifications for (2).

This mistrust of directors was part of his reason for rejecting an invitation to play Ariel in an open-air staging of *The Tempest*, in Regent's Park; also, he suspected that Shakespeare was incongruous in the 1950s, and that actors should not be playing Renaissance myths on lawns when they could be acting human dramas, speaking real dialogue.

Williams understood human dramas. He observed them constantly, though he drew back from participation. He listened to their language, recording it in long letters laid out like scripts. Annette Kerr, in the mid-fifties, was the usual recipient, as he described the relationship between Michael Harald and his girlfriend, Susan Sylvester, who were living next door in Marchmont Street. Harald was a writer, with ambitions to stage his own plays: in early 1955, he was trying to find a theatre for his unpublished *Face of Doubt*. Williams paints him as a stereotype of the fifties intellectual, a man like Osborne's Jimmy Porter – sincere, frustrated, a chauvinist bully, and very angry.

After one drunken lunch at a hotel, Sylvester had to drag Harald home, shouting and falling down. She fled from the flat when he began to be violently sick and ran to Williams; he calmed her and listened to her as she sobbed out the story, then went next door to clear up the worst of the mess and scrub the floor with a brush. The same practical aspect that enabled him to put up shelves or hang wallpaper also helped him to cope with messy little crises. Other people's illnesses disgusted him, but he was not afraid to deal with them.

After a life with Charlie Williams, he accepted that men would harangue and abuse women, but he disliked hearing Sylvester be told to shut up whenever she opened her mouth. Between the two productions of *Saint Joan*, he discussed the idea of moving into a flat with her. It was partly pity, but also a sign that, at twenty-eight and established in his career at last, Williams was almost ready to leave his parents' home.

The routine of nightly performance began to wear – 'Lots of giggling in the Epilogue which I started quite deliberately and with malice aforethought.' This was his longest run in a role since *Peter Pan*, and that at least had not taxed his emotions. The strain and technical demands of *Saint Joan* told on McKenna as well, and on 19 March 1955 Williams's handwriting betrays disgust and anger. He complains that her voice had gone, that she was bad-tempered with all the cast and that people were becoming sick of her self-pity; such criticism was comparatively mild, but the slashing calligraphy on the page told of a deeper hurt. The next two entries were written with a compressed fury, which simmered for a week before erupting in a three-day demolition of everything McKenna was doing on stage.

He accused her of being incapable of trust, which suggests the row may have started with some breach of a secret; Williams loved to let colleagues know what other people thought of them, especially if he'd heard it in confidence.

Unable to vent his resentment to McKenna's face, he transferred it to the actor who played the bigoted cleric Stogumber, David March. On stage, Williams bullied him, trampling on his lines in the epilogue; off stage, he behaved with disdain and mocked March for taking his complaints to the director. Later, he was suddenly scared of the consequences – he never could be openly defiant of authority, and the thought of a reprimand from Fernald frightened him. Still bubbling with venom for March, he composed an abject retraction: 'It would be wholly undignified for me to EXPLAIN myself [. . .] Therefore I shall say, "My behaviour was inexcusable, unprofessional and has caused me to feel ashamed."' This sort of spat, which seems at first so trivial that it must be irrelevant, shaped his career. The reluctance he felt in risking a debut in America was compounded by the knowledge he was neither liked nor trusted by others in the cast. He had the excuse he needed to turn Sherek down when the Broadway transfer was proposed.

He need not have bothered. Orson Welles supplied a better excuse for abandoning *Saint Joan* when he invited him to join his company at the Duke of York's Theatre. The audition was affable. Another in the cast, Peter Sallis, recalled that Welles sat drinking and chuckling in the stalls with friends, before greeting the actors with a handshake and a joke. He welcomed Williams by praising his versatility and proved he meant it by giving him a fistful of parts to play in *Moby Dick Rehearsed*.

Its script was by Welles himself, adapted from Melville and Shakespeare, and opened with a troupe of actors on a bare stage, at the turn of the twentieth century. The set, the lighting and the switchback narrative were in radical contrast to the material: all the cast were always on stage, frozen in a band of shadow when they were not speaking; the curtain was already up, revealing brick walls, boxes and coiled ropes, as the audience came in. The play began with a reading from *Lear*, with Welles as the senile king and Joan Plowright as Cordelia, before plunging into the story of Ahab and the *Pequod* and the pursuit of the great white whale. All of the vast scenery, the ship and the whale and the ocean, existed only in the imagination: the effect was avant garde, and won critical adulation.

Many in the audience, which was sold out every night for the three-week run, returned to marvel as often as possible – Tony Walton, who later designed the sets for two of Williams's revues, saw all but three or four of the performances. Welles altered his performance every night, even changing his make-up in mid-show so he would play some scenes clean-shaven and others with a straggling white beard. The prompter, his new wife Paola Mori, could not follow his violent shifts of pace, and all the cast were subjected to ferocious ad libs and changes.

Williams was nonplussed. He understood how to unsettle his fellow actors with subtle trickery, and he knew how to dominate by stealing slivers of a scene. He had never seen any actor cow an entire company with sheer bombast.

Rehearsals had been gruelling. Once *Saint Joan* finished on 28 May 1955, Williams was plunged into practice runs of *Moby Dick* that could last fourteen hours, from mid-morning to midnight, seven days a week. His only break would be the read-through and recording of a Hancock episode, with stage rehearsals both before and after. Welles constructed the play by inches: by 3 June they had worked out only the first half of the first act. 'Dead, but dead tired,' Williams moaned. 'I don't think I could stand much more of this kind of work.' The star directed from off stage, with much emphasis on the lighting, which radiated across the set in spokes. Sallis claimed it was not until the dress rehearsals that Welles rehearsed his own part, and then discovered that the force of a spotlight directly in his face could send him stumbling.

Williams played 'A Very Serious Actor', as well as Elijah, the Ship's Carpenter, an Old Bedford Sailor and others. Welles was amused by his affectation and began calling him 'Miss Bankhead' – 'If Miss Bankhead is ready?' he would roar. Williams enjoyed that, but he was upset by Welles's abrupt changes to the text, sometimes in the middle of a performance. As Ship's Carpenter, Williams had a moment of poetry, promising to carve his captain a false leg of gold and ivory. Welles cut short the speech one night with a curt whisper:

'Piss off!' Williams retreated to stand beside Joan Plowright in the shadows, burning with indignation; afterwards he gathered his courage, knocked at Welles's dressing-room and asked, deferentially, why he had been ordered off the stage. 'Kenneth, you bore me,' Welles replied. 'You've been boring me for weeks. Now piss off.'

On the opening night, 16 June, the assistant producer, Billy Chappell, invited Williams to audition for a musical which he was to direct at the Lyric Hammersmith. He had heard Williams singing backstage at the Duke of York's and complimented his voice: 'I said, "That's very perspicacious of you," because modesty forbade overt agreement.' The show's composer was Sandy Wilson, whose first musical, *The Boy Friend*, was running in triumph both in the West End and on Broadway. The musical was *The Buccaneer*, the tale of a *Boy's Own* newspaper and its own boy editor, twelve-year-old Montgomery Winterton.

'The problem was to find someone who could look like a small boy but behave like a grown-up,' Wilson explained. 'It was difficult to cast. But Billy Chappell had been working on *Moby Dick*, and I had heard of Kenneth because he had played the Dauphin. So he was brought, very reluctantly, to audition for this musical, which he didn't really want to do – he was a very serious actor. We asked him to sing, and he launched into a marine song called "Rocked in the Cradle of the Deep", singing baritone. We said, "Kenneth, don't be silly, you know perfectly well it's for a young boy." So Kenneth rather reluctantly sang the national anthem. But I'd already decided that we wanted him in any case, because he was obviously *it*, because he did look so very young, and yet was a very grown-up, sophisticated actor, and could sing.' Williams was so strained by the weeks of rehearsal with Welles that after this audition he walked to St Giles's churchyard in Camden and sat down among the tombstones to weep.

When Welles learned that Williams was rehearsing a musical, he disapproved. Light entertainment was a waste of serious talent, and he asked Williams to make films with him instead. A few days later, he proposed two definite roles, with his Shakespeare company in New York, to play Octavius in *Antony and Cleopatra*, and the Fool in *King Lear*. Williams squirmed. The thought of acting with Welles again was daunting; the idea of living in New York, with no family and no friends, horrified him. He had already dodged one Broadway booking that year, and at least he would have been with a cast he knew in *Saint Joan*. To be unknown and know no one was his worst nightmare – Williams needed always to have immediate access to companionship, an audience, even if it comprised just one person. And then, a season in New York would mean moving away from his mother, and though he was almost ready to do that, he did not intend to put more than a couple of streets between them. Louie could not go to New York with him: Charlie would not have permitted it. Grateful for an excuse, Williams told Welles he could not walk out on *The Buccaneer*.

To be so much in demand was doubly unsettling, because he was feeling the lack of anyone to comfort him, especially over his health. His mother would be busy in the shop as he ate a hurried breakfast, and he would not return to Marchmont Street until late. When he cut his leg on a prop one night, Williams was despondent: 'it was sheer agony' and nobody cared. He was always abnormally sensitive to pain, and the sight of his own blood filled him with anxiety. After nursing the cut for a week, he decided to go to hospital, 'but they acted disinterestedly and stuck a bandage on. I think I shall have to handle this myself.' Two days later he visited a different doctor, who was attentive: 'He said it would be rather slow in healing owing to bad blood circulation. He has prescribed some remedy + it must be dressed once a day.'

Williams was gratified and relieved. He had found a simple and obvious solution, a way to procure sympathy for his ailments, with the advantage that he would not be expected to show reciprocal interest in the doctor's problems. This began a lifelong relationship that intensified over the decades: the doctors changed but their role was constant.

Filming began at the Hackney Empire, as Welles attempted to record his extraordinary version of *Moby Dick*. He drove the actors for long sessions that stretched into tortured marathons – first ten hours, then twelve, then fifteen. After two weeks the project was abandoned, unfinished: the innovative lighting looked murky in the rushes, there was no money or time for reshooting, and the star was distracted by his television series.

With rehearsals for *The Buccaneer* under way, Williams had a new burden: his parents were away on their annual week's holiday, and Pat Williams had returned from Australia, after her divorce, to a heat-wave. 'This week has been sheer disaster with the sister back and, supposedly, in charge of the house, and Louie and Charles away, the place is like a pig sty. Of course there is a mad clean up on Saturday so that it will look good to the folks. Not a thing done until Saturday though! She is so utterly slothful that it is almost horrible; and there is a quality of imbecility about the physical nature of her that amounts to nausea. No wonder she flopped in Australia. This one is so drear, she'd flop anywhere.' Now that Pat was home, Williams was almost certain he could move into a flat of his own.

The Buccaneer went on tour, to Brighton and Southsea, at the end of August 1955, and was well received. Wilson's score was crammed with jaunty, wholesome melodies and arch lyrics: Williams found he could deliver them best in a rhythmic, nasal recitation, with just a hint of a tune. His character, the boy editor, was determined to remain adolescent and avoid the opposite sex. Williams was afraid of looking amateur, and early in rehearsals he berated himself for taking the part: 'This show is really frightful. The production is utterly conventional. The material is practically non est [non-existent] and the talent is questionable. It's all so bloody dull. Billy Chappell might be an excellent choreographer but he has no idea about production. Parrot inflexions to artists!! The old old story. Nothing of individual-ity. I hope it flops, that's all. I just hope it flops.' At the theatre, his depression receded, and none of the other Buccaneers had any idea of his private torments.

'He was depressed, but we didn't know it,' said Sally Bazely, who played the heroine, Mabel. 'It all came out in the diaries but he wouldn't show that to any of us. I didn't feel he was performing all the time off stage: he would fool around in the wings sometimes, just trying to get the laughs, but he certainly wasn't on show all the time like that. He was quite serious really.'

The Buccaneer ran for seven months. It is clear that Williams was not feigning enthusiasm – someone would have sensed it eventually. His buoyancy, dedication and spirited mischief at the theatre were all genuine. 'God, he made us laugh,' said Wilson, 'not just on stage but off stage too. He shared a dressing-room with John Faasson, and they were a very funny pair, because he was a very straight, very handsome leading man, and Kenneth was a wild . . . you know what Kenneth was. They were an amusing couple.' And yet Williams returned to his room above his father's shop, and castigated himself for betraying the theatre: 'It is difficult to sustain a standard in one's own work, when ignorance prevails about one: nonetheless it's obviously one's duty to try – and it is in the periods of not-trying when depression + melancholia seize me and drag me down a hundred dark passages into a temporary despair.' These two personalities seemed to live within him like guests in a boarding-house who only ever passed on the stairs.

His conflicting emotions could produce what seem, at first, to be shocking hypocrisies. Here is Williams on 8 November, savagely indicting the man who gave him his first West End starring role:

> Lunched with Billy Chappell and Tom Eliot. It was very interesting to see at close quarters the level at which these two live. It was the most debilitated atmosphere. Such futility. The sadness – the tragedy of Billy Chappell is the tragedy of the man in circumstances beyond his control. Not tragic in the sense of greatness unrealised, but in the sense of lack of self-discipline. The man who finds himself in a position of authority without the ability to wield that authority becomes an evil man [. . .] Tom Eliot is the universal sycophant – yes sir, no sir, three bags full sir.

And three weeks later, a presentation from the whole cast to the director: 'It went well, and he liked the silver box and illuminated address which I drew up.' The loathing is real, and never retracted, but the pride Williams evinces in pleasing his employer is real too. The contradiction is not dishonest: he is a child, despising and adoring his friends on the least provocation. When Chappell cast Williams as a twelve-year-old, he was possibly asking for an emotional maturity that the actor himself hadn't developed.

Thelma Ruby, who played Williams's mother, recalled his gift for creating a conspiratorial intimacy. 'At the curtain of one act, where Betty Warren and Eliot Makeham were on stage, the last line was,

"And the rest doesn't really matter." And Kenneth whispered to me at that moment, "There's you, and there's me, and the rest doesn't really matter!" He was a delight and I was very, very fond of him.'

With the *Hancock* team, he rarely went to the pub after a recording, and in his parallel life on *The Buccaneer* he followed the same pattern. 'He was very private, he never socialised after the play if we all went for a drink,' Bazely said. He sometimes invited one or two of the cast back to his parents' home, though, or dropped in on one of Sandy Wilson's parties. 'The thing was,' Wilson said, 'if you asked Kenneth anywhere, that was it – nobody spoke, we just sat and listened, which was fine. He took over. Not dominating, but once he started you wanted to listen to him. He wasn't pushy or anything, he just started telling a story and we listened and we all laughed. I was fond of him, I admired him tremendously, but I didn't feel I really knew him.'

Williams usually regretted his revels. After drinks at 57 Marchmont Street with Faassen, he noted in hungover handwriting: 'Woke feeling utterly jaded and determined not to stay up late for frivolous purposes ever again. Simply isn't worth the loss of energy. I feel just terrible. Performance at night ghastly.'

One regular visitor to No. 57 was the show's assistant stage manager, Nora Stapleton, four years younger than Williams. Affectionate, maternal and armed with a robust sense of humour, she fussed and worried over him, and he played up to it. Others in the cast assumed it was a love affair; for Thelma Ruby, the backstage gossip about 'Ken and Nora' was one of the defining memories of the production. Nora showed every sign of being infatuated: 'I do think she had fallen in love with him,' Ruby said.

They sometimes behaved as a couple, calling on other Buccaneers at home, dining in favourite restaurants and frequenting bawdy shows. When one of the cast, Eliot Makeham, died in February 1956, however, it was not Nora but Sybil Burton who accompanied Williams to the funeral. They were overcome by giggles during the service and had to leave. They retreated to a pub, but were confronted by the other actors later: 'Betty Warren came in with the rest of the company,' Williams wrote, 'and went on and on in terrible taste.'

The show's producers, H.M. Tennent, made a late decision to transfer *The Buccaneer* to the West End, opening at the Apollo on Williams's thirtieth birthday. It was six months since the first night at the Lyric and, without momentum or fresh reviews, the show closed four weeks later. During that short run he also took the role of Justice Shallow in a BBC radio production of *Henry IV Part Two*, and took steps to move into his own apartment. The combined stress almost brought him to a breakdown: in the street he imagined that every stranger was staring at him and that their footsteps followed him. He wanted to cry constantly and took refuge in cinemas, sometimes seeing three films before going to the theatre.

But he could no longer continue to live with Charles and Louie. The lack of privacy was stifling, and now that he was an established star on both stage and radio his relationship with his father had become impossible. 'My work suffers and my existence is utterly wretched. I don't suppose it's anybody's fault, for in the fundamental sense I'm obviously the one to live alone.' He tried to assert himself by buying presents for his mother – a Hoover washing machine and electric wringer, for instance – but Charlie just sneered at the waste of money.

Williams asked Peter Eade to help him find somewhere to live and together they viewed a one-bedroom flat in Trinity Court: in a surge of optimism, Williams spotted the newspaper advert, inspected the rooms, and paid a £50 deposit on the £500 fee all in one day. A week later the property was withdrawn. Determined to escape, Williams saw another apartment the next day, on Upper Woburn Place, between the Euston Road and Tavistock Square. The building, Endsleigh Court, was a brick-built, inter-war mansion block divided into eight storeys of apartments, all with metal-latticed windows. Flat 817 was tiny: one long step through the front door took him into the bathroom; the hallway dog-legged into a cramped living-room with a curtained alcove for the bed, and the kitchen was barely wide enough to stand in. The walls needed painting; the furniture needed burning. The lease was £800. Williams paid it.

Stanley Baxter, whose success in Scotland was now bringing him TV work in London, suggested he could share the apartment when he was in town. Williams was aghast. 'I could no more share a flat with Anyone than I could fly. The very *idea* is absurd.' He obtained the keys on 24 March 1956, arranged for his books and possessions to be transferred two days later, and moved in that evening to discover that the electricity had been cut off.

If he had more than two visitors, he had to pull back the curtain and sit on the bed – and even then there was barely room to stretch. As a retreat, though, it had all that he needed, and it was only three minutes' walk from Marchmont Street.

Before *The Buccaneer* ended, he was already in rehearsal for *Hotel Paradiso*, a farce by Georges Feydeau, translated and directed by Peter Glenville. The star was Alec Guinness, and Williams's part, as Maxime, one of the guests, was a minor one. His demotion was a relief. If the show flopped, or the audience didn't laugh, that would be a public rejection for Guinness, not for him. The play was tried in Birmingham and then Glasgow, where Baxter met him at the station and took him back to his house to see Moira and share their supper. Bill Kerr was also in the city, and they met for coffee.

After a week in Newcastle, and a London dress rehearsal that went on till midnight, *Hotel Paradiso* opened at the Winter Garden on 2 May 1956. Guinness sent champagne to Williams's dressing-room, with a card that was pasted in the diary: 'Good luck Kenneth to your charming performance. Alec G.' A telegram from the Tennent's management, signed 'Binkie and John', was also preserved. The reviews were good, with Tynan describing Guinness as a 'most creative *farceur* [. . .] notably assisted by Kenneth Williams as a blond prig'.

If such glancing praise smacked of a return to rep, Williams was unconcerned. He was more interested in decorating his new home. His aunt Daisy and her husband Cliff, two of his favourite relatives, helped him to hang the alcove curtain, and he treated himself to a Rambler radio and three chairs, at 9 guineas each. He painted the living-room, the electric fire, the doors and the window frame himself, and hired decorators to do the rest of the flat; when he wasn't satisfied with the work they did in the bathroom, he made them come back. With the decorating done, he could occupy himself with cleaning; it was a pastime that would soothe him for the rest of his life.

He did not want to share his home, but he felt he would like to have his friends close by. When a fifth-floor flat became free, he tried to persuade John Vere, a regular on the *Hancock* television shows, to take it; later he invited Annette Kerr to move into a cubbyhole built around the staircase on the second floor. When she declined, he offered it to an eager Nora Stapleton, who lived there for more than thirty years. Stanley Walker, a friend from his days at the physical training camp in Herefordshire, in 1944, also moved into the block, and regularly borrowed money from him.

Dennis Main Wilson suggested a radio panel game with Harry Secombe and Ted Ray, and though Williams agreed to record a pilot, he was wary and doubtful, and backed out a week later. A sketch with Zsa Zsa Gabor at the Palladium in *Night of a Hundred Stars*, with Williams playing a 'daft reporter', pleased him more. Gabor, the ex-wife of Conrad Hilton and George Sanders, epitomised international glamour to him, and he was flattered to be chosen for her foil. He must have been dropping her name madly, backstage at the Winter Garden, because 'Guinness suddenly hissed at me "Zsa Zsa Gabor to you too!" before sailing on to the stage.' But Williams continued to brag of the association, and years later, after a lively dinner, even boasted wildly to a group of friends that Gabor was the only woman he had ever tried to sleep with.

Guinness displayed a dignified generosity, the noblesse oblige of the cinema star, often treating members of the cast to dinner and giving a party on stage to mark the hundredth performance, on 30 July. Williams would have panicked in such a patrician role; he was happier as the naughty boy of the company. In his autobiography he told with delight how he had taunted a junior actor, John Salew, that he was being taken for granted as the star's understudy. At last the man was goaded into making a complaint, to which Guinness replied graciously with a gift of whisky. When Williams realised that Salew did not like whisky, he ordered him, with spiteful glee, to take the bottles back and ask for gin. Whatever the truth of the incident – and there is no mention of it in the diary – the story reveals a streak of malevolence that most people would deny or conceal. Williams revelled in it and was especially pleased that none of the other actors seemed to find his machinations funny.

At other moments, he was gripped by a fear that his life was wasting, and that he lacked the resolve to grasp his talent and wring greatness from it. 'O! for the real courage to speak out bravely, to do ONE decisive, unselfish and creative deed. Instead of watching the sand run through the glass.' These moods came on when he was in pain, and for weeks he had been suffering from backache, exacerbated by his habit of rocking back on a chair with his feet on the dressing-table while he read. At the National Orthopaedic Hospital, 'I was X Ray'd and blood tested – both shewed nothing wrong. So I'm to be given heat treatment and exercises for the back. What a lot of balls. They simply don't know what is wrong with me, at all.'

Williams was not merely sensitive to pain, but afraid of it. Even a pain that came from outside, such as intrusive noise or oppressive heat, could distort his thoughts. Pain that was constant for more than two or three hours would set him sliding into despair. He imagined that only death was a sure panacea, and he castigated himself for failing to appreciate his life before the pain began. While he suffered, he found more to praise in his friends. Throughout these weeks in the late summer his back throbbed; it was eventually diagnosed as lumbago. Like an animal licking a wound, Williams seemed subdued and pathetic and pitifully glad of his friends. He could only summon the energy to be vicious when he was in good humour: when he was at his most monstrous in his diary, he seems to have been at his most likeable in life.

The *Paradiso* run ended during the Suez crisis, a political mess that Williams deplored. Eden was weak, Macmillan a 'mediocre fossil' and Churchill was 'that old hypocritical ratbag [. . .] He excelled so greatly in the oratorical sense – in the corruption of the poetic consciousness.' Williams escaped from current affairs into Margaret Yourcenar's historical novel, *Memoirs of Hadrian*, which captivated him: 'The atmosphere is incredibly real. For the first time I seem to "experience" history myself, and to live these events. The writing is so full of sweetness and poetry and light; it is a joy to read. I am reminded of all that was most noble in pagan civilisations.' The Baxters were in London; when they waved goodbye to him from the night sleeper at Euston, he promised to come and visit them in Edinburgh.

By now his lumbago had eased, and in the barometer of his moods the vitriol was rising. Peter Ashby-Bailey invited him to tea in his new flat: 'It was all terribly Victorian – overstuffed and faintly squalid. It's fantastic, the way some people live.' A party thrown by John

Schlesinger revealed 'the looking glass world. Over and over again I see it for the first and last time; over and over I say I won't look again, it only aggravates and hurts.'

This disquiet that his friends roused in him was trivial in comparison to the five-page diatribe provoked by his trip to Scotland. Baxter met him from the King's Cross express, and the only grumble on Monday 14 January 1957 was about the sleeping arrangements: Williams realised he would have to bed down on the settee. But what followed was slaughter. Every aspect of the Baxters' marriage, of Stanley's career, of their conversation, their home, their life, aroused their guest's disgust. From this carnage of character assassination emerged the chief complaint: that Stanley and Moira were absorbed in their own relationship, with its private jokes and shared memories, and they were insufficiently interested in Williams. He felt excluded. On the Friday he walked out and caught the sleeper: 'I can't stay here any longer [. . .] It's something of a victory in me, NOT to have been at all offensive in my stay.' At 6.30 a.m. the next day he arrived at King's Cross 'and practically kissed the ground in gratitude. Never again.'

With *Hancock's Half Hour* now in its fourth series, Williams felt confident about turning down work. He refused the role of Androcles in Shaw's play for BBC radio – 'a character performance I could easily sustain on the stage, but never on the air' – and he claimed he could not manage the authentic accent to take over as Willy Nilly in *Under Milk Wood* at the New. Both these excuses were nonsense: the work simply didn't appeal to him. But he accepted the chance to return to the Arts Theatre, as Kite the valet in Mervyn Peake's *The Wit to Woo*, even though it clashed with an offer to appear on independent television, in a production of *Venus Observed*.

When he read the play, he 'was struck by the nature of the dialogue. It is always the words that interest me,' he later wrote to Peake's biographer, 'and I hardly ever find myself thinking in critical terms of construction or plot or technical details of stage mechanics.' Kite was intriguing, a spectral manservant who enables his master to declare himself dead and be resurrected as a flamboyant cousin – 'it glittered with malevolence and vituperative wit + I knew I could encompass it vocally. I was a bit perturbed about the physical side of the role but I know that I managed to get a lot of slithering into it.'

Rehearsals for the play, presented by Michael Codron, began in mid-February, and at first he was thrilled to be working for the director, Peter Wood. It was 'wonderfully wonderful' but he suspected the feeling wouldn't last. It did not. Within a week he had a stinking cold, a boil on his neck and sore feet. Denis Goacher, a friend since they had worked together in Salisbury rep, tried to persuade him to join relaxation classes, but Williams would not hear of it: 'I *KNOW* it's no good to me. That isn't stupidity or stubborn refusal to try – it's simply that I *know* it would not help.' Instead, he was taking sleeping pills.

As Kite, he provided a running commentary on the play, and Wood had him appear through a window, from behind a screen and once from within a long-case clock. 'This is going to be murder to stage,' Williams muttered. The production was left-field and unconventional: for Codron, who went on to make the names of Harold Pinter and Joe Orton, it was an early indication that he should concentrate on theatres at the fringe, such as the Arts and the Lyric Hammersmith.

When the play opened on 12 March 1957, Williams found his nerves were soothed by good notices: 'A joyous joke so long as Kenneth Williams is on the stage,' said Cecil Wilson in the *Mail*. '[He] slithers about the stage like some reptilian Jeeves.' Milton Shulman in the *Standard* said, 'Kenneth Williams, as a fey valet, is a delicious concoction of criss-crossing knees and throttled vowel sounds.' 'A continual delight – razor sharp, gilded with subtlety, wickedly expressive,' praised the *Liverpool Post*. What really quelled his fears was a letter of applause from Michael Harald. Praise from friends, especially when it was written down and could be re-read often, gave him lasting encouragement. The applause from an audience was over before they left the theatre, and it sustained him for about as long.

His feud with the Baxters was quickly forgotten. They visited in March, and a couple of months later he was taking them to dinner with his other favourite couple, Gordon Jackson and his wife, Rona Anderson. The next day, he 'saw Stanley and Moira off at Euston. Stayed too long on the train and had to jump from the moving carriage.'

The problems with his family were more entrenched. A year after he had moved into his own flat, he found it difficult to return to Marchmont Street. Following a meal to celebrate his thirty-first birthday, he wrote:

> The more I visit home nowadays the more I want to get out quick. I spend v. little time there, and leave as soon as possible. The atmosphere is full of ferment and it's largely due to Pat – there is something in her nature, which Charles is antipathetic to. I am, as well. She rouses in me such inner discomfort and such psychological irritation, I could scream at her with loathing. Louie is not sensitive to this feeling, for she is obviously fond of her. But I admit defeat. I just *can't* like her, and I never will. I am conscious of the sinfulness of this.

He tried to overcome this by being friendly, giving her his old record-player when he bought a new one – this was more than just the practical gesture of a man who hated throwing things away, since the gramophone had been almost a companion in the tiny flat.

To share his emotions, even on medical advice, was impossible. All year he had been suffering from piles, and visiting a doctor called Newman, who 'seems lackadaisical, but he is kind, and says not to worry'. On 14 May Newman prescribed an ointment and a treatment: sexual activity. All Williams's fantasies centred on submission, on giving control to a sexual partner and, though he longed to do this, he did not dare. Instead, he engineered an encounter that he wholly controlled. After booking a train ticket to Glasgow that same evening, to visit the Baxters again, he invited a young ex-serviceman back to his apartment: 'David – a charming fellow – just demobbed, been out in Cyprus, entirely unspoiled + honest [. . .] It was charming. The first time I've had physical relaxation with anyone – it was superb.' At 11 p.m. David was bundled out, with the excuse that Williams had a train to catch.

This trip to Scotland went no better than the last. Baxter remembered the debacle and how it ended: 'There was a fight and he left in the night, leaving a note on the pillow.' Williams had to bribe a porter to get a berth on the night express. Unable to commit himself to a lover, or indulge his friends, or embrace his career, he needed a figure of authority, someone to force him back on to his feet. The man who took up that challenge was Michael Codron.

7

'Lots of old pals. It was all delightful'

May 1957–April 1959

M ichael Codron, the nascent impresario who had staged *The Wit to Woo*, was under pressure to abandon theatre and return to the family business. His two other productions had folded after short runs and he needed a success. 'I was being told by my father that it looked as if I hadn't got the skills to be a producer,' Codron said, seated behind an expansive desk in his office over the Aldwych Theatre on Drury Lane. 'I must have prevailed on my father to let me have one last go, with a project that wasn't like the other plays.' After seeing *Share My Lettuce*, a mix of sketches by Cambridge Undergraduate Bamber Gascoigne, he decided to stake his career on a revue. If he could persuade Williams to star, he felt it could be a hit.

'*Share My Lettuce* was the thing that changed my whole career, my make-or-break production. I must originally have met Kenneth at the Grill & Cheese, which was in Lyons Corner House. On the first floor was a place where all the actors went after the shows and Ken would hold court there. We became friends; I had fallen under his spell, as one did, because he would hold the whole table in great thrall.' Codron knew that Williams was perfect for revue: 'It was the voices.'

It happened that, on the day Codron invited him to discuss *Lettuce* over lunch, Williams had received a tax demand for £210. *The Wit to Woo* had earned him only a nominal sum, and after six months of living on his BBC income he had just £200 in his deposit account. When Codron proposed a starring role in a revue, Williams was stymied. This was exactly the sort of opportunity he had spent years avoiding, but he needed to earn money somehow. A week later, on 13 June, he met the director, Eleanor Fazan, at the Cambridge Theatre, and realised he had committed himself.

The revue needed a charismatic personality to connect the scattered sketches. Williams was flattered and frightened, but when rehearsals started he saw that he would be the star only in name – 'all this talk about it being built round me is so much cock'. The set pieces relied on quickfire ensemble playing, the lines and lyrics whipping around each other. One sketch was set at a party where all the men were called Michael and all the girls Susan, and conversations were chanted in unison; in another, a waitress echoed every order as four diners sprinted through the menu. The show opened with a drum solo and seven dancers who called out the colours of their costumes – 'Pink! Maroon! Grey! Violet! Brown! Blue! Orrrr-ange!' – until Williams sauntered on and announced that he was Green.

'What a ridiculous colour for a suit . . . green?' chorused the dancers. Williams tailored his monologue to reprise his opening line from *At Your Service* with CSE, and closed with a gag that he would reuse for thirty years: 'Lettuce green, if you don't mind. Oh, don't worry about them – they don't like my lettuce-green suit and they don't like the fact that I grew my own lettuce just from an ordinary packet of seeds. Course, they're all standing there behind me, waiting for me to open the show. Nnn-yess! They expect me to sing some terrible opening chorus. I told the producer, I said, "Oh no!" I said. "I am an Ac-tor." She said, "Your secret is safe with me." Charming.' The rest of his links pursued a running gag that he had something in a box, and that he had brought the lettuce to share with it. At the denouement, he produced a white rabbit.

The real star to emerge from *Lettuce*, though, was the girl in orange, Maggie Smith. Williams was entranced by her. She took a weak number, where a hostess cajoled her guests to play party games, and turned it into a stifled scream, on the brink of hysteria. At another moment she was a lovelorn waitress at a railway station, waiting for some Trevor Howard to transform her into Celia Johnson; then she was a streetwalker, taunting the newspaper vendors; then she was a char, grumbling at the soapy mess on the stage after the dance of the bubble-blowers.

Williams felt sick with nerves at first: 'Very worried [. . .] The material is very thin. Feeling like absolute DOOM. This revue is going to die die die.' It got worse: 'Now it is bitterly apparent that there is no substance whatsoever in this "revue". It isn't even a "revue" – just a collection of Bamber Gascoyne's university eccentricities. The kind of company to make this a success must be all as eccentric and odd, themselves. The depression has eaten deep into everyone. Only a miracle could now save this mediocre mess of pottage. I am sick, sick inside and can hardly think straight.'

Tensions were running high across the production, Codron remembered: 'Barbara Evans was one of the girls in it, a very good singer. I remember peeping through from the wings, just before we opened, and she said, "Well, I hope it goes well, but you know they booed John Gielgud here." Not the most charming thing to say. Roderick Cook [who played Grey] had given us a whole lot of grief and was rather anti-Ken. But Maggie Smith and Ken hit it off straight away, so I had two huge pluses there – they both looked as if they were potentially going to be stars.'

The try-out in Brighton was 'iffy', Codron said, but at the opening in Hammersmith, audiences loved it. What could have been insignificant was innocent, airy instead of empty. The critics were kind too: 'Evening papers are excellent for me. Schulman is quite a rave. V. nice – and gratifying after all the sufferings.'

'It opened well,' Codron said. 'Roderick Cook burst into tears and asked to be forgiven at the curtain call, and we then woke up to a rave review from Milton Shulman. If he hadn't liked it . . . but he did, and it was as important as that. A make-or-break review from the man in the *Evening Standard*.' Shulman called it, 'fresh, crisp and very young [. . .] a rare divertissement that you should do your best to keep with us for a long time [. . .] Kenneth Williams has the baffled nonchalance and the masterly timing of a real comic.'

Edward Goring in the *Mail* said, 'the show was saved, for my money, by Kenneth Williams, who effortlessly proves himself the funniest unknown actor on the English stage'. Williams 'ought by now to be recognised as the funniest young comedian on the British stage', echoed *Punch*. 'Kenneth Williams, bursting with aplomb and totally heedless of what is going on around him, emerges as a magnificently assured revue performer,' said Tynan in the *Observer*. 'A Great Star In The Making' announced the headline in the *London Chronicle*. From J.W. Lambert in the *Sunday Times*: 'A very clever actor, Mr

Williams is clearly building himself a wholly comic persona: that of an epicene elf – mincing, sibilant, sly; a commedia dell'arte figure with, when he actually opens his mouth, an enormous voice.' *Plays and Players* said, 'Mr Williams, dressed in Lettuce green, fulfilling the function of both leading man and compere, looks like some horrible little schoolboy – a kind of male Searle's girl – from which there issues a voice delightfully unexpectedly out of keeping with his appearance.'

Share My Lettuce opened at the Lyric Hammersmith on 21 August 1957, transferred to the Comedy Theatre in the West End a month later, and arrived at the Garrick Theatre early in 1958. 'This must be the longest tour in town,' Smith said. Codron was pressing his advantage in an attempt to persuade Williams to sign up for a nine-month run, a longer commitment than he had ever made. A stream of his friends came round to congratulate him backstage, from Joan Plowright and Thelma Ruby to Billy Chappell, Binkie Beaumont and Clifford Evans, and he was thrilled when Terence Rattigan looked in and called Williams 'the funniest man in England'.

Codron's confidence had swept aside the prickly doubts that Williams drew around himself in a hedge. Without this defence, he tumbled into every kind of work, in television, on radio, in cinema. Before *Lettuce* even opened, he made an appearance on independent TV, in a sketch with Alan Young, both playing thumb-sucking children. At the beginning of October he spent a week filming an episode of the MGM comedy series *Dick and the Duchess*, rushing back to do the show at the Comedy every evening, and on 3 October he recorded the pilot episode of a radio ragbag of gags, songs and sketches, with Kenneth Horne as the ringmaster: it was called *Beyond Our Ken*.

Williams used his desk diary as a record, rather than an appointments book. He might make a note when he was due to pay an insurance premium or visit a doctor, but he did not mark out his schedule, to remind himself of when he should be at the theatre or a recording studio. Nothing of that kind has survived, even accidentally, in the archive, and he must have carried all his engagements in his head, relying on his exceptional memory.

On 23 October 1957 his memory slipped up. The cast had rehearsed a new sketch in the morning, and in the afternoon Williams took a nap at his flat. He forgot the early evening show, and arrived at the theatre at 6 p.m. to find the 5.30 audience had been turned away. In their Fleet Street offices, a mile away, the press heard of the cancellation, and Michael Codron advised Williams to admit that he had overslept. The story made all the national papers, including the front pages of the *Express* and the *Guardian* – 'Fabulous publicity'. He was interviewed by Ned Sherrin on *Tonight*, the BBC's teatime news magazine, before being presented with an alarm clock on stage at the Comedy.

The clamour for tickets increased, and by Christmas the show was so popular that the cast were invited to perform a condensed version for the BBC. Williams affected such venomous disdain for the broadcast that he must, in fact, have been flattered to pieces: he called it 'Share My Pisspot' and 'a ghastly TV excerpt + we died a death'. His comments a day earlier about the stage production reveal, without dissimulation, the pride he took in every performance: '2 shows today. Both well performed. Voice still not very good, and it buckled a bit in the 2nd house.' More television followed, with a potted *Lettuce* for Granada.

Suffering from a cold, red-eyed, sneezing and hoarse, he dragged himself through the January shows, negotiating through his agent for a pay rise while refusing to discuss his demands with Codron. At last his doctor, John Musgrove, signed him off: 'This time I obeyed him, unlike Ham'smith when I flogged through "Lettuce" every night with a voice like a nutmeg grater.' He treasured the letter that came next day from Maggie Smith, telling him how miserable the show had been without him but ordering him to remain in bed until he was well; she signed it with a doodle of herself bearing a bouquet.

The *Tonight* show asked him back, to perform the 'Peter Patter' routine from the revue with Dilys Leahy. By the time he had collected all his TV earnings, he noted he had £1,000 in the bank for the first time in his life. The show celebrated its 200th performance, John Gielgud saw it again, Charles Laughton came round, and two ambitious but little-known film-makers appraised Williams from the stalls.

One of them was Peter Rogers, a writer and producer. The other was his director, Gerald Thomas. They were adapting R.F. Delderfield's romantic novel, *The Bull Boys*, in the style of the hit television comedy *The Army Game*, and after trying a succession of writers had settled on Norman Hudis, a colleague of Peter Eade. 'The script had been left hanging in mid-air,' Hudis said. 'I retained the first part, wherein a recently married conscript wants to consummate his marriage with his new wife. Smuggles her into the army camp . . . Frankly, I thought this was highly unlikely, but it was OK and it worked. And then, sometimes what people regard as great innovations happen in a mixture of desperation and luck. Looking for the rest of the script, I thought, Why concentrate on one conscript? Dozens come in with every intake, so I'll invent a few.' Kenneth Williams looked ideal for the part of an effete recruit who would rather lie on his bunk with a book than learn rifle drill. Charles Hawtrey, Kenneth Connor and Terence Longdon were among the others, with William Hartnell as their sergeant, Hattie Jacques as the medical officer, and Bob Monkhouse and Shirley Eaton as the newly-weds.

Rogers approached Williams through his agent and offered £800 for a month's work on *Carry On Sergeant*; the fee 'seemed astronomical to me and I didn't hesitate'. Money was rarely an incentive to him, but a few days earlier he had cancelled an insurance policy, in order to lend money to John Hussey. 'It is wrong that artists be worried by money – or lack of it,' he reasoned. 'It drives them to despair.'

He had two fittings for the film with the costumiers Morris Angel in Shaftesbury Avenue, and at the beginning of April Charlie gave him a short back and sides in the shop, an army cut. The feeling of déjà vu intensified when the cast were drilled at Pinewood by a sergeant-major of the Queen's regiment.

He was surprised to realise the filming was fun, too – his last experience at Pinewood, soaked and tired during long night-time shoots on *The Seekers*, had been miserable, but actors and crew on the *Carry On* set were a joy: 'Bob Monkhouse is sensitive and kind, Ken Connor is v. amusing [. . .] Gerry Campion is on it too [. . .] gossip, v. lovable.' The source of this amiability, Williams found, was the affable competence of the director, Gerald Thomas. He was an experienced film editor who could tell how the scenes he was shooting should be recut for continuity and pace, so that he rarely had to ask actors to film more than a couple of takes after rehearsing their moves. In return, he expected the cast to know their lines and get them right. This professionalism was a boon to all – to the producer who was able to make the film for under £80,000, to the cast who were able to keep the comedy fresh, and to the crew who were treated with respect, even though they had to accept that Rogers and Thomas knew all the tricks. (The sound stage was locked up at lunchtime, for instance, so that the electricians could not claim overtime for working on the lights across the break.)

Throughout April, Williams was filming Monday to Friday, with evening shows at the Garrick from Monday to Thursday, two on Fridays and Saturdays, and the *Hancock* recording on Sundays. He squeezed in a one-off variety performance in *Follow the Stars* on 27 April, and he could hardly be blamed for rejoicing when Codron announced, on 6 May, that *Share My Lettuce* was to close: 'This is a wonderful let out. More than I had dared hope for [. . .] Michael asks if I will do a tour of "Lettuce" – of course I don't want to. I just want to get shot of the whole wretched business.'

After two parties to celebrate the last night, he spent most of the next day in bed before starting rehearsals on *Hancock's Half Hour* at the Playhouse at 5 p.m. The combination of revue, slapstick movie and radio comedy had eroded his enthusiasm for avant-garde theatre, and when he attended the première of *The Birthday Party* the following evening, he was disparaging – 'it was an awful rubbishy play'. Instead, he recorded his first advertising voiceovers, for Murray Mints, with Michael Bentine, Kenneth Connor and Bernard Bresslaw.

Carry On Sergeant became the hit comedy of the summer, and the third biggest-grossing film in Britain that year. Today it seems like a frozen farce, preserved in the permafrost of the Cold War, but it contained grains of the theme that ran through all the series – that class boundaries were collapsing, and friendship and co-operation were possible between everyone when prejudice (and inhibitions) were abandoned. Hartnell the sergeant drops his bullying façade, Williams the graduate discovers the pleasure of teaching the uneducated, Longdon the public-school boy abandons privilege to be one of the lads. Even more than hackneyed jokes or sentimental asides, the film is full of affection, for officers and conscripts and canteen girls. It also featured a dozen moments for Williams to demonstrate the subtle comedy of his expressions – admiring himself in his new beret, cocking an eyebrow at the corporal who orders him to stand by his bed, disapproving of bayonet practice, staring down his nose at the captain during a parade. On radio he was celebrated for his voices, on stage for his range and timing, but now he announced himself in a new medium: as a character clown.

His potential for television was obvious, and on 23 July Eade arranged an 'interview about "The Army Game" with [producer] Peter Eton. Too grand by half. An audition suggested. I told Eade to scotch that. I'm a little past auditions for such a programme.' He did not refuse entirely to work on television, and recorded an episode of 'epic banality' in Granada TV's *Time Out for Peggy*, with Billie Whitelaw. 'Banality' was mild condemnation – a month later he played Captain Chalford, the romantic lead in Somerset Maugham's *The Noble Spaniard*, for BBC TV, and that was 'a crock of shit'. The producer, Adrian Brown, had approached Williams personally, phoning him at home to invite him to tackle this 'daft Victorian comedy [. . .] a pleasing trifle, to be performed with style and dash', opposite Margaret Rutherford. The broadcast was well received, with *The Times* praising Williams for his 'idiosyncratic tantrums and an unctuous delivery compounded equally of syrup and suet'.

On stage Williams reprised the Bubble Man sketch from *Lettuce*, for *The Night of a Hundred Stars* at the Palladium, with Rutherford, Daniel Massey and Jeremy Brett, and received a note of thanks, signed 'Ever Larry Olivier', for helping to raise funds for the Actors' Orphanage. His most rewarding work, though, was a run of radio shows that had started three weeks after the end of the fifth *Hancock* series: *Beyond Our Ken*.

The series almost never happened. Kenneth Horne had suffered a stroke after recording the pilot, but recovered from his initial paralysis. Once part of a successful double act with Dickie Murdoch, he had been appearing during the mid-fifties on *Henry Hall's Guest Night* and as the compère of *Variety Playhouse*. Eric Merriman, a *Playhouse* writer, had been petitioning BBC producers in light entertainment to try a series, anchored by Horne and featuring regular character actors to supply a panoply of voices in a sketch format.

The reponse was tepid: 'It seems to me,' wrote the assistant head of variety to his manager, 'the title [originally *Don't Look Now*] is nothing but an excuse, stringing together a couple of flimsy situations.' The proposal was championed, however, by producer Jacques Brown, who liked Merriman's idea that Horne would preside, like an amused schoolmaster, over a gaggle of artistes in panel games, parodies and cod documentaries, or Horne-a-ramas, on topics such as 'wine gum addiction in the United Kingdom'. It was Horne's personality that made the pilot a success – his warm, deep voice was full of kindly reproof, like a bank manager refusing an overdraft to an elderly nun. He made the most outrageous puns seem permissible, though Merriman's puns could be as painful as stomach cramps.

Another writer, Barry Took, was drafted in to help create characters with catchphrases, and they built the format around musical spots by Pat Lancaster, the Malcolm Mitchell Trio and the BBC revue orchestra. Instead of a signature tune, the first episode opened with Williams as Snide, goading the announcer to repeat, 'This is the BBC Light Programme' ('Oooh, go on, say it again . . . inn'ee good!'). *Beyond Our Ken* epitomised everything Galton and Simpson had rejected with *Hancock's Half Hour*. Kenneth Williams, feeling rejected by Hancock, embraced it.

Within a few episodes, he was relishing the Wednesday broadcasts from the Aeolian Hall in Bond Street, and inscribing the name of the show in florid letters at the top of his diary page. 'The broadcast went excellently well,' he wrote on 9 July; almost every week he made a note of approval, and he would sometimes make a point of tuning in to hear the show after the recording. As the series progressed, he developed characters such as Arthur Fallowfield, the rural lecher who claimed that 'the answer lies in the soil', and a gin-sodden old man who boasted he'd been doing it for 'thirty-five years', whatever 'it' happened to be that week. Between sketches he supplied links and announcements in a BBC voice dripping with supercilious disgust.

He and Hugh Paddick played a precious pair of actors, Rodney and Charles, fervently outdoing each other in praise. Paddick also played Ricky Livid, a teenage rock'n'roll star with a mind as banal as his lyrics; Betty Marsden was Fanny Haddock, a celebrity chef who had been basted in red wine, and Douglas Smith was the announcer. Ron Moody was hired to supply stock accents, but Williams quickly supplanted him. In one of the earliest surviving broadcasts, from 26 August 1958, he plays a French chanteur and an Irish car salesman, selling the Flaherty Mk 12; his sales slogan was, 'Flaherty gets you nowhere.' Rodney and Charles made one of their first appearances, as Noddy and Big Ears.

Horne ruled the shows with self-deprecating ease; surrounded by actors who could change their voices as though they were flipping between radio channels, he kept always to his slow, rich diction. At rehearsals, he would sometimes look up from his script and remark, 'Now, I wonder which voice I should use for *this* part . . .' His stroke had left him with constant pain in his left leg, but he rarely spoke of it; when it was bad, he would ask Bill Pertwee (who joined the team from the second series) to bring him a tot of whisky from the Captain's Cabin, and he sometimes leaned on Williams's shoulder at the microphone. He made all the cast feel he knew how talented they were, how much the show depended on their performances, and he showed his gratitude: halfway through the first series, 'Ken Horne took us all to lunch at the Spanish Club in Cavendish Square – it was splendid.' Meals and parties became a tradition throughout the seven series of *Beyond Our Ken*, and the four series of *Round the Horne* that followed with the same cast.

In his small flat on the top floor of Endsleigh Court, Williams was experimenting with the decor. He decided to have the apartment redecorated, and hired the Patent Steam Carpet Beating Company to remove and clean his two carpets while he stayed for a week with John Hussey in his rooms at Queen Alexandra Mansions, in King's Cross. After solitude, it was hard to share lodgings: 'Living with J.H. is torture because he snores v. badly.' By the following weekend the decorators were gone and Williams threw himself into home-making. His immaculate apartment was nearly destroyed when he barely avoided a house fire: 'Went in to see Frank Jackson and we talked of this and that [. . .] I left about 9 – discovered the kitchen full of smoke. I'd left some sausages burning in the oven. They were burned hard + the place smelled dreadfully. Had to clean the oven.'

Bob Monkhouse invited him to guest on his Saturday evening BBC variety show, and he was reunited with Siobhàn McKenna to perform an excerpt from *Saint Joan* on Granada's *Chelsea at Nine*. Though he hadn't enjoyed his first appearance on the show, he agreed to return to *Time Out for Peggy*, broadcasting from Manchester – 'it is perfectly foul rubbish. I foolishly said so, to the director (Philip Dale) and he said he thought I was being vitriolic!' A second film for Rogers and Thomas gave him much more pleasure; it was *Carry On Nurse* and, after a lunch with Peter Eade and two fellow clients – the writer Norman Hudis, and Joan Sims, who would be co-starring with him for the first time – he started filming at Pinewood on 5 November. 'Lots of old pals,' he remarked. 'It was all delightful.'

The success of *Sergeant* made a follow-up imperative. 'We didn't expect to make a series,' Rogers said. 'You don't set out to make a series, that's rather a conceited thing to try to do. I never thought we'd make more than one. And when we made two, I thought, that's not bad – and when it got to six, I thought, my God, what's happening? Kenneth used to amuse us on the set with his own version of Shakespeare, which he made up as he went along. Talented little chap. It sounded like Shakespeare but it wasn't. He was imitative, he could do any voice. He loved to have an audience around him. You can say without any derogation that he was a wonderful show-off. He was so professional, you didn't have to teach him anything. He knew the game so well, exactly what he wanted to play and how to play it.'

The germ of *Carry On Nurse* was a play called *Ring for Catty*, by Patrick Cargill and Jack Beale, though Norman Hudis retained almost nothing from it but the hospital beds. Williams once again played a studious, sarcastic loner, with books stacked on his bedside table. This character was more rounded, with his own story arc – he is befriended by a girl, Jill Ireland, and gradually realises that his feelings for her are more important than his physics textbooks.

'Kenneth baulked at the idea of playing a heterosexual love scene,' Hudis said. 'He said, "I'd rather play Lear on stilts." We weren't great bosom friends, because I wasn't at the studio much, I was too busy writing the next one, but on that one, he did turn to me and say, "What the hell am I going to do? I can't play this." I said, "This is ridiculous. You've played the French Dauphin. Why the hell can't you play a straight Englishman?" I think sometimes actors set up a difficulty that they have already decided they can conquer, so they look wonderful in the eyes of the people they've complained to. I think he was capable of that. The point is, he was all actor, no matter whatever else there was about him. An actor by definition.'

The diary entries dwindled during the five weeks of shooting, and on 18 November, in small, neat lettering, he set out his complaints in eight lines. Under the heading 'Film all day', in a different ink, the words were arranged in a blank verse:

> Feeling really terribly tired,
> Especially round the eyes.
> I can't sleep well at all.
> It shows in close-up.
> I don't like filming hours.
> Always having to be up
> At 6. It's quite ridiculous.
> Absurd. That's what it is.

He frequently relied for sleep now on prescriptions from Dr John Musgrove in Wimpole Street, made up by Boots the Chemists in Piccadilly Circus. Thirty sleeping tablets would last him about ten weeks.

For the first time since *Peter Pan*, he had agreed to play in panto, as Portia, one of the Ugly Sisters in the Rodgers and Hammerstein version of *Cinderella* at the Coliseum. Reluctant to play in drag, he was swayed when he learned the other Sister would be played by Ted Durante, his comrade from the troopship *Devonshire* in 1947. The choreography in *Cinderella* included a moment where Williams, in a ballgown sewn with lights that were powered by a battery in his bustle, was hoisted into the air by his partner: Durante, a former circus acrobat, had the strength and agility for the manoeuvre. They had one duet, 'The Stepsisters' Lament', in which they pleaded with the Prince to stop dancing with the girl of his dreams – Williams sizzled with malice as he offered to make Cinderella less attractive, by breaking her arm. Throughout rehearsals, the costumes gave

him problems, and under the outlandish wigs he had especial difficulty with hats. A week before the opening, the director, Freddie
Carpenter, 'took me aside and apologised for the costumes which he
admitted were all wrong'. Williams was mollified.

On the opening night, all his family came to his dressing-room
for drinks – his parents, his grandmother, and his aunt Edie. Gordon
Jackson was in the audience and wrote a note of fervent praise: 'I
thought you were really fabulous, and the best thing in the show!
Quite brilliant – in fact too brilliant! cos you're going to have a great
struggle getting out of drag parts after your *grand succes*! Altogether
a tremendous debut in panto. Of course, I disgraced myself at the
National Anthem! I was in hysterics watching you playing it straight
– and I'm *sure* you were singing God Save This Gracious Queen!'
Always grateful for written praise, Williams preserved the note in his
diary.

The critics were effusive too. In the *Evening News*, Felix Barker
described it as 'the most sumptuous and beautiful *Cinderella* that I
should think London has ever seen'. Angus Wilson in the *Observer*
wrote: 'Kenneth Williams as the blonde, smart, dominating sister
created a brilliant take-off of a certain kind of lady – a sort of vulgar,
Hendon *grande dame* who couldn't keep it up and was forever slipping back into plain slum shrew.'

Williams was beginning to warm to the show – 'Children loved
the slapstick of course' – and by Christmas he had recorded his role
both for a Decca LP and for radio. A visit from Noël Coward, after
a matinée, compounded his pleasure: 'He said, "You were wonderful – such a dreadfully vulgar walk".' Williams treated himself to a
stereo hi-fi set, and made a present of his mono gramophone speaker
to the dresser, Bill Beresford Hobbs, who helped him nightly into
his costumes. In his summary of the year, at the back of the diary, he
had only kind words for his co-stars, Tommy Steele, Jimmy Edwards
and Yana, who played Cinders. Of himself, he said: 'Sexually, still
unresolved, professionally in the middle and not quite defined, and
spiritually – mercurial [. . .] for the first time in my profession I am
earning over 100 pounds a week + I feel I am working for it.'

'Mercurial' was an understatement: his moods were like pluto-
nium, and could decay in a split-second. On New Year's Eve, he

woke to 'a lovely morning – overcast and raining – *my* kind of day'. He took a cab to the Jacksons' from the Coliseum after the show, to join their celebrations, but baulked at the party games. A taxi ordered for 1 a.m. failed to pick him up – Williams believed it had been deliberately turned away. Marching out of the house, without saying goodbye to his hosts, he walked and fumed before hailing a cab and arriving in Bloomsbury almost an hour later. Gordon, always a peacemaker, took him to lunch a couple of weeks later.

Even before the release of *Carry On Nurse*, which would become the most successful film at the British box office in 1959, Peter Rogers was preparing a sequel, an ensemble comedy as before, broad and sentimental. After the hospital and the barracks, the institution he chose was a school, for *Carry On Teacher*. Once again Kenneth Connor was a clumsy romantic, in probably the best version of the character that Hudis wrote for him; Joan Sims, who had stolen *Carry On Nurse* as a trainee who takes one patient's temperature with a rectal daffodil, was the gym mistress, and the radio comic Ted Ray played the head teacher. Williams's role was more central this time, as a progressive-minded English teacher who disdains the cane until rebellious pupils blow up a classroom and shower the staffroom with itching powder.

Cinderella was expected to run for months, and the producer, Harold Fielding, was unwilling to release Williams for filming: 'Peter Eade telephoned to say that H. Fielding is being bloody-minded over my film, and may stop me doing it. I don't care. Eade is furious and says the studio will be thrown out etc etc. I don't care. I'm not going to shed any tears or energy over WORK any longer. I think Eade would like me to tackle Fielding but I'm not going to. I couldn't begin to care.' A postscript hinted at the anxiety below the insouciance – '2 performances and pretty ghastly at that'.

Fielding withdrew his objection, and a month later Williams returned to Morris Angel for his costume fitting. After the panto gowns, his teacher's tweeds were a relief, and he was glad to be reunited with the regulars at Pinewood, for the atmosphere at the Coliseum was becoming confined. 'Ted Durante was most hurtful and rude apropos the smacking scene of which he sarcastically and rudely said – "Why don't you hit me harder . . ." etc. inferring that

I hit him hard on purpose. What really hurt me was that I believed there was trust between us. It is a pity, because the relationship will not ever be the same now.'

Leslie Phillips returned for *Carry On Teacher*, after the debut in *Nurse* as Jack Bell, which gave him his lifelong catchphrase, 'Ding Dong!' He saw Williams as 'permanently attention-seeking', and 'colossally irritating if he felt he was being ignored for more than a minute or two. He craved the response he got from perform-ing, as if it was a drug.' The good-natured fun on the set affected everyone, Phillips said, and for one scene Alan Hume, behind the camera, had to be gagged with a handkerchief to stop him from laughing out loud.

The second series of *Beyond Our Ken* brought another reunion, with Horne, Marsden and Paddick; now Williams was rising at dawn for the morning shoot at Pinewood, appearing six days a week at the Coliseum, with shows twice nightly on Mondays, Wednesdays and Saturdays, and recording for the BBC at the Aeolian Hall on Wednesdays. *Beyond Our Ken* had settled now into a smooth routine, with Horne's urbane delivery making the puns seem ironic instead of laboured. Each episode opened with a sketch, which Williams, in the voice of a merciless newsreader, would reveal to be an excerpt from 'another of the books we recommend you to read . . . especially during the next half-hour'.

Cinderella closed on 11 April, and the cast exchanged presents. Three days later it was the end-of-filming party at Pinewood, a tradition Peter Rogers had cannily revived to distract his cast and crew from the broader parsimonies. Williams enjoyed the free gin, flirted drunkenly with one of the electricians, and woke the next day to realise he had made an assignation for the weekend. The electrician turned up that Saturday at Endsleigh Court in a car with two other men – Williams gave them £3, which he pretended was petrol money, and to his relief the men agreed to forget all about it.

The Pinewood party led to another, more salubrious date – a dinner with Thomas and Rogers in Harrow, followed by drinks at Kenneth Connor's house. More *Carry Ons* were planned, and Williams took the opportunity to ask whether his shooting schedule could be arranged around theatre commitments. Ten days earlier, he had lunched with Michael Codron, who had proposed another revue. Peter Eade advised him to take it, believing he could command £100 a week. The show, which would become Williams's greatest West End triumph, was called *Pieces of Eight*.

8

'Throwing temperaments in sapphire mink'
April 1959–December 1960

Williams never learned to drive. The reasons, as with all the things he did not do – appearing on the New York stage, or filming in Hollywood, or sustaining a sexual relationship, or acting in a television series – defined the limits of his personality, and revealed the lengths to which he would go to avoid breaching them. He was afraid, rightly, that he would make a dangerous driver: when he was talking, his movements became exaggerated and uncoordinated, and so he disliked holding even a cigarette or a glass when he was acting; at the wheel, he would be easily, and probably fatally, distractible.

He resisted spending money on possessions, in particular anything – such as suits, shoes and watches – that pretended to wealth and status; a car would have been an impossible purchase. He reasoned that the expense and inconvenience of public transport, as well as his chauffeur to Pinewood, for which Peter Rogers refused to pay, would be outweighed by the cost of buying, taxing and insuring his own car. Most of his friends lived within walking distance of Bloomsbury. He enjoyed the luxury of being driven. There was, anyway, almost nothing the world could offer that he could not find in north London. And, at some level below conscious reason, he felt that driving was an adult activity, something his father did, and that no one holding a driver's licence could remain an adolescent.

Instead, he bought a bicycle, second-hand, for £3. To emphasise that he should not be allowed on the roads, he rode it into a car on his second outing. He bandaged his bruised ankle and had the bike repaired: when he was sixteen, he had ridden to his first job, at Stanford's, and at thirty-three he would continue to ride.

Before rehearsals began for *Pieces of Eight*, Williams treated himself to two holidays, the first in Germany with a friend called Terry Duff.

They stayed in Hamburg, and a street photographer's snap shows them standing on a crowded Elbe quayside, waiting for the ferry on an excursion to Cranz. Williams seems relaxed and happy. Back in London, he went boating on the Serpentine with Stanley Baxter, Michael Hitchman and John Hussey, and had 'a fabulously lovely day' in Clacton with another group, before setting off on a motoring tour of the West Country. He was chauffeured by Philip Gilbert, who had played Blue in *Share My Lettuce*, and they stopped at Stonehenge before touring Devon and Cornwall.

As *Pieces of Eight* took shape, he had a series of lunches with Michael Codron. Williams had suggested several sketches by his CSE comrade, Peter Nichols, but Codron had 'found some v. good material from a boy called Peter Cook from Cambridge. It sounds excellent'. The producer also suggested that Williams should direct his own skits, an idea that, though it appealed to him, was soon dropped. The designer would be Tony Walton, who had worked with Codron before, and who also happened to have been at school, at Radley College in Abingdon, with Cook. 'Peter of course wanted to star in it himself,' Walton recalled, 'but Michael said, "You're not interesting as a performer and I have to get somebody much better to do your stuff."'

Codron's ambitions for this revue were expanding. The choreography, by Paddy Stone, would be spectacular; the music would feature show-stopping numbers by Sandy Wilson and Lionel Bart; the sketches would include modernist fragments by Harold Pinter as well as Cook's surreal whimsy. Williams, who had never helped to construct an entire programme, began to be anxious: 'Wrote long letter to Codron saying I thought the revue was being planned on the wrong lines – not verbally funny enough, and pro' jokes which are not funny, to an audience.' A long talk allayed his fears, but Codron had seen a worrying side to his star: 'I started to realise, with *Pieces of Eight*, that Kenneth was not going to be an easy ride.'

Long theatre runs exhausted him, but the uncertainty of this nebulous stage before rehearsals brought a different kind of enervation. Williams was unsettled too by the death of his favourite aunt, his mother's younger sister Daisy: her parties after the war, with sing-songs and showing-off, were the family occasions he had loved best.

A few weeks earlier he had received a desperate letter from a friend, 'asking what is the point of life. How is one to answer? How long is it going to take for that good boy to discover faith?' Now his own faith was tested. As Daisy's cortège wound through the streets where he had often walked with her, Williams found himself sobbing. 'There is no real answer to the life of suffering, or unreasonable death . . . it just remains a mysterious, illogical fact.' At these times he needed the distraction of work; apart from the radio series, there had been just two days of filming, at Elstree with Tommy Steele. Rehearsals for the revue began at last on 4 August 1959, at King George's Hall in Bloomsbury.

Williams was impressed by his leading lady, Fenella Fielding, but liked Myra de Groot, a singer, less: 'Common as muck + a sycophant to boot.' He was no easier on Peter Cook, as Walton explained: 'It was very hard for Peter to sit down and write but he could do stuff extemporaneously. He could be brilliant like no one ever – hysterical, out-of-control eruptions – and then he would dash away, try and remember it, and write it down. And Kenneth was very slightly superior and dismissive with Peter, because he could respond very fast to any of Kenneth's ideas. There was a sketch in a restaurant, Kenneth calling it all filthy foreign muck: I remember a lot of that was simply devised on the spur of the moment, with Kenneth saying, "Oh for goodness sake, give me something better than that! God! I mean, is that as funny as you can be?"'

The haggling over material began to cause tensions within the small cast. Williams felt the jealousies were mostly musical, since de Groot had the best songs. Fielding saw it differently. She had accepted the revue with misgivings: 'I didn't really see what Kenneth and I were going to be able to do together. But the producers were very persuasive and they gave me co-star billing, which means that you're equal. What they didn't actually tell me was that the show was built around Kenneth, and however equal I was, it wasn't going to be equal. Kenneth had all kinds of starring pieces – entrance and exits, first-half opening and closing, second-half opening and closing, so if you're in the audience you know who the star is.'

As rehearsals progressed, Fielding felt she had been lured on several false pretexts. Many of the sketches she had liked best were disappearing from the set and, when she challenged Paddy Stone, he explained that cuts had been demanded by Williams. 'This happened again and again and again, and I realised that all the material where I'd thought, Yes, I love that, that's very good, it wasn't going to be done.'

Williams's pieces were not immune to changes. Three days before the revue opened on tour at the New Theatre in Oxford, he made a diary entry in his angriest hand, with ligatures strung between the words: 'Infuriated by cuts on my sketches that were totally wrong. Couldn't even bring myself to say goodnight to M. Codron. He is behind the cuts I am sure.' Two days later he was furious again: the posters and flyers gave Fielding equal billing.

Rehearsals at the New continued to within an hour of the first curtain. For the opening number, the cast sang 'Hallelujah' as Williams swooped from the flies on a Kirby Flying Ballet wire. On the first night this descent was 'unadulterated agony' and on the second, 'I cut my leg coming down on the wire. I am sick sick sick of this entire show. I HATE it bitterly.' More changes were made: frantic with frustration, Williams blamed the producer: 'I was incensed to receive a new running order which is sheer madness – I have never seen anything so daft [. . .] Of course it's Codron at the bottom of it all – that much is obvious. I've had "I Need" cut right out of the show! without so much as an explanation. I feel utterly sick.'

The producer's efforts to soothe him were wasted. 'I thought he realised that he had in me a great ally,' Codron said, 'but when I read all the letters and the diaries, I saw he thought of me as the management.'

The situation grew worse in Liverpool, where a song-and-dance routine was introduced at the Royal Court for Fielding and Peter Reeves; it didn't feature Williams. 'It's a disgraceful insult + I've decided to swallow it. It is obviously a sop to Fenella, who must be indulged at all costs + to hell with the rest.' Two days later: 'Wrote rude letter to Codron + tore it up because it was temper, not wisdom. Though a lot of it was justified.' Instead, he listed his complaints in the diary: the revue was all clunking, grinding labour, performed by men with no sex appeal and women with no talent. And in this mood, he travelled with the show to Brighton's Theatre Royal.

'He did something awful before we opened, really terrible,' Fielding said. 'When we were in Brighton, the week before the show came in, I had the most marvellous notices, just wonderful. Kenneth was outraged – terribly angry with me. He kept coming up to me and reading bits out, and sneering at them. And then he began to threaten me. I can't tell you how awful it was. It was about two or three days before we opened, and he was actually uttering threats about what happened to people like me who had the nerve to provoke these kinds of notices. He could be so nice, so sweet, but he could be just vile.'

Assertive and witty, Fielding found ways to retaliate. After opening night at the Apollo, Shaftesbury Avenue, on 23 September, the notices had been good, with John Mortimer in the *Standard* calling Williams a genius: 'A good deal of expendable material is saved by this small urchin actor who can deafen the upper circle with a single sniff of disapproval and apparently rearrange his features at will. His performance is continually kept from affectation by underlying cockney savagery.' The stars were interviewed on Independent Television news, and Fielding interrupted the questions with a small bombshell: 'We're engaged,' she purred. Williams looked at her aghast. Fenella smiled archly for a few moments before revealing the joke with a peal of giggles, while her co-star floundered.

Codron tried to keep the peace. 'Fenella knew I sided more with Ken than I did with her,' he said. 'She was a very talented but very tricky girl. I knew all about Fenella and how to handle her, because of *Valmouth*. But they fizzed together, they really did.'

A week after the opening, though, he gathered the cast to dispense notes on their performances: Williams felt he was being criticised in public, and erupted. 'After the performance we were all lined up for a telling off. M. Codron said we were all slacking off and not doing our best. I started shouting the odds and saying I did my best every night + couldn't do any better etc etc + he shouted back at me "I am the management . . ." it was awful. Afterwards in my room he told me it was really aimed at the other members of the company.' He kept the note that Codron sent, which reiterated concerns of 'chaos in the first half' while offering an elegant apology.

Pieces of Eight glittered with brilliant wit and characters that showcased Williams across his range. In one sketch, he clutched a shoebox to his furtive chest as he droned on about its contents – 'I've got a viper in this box. It's not an asp, if that's what you're thinking . . .' – and managed to be suffocatingly funny while playing a bore. This character, a brother to Snide, was called Mr Grole, whose inspiration was the butler at Radley College, Arthur Boylett: a dry-spoken man, Boylett held eccentric convictions about the paranormal. Cook insisted to schoolfellows that the elderly butler had told him of seeing stones move and sticks levitate – 'I thought I saw it move!' became a college catchphrase.

In another sketch called 'Balance of Trade', which was not recorded for the Decca LP of the show, Williams was a shopkeeper selling fifth-rate shirts, guaranteed to shrink – 'very rapidly too. I remember last week ten of our customers were strangled in a thunderstorm.' He also played Mr Oates, president of the Society for the Prohibition of Snail Racing, dedicated to stamping out a corrupt sport where champion gastropods were doped and slugs were disguised with artifical shells. With Fielding as his sympathetic wife, Williams was a disappointed man called Arthur Grangeleigh, who could have made a fortune as the fattest man in the world, 'if only I'd had the flesh!' And there was 'Buy British', where his bigoted Blimp salivated over delicacies such as sheep's eyeballs in baby goats' blood, until he discovered the dishes were foreign – 'Filthy Spanish muck, is it? Nothing but beggars and bishops trying to lay their greedy hands on Gibraltar!'

All these were written by Peter Cook who was then just twenty-one, and still at Pembroke College, Cambridge, where he was reading Modern Languages; the Establishment Club, *Private Eye*, *Beyond the Fringe* and *Not Only But Also* were still years away, and he would not even become president of the university Footlights Club until the following year. His sketches still obeyed some conventions: they had punchlines, for instance. An extraordinary piece by Harold Pinter, which cast Williams as an old newspaper-seller, had no restrictions – no tagline, no jokes, no story, just a rhythm and a pathos that made audiences want to laugh and cry together. Williams had often played old men, but this one he invested with a hopeless dignity, and a senility that trembled between the pathetic and the noble. It is impossible to hear the recording without wondering how he would have played Estragon in *Waiting for Godot*.

Fielding believes that Williams was unable to sustain similar restraint with another of Pinter's sketches, one that drew on the playwright's obsession with cricket: 'Kenneth was to do this particular piece with Peter Reeves, and it was fairly serious. They rehearsed it and I thought it was rather beautiful. That night Kenneth simply couldn't resist it and he got laugh after laugh after laugh. The whole thing was wrecked. That was it, it came out, because he'd spoiled it.'

For weeks Williams had been dithering about his need to leave Endsleigh Court. He felt the flat was too noisy, though his sensitivity was probably heightened by anxiety and a bout of haemorrhoids. He paid down a deposit on a flat off Great Portland Street, at Devonshire Mansions, but pulled out when he learned that, in addition to the price of £800 with £375 annual rent, the apartment needed at least £300 of repairs. When John Hussey invited him to share a two-room flat in St Pancras, next to Williams's old primary school, he accepted: if living with Hussey did not work out, he reasoned, he might be encouraged to find somewhere he did like.

He moved into 66 Alexandra Mansions on 7 October, got drunk with Peter Eade and Annette Kerr after the show, and fell into bed at 2 a.m. The next morning, he discovered the massive apartment block, shaped like a brick and adjacent to the Cromer Street flats where he grew up, was a good place to nurse a hangover: 'Woke feeling awful. This flat is so very quiet, unlike that ghastly Endsleigh Court.' With Manchester Street Junior on one corner and the Skinners Arms on the other, this was almost like living at home again. Though he stayed in Hussey's flat for less than six months, he would return to the block ten years later.

Pieces of Eight had become a spectacular hit. Audiences adored it, not only for the wild laughter but for the music. Fenella Fielding was winning rapturous applause each night for a Sandy Wilson number. Determined to set the pace, Williams started to ad lib through the sketches, and ordered Fielding to follow his lead. 'He said, "Look, what you've got to understand is that all this material is rubbish. It's all crap and it's terrible, and you've got to be prepared to ad lib, go all round it, improvise, do anything, but don't just say what's on the page." I couldn't understand what he was on about,' Fielding said. 'I thought, if we do as he says we might very well spoil it. But he was very insistent. I decided to go along with him, and those particular sketches were outstanding – the audience shrieked, and people used to come and see the show over and over again to hear what different things we were saying.'

In his dressing-room, Williams was fêted by admirers including Julie Andrews and Sir Malcolm Sargent. Princess Margaret attended, and, on 12 October, 'Cardew Robinson, Eric Merriman, Maggie Smith + Ian Bannen came round after'. Williams, who never encouraged callers at home, loved to be visited backstage.

Filming began on *Carry On Constable* on Monday 9 November 1959, a six-week shoot timed to avoid disrupting the various panto commitments of the cast. Williams was able to leave the set in time for his evening shows, though an understudy stepped in for some matinées. The work was tiring: 'I hate getting up at 6.30 in these mornings. Everything v. dark. But in a way it's good for me – and the film unit is enjoyable – they're a good crowd.'

Actors' tales grew up around the escapades on location. Peter Rogers remembered that after the sequence where Williams helps an unwilling Esme Cannon to cross the street, a member of the public demanded similar assistance; Kenneth politely obliged. He and Leslie Phillips dared each other to step into the road and direct the traffic – Phillips claimed in his autobiography that, after holding up cars for several minutes, Williams called out, 'I want a piss,' walked to the kerb and, in his policeman's uniform, pretended to urinate into the gutter. Williams was never shy about exposing himself in front of friends, and he revelled in the sequence where he, Phillips, Charles Hawtrey and Kenneth Connor dash naked from the ice-cold showers. All four had such white skin that the make-up man, George Blackler, had to dust their backsides with powder to prevent camera flare.

Victor Maddern made his first appearance in the series, playing an undercover CID officer arrested by the bookish PC Stanley Benson – as in all the Hudis scripts, Williams's character has to learn that human beings are not textbook cases. 'On the set it seemed to me that Kenneth Williams's mouth was never closed, except when he was swallowing lunch,' Maddern said. 'Sometimes I had to walk away for fear of the laughter pain becoming too much to bear.'

The Christmas special of *Beyond Our Ken* was recorded at the Paris Cinema in early December. Ten days earlier, Eric Merriman had phoned Williams to explain that he could no longer stand working with Barry Took, and that their partnership was over. Merriman was a combative, prickly character, and all Kenneth Horne's emollience could not change his mind. Horne feared the show would fossilise with only one writer, and pleaded that Took should retain some role, even if it was only in supplying the opening monologue. 'Surely Eric is not so bitter as to refuse such a request?' he wrote. He was wrong, and the next five series were scripted entirely by Merriman. The same formats and characters would recur and never evolve, even while trends in humour changed rapidly and stand-up comedy, sitcom and satire went through transformations on television. *Beyond Our Ken* featured the most talented and experienced ensemble on radio but, chiefly because of Merriman's intransigence, it seemed old-fashioned before its run was halfway over.

Pieces of Eight attracted packed, rowdy houses across Christmas, and by the middle of January the cast were on bonuses and all the backers, including Williams himself, were in profit. His great extravagance continued to be private medical attention: since the revue opened he had been visiting Desmond Mulvany, a surgeon at 112 Harley Street, for a series of injections to cure his piles. The course ended on 7 January 1960 and brought little relief: 'I only hope this last one results in some permanent cure because I don't really want an operation. [Mulvany] became very Biblical + said at the end, "You're like the man worrying about his big toe, when the leg has been amputated . . ." Charming.' The implication was that the haemorrhoids were gone and any lingering pain was imaginary.

With his nerves on edge, he began to find John Hussey's flat intolerable: 'Noise above atrocious. They were having a party. Lot of uncivilised yobs from the sound of it. Disgraceful. I must get out of here.' He looked at a flat on St James Street – 'unfortunately *no* bathroom or lav. Otherwise perfect. But at 350 ex. a year, I think one should have a lavatory.' In this froth of pain and irritation, it was impossible that he would consider a proposal, tentatively proffered over lunch with the American producer Alexander Cohen, to take the revue to Broadway with Diana Dors.

Tensions had not eased between Williams and Fielding. She felt she had carried him during the *Carry On* filming: on evenings when they had two houses, he expected her to work the audience at the early show, and retreat when he commandeered the laughs in the second. 'That was hell,' Fielding said. The competition over ad libs had reached a breathless pitch: 'If I came up with something that he thought was terribly funny and the audience liked, he would be over the moon, you could see he was. But the next night, I possibly wouldn't get the cue. Or else he would say it himself.'

The crisis came on a Wednesday night, in the sketch that wrapped up the show before the final chorus of 'Hallelujah'. Williams and Fielding were two spies meeting in a hotel room, she in a sequined ball gown, he in a fedora and shifty raincoat. They began to compare spies' gadgets – 'We behaved very childishly – "My stuff is better than yours",' Fielding said. 'Finally we had the big row about who had the most efficient death pill. We took them, then waited to see what happened. We got into agonies and staggered about, and then felt better, and didn't . . . and in the end I was the one who died first. I fell on the floor, and lay there in the wings while Kenneth did the punchline, and then I scrambled to my feet and did my quick-change for the finale. And one night he wouldn't let me die in peace. He went on and on, so that I didn't know what to do – I was getting more and more extravagant in my death agonies, and it didn't make any difference. He just wouldn't stop. So I just went completely still and silent, and then I said, "Last one dead's a cissy," and died. And it brought the house down. He was stunned, his face was white, and I couldn't understand why, except that I'd got the laugh and got off. But I didn't mean it as "You are queer" – it never even occurred to me. It was a childish remark, in the style of the whole sketch. But he went to Codron and said that I'd called him a homosexual in front of the audience. It was awful.'

Williams must have expected to win this clash, and he was furious when Codron told him to apologise. His handwriting became increasingly angry in a series of entries: 'To Eade to ask him to speak to Codron about Fielding – I can't tolerate this any longer [. . .] Then the show. I don't speak to her at all. Just did my job. In the middle of the spy sketch she broke down and had hysterics, tears etc. Codron came b/stage [. . .] the long + s. of it is, I have to make a rapproche-ment. You can't win.' The following day, he noted he had 'made up with Fenella', but for the next nine months their partnership was as brittle as frosted sugar. On 1 April he wrote, 'Still not talking to Fenella. I know it's futile, but I simply can't face discussing even superficialities with such a transparent inanity.'

For Fielding, it had become exhausting. 'I was so sick of crying my eyes out that I said to my agent, "Really I don't want to go on with this any longer. I can't stand it." Michael Codron came to see me, and in the end I agreed to go on but I said, "It can't be like this back-stage. I really can't take it. He's got to decide to change his mindset." There was a kind of truce, it was all meant to be over and done with. Kenneth had a really bad effect on me. I would say in a way he ruined my life, because it changed me completely, that experience. It's a question of trust. I really was a bit of an innocent, very trusting, and I don't know how much I lost of that.'

Williams would have liked to issue the ransom demands, but the revue was too much his own triumph for him to quit it. With his name blazing over the Apollo and the house packed every night, he was the biggest star on the West End. When he told Codron, over lunch, that he intended to leave the run in March, two pages of praise on the producer's blue notepaper bought his retraction; instead of leaving he signed on for a further three months, soon extended to six, with no matinées after 1 April and the promise that Codron would try to find him a serious play.

His spirits reached a peak when he found an apartment he liked, at £525 for the lease, off the Edgware Road, at 76 Park West. This sprawling complex of flats was well named: for the first time, Williams would be living closer to Hyde Park than Regent's Park. He loved the setting: 'Walked with folks in Hyde Pk then they came back to my flat for tea. The day is full of bright sunshine and warm. Crocuses are all out. Everything quite beautiful.' Park West's entrance was set back from a side street, on a horseshoe driveway, and it had a private swimming pool in the basement. Williams took almost no furniture, just his bed and a desk, and enjoyed fussing over the new fittings.

It made a change for him to be spending money on himself; always an easy touch, he was being pestered for loans by everyone from acquaintances to close family. Often he said no. 'Long letter from Ralph Hallett about owing his tailor £100 and asking me for it. Of course I've refused. I think this kind of self-indulgence is utterly contemptible.' On his thirty-fourth birthday, he took his sister to dinner: 'We went to the Grill + C. She started on the old tack, "if only I had 100 pounds, I could really start to live properly etc etc." I'm NOT buying any more hard luck stories. I scotched that one.' When Stan Walker and Terry Duff approached him with a proposal for opening a café in East Ham, he did agree to invest £250, which eventually rose to £1,600. He lost it all. He preferred giving presents that might be inexpensive but showed thought – over two days, for instance, he recorded a tape of poetry and prose for a friend in Canada.

He spent the days before most shows with friends. Sometimes he would drive out of London with a group for a picnic, or take a river trip; more often he would visit the cinema with just one companion.

At the cinema Williams demanded distraction. He wanted to be absorbed, by a storyline with a moral theme and by strong acting. Maggie Smith joined him for a preview of *Inherit the Wind* – 'Spencer Tracy was exceedingly good.' He visited the theatre often, taking in a matinée of Pinter's *The Caretaker*, which was 'marvellously well done', and Robert Bolt's *A Man for All Seasons* at the Globe. A friendship between Williams and Bolt had been developing for eighteen months. Williams admired the playwright's idealism and regularly visited his Richmond Green home; Bolt was already talking of writing a play for him.

If he was not having supper with well-wishers who continued to come round after a show – that summer they included Richard and Sybil Burton, John Schlesinger, Thelma Ruby and Stanley Baxter – Williams would sometimes take a taxi to a private club called the Spartan in Tachbrook Street, Pimlico. The Spartan was licensed till 11 p.m. (pubs had to close at 10.30) and was ten minutes by taxi from the West End without being part of Theatreland. For one other reason it was the most popular club in London for prominent, gay men: it was discreet. 'Some nights it could be rather like a gentleman's club,' said a former barman at the Spartan, Richard Caswell. 'It was somewhere that people could go and relax. I think Kenneth

Williams felt he could go there and not be hassled. There were no knees-ups, no screaming queens – they knew it wasn't their sort of place. It was theatrical.'

The club, run by Patric Walker, comprised a main bar with a piano, a smaller bar behind, and in the summer a drinks marquee in the garden. 'I particularly remember that [Williams] always used the smaller bar. So there would be fewer people around him,' Caswell said. 'He came two or three times with Hugh Paddick, but I remember him often turning up on his own. And he used to tell us these wonderful stories, but not in a flamboyant way. No screaming, raised voices like he did on the radio. I can't remember him being particularly bitchy either. He told them as amusing anecdotes. There would be three or four of us round him. Everybody else was far too busy talking to one another, which I suspect is what he liked about it. He didn't arrive and say, "Look! I'm here! Gather round, folks!" He'd just come to the bar, where a small group of us would just be gobsmacked with these fabulous stories. The other end of the bar wouldn't have been able to hear them.'

Unlike Peter Cook, whose volcanic creativity could not be controlled, or Tony Hancock, who was able to sightread a script with an instinctive timing that he could not himself analyse, Kenneth Williams was a conscious artisan. His anecdotes were crafted, as a jeweller crafts necklaces; his voices, his faces, his embellishments, distortions and inventions all sparkled on the thread, and always there was a glittering gem of a phrase or a retort set at the apex. His stories came to a point, as though this was the reason that people listened, but it was the way that he spoke, the sound of the words, that earned the laughs.

At the start of the third series of *Beyond Our Ken*, Kenneth Horne upset Eric Merriman when he told a reporter that his cast were so talented they could read a phonebook and make it funny. Merriman tried to take revenge by handing out telephone directories instead of scripts at the first rehearsal: Williams flipped his open and began to drawl, with the greatest exaggeration, through names and numbers, finding esoteric, ridiculous comedy in the most banal addresses. The actors roared with laughter; Merriman admitted later he too had found it devastatingly funny. Their microphones were not on, and the performance was never repeated – a shame, since *Kenneth Williams Reads the Phonebook* would have been an absurdist classic.

This was comedy of technique, not original wit. In conversation he plucked and scattered brilliant lines from his storehouse of quotations, taxing his memory rather than coining fresh phrases. For an actor, this was no limitation. When he was invited to perform on a television panel game, which demanded spontaneity, he had to adjust his method. In May 1960, he guested on *Laugh Lines*, from the BBC's Shepherd's Bush studios, inventing captions for cartoons. Even though he had a day to prepare, it was 'murder' to think of new jokes, and the first show was 'lousy'. Two weeks later he was invited back, and this time he 'rang Stanley B. who helped me enormously with ideas'.

Pieces of Eight wound down over the summer, with audiences falling by about a third from the packed Christmas houses. His euphoria ebbed with it, and he began to sidestep other work: 'Peter Eade arranged fr. me to talk on the BBC "Woman's Hour" – I have now returned the contract, and bowed out of it. I just know it's not me. Must have been out of my mind in the first place.' At the end of July he was offered a seven-year film deal by Charles Schneer, a producer at Shepperton, and turned it down: only one of Schneer's suggested synopses appealed to him, and Williams would not consider it without the promise of 'some excellent money'. Barry Took proposed a radio series, *The Proudfoot Family*, for him – Williams responded by taking Eric Merriman to lunch and asking his permission. When Merriman objected, 'I wrote [to] Took to tell him I must withdraw.'

Michael Codron 'returned from America where, he says, my stock is v. high!'; if this was flattery, it was ineffective, for Williams had no intention of taking the revue to New York, nor of staying with it in London. The closing night was set for Saturday 29 October, and he ordered commemorative ashtrays for all the cast and crew, at a cost of £62 10s.

On the day of the last performance, he was woken in the small hours by the police, to inform him that his friend Michael Hitchman had been found dead. Williams was appalled. 'I really loved M,' he wrote. 'I know I was better for knowing him.'

The last show passed in a daze, and the following day Williams was admitted to St John and St Elizabeth Hospital for an operation on the haemorrhoids that had tormented him all year. He spent a fortnight there, in real pain at first and plaintively grateful for visits from his friends. As he recovered, his spite returned: 'Val [Orford] was here for hours! He wouldn't go at all! Don't any of them realise the need of a human being for privacy!! It's all too much.' By the time he was released, he was well enough to settle straight into his routine of cinema and outings, including a long weekend in Brighton. When shooting began on *Carry On Regardless*, at the end of November, he was well again, and no longer felt the need to record details of his daily bowel movements in the diary.

Regardless was the weakest in the Hudis series of *Carry On*s, a sequence of vignettes that showcased the cast individually, ending with a slapstick ensemble scene where a house was demolished. Williams had the best sketch, babysitting a chimpanzee called Yoki and taking it for tea at London Zoo. The script lacked continuity, a ragbag stitched together in a hurry, and Williams was concerned that the film was being rushed.

During the shoot, he recorded a reprise of 'Buy British' from *Pieces of Eight*, for television – the cast included Amanda Barrie, to whom Williams took an immediate dislike. The American singer Kathryn Grayson, star of *Show Boat* and *Kiss Me Kate*, was also on the programme, 'throwing temperaments in sapphire mink. Ostentation gone mad.' Filming at Pinewood continued on the *Carry On* across the New Year, and before it was finished rehearsals had already begun on another theatre revue. Its title made clear this was a sequel, brazenly cashing in and going too far: *One Over the Eight*.

9

'I have been taught the severest lesson of the theatre, and taught it pitilessly'

September 1960–December 1962

Michael Codron had first broached the idea of a second revue over supper at the Ivy in May 1960. Knowing that Williams and Fielding would refuse to work together again, he suggested Maggie Smith as the co-star, perhaps supported by Joan Sims. Williams warned that he would expect a say in the casting, and the discussions continued through the summer, until in early August Smith ruled herself out.

By the end of September, Williams was meeting Codron and Peter Cook to voice concerns over the script: 'I am not happy over the way this material is shaping. Too much of it is in the same amateur state we found ourselves with at Liverpool. It's not right that I should continually have to salvage mediocre material.' To make it worse, his closest friend in the cast, Terry Theobald, was told he would not be needed in the sequel. Theobald shared Williams's taste for racy European movies, such as *La Notte Brava*, and his dismissal would mean the loss of an ally.

'*One Over the Eight* might have come too quickly after *Pieces of Eight*,' Codron said. 'We did it that way because we'd had such a good time, and the first show had been a hit. But *One Over the Eight* wasn't so happy.' Codron had tried, and failed, to divert Williams into more serious theatre, inviting him to read plays by David Perry: 'I am amazed and naturally disappointed that you did not like [them],' he wrote, 'but anyway the temptation to feel frustrated that you cannot appear in one of his works will now be removed.'

Rehearsals for the revue began badly on 4 January 1961. Williams warmed to Lance Percival, one of the cast of nine, but immediately pressed for another, Ian White, to be dismissed for 'pedestrian dullness'. Codron asked him to be patient. 'Michael dislikes doing a sacking in rehearsal and thinks the whole thing foul. He is a curious enigma of shrewd business plus a compassion which sometimes overwhelms him. I suppose it is why one adores him.' Two days later Harold Pinter attended a rehearsal: 'He thought Ian White terrible so that clinched it.' The sacking didn't help. White's replacement, Robin Hawdon, proved both talented and harder to bully, even speaking up during rehearsals to suggest cuts in the star's sketches.

The material was disjointed, and Williams could not find a voice to do justice to some of Cook's funniest work. 'One-Legged Tarzan', which would become one of Cook and Moore's best-loved sketches, failed to spark, with the bemused impresario played as a mixture of Snide and Lew Grade. It was recorded for the Decca LP of *One Over the Eight*, but dropped before the revue reached the West End: to hear it now is bewildering, as Williams forces an anticlimax from the line, 'I've nothing against your right leg . . . the trouble is, neither have you.'

The show's strongest point was its co-star, Sheila Hancock, whose resilience seemed to calm him: 'Sheila came back to flat for a cup of tea + we talked about the drear of it all – and discussed the idea of faith – and did the crossword puzzle, in a sort of quiet desperation.' When they took the train to Stratford-upon-Avon two days later Williams travelled with the songwriters, Lance Mulcahy and John Law, who raised his spirits; Law's facility with jokes and his genial absence of ego would later make him an ideal writing partner for Williams.

The revue opened at the Memorial Theatre on 31 January, with scenery – some of it abstract, some cartoon – projected from slides on to a curved background screen. Such ingenious staging deserved innovative material; it didn't get it. Williams filled his diary with pages of complaints, as he analysed every sketch, not so much dissecting as ripping each one to pieces.

Mr Grole returned, without his viper but clutching a notebook of Interesting Facts. Pinter's contribution was cut by the third night, and a nightclub scene written by John Mortimer, featuring Williams as a repressed manufacturer of string and Hancock as a prudish hostess, sounded derivative. Codron particularly liked a Cook sketch where

Williams, as a playwright called David Frost, explained how he had lifted words and even individual letters from his condemnation in the newspapers to create the rave notices emblazoned outside the theatre.

The show opened, after a musical overture, with an inept bank robber falling over his words as he waved a gun at the manager – 'Hold hands! This is an up stick!'; it closed with Williams standing in a hollow tree stump, expounding on the perils of bird-watching. This was even more his showcase than *Pieces of Eight*, and the responsibility of it weighed miserably on him. At a production conference after the opening night, his protests upset almost everybody. He took ample offence in return: 'Michael Codron said to me, "If you have no faith in Paddy Stone, or me, it is best not to work with us in the theatre." Certainly good advice, but my contract forbids me acting on it. Like the coxswain of a lifeboat telling one of the passengers to get out if he doesn't trust the cox!! – only I haven't got a lifeboat. But my God! I'll remember this crack when the time comes.'

Codron tried to solve the problems, asking Cook to supply a new sketch for the opening: the result was a mélange of jokes from the first revue, with Williams as an angry customer in a music shop, brandishing a British-made triangle that had fallen to pieces at a climactic moment. 'By that time,' Codron said, 'Peter Cook was rather involved with *Beyond the Fringe*, so his whole mind was not on it, though it has got wonderful sketches.'

The tour reached Brighton where, during a dressing-room talk with Codron, Williams raised the possibility of quitting the show. The force of Codron's reaction shocked him. The next day, he tried to write, asking for forgiveness. Two efforts were filed away: 'Dear Michael, I've written you loads of letters and torn them all up. I think you know me well enough by now, to know I would not want to jeopardise the work and reward of the many people associated with this show [. . .] When I said in the dressing room it would be wonderful if you could withdraw the show, I was speaking very selfishly, I know.'

Both letters tailed off when he began to explain his anxieties, but after a week at the Liverpool Grand Theatre he returned to Park West and his typewriter, and his fears poured out:

I am typing this because I don't think I could write properly. I've written so many letters to you since this production began – all of them remain unposted. The really terrible things that have worried me, have all got confused when I tried to commit them to paper, but I think I have got to try now, because I don't seem to be able to talk to you any more – something inhibits me, and what comes out is far from what I want to say. One thing I do know – that I have got to make a stand about this material, because you don't seem to realise what it is doing to me. To lose faith as much as I have, in the work that one is doing, is to cut deep into the ego and to eventually destroy the very thing that might have given life to something mediocre [. . .] I have been suicidally depressed since Stratford, because I have felt this show to be a bad show [. . .] To go on to the stage and actually PERFORM the triangle thing is humiliating – I am trying to rid myself of shame while lines are coming out [. . .] I honestly don't know how I have got through the past few weeks – that finale entrance makes me crawl with embarrassment but I try not to show it. That is why I felt like I did when I asked if it was possible to withdraw the show at Brighton in the dressing room. Now I am really frightened about doing the show at Streatham etc. because perhaps it is ME that is no good. I have got to see a doctor or something because I feel on the verge of a breakdown – my inside just goes over and over.

He kept both the top copy and the carbon, and wrote at the bottom of the latter, in pencil, 'unfinished, and of course, unsent'.

At both the Adelphi and the Streatham Hill Theatre, audiences were enthusiastic, and Codron suggested Williams should commit to the show for a full year, instead of the six months his current contract stipulated. Peter Eade applied gentle pressure too, hinting that his half-heartedness was tantamount to blackmail: no West End theatre would take the revue if its star was signed for only six months. Williams felt bound by duty, friendship and contract, and the constrictions were strangling him. Happy news from his closest friends helped him to face the decision. Gordon Jackson's wife, Rona, came backstage after a show – she was nine months pregnant and gave birth to a son, the couple's second, two days later. Williams visited the maternity ward and was cheerful again. He told Codron he would sign up for nine months.

After another week on the fringes and a second trip to the provinces, in the 'English Siberia' of Blackpool, the revue opened at the Duke of York's Theatre. The critics confirmed his fears. 'This gay, trivial and frequently tedious little extravaganza,' wrote Clive Barnes in the *Express*, 'seemed as old and dated as last year's calendar.' His only praise was for Williams, who 'triumphantly rose above his material in a positive feat of levitation [. . .] Mr Williams, with his ice-cold face and tortured vowels, was a delight.' The following Sunday, Ken Tynan in the *Observer* was blunter in his condemnation: 'There is almost nothing in the show that could not have been written twenty years ago.' And he was more arch in his praise – Williams 'has a matchless repertory of squirms, leers, ogles and severe, reproving glares, and must be accounted the petit-maitre of contemporary camp. As such, I salute him; but I wish there were more to English comedy than this.'

Camp, in 1961, was a word of lurid and unexplored resonances, and it was often bracketed with Williams's name. It became gradually coarsened by twin implications: that a camp performer was homosexual and a camp performance consisted of gay clichés – the limp wrist, the mincing walk. 'Camp' became the opposite of 'butch', but Tynan's meaning and Williams's interpretation were far deeper. It signified a love of artificiality, the patently fake, and permitted its enthusiasts to enjoy the cheap, plastic emotions of mass-produced art.

Susan Sontag defined it in her 1964 essay, *Notes on Camp*, as a love of exaggerated style – the extreme carried so far that it made comparisons irrelevant. Camp art would seem ridiculous, except that it took itself so seriously. A reverence for fantastic flamboyance, amounting to an addiction to exuberance, was blended with an awareness of double meanings. True camp was naive, and narcissistic, and self-absorbed, and precious, and precocious. Frequently it was gay, but that might be part of the pretence too – and in Britain before the 1967 Sexual Offences Act, this double meaning protected everybody. The comic could indulge in filthy innuendo, and the audience could applaud without condoning sexual deviance.

In the theatre, camp was the antithesis of tragedy, Sontag decided; it demanded two-dimensional characters portrayed with ferocious intensity. Camp could be cruel, or excruciating, or immoral, because it judged life by an alternative set of values. It elevated bad taste to an artistic pinnacle; those who savoured it were aristocrats of sensibility, declaring their capacity for deep undercurrents of passion, which conventional society ignored and denied. Camp at its most perfect was detached and elegantly heartless, but it also demanded an appreciation that was tantamount to love, for people and for low culture. 'Camp is a tender feeling,' Sontag said, inadvertently coining an alternative title for this biography. Kenneth Williams defined it more briefly: 'The sceptic finds refuge in irony, and camp is the JUNIOR version.' Camp, like Williams, could be childish and childlike. It was an immature aesthetic.

One Over the Eight drew packed houses. 'To my absolute surprise, and this will indicate that Kenneth had become such a huge draw,' Codron said, 'despite the carping reviews, it got off to an enormous start. It was full. We had the Duchess of Kent come on the third night, and that sort of thing made me realise that we'd got a hit.'

When Noël Coward came round to Williams's dressing-room, 'I mentioned the bad reviews + he said – "of course my dear, that's why you're doing good business . . ."' Coward lavished praises on him – '"everything you do is completely authentic . . . I can't imagine it being done by anybody else"' – and to add to this surfeit of flattery, Roy Plomley invited Williams to be his castaway on *Desert Island Discs* the following day. His choices included a Beethoven sonata and a Bach Brandenburg concerto; for his luxury he took Michelangelo's *David* ('It's the god-like head I admire').

Codron was trying once more to nudge Williams towards New York. The leading Broadway producer Alexander Cohen took him to lunch at the Savoy. 'I like Alex more every time I see him,' Williams admitted, but he had no intention of being persuaded. 'I have decided not to go to America fr. revue,' he wrote a month later, 'or indeed to do ANY revue. Any more.' He was right to stay away from America, believed Norman Hudis, who moved to Hollywood in the early sixties: 'The atmosphere would have been too fervid, too fanatical for him.'

His reluctance to brave New York was not fear of exertion: he was working constantly, rising early and leaving his flat at 7.15 a.m. to be at Pinewood for *Raising the Wind*, which had gone into production as the revue opened. On 11 May he shot probably his funniest movie sequence outside the *Carry On*s, working himself into a frenzy as he tried to conduct an orchestra and finally crashing from the podium. It was strenuous work, but he had to be at the Duke of York's that night as always.

He was relieved to be working in another hit, though he did resent the burden of carrying weak material. His relationship with Sheila Hancock was uneasy – like Smith and Fielding, she could match him when he started to ad lib, and he admired that, but when he goaded her she was neither forgiving nor hurt, which was exasperating. 'She said to me when I asked if she was upset once . . . "No . . . and when you are, I just want to laugh . . ."' He was thrilled, though, when she gave him lifts to Park West on the back of her Vespa scooter.

That summer's heatwave made him still more restless; he was disgusted and enthralled by the Hyde Park sunbathers in their underwear, the stifling nights kept him awake, and his only respite was to swim in the pool at his apartment block. When he developed a tic under his right eye, tiredness was diagnosed, and he used it as an excuse to back out of a film with Norman Wisdom. He also rejected every script that Codron proffered, and when Hal Roach, who had been Laurel and Hardy's producer, promised to take him to Hollywood and make him a bigger star than Danny Kaye, he refused with a shudder.

To sustain himself, he prayed frequently, for strength and patience to tolerate others. Though he regarded himself as lacking self-knowledge, he recognised that he was too quick to judge and to condemn. He read the Gospels, grappling with the recently published New English Bible as well as taking comfort from the King James. When he had been vicious, he tried to understand what had happened and how he could avoid a repetition; when he could see a way to help friends, by lending money or writing letters, he did it.

'I must try to keep up this correspondence,' he wrote, after replying to an unhappy fan. 'I feel it might do some good. And it's time I did some altruistic good . . .' The imprisonment of Robert Bolt, for protesting against nuclear weapons, horrified him – he sent a telegram of support to Bolt's wife, Jo, and visited her at their home in Richmond Green the next day. She wrote in thanks: 'You are a good person to have about at any time; a particularly good person in a crisis; and in fact a good person. Your telegram yesterday and your toiling out here today, tired and occupied as you are, were absolutely typical of you.'

Williams wanted to do more good; to see his friend jailed, with the octogenarian Bertrand Russell, filled him with outrage, but he was afraid of being arrested. In his diary he tucked a CND leaflet calling for a non-violent demonstration that Sunday, in September 1961: 'Pack Trafalgar Square for the rally with numbers such as have never been seen before,' it urged. 'War is imminent. We resist. The Government represses. Help us.' He did long to help, and steeled himself to attend the rally, though the police cordoned off the square and he could not get close enough to be in danger of arrest. The sight of protesters being dragged away sickened him: 'The Police used filthy methods [. . .] One saw the fascist, and the savagery in them start to emerge [. . .] uniformed bullies that enforce an unjust law.' He wrote letters of support to John Osborne and Vanessa Redgrave in jail, and was gratified to receive notes in return.

Though the government policy, and the absence of support in Fleet Street for the protesters, angered him, he did not set out any political objections in his diary, and when he joined in debates, at the Bolts' house or over supper with friends, his grasp of international complexities was shown up to be flimsy. His anger at the H-bomb was a moral indignation, not a practical one. When he tried to analyse it he found himself confronted by deeper questions: non-violent protest was right because it was one of Christ's precepts, and if Williams lacked the courage for civil disobedience then he ought to strive harder to obey the other Christian injunctions. The greatest of these was love.

'When you talk about love, I think you mean idealised love,' Melvyn Bragg remarked, 'and God as an idealisation: Williams was always looking for an ideal. And of course it is unrealisable.' This exalted conception of love was matched by more mundane feelings such as 'the extraordinary relationship with his mother, which was way beyond normality, with the interdependence they had. I don't think it's all that unusual, but in his case it seemed to be exaggerated to as high a degree as you could get. Nobody is going to equal her.'

Williams seems not to have been aware that his devotion to Louie might have coloured all his other relationships. He was conscious instead that his respect for Charles and his affection for Pat failed to attain the same heights. He had always admired his parents' marriage, and wanted to emulate it, but the idea of a sexual union with a woman was impossible. It was not just that he was homosexual; he could not endure the presence of a sexual element in a friendship.

'I think that people who manifest their love for you, physically, when they know your lack of reciprocation, are abominably selfish,' he wrote in 1953. 'Sooner or later, the relationship *must* suffer, however noble its beginnings. I must be comparatively undersexed or something for I have never particularly wanted to make physical love to anybody. All this touching and kissing which seems so popular among others passes me by.' The men he found gorgeous had to be fantasy figures – new acquaintances, or figures on the screen, or young men seen in shops or parks. To be attractive they must be ideal, and to be ideal they must be unknown. Marriage, the closest friendship imaginable, was the negation of sexual desirability. Given this restriction, there were two women who might have coped with Williams as a husband, and during the weeks of political and spiritual questioning he proposed to both of them.

For more than a decade Williams had been drawn to Annette Kerr's gentle, practical, forgiving character. With her he could envisage a celibate alliance, without the 'abominable selfishness' of sex. When she had visited him during the West End run of *Peter Pan*, again in 1953, he'd suggested he would like to share a flat 'with someone'. Without acknowledging the invitation was aimed at her, Kerr replied: 'My dear no. You know how you loathe people when you see them often.'

Two days after Trafalgar Square, Williams noted: 'Supper with Annette. I suggested we get married but she didn't think it would work.' A year later, in 1962, he tried again: 'Annette Kerr arrived at 4 o'clock and we had some tea. "You do make a lovely cup of tea," she said, so I replied, "Well, why don't you share a flat with me?"

'I found this old snapshot taken in Mesopotamia [in 1919] of my father Charles in the Royal Berks. Regiment. He had an enormous portrait of the entire regiment over the fireplace'

Kenneth Williams, aged about one. This formal portrait was probably paid for by his mother's older sister and her husband, Edie and Siegfried Kaufmann

The boys of Bolt Court school, June 1940; Williams, bottom left. His diary hints at an early sexual experience with 'D.P. [top row, centre]. Always remember him saying, "I'm enjoying this just as much as you are . . ." '

Corporal Pat Williams, a wireless operator, and Private Kenneth Williams, not yet attached to the Royal Engineers, shortly after his call-up in 1944

Williams in his first stage role, as Princess Angelica in *The Rose and the Ring*, performed on the roof of Manchester Street Junior School in St Pancras, 1935

Louie Williams, July 1957, in the back yard at 57 Marchmont Street, where Charlie had his hairdresser's shop. Louie is holding the family dog, Bob

With CSE in Singapore, 1947. Williams jotted on the back: 'Self and Peter Stretton – "Cat's Cradle" sketch from *High and Low* – me with the lorgnette!'

Williams's first professional portrait, from the programme of *High and Low*, January 1947. The forces show included a spoof Mexican number, 'The Three Caballeros', starring 'Bamba', 'Samba' and KW as 'Caramba'

With Sonia Moray, in rep at Newquay: 'Came out with the wind blowing a miniature gale, and a photographer snapped us, almost before we knew it!'

Williams in his first television appearance, with Barry Jones in *The Wonderful Visit* by H.G. Wells. The second performance was cancelled by the BBC following the death of King George VI

With Peter Ashby-Bailey, August 1949, when they were both in the Newquay Repertory Players. Ashby-Bailey would be Williams's last director in rep, at Bridgwater in 1954

1952: 'My new *Spotlight* photograph. Don't really like it, but what the hell?'

Williams in his first major film role, as Peter Wishart in *The Seekers*, 1954, with Glynis Johns

As the Dauphin in *Saint Joan*, autumn 1954, pictured in *Plays and Players*: 'He is convinced that only the actor who does not claim that his work is creative has the necessary humility to do his job well'

One of three snaps pasted into his diary at the end of April 1955, showing the severe haircut Williams wore as the Dauphin

On holiday at Shanklin, Isle of Wight, July 1955, with Phyl Hussey, the sister of his friend John. Williams always enjoyed the company of other people's families

Sid James, Tony Hancock, Bill Kerr and Kenneth Williams, the cast of *Hancock's Half Hour*. 'We had to stop ourselves from corpsing all the time,' Kerr said, 'because everybody was so terribly funny'

Williams as Montgomery, the boy editor of *The Buccaneer*, with Thelma Ruby as his mother. 'He was developing that persona that became him, very quick-talking, and he lit the place up,' Ruby said.

From Bamber Gascoigne's revue, *Share My Lettuce*, at the Comedy Theatre, autumn 1957, a sketch called 'The Nutmeg Tree': Williams is the tree, Barbara Evans the King of Spain's daughter

A break in rehearsals for *Share My Lettuce*; taken by Gordon Jackson in Brighton, on the weekend of 8–9 August

With Maggie Smith in *Share My Lettuce*. They would work together again in 1962, in Peter Shaffer's *The Private Ear and the Public Eye*

With the cast of *Share My Lettuce*, as Maggie Smith lays down the rules for 'Party Games'

'The mouth is the key, and it's all a question of what goes on inside it. Restrict the larynx and you get a silly fat boy's voice, flatten the vowels and you get the voice of the governing classes.' Williams in *Pieces of Eight*, 1959

Charlie and Louie Williams arrive on holiday in the Adriatic, 1961. 'I've missed them both this year more than any other. The darlings. I hope they're adoring every minute of it'

With Barbara Windsor and Louie in Funchal, Madeira, April 1964 – the *Carry On* actress and her husband, Ronnie Knight, were on their honeymoon. 'He was an absolute pain on holiday,' Windsor said

But she said it would never work out – her smalls in the bathroom, she said, were inevitable . . .'

The other, more likely candidate was Nora Stapleton. Submissive, with a bawdy sense of humour and a sycophantic admiration for Williams, she had been his loyal satellite since falling in love with him during *The Buccaneer*. The possibility of marriage was raised, and buried, and resurrected; Williams suggested it over supper at his flat in Edgware Road, ten days after he was rejected by Kerr in 1961, and Stapleton promised to think about it. Probably the offer was made in an offhand way, for if he had pressed her she would certainly have acquiesced.

In July 1962, she timidly brought up the proposal again. 'I told her we ought to go through with it,' he wrote, though three days later he was backing out: 'This marriage is something I'll always baulk at. I shouldn't be allowed out. I shouldn't.' He continued to agonise over the idea with friends. Thelma Ruby said: 'I went round backstage [at the Globe, during *The Public Eye*] and we went out for dinner some-where in Soho afterwards. He said to me, "Nora thinks we should get married. What should I do, what do you think?"' Ruby was surprised, and said so: wouldn't he prefer, she wondered, to live with another man? 'He said, "It's against the law and I don't want to go to prison. And it might be nice to have children . . ."' Ruby warned him that marrying Nora would create more problems than it solved. 'Poor chap, this was in the days when it was illegal and he had to suppress that, and I think it was responsible for a lot of his problems.'

He did like children, and they liked him. 'Lovely sunny day,' he jotted in his most carefree hand, 'so went into the park, where I met two sweet little children. They chatted away + so did I. That's where I belong. With children.' Conversely, the fear of prison was a convenient lie. Gay men were certainly justified in being wary – the law still threatened to inflict misery and opprobrium, and John Gielgud's arrest a decade earlier had cast a long shadow. Williams, though, never worried about that. It was not simply that he knew he was immune from arrest because his occasional forays into 'tradiola' were too mild to break the law; the threat of prison was academic because he had no desire to commit the crime. Nowhere in his diaries does Williams meditate on the risk of imprisonment for his sexuality.

It was an irrelevance for him. He was no more likely to be jailed for being gay than for drunken driving: he was sometimes intoxicated, but he didn't own a car or possess a driving licence. And he was often attracted to men, but he was never licentious.

Despite the reputation for sexual frankness his diaries acquired after his death, they were explicit only when recording a dream or a fantasy. He referred to real encounters using the oblique code he had used since the army, a cautious habit. It was not that he was ashamed to confess his sexual adventures, since he would relate them with flagrant candour in restaurants or studios, often when his mother was with him. Those encounters were mostly flirting and, however much he made of them later, he was adamant that he had never had penetrative sex. Like a fifties prom queen who wouldn't go all the way, he preserved a smutty purity that was more immature than innocent.

'He was a sort of Virgin Queen, and projected that,' said the playwright Trevor Baxter. 'That's the way he got away with it with the public – for most of his career, homosexuality was against the law, and I think people just didn't believe he did it, which on the whole he probably didn't. He allowed them to think that, and that somehow made it acceptable. There were always stories of him going around Piccadilly Circus in an open-topped motor car, calling out, "Arrest me, officer, I'm a homosexual." But that was all right because he wasn't actually doing it.'

For three years he had been spending occasional evenings with an Australian student named Paul Florance, who had been twenty when he stayed the night with Williams after a party in 1958. This was the only relationship of his life that began with a sexual episode and became a lasting friendship. Florance returned to Sydney in the mid-sixties, to study law and join the family firm of solicitors, but he continued to visit England and to write sprawling letters to Williams. 'Lovely letter from Paul. Felt a wave of affection pour over me as I read this letter. Suddenly realised how v. fond I am of P. He was always a lively companion, he was always honourable, and he was loyal. Very good to me. O! dear! I wish he wasn't so far away. Didn't know how lucky I was, I suppose. And now it's too late. "And you lacked the courage to choose, and you've only yourself to blame . . ."'
Other episodes were isolated – with an assistant stage manager at the

Grand Theatre in Blackpool, for example, who stayed in Williams's hotel room till 4 a.m. and came backstage at *One Over the Eight* when he visited London, but otherwise was never mentioned again.

Williams's caution even extended to rewriting his diary. He almost never removed pages, but one instance occurred over the weekend of Sunday 24 January 1960. He carefully cut a blank sheet to size and tipped it into the book; the entries copied there are busy with names and events – for instance, 'Lunched with Celia Johnson at the Ivy with Nora – it was a v. pleasant surprise.' But something had been excised. The only hint to its nature was a cryptic comment the following Friday – 'Robin Tutt for lunch. Told him everything + was politely + firmly rebuffed. I think I always knew in my heart, that this would happen.' Whether the lunch followed on from events at the weekend, and whatever it was that Williams had told Tutt, a bitter reaction set in: 'Robin Tutt . . . he's just one of those culture hungry Americans – the search for him is almost as avid as when people in another period were searching for God. He's a restless, boring man, who must keep changing trains. I dread to think how he'd react to an empty platform.'

One method of imbuing his lovers with mystery was never to meet them. He maintained a succession of penfriends, some in the services and others in Europe or America, most of them gauche and dull correspondents: it did not matter that they were boring, providing they were kept at a distance. He made the mistake of inviting one of the first, a Dane, to London: 'Met Bent Ore Petersen at the Airport. Bleached and boisterous Bloomsbury Blonde – v. vain and a fancy piece – O well.' 'Took her round the city etc. O! She is such a bloody bore. O drear drear drear.'

The friendships that endured were those where Williams could expound the ideas that grew from his reading. He had to share his latest discoveries, whether they were factual or spiritual or just gossip. One Sunday in October 1961 he visited the Baxters, who had been holidaying in Sicily, and sat late into the night discussing religion. The following week, eager for conversation, he dragged Stanley and Moira to the Bolts' house, but any arrangements he'd made to do so had been forgotten, for Robert was at a CND rally and Jo was not expecting company. In the end, they stayed for seven hours, with

Williams chain-smoking to disguise his nerves; the conversation, to his disgust, never rose above chit-chat.

He had refused to sign an extension to his nine-month contract and, at a party to mark the 200th performance of *One Over the Eight*, Codron announced that Kenneth Connor would be taking over at the end of the year. Williams counted the days – 'Artistically it has been complete stagnation to me. A marking time. Money at the expense of talent' – and returned to Pinewood for another Thomas/Rogers film, *Twice Around the Daffodils*, to play a TB patient. The film was Norman Hudis's second adaptation of *Ring for Catty*, and co-starred Joan Sims and Lance Percival. Hudis later admitted it had been poor judgement to make a comedy about an illness that was still killing 2,000 people in Britain every year. 'The kindest headline we got was *Carry On Coughing*,' he said.

When anxieties caused physical ailments, even as petty as a pimple or a blister, Williams had an outlet for his fretting. The revue, though, had depleted his emotional reserves but left his body unscathed. His skin, his teeth, his piles, all the usual psychosomatic weak spots, were quiescent, and yet he was still ill; this nebulous sense of malaise was as tiring as any sickness.

'This week will see me into December and when it's the 6th I'll know that there's only one more month of this muck to be performed,' he promised himself. 'It will be marvellous to get out. Only spiritual care has got me through this nightmare – only the result of God's help, and prayer. Nothing else. It's been little short of a miracle.' When the 6th came, he was still counting: 'Now it is a month before the end of this nightmare of a run, and monstrous humiliation. I have been taught the severest lesson of the theatre, and taught it pitilessly. That is – that when what you are offering is inferior, it should be stopped. It's as clear as that.'

He turned down an offer of a radio show with Bob Hope, but agreed to make another *Carry On*, with the proviso that his salary must be £5,000 – a sum he had demanded, and been refused, for *Twice Around the Daffodils*. It was the offer of another stage play, though, that restored a gleam of optimism.

The play was a one-act comedy called *The Public Eye*, by Peter Shaffer. It was to be staged by Binkie Beaumont at Tennent's with its twin vignette, *The Private Ear* – Williams would appear only after the interval, but the part was a rich one. 'Julian Cristoforou,' Shaffer described him, is 'a man in his middle thirties; his whole air breathes a gentle eccentricity, a nervousness combined with an air of almost meek self-disapprobation and a certain bright detachment. His speech in the main is rapid and virtuostic in effect.' The writing was resonant: 'I realised something shattering about myself,' Cristoforou declares. 'I wasn't made to bear the responsibility of a private life. Obviously nature never intended me to have one.'

Over supper, Nora Stapleton urged him to take the play, but he was wary of being embroiled without knowing who the other actors would be. The play centred on a bored, decadent wife, escaping from a stagnant marriage into horror movies in back-street cinemas; she falls in love with a private detective, Cristoforou, as he follows her around Soho. Williams cringed at the thought of professing adoration while some actress made a hash of the character. If he was to accept it, he needed to be opposite someone adorable. He phoned Maggie Smith. When she told him that she had already agreed to play Belinda in *The Public Eye*, and Doreen in *The Private Ear*, he was almost decided, but Beaumont had to ratify his terms: 'I am asking: 1) 6 month release. 2) Top billing. 3) No rehearsal after London opening. 4) No alteration of text. 5) No more than two matinees in any one week.' Salary was less important; he accepted what Eade had negotiated, but he did loathe matinées. In addition, he insisted that he should not have to arrive at the theatre until the first play was halfway through. The director was Peter Wood, who had directed Williams in his last drama, *The Wit to Woo*, five years earlier.

Dinner with Shaffer helped to reassure him. The playwright was sparkling company, 'v. funny, and I laughed more than I've laughed in years. He has the most incredible fluency, + a very quick dramatic quality in conversation. Quite charming and endearing.' What Williams did not realise, as he sized up his colleagues, was that Shaffer also had doubts: he had asked Fenella Fielding whether she thought that, after so long in revue and in radio comedy, Williams could sustain a performance throughout a run without resorting to gurning and voices for easy laughs. Fielding, aware that her co-star had spent months decrying her to the whole of London, assured him that Williams could be trusted – 'which was very nice of me!'

Filming for *Carry On Cruising*, the last time he would play one of Hudis's supercilious know-it-alls, began on 9 January 1962. The writer continued to hope for further commissions in the series, and sketched a couple of ideas, both with starring roles for Williams. 'He was a sparkling intellect,' Hudis said, 'with a wonderful mind, very very fluent, a bloody good writer, could ad lib anything. I'm going on as if he was the only actor who ever breathed, but he was the best of a very explosive breed. Right up there with the top ones. I'm talking about Olivier and Coward. I think he was their equal as a performer.'

Hudis's first idea was based on a seaside concert party – *Carry On Under the Pier if Wet*, with Williams as a mime, who would not speak a line in the whole film. 'He was an English version of Jean-Louis Barrault,' Hudis pointed out. 'If you put their photographs side by side, they are very much alike. The flared nostrils, the sensitivity, the spark that flies off them. I would have had enormous fun with that.' Williams was aware of the resemblance, and claimed Olivier had remarked on it during *The Beggar's Opera*. Hudis's second secret hope was for a *Carry On Sherlock*, with Williams as Holmes: 'Self-sufficient, arrogant, that would have perfectly suited Ken's superior approach. Completely insulated against any criticism, and always with the right answer, done in a dismissive fashion.'

Williams, who adopted Noël Coward's voice when he played Holmes in later radio sketches, would have relished the role in a *Carry On*. The mime he might have resisted: he was not an adroit physical comedian, nor was he naturally silent. Film-goers wanted to hear his voices. But if Thomas and Rogers had promised that the camera would never leave his face, and told him that his expressions were funnier than any script, he might have agreed. He loved the series so much that, when the director and producer took him for lunch at the Bull in Shepperton, the day after the press showing of *Daffodils*, he arranged to buy the pyjamas he wore in the film.

He adored *Beyond Our Ken* too, not for its bad puns and close harmony quartets, but for the reliance it placed on his talent. He made the show fly: he was its wings, but not its pilot.

Horne, a demon-ridden worker who would regularly journey to Newcastle from London to record his *Trader Horne* show for Tyne Tees TV, had never recovered fully from his stroke, and he sometimes sounded weary. His blissful gift for deadpanning turned many of his lines into feeds for Williams, who would ad lib an aside to the audience so that he coasted into his own lines on the crest of a laugh. He worried about Horne's health, commenting after one broadcast that the ringmaster had suffered a nosebleed throughout the recording. Horne knew that Williams held the show together and was grateful: 'My dear Ken, to say that we've had our difficulties would be the greatest understatement of all time! Without your inspired fooling around before, after *and* during the "read-throughs" (whenever you could obviously see the danger signal) and your fabulous performances during the actual recordings, we could never have kept up such an incredibly successful standard.'

Williams and Marsden shared a prickly enmity, and he was disdainful of the versatile Bill Pertwee, but he liked Paddick well enough to suggest a holiday together to Spain − 'I *feel* I ought to go to Malaga.' Two days after appearing on *This is Your Life* for Horne ('I did a terrible load of rubbish ad lib . . . just hope they're not too critical'), they flew to Gibraltar and hired a car to drive to Torremolinos. Williams was disappointed by Malaga, which was damp and 'full of awful English and dirty Spaniards', but Gibraltar, when they drove back, was worse − he became bored with 'travelling incognito', Paddick said, and made sure he was recognised. 'He was mobbed and [. . .] before we had been [at the hotel] five minutes, Radio Gibraltar was down to interview him. We ended up doing a Rodney and Charles routine about the apes.'

They returned to Torremolinos on Williams's birthday: it was 'full of drears [and] deathly types', so they flew to Nice, by now fed up with each other and 'stuck together with stamp paper'. Paddick wanted to relax and his companion literally refused to unbutton: 'I'd be on the beach sunbathing and he'd be sitting there in a suit, collar, and tie and black shoes. Not really my idea of how to spend a holiday.' They spent the last night sharing a room at the Hôtel Méditerranée in Cannes, where Williams caused a scene by singing to the violinist in the restaurant. That night he took a sleeping pill, while Paddick lay in a state of nerves in the next bed, 'worrying about the chaos he had caused'.

'The south of Spain,' Williams remembered later, 'I thought it sounded rather grand. Only I'd never been anywhere except in the army and, as it turned out, the holiday was a disaster. I'm really terribly insular. I couldn't stand the plumbing and the garlic.'

Rehearsals began on his return for *The Public Eye* in Peter Wood's flat in Little Venice, and Williams bristled at the director's technique of trying read-throughs in different styles. 'P. Wood is asking one to do the reverse of what one was told yesterday. Far from artificiality and style, we are now being told to play for naturalism and be real. All v. confusing.' Shaffer's dialogue, polished and pointed, stood up to any amount of experiments, but the rehearsals foreshadowed a crisis to come three years later.

Williams strove to be obedient: when Wood accused him of being too knowing, or lacking authority, or playing too fast and missing cues, he noted the criticisms and conceded they might be right. He and Richard Pearson, who played Smith's husband, practised talking over each other's lines to create a sense of spontaneous conversation; when the plays opened on tour in Cambridge they talked nonsense during the laughter, to complete the impression that this was natural dialogue. He was merciless with himself, counting all the instances when a word or a cadence did not sound exactly as it should – 'One fluff from me over anticipating a word. I really must stop this sort of thing. I don't think I've ever given a perf yet that has been immaculate.'

But not since *Saint Joan* had he found less to fret over at the start of a run, and as they travelled to Birmingham for the tour's second week the praise from the producers, the director and the critics was unanimous. Any problems at the Hippodrome – 'somehow this theatre nullifies one's acting. Like farting at a wet blancmange' – were alleviated by his delight in Smith's performance and her company off stage. As they dined, drank coffee, visited museums and saw films together, one moment epitomised everything he loved about her: amid a cinema audience all weeping at *Pollyanna*, Smith was laughing and crying simultaneously.

After a week at Oxford, Williams approached the opening night in May 1962 at the Globe with more trepidation than he had ever felt before a performance. Wood sent him a card with the slogan, 'You do things to me!' and added, 'that is nothing to what you'll do to *them* this evening [. . .] don't speak too quickly, will you?' The plays were a triumph, the dressing-rooms overflowed with well-wishers and wine afterwards, and after taking his family to dinner at the Ivy, Williams went on to a party thrown by Shaffer and then returned for more drinks at Wood's flat. It was almost 4 a.m. when a taxi returned him to Park West.

Over the next few nights he was fêted by Sybil Burton, Michael Redgrave, John Osborne, Tony Hancock and Noël Coward, who was 'full of praise for me. He is a wonderful person.' The reviews were all flattering: 'Harold Hobson prints a fabulous notice, Tynan a good one and Telegraph marvellous. I am really v. grateful.' He preserved letters of praise from the *Mail*'s critic, Robert Muller, and from David Tomlinson, John Perry at Tennent's, and Kenneth Horne, who wrote, 'What a superb performance. I'd heard about it and though I'd never say I didn't believe it, I thought that reports must be exaggerated. But they weren't.' Shaffer wrote a letter of extravagant acclaim: 'The brilliance of your playing (I mean brilliance in the true sense of the word – the sheen, polish, lustre), the attack and the gorgeous cleverness of it [. . .] have projected my Cristoferou into realms of pure wit, into skies of fantasy [. . .] You are a superb professional and a unique artist.' When Eade suggested the play might transfer to Broadway, Williams almost felt disposed to agree.

In such a benign mood, he thought seriously about moving away from the Marylebone and Euston Roads, and buying a house. His affection for Park West had soured when the superintendent asked him to stop inviting friends to share the free swimming pool, and the noise of neighbours overhead was distracting him. On a wet afternoon late in May he joined a friend from his days at Bridgwater rep, James Roose-Evans, walking his dog on a drenched and verdant Hampstead Heath, and loved the surrounding streets (though he was sure the rates would be prohibitive). Three weeks later, he drove out with Stanley Baxter to look over a cottage in Southgate: 'Everyone keeps on at me to buy property!' On an impulse, visiting the Bolts in Richmond Green, he viewed a terraced Victorian villa that was for sale, and made an offer of £4,250. He had left a cheque with Robert

Bolt, who had offered to be his partner in the purchase, but the following day he cancelled it when he saw the surveyor's report. His courage, when he was not with his friends, ebbed away.

He did own property, a leasehold flat at 26 Brunswick Gardens, Kensington, which he had bought in January the previous year for his parents. They had been living at Queen Alexandra Mansions for two years, after Charles had been forced to sell the Marchmont Saloon: faced with a bill for unpaid taxes, he had been declared bankrupt. Since the late forties his health had been failing and he had been treated in hospital frequently, for pleurisy, bronchitis and shingles. Charles was a heavy drinker and smoker; what the family did not realise was that, after his bankruptcy, he had become addicted not only to alcohol but to opium, purchased over the chemist's counter in Gee's Linctus, a cough medicine. This concoction contained 4 per cent powdered opium and about 20 per cent alcohol, with a flavour so foul that most abusers could swallow it only if they held their noses and swigged in gulps from the bottle, to avoid tasting it. Although it could be bought without a prescription, pharmacists would not sell it to any customer in large quantities, so Charlie would have been forced to purchase it from a series of shops.

Family meals, always an ordeal, had become grim: 'Lunched folks. Pat was there + we went over and fetched Gran. Awful atmosphere with P. being her jocular aggressive self – and Charlie quietly feeling sorry fr. himself + bursting into anger, and Louie doing that perky one. Gran just sat. I was glad when it all broke up.' Pat had found her father a job as a messenger at ICT, the electronics company where she was an executive, but he was laid off because of his continual sicknesses.

Williams recognised that his father was becoming increasingly frail and difficult, though he was more concerned about Louie's health, following a thyroid problem that had left her tired and thin. She collapsed at the end of a meal at Biagi's, falling forwards on to the table, and was unconscious for nearly ten minutes despite her son's panicky efforts to hold her upright: 'the face was askew on the shoulders – grotesque – the mouth open and the breath gasped noisily like a frightening drunken snore'. After this scare, he sent both parents to Butlin's in Minehead, but the holiday was a disaster, with constant quarrels and a bronchial relapse for Charles, which meant he was readmitted to the Royal Brompton Hospital in Chelsea.

The worry and distress broke Williams's confident mood. Sweltering in a humid summer, he was convinced he would contract a cold and dosed himself with quinine tablets, but his anxiety rose up in his throat, forming a lump, a globus hystericus, that felt as though it would explode. Every time he and Louie visited Charlie, he felt his spirits dragged down: 'He has caused a lot of trouble in the ward + is obviously the bane of the nurses' life! The sister told Louie that he had been most objectionable [. . .] He works himself up into tempers, is full of persecution complex and hints darkly at revenge. He shakes a lot, and looks at times as if he was going to weep. It is difficult to feel any pity for him. He is so argumentative and cantankerous.'

Out of work, sixty-two years old, and without cash to buy drink or Gee's Linctus, Charlie had begun to talk of bizarre plans for making money, such as selling pigeon food in Trafalgar Square. After he had been discharged from the Brompton, he waited for his son in a pub near the Globe, and began to outline a plan for adjustable beds, which, he claimed, would make him a millionaire within three months. For the first time, Williams faced the fact that his father was mentally unstable.

Charlie's behaviour became frighteningly odd. He phoned his son's friends at all hours to urge them to go into business with him. One morning he ushered his mother into a taxi and declared he was taking her to Eastbourne. She panicked and jumped out at traffic lights, leaving her son ranting and gesturing. Once he had refused to see his son's plays, but now he kept turning up in the dressing-room, to cadge money, which he claimed he wanted for meals, or to expound on his plans for telescopic scaffolding or some other invention. On one occasion he arrived in his pyjamas and, instead of lending him a coat, Williams shooed him away; he brooded on this and felt he had been unchristian.

By the beginning of October, Louie was in despair. 'He is now demanding money from her the whole time. I told her to leave her cheque book with me in case of trouble + I've got her Building Society book as well [. . .] It is incredible that he is making lives so wretched. There seems to be nothing one can do, except watch him drive Louie to a nervous breakdown.'

On Saturday 13 October 1962, Williams lunched at Brunswick Gardens, with Louie anxious because her Post Office savings book had disappeared. Charlie claimed he had never seen it, and left. The next afternoon, Williams was called to St Mary Abbot's Hospital, to be told his father had been admitted that morning after drinking poison. Louie was at her flat with her daughter; when Williams arrived they told him Charlie had swallowed Thawpit, a cleaning fluid, from a Gee's Linctus bottle. Louie had found him, vomiting and doubled over. She had put him to bed, where he fell unconscious; she then dialled 999 for a doctor and later told the story to the police.

There was no performance at the Globe on a Sunday, so Williams went home and, after recording the events in the neutral hand he used for writing letters, took a sleeping pill. The next entry revealed his tension in neatly printed block letters: on the Monday, Charlie seemed to be recovering, and Louie had discovered her savings book in his pocket – he had forged her signature to draw out £8. Williams met Gordon Jackson for lunch and saw *Dr No* at the cinema. At 7 p.m., as he was preparing to go to the theatre, Louie rang. His father had died at three that afternoon. Williams gave his performance – 'Show went OK. Audience good' – and went to supper with Smith and Beverley Cross. He took comfort in the doctor's comment that Charlie's heart, brain and kidneys had been so badly damaged that his death was a mercy.

Williams decided not to attend the inquest and asked Eade to accompany Louie in his place, fearing his presence would attract newspaper attention. He was avoiding Pat, who had a bad cold, but took his mother shopping for a black coat, hat and gloves, although her tears upset him. 'I shall be so glad when this wretched inquest is over,' he complained. 'I've read about this situation in books but never dreamed it could happen to our family.'

The inquest was held at Hammersmith Coroner's Court on the Friday morning. The court records no longer exist but two local papers reported the hearing. On its front page, the *Kensington News* quoted Louie: 'Early last Sunday morning I heard him calling out to me. "Lou! Quick! What have I done?" he said. I rushed into the bathroom and saw this bottle that he had in his hand.' The report noted that Charlie frequently had severe attacks of coughing, and continued, 'Mrs Williams stated that her husband always took the medicine from the bottle. She could not explain how this other bottle had come to be in the medicine cupboard in the bathroom. "I've never seen it before," she emphasised.'

The paper went on to quote a house doctor at St Mary Abbot's, Michael Henderson, who said Charlie had been conscious for a time and had told him that 'he had swallowed a fluid that he thought was his linctus'. The second paper, the *West London Star*, reported that the coroner, in his summing-up, had suggested the police should try to discover which chemist's had sold the bottle of linctus, though he accepted the chances were 'rather slim'.

The death certificate recorded a verdict of accidental death – not misadventure, as Williams wrote in both his diary and his autobiography – and gave the cause as 'bronchopneumonia and acute gastroenteritis following carbon tetrachloride poisoning self-administered by accident'.

After the inquest Williams took his mother and sister to Scott's, the restaurant where he had lunched just a couple of hours before Charlie died. 'I ordered champagne. It was all v. gay and forced.' He was indignant to learn that his grandmother and Charlie's sister, Phyllis, expected Louie to take them to view the body at Golders Green crematorium chapel – 'I told her she was NOT to do anything so morbid.' The service was held that Tuesday and the following day Williams settled his father's overdraft. Since Charlie had left no will, Eade accompanied Williams and his mother to the courts, to apply for letters of administration.

Despite the verdict, Williams suspected his father had committed suicide. That one of his parents had carelessly decanted cleaning fluid into a medicine bottle, which had then been replaced in the bathroom cabinet, seemed an improbable accident. Thawpit was so corrosive that one teaspoonful was enough to kill. The idea that Louie or Pat could have deliberately replaced the linctus with this poison, knowing Charlie would down it in one draught, was too preposterous to be considered. The least unlikely possibility was that

Charlie had deliberately disguised his suicide as an accident, a piece of muddled cunning of which he was certainly capable. Suicide was no longer illegal, but Williams was anxious to see his mother receive the life insurance dividend. The claim dragged on into December.

Eventually Louie did receive both a pay-out of £2,000 from the mutual society and a rebate of taxes, and Williams arranged to pay £15 a week, by three deeds of covenant, into her bank account. 'So all in all,' he noted, 'she's not done too badly out of all the misery.' His summary of 1962 was more callous still: 'It was a good year really. Charlie's death released Louie from that rat trap of a marriage, and now she's happy.'

10

'God has given me the opportunity to use the theatre in its moral sense'

January 1963–April 1964

Kenneth Williams had learned now to exert control over every possible aspect of his existence. When he spoke, he knew the weight and value of each syllable. When he slept, he measured out his grains of sleep in 600mg doses of Seconal and Noludar. He saw his friends constantly but by appointment, rarely permitting them to overlap. Where his life was touched by circumstances beyond manipulation, he permitted anger in proper proportion – at the neighbours in the flat above who walked on bare floorboards, and the bus schedules disrupted by snow, and the playgoers who dared to offer criticism. His self-control attained its peak during the run of *The Public Eye*, an extraordinary comedy with exceptional actors. He mused on the importance of vulnerability in a performance, and claimed an actor could be good only when he had the courage to expose his raw self, but he had sealed his emotions within a glass tank.

The mental disintegration and death of his father drove a wedge between the seals and started his emotions trickling out. He had not even felt the damage, though his friends saw it: Robert Bolt warned, 'It would be very odd if both Louie and yourself didn't have some distress, at some level of consciousness about your dad's death and the manner of it, particularly since it wasn't humanly possible to have much love for him immediately prior to his going.' The distress became displaced: instead of mourning his father, he worried for his mother and his sister. They were a widow and a divorcee now, and he felt the pressure to become their protector, a supportive, established man – an adult. Extreme control is an adolescent state: it cannot be maintained in a mature relationship. Barely aware of the change in him, Williams had become what he advocated all actors should be: vulnerable.

He felt it first with the departure of Maggie Smith. Peter Shaffer had favoured Joan Sims to replace her, though he conceded her earthiness wouldn't suit Belinda. Juliet Mills was considered, but when Judith Stott read, she was the clear choice. An experienced Shakespearean actress who had played opposite Coral Browne and Wendy Hiller in the West End, she revealed her nerves after the audition, and at the first rehearsal she was 'shaking all over'. Privately Williams was alarmed – 'she puts on an emotional heave that would be more appropriate to Strindberg or something' – but he was encouraging to her face.

Stott, who was going through a divorce and had a young son, was earnestly grateful, a new face relying on the established star, and this set off emotional resonances that left Williams bewildered. In the theatre, just as at home, he felt he had grown up, and the instinct to respond almost swept him away. After they had supper at Chez Victor, he was shocked to realise he was falling: 'I think she is the sort of girl who might easily become an involvement. Continually suggesting we do things together, and meet people all the time.' A couple of weeks later, he warned himself that Stott was 'converging on me more and more. It would be terribly easy to get involved here. I must tread v. warily.' Fearing he would plunge into a relationship that he could not imagine, impelled by an attraction that he could not comprehend, he did not tread warily; he literally ran away and hid.

At a party after the 300th performance, he panicked. 'I just walked out. She telephoned my home and rang the doorbell but of course I didn't reply. This must be stopped and stopped quickly.' He was too embarrassed to speak to her at first, but two days later, at the end of January 1963: 'Told Judith Stott I was not seeing her socially again. Just do the job and leave. I can't have any more of this sort of emotional interference. Should never have allowed it to occur in the first place.'

Jack, a terrier that he and Pat had bought to keep Louie company, aroused something even more immature in him. He became jealous of his mother's dog. The Jack Russell, eleven weeks old and not house-trained when he collected it from Harrods, was a favourite at first; Williams enjoyed walks in the park with the dog cavorting in mud and slush. As the animal got bigger, he worried that it was diverting too much of his mother's energy and affection. Though Louie insisted she was fond of it, his dislike became intense: 'Went over to Louie [. . .] Pat came too for lunch. I bashed the dog cos it misbehaved + she started crying (P) and carrying on dreadfully. She's obviously hysterical. She went out of the flat crying. I can't cope with all this drear. Of course I dislike cruelty as much as anyone else, but a dog has to be given a hiding occasionally + if one sometimes overdoes it, one has to remember the natural instinct for cruelty that is in all of us.'

The next day, 'Louie looked a bit faint: I think it's partly worry and partly the dog which she has to keep taking out. That dog is a nuisance, + I will have to see about getting rid of it. It's no good allowing an animal to dictate yr. way of life. Bloody ridiculous.' Within forty-eight hours Jack had been adopted by Judith Stott for her son. When Louie protested that she missed her pet, Williams took her to see it in its new home and insisted that, after one week, the dog no longer recognised her.

The play was as popular as ever. At the front of his 1963 diary, he kept a ledger of every week's attendances – the date, the length of the run so far (circled, in red) and the weekly audience. The weekly houses were still well over 3,000, but he was growing bored. He could speak his lines without thinking, but if he tried to recall them consciously, they meant nothing. There were fan letters, including one from Dirk Bogarde – 'I laughed like an idiot . . . I really have'nt behaved so badly in a Theatre for years!' – and he still got a round of applause on his first exit every night, a spontaneous indication of his popularity. But Williams wanted to get out and take a holiday.

He was sidestepping other proposals easily: a television series by Eric Merriman, a play by Adrian Brown, a radio show by Barry Took, even a night at the *Evening Standard* Drama Awards ('they can stick their awards up their arseholes'). A suggestion from John Perry at H.M. Tennent's for taking the plays to Coventry Cathedral drew his incredulous laughter – 'I said certainly not. What a fantastic raving barmy idea [. . .] O! it's a disgrace. I wonder the C of E is still going. It certainly should be dead by now.'

Williams did almost agree, at a party in Scott's thrown by Binkie Beaumont, to take *The Public Eye* to New York: 'I rather wilted a bit in my resolution. There is no point in going to N.Y. for me. It would achieve nothing. But when people are excessively charming to me, I always wilt. I shouldn't be allowed out.' The prospect of Broadway had been looming for months – in December 1962, George Rose had tried to twist his arm: 'We had supper at the G+C [Grill and Cheese]. He raves about America and the rest. He says it's all fantastic. Can't help feeling that, really, it isn't. Of course he said I'm mad not to go, that I'd have a ball etc. None of them KNOW me!' Through Peter Eade, he warned Tennent's that he would leave the production in May, and would not go to America. Perry, unsurprised, replaced him with Richard Pasco.

Two forays did reveal the versatile uses for his voices, and hinted at the genius for serious drama he had kept under dust-sheets since the beginning of *Beyond Our Ken* and the *Carry On*s. On BBC2's arts programme *Monitor*, he read five poems that, as defined by the BBC's audience survey, took 'a satirical look at the characteristics of certain types of English gentlemen. Though it was evidently a surprise to some viewers to find him so much at home with this material ("suited him perfectly"), others made it clear that they regarded him as a very talented artist, and that this "brilliant performance" as an interpreter of poetry confirmed their opinion of his versatility. On the debit side, it was "all rubbish" to a reader describing himself as "a Regimental Soldier".'

Williams had misgivings: the programme was originally conceived as a selection of amusing Victorian verse, and he worried that it had turned into something self-consciously arty. Humphrey Burton, *Monitor*'s editor, wrote to praise him: 'We enjoyed it enormously and would like to do a lot more in the future. The Waste Land and D.H. Lawrence on the Bourgeoisie for a start.' That encouraged him and, though he sidestepped director Patrick Garland's invitation to read at a poetry festival in Stratford, this would be the first of several recitals on radio and television.

He also agreed to narrate an animated version of Gogol's *Diary of a Madman*, for the film-maker Richard Williams, whom he had met two years earlier when he supplied the voices for a cartoon short, titled *Love Me Love Me*. The animator was a perfectionist, who courted Williams by visiting Park West and playing him two recordings of Peter Shade's soundtrack music. 'It opens a world of loveliness to one. It makes life richer, it gives a new conception, it makes this rainy afternoon miraculous. I begged Dick W. to let me keep these records.' Gogol's story gave lunatic scope to Williams's voices. It told of a lonely clerk, who is driven out of his wits by unrequited love until he succumbs to delusions that, as the uncrowned king of Spain, he is spied upon by talking dogs.

In a recording session that stretched for more than six hours without a break, Williams read from the clerk's diary in a halting voice, like a man on a window-ledge who cannot will himself to suicide. Other personalities pierced the reading – the sadism of the office supervisor, the contempt of the boss's daughter, the shrill proclamations of King Ferdinand VIII. 'I was pretty hard on him, and made him read passages again and again to get the right effect. It freaked him out,' Richard Williams recalled. 'At one point he walked out of the studio and I had to run after him. It was a block and a half before I caught up and persuaded him to come back.' Full of repetition and bitter nonsense, the piece is almost nauseating as the clerk slops and flounders towards insanity. While no recordings exist of Williams in his most unsettling stage roles, *Diary of a Madman* is proof of his merciless gift for a sustained, upsetting performance. The animation was not completed, but the voiceover survives and was broadcast by the BBC, three years after his death.

That night after the recording sessions, he was 'strangely nervy + upset' at the Globe. Years later he blamed the Gogol adaptation for his low spirits after leaving *The Public Eye*, though the chief cause was his anxiety over another discomforting role, which was being urged on him by Robert Bolt. The playwright wanted Williams for the nature god, Jack o' the Green, in a violent story of lust and feudal cruelty titled *Gentle Jack*. Bolt first hinted at his desire to cast Williams in October 1962, at a party, and by Christmas was talking obsessively about the play whenever they met.

He was buoyed by the success of *A Man for All Seasons*, and his ambition was unlimited: he wanted Richard Burton for the timid hero, Jacko, and Edith Evans for his employer, a fascistic millionaire.

Williams introduced him to Burton, who turned down the role. Jack the god was inspired by the carvings seen in many English churches of the Green Man, a face made from fruit and curling leaves, which peers through foliage, with an indecipherable expression that seems mocking, loving and murderous: 'a pan – a symbol of the Animal in man. It sounds v. diverting and fascinating – of course I'm v. interested.'

Flattered at first by the energy of the writer's intellect, Williams recoiled when he realised the character was based on his own persona. 'I am,' Bolt declared, 'quite helplessly writing it – I will not say for you since that implies some sort of moral suasion on you – but in your theatrical mode and what I have learned from it. I describe him in my List of Characters thus: A God and immortal. A charmer, a liar, a teacher, a murderer. He must be funny, and alternately despicable and terrifying; he must disturb; and you do disturb, when you have the lines to do it on.'

Dismayed to discover how his friend saw him, Williams wrote to protest that he could not bear the responsibility of living up to Bolt's masterpiece, and asked to hear nothing more of it until the play was finished. Bolt replied immediately, with another tightly typed page of eulogy for both Williams and Gentle Jack. He signed his letters with an ambiguous squiggle that was part pal and part auteur, both 'Bob' and 'Bolt'.

The more he heard of the role, the less Williams liked. 'I'm not at all sure about many aspects of it,' he fretted. '(a) It's not enough of a star role. (b) Only 2nd half of play. (c) Don't like the idea of the costume. (d) Not keen on the style of character. (e) Staging would be very compliqué.' And the following day, 'in the afternoon I went down to the Bolts. R. started on about the play as soon as I arrived in the most embarrassing enthusiasm! This, after writing to me and saying he wouldn't talk about it any more. Twice the children asked if I was playing the part – in front of him – and he hardly helped me out. It's all so damned selfish . . .'

The script arrived as Williams was preparing to go on holiday. It came with more flourishes of praise and an assumption that the part was irresistible. Of course he resisted: 'The whole thing is so "surprise for the little boy who never knew he would land such a plum . . ."

But not everyone's idea of a plum is the same.' That Sunday he flew to Venice with Beverley Cross, and before boarding the cruise ship *Romantica* he posted a letter to Bolt, withdrawing from *Gentle Jack*.

His friendship with Cross and Smith was the antidote to his worries. Whenever he dined late with them after a show, the last notes in his diary would be contented, satiated with the pleasure of acting and London and life. He joined them on sallies into the country, searching for a property to buy and renovate, and even played the game himself, putting down a deposit of £495 on a mews cottage in Earl's Court – this fantasy lasted an unprecedented three days. Over tea, 'I said to Mags I don't think it will ever be as good again – getting what one wants, and being a success, + having sunshine, going to Venice + Greece [. . .] I have reason to thank God.'

As a companion, Cross was incomparably better than Hugh Paddick: he was tolerant when Williams showed off to the ship's officers, he was gregarious and erudite and amusing, and both sightseeing and sunbathing suited him. They visited Corfu, where Williams dared to remove his shirt and got burned; drank retsina under the Acropolis; saw the mosques of Istanbul, and returned via Rhodes and Dubrovnik to Venice, where a gondola took them to the Danieli Hotel. Williams was a tourist, not a traveller; just as in Burma and Malaya he had been a cockney abroad, he had no pretensions about entering into the Mediterranean lifestyle. The café where they ate in Athens was 'all v. peasant and quite revolting', the birthplace of Apollo on Delos looked 'like a ruined graveyard in a borough like St. Pancras', and his last self-indulgence before flying out of Marco Polo airport was to have a coffee at Florian's in St Mark's Square.

He returned to a 'sharply disappointed' letter from Bolt, and an offer from Michael Codron to play Lord Goring in Wilde's *An Ideal Husband*, with John Schlesinger to direct. Williams liked the idea, and demanded full involvement with decisions on casting and staging. In the production meetings that followed, he bickered with Schlesinger about dates, and names, and styles, until within six days they had talked the idea to a standstill. Peter Rogers was pressing him to star in *Carry On Sailor*, which started filming in September, and Williams, tired out by indecision, opted to make the movie instead: he and Codron buried Oscar Wilde over dinner at Biagi's.

Rogers plied him with charm. He sent the script with a covering note, to point out that the writer was not Hudis this time but Talbot Rothwell, and offering him a choice of roles, as Captain Fearless or the hero, Midshipman Poop-Decker. A week later he sent a fresh draft, with the apology, 'Sorry to be a nuisance but would you please read *this* script [. . .] this one has pink pages and I know how you love pink.' Amiably ruthless, Rogers would not hold up production for anyone. He kept costs low by refusing to concede top billing to any actor. 'We never wrote a script for anybody in particular,' he said. 'If you start doing that, one gets above the other. Before you know where you are you've got a star on your hands.'

He had proved his point the previous year, when Eade was holding out for more than £5,000 for *Carry On Cabby*; Rogers derided his client as 'terrible' in *The Public Eye* and hoped they would never work together again. To show he didn't mean it, he and Gerry Thomas took Williams to dinner at Mirabelle and promised all manner of petty concessions, such as Wednesday mornings off to record *Beyond Our Ken*. But the producer was adamant about salaries, and the actor was hurt, and *Carry On Cabby* had gone ahead without him.

Bolt attacked from the opposite angle. On 13 July he sent a telegram: 'DEAR KENNETH WILL YOU OTHER CONSIDERATIONS APART BUT AS A CONSIDERABLE PERSONAL FAVOUR CONSENT TO PLAY JACK FOR VERY LIMITED PERIOD SAY EVEN THREE MONTHS?' Williams took a car to Bolt's new house in Hampshire where, for almost the only time in his life, he agreed to spend the night in a friend's spare room instead of returning to London. Noel Willman, who had staged *A Man for All Seasons* to acclaim and would direct *Gentle Jack*, was also there. Pursued, flattered, and now charmed by Willman whom he thought sensitive and frank, Williams told himself that to refuse would be unprofessional. He arranged to start rehearsals as soon as filming finished at Pinewood on *Sailor*, now renamed *Carry On Jack*.

Worry over the play tormented him all summer: it was a 'fundamental feeling of gloom' and at its worst it drove him to despise himself for his loneliness – 'I've spent all my life in the mind. I have existed. I know everything vicariously. I have entered into nothing. I've given some sympathy but never empathy.' He tried to drive away depression by swimming every morning and, as he always did at a low ebb, was humbly thankful for his friends and possessions: 'My little electric clock on the desk is a continual delight. The timing is perfect.'

After another attempt to buy a cottage, this time in Bayswater, he decided he could be happy only in a flat, and chose one next to Baker Street tube station, overlooking the Planetarium, on the top floor of Farley Court, a nine-storey brick Victorian block. Though it was barely bigger than the rooms at Endsleigh Court, and had no pool in the basement, and the leasehold was £8,000 with annual ground rent of almost £500 – though, in other words, it was far more expensive than a one-bedroomed cottage – Williams believed he could afford nothing else. 'I suddenly don't want to know about all the wood rot, and cleavages in walls + bad ceilings etc.' The move served its subconscious purpose, for he was chivvied out of despondency. Suddenly he was measuring up for carpets, and blinds, and a wardrobe; it gave him the energy for an overnight trip to Stratford to see three plays with John Hussey, and for the first time he felt optimism about *Gentle Jack*.

Shooting started on *Carry On Jack* at the end of August, and Williams was restored. He loved working for Thomas, and he relished the uninhibited mood of the set. Almost none of the usual actors was involved – only Hawtrey, as a drunken cesspit cleaner, Jim Dale as a cut-rate sedan cabman, and Bernard Cribbins in his *Carry On* debut. Many of the crew were regulars, however.

'He used to chat with the crew a lot,' said Alan Hume, the director of photography. 'He was very popular with everybody, very easy to talk to, and I don't think I ever saw him get moody – only if he was trying to get himself into a character, get himself ready for a scene. Not the stroppy sort, quite the opposite. A lovely chap to work with: he was always up for a joke or a laugh. Quite a character in that respect. He'd be telling you something, and it was all rubbish, but he'd be telling you seriously and you'd swallow it.'

The expertise and good nature on set, and the pace of the work, appealed to Williams's artisan pride. Hume believed the film crew responded to this working-class ethic: 'People probably think it's a soft old cushy number but the actors are making their living, and it may not be tough physical work but it's tough mental work. When I was working on the *Carry On*s, at the weekend come Sunday morning, I was looking forward to going back to work on Monday. So much fun. We enjoyed making those pictures – it was always fun on the set, always.'

Carry On Jack, the first period comedy in the series, gave Williams an opportunity to play manic and melodramatic after so many prissy characters. He threw everything into it, pompous and lecherous, naive and noble and cowardly, outraged . . . all the elements that came to typify his best *Carry On*s. 'His humour hasn't dated at all – what I call real comedy doesn't date,' Rogers said. 'It's when you start getting topical and political that it starts dating. Our stuff was almost music hall. He was a dear man. I don't think he was always happy, but he was a dear man, and he made other people happy.'

Bolt continued to press ideas on him for the playing of *Gentle Jack*. He sent letters explaining scraps of Middle English and Welsh that he wanted to slip, like magical incantations, into Williams's speeches, and decreed how each syllable should be spoken. When rehearsals began in October, both Bolt and Willman were telling him how to play it; just as he had predicted, they had sworn he was the only actor alive who could embody Jack, and then they started by criticising his interpretation. Bolt took him to dinner at the Pastoria Hotel, and 'it all got v. hot under the collar. Bob being v. didactic and at times perverse, and thro' the drink, a lot of conceit and arrogance came out. It wasn't a very edifying evening.' All his instinctive reactions to Jack were dismantled by the writer and director, who argued their analyses until the lines, instead of developing deeper meanings, became nonsense: 'I want to shout, "Do it yourselves – you're all so bloody clever – get a load of puppets that will mirror your thoughts . . . to hell with you . . .'"'

Filming at Pinewood had not ended, which meant Williams was rising at five on dark mornings, when the feverish narcissism surrounding the play seemed tiresome and petty. To soothe his nerves he sought out maternal figures – not only Louie, who was helping him prepare for the move to Farley Court and being 'a doll', but also his co-star Juliet Mills, who was 'lovely, lovely [. . .] quite adorable', and of course Nora Stapleton, who came to inspect the new flat and to hear him read his lines.

Farley Court delighted him. The bliss of being insulated from his neighbours' noise could not be exaggerated: it felt like a state of spiritual grace. It was true that there were fans thrumming in the roof space, part of the heating system, but he was sure he would become used to their impersonal noise. And the views were glorious, all down the Marylebone Road and across Regent's Park, the vista of that London to which he really belonged. 'The sky is all pearly grey and shot thro' with rays of the sun: from this flat, you can certainly see the weather.'

The cast of *Gentle Jack* were intimidatingly good, though he took spiteful glee in sneering at Dame Edith Evans – behind her back he called her 'Sans Merci', meaning 'La Belle Dame'. She had difficulty learning her part, which was not a long one, and Williams hinted to Willman that she must be growing senile. When she conquered the lines, though, he had to admit her delivery was brilliantly comic and a match for any of the others. As he relaxed and allowed himself to trust Willman's direction, he started to believe the play was at least as good as *The Public Eye* and was going to prove a hit. He was wrong.

Gentle Jack was confused, dull and shapeless. Its message seemed to be that repression made us vicious but our unfettered animal impulses would kill us. The luckier characters are a bickering middle-aged couple who realise their love isn't enough to make them happy, and so divorce; and a debutante who manages to slough off her virginity with a suitor she never wants to see again. The rest fare worse. Bolt urged Williams to make the nature god Jack an amoral, anarchic symbol of wishes fulfilled, but his first deed was to disembowel a dog and spill its entrails towards the audience. They were not going to love him after that.

The play opened at Brighton's Theatre Royal, with Binkie Beaumont out front. Afterwards, he commented to Dame Edith that Hardy Amies had designed very regal costumes for her, and that she should endeavour to be equally regal in them. 'What a daft thing to say at this stage of the game,' snorted Williams. 'Of course it upset her all through supper.' It also provided him with a favourite anecdote, of how he comforted the actress that 'any criticism of her deportment was tantamount to impertinence' and how she replied, 'You're a very pleasing young man, and there isn't any reason why the right girl shouldn't come along.'

Audiences were baffled by the production. After a Thursday matinée, when he was eating at a café with cast members Timothy West and Michael Bryant, several customers asked them what they thought the play was supposed to be about; West felt the implication was that the actors owed the audience a refund. But Williams continued to believe in it: 'I have waited a long time for this – and now God has given me the opportunity to use the theatre in its moral sense.' Bolt left a letter in his dressing-room, praising '[your] conscious artistry' and 'your application of the harshest discipline to your most vulnerable states of mind'. Some in the stalls did appreciate what Williams was attempting, to project the character without playing for laughs. Ned Sherrin wrote, 'it looks lovely and *you* look impossibly attractive & your switches of mood and the authority with which you carry them off are breathtaking.' But Eade loathed it, Richard Williams called it pretentious, and even Kenneth Horne could not hide his disappointment.

Gentle Jack opened at the Queen's Theatre on Shaftesbury Avenue at the end of November 1963, to mixed reviews – the best were Bernard Levin's in the *Mail* ('Though his first act is a little arid, his second, with the arrival of Pan-Bacchus, played by Mr Kenneth Williams, who was clearly born to do just this, is a thing of terrible beauty and soaring imagination') and *The Times* ('No idea in which Mr Kenneth Williams can be occupied seems to exhaust his reserves of fantasy'). The rest were scathing. By the following Friday, Williams knew he had to get out of the production. All the encouragement of friends could not disguise the nightly failures.

Maggie Smith wielded the fatal sliver of praise: Williams was wonderful as Jack, she said, but his lines were not strong enough to salvage the play. That night, he resolved to leave as soon as possible: 'It is a lonely part + it is a miserable part and it would be too frustrating to be in it for long.' A recorded excerpt for the BBC's *Monitor* programme did boost the audiences, who were drawn by the names despite the notices, and Princess Margaret came, but before Christmas the takings had collapsed. *Plays and Players* summed it up as 'disastrous. Not only was it a bad play, a sort of star-studded pastiche of Afore Night Come, but Williams was miscast. He *could* not play anyone but himself. One critic at least has compared him with Peter Pan. Well, yes: but the god Pan, never.'

The friends ceased their encouragement, and came backstage to criticise. 'Shaffer's brother came round and raved about the awfulness of the play. "What a bloody TRICK it all is," he said, "a rotten cheat of an evening." He went on to say that his brother could've done it infinitely better. I said it was v. probable + that it was all awful, and M. Bryant said, "O! You're such a traitor + so disloyal to Robert Bolt . . ."' For a month the production struggled on, until Williams arrived at the Queen's for a matinée to find a note in his dressing-room from Binkie Beaumont, announcing the play would close on 1 February 1964. The producer laid the blame upon Bolt: 'I am sad that in spite of the cast production, Bob did not bring off Gentle Jack – but let's hope his next will have a clear line.'

Bolt wrote to apologise: 'I will now confess that the chorus of sneers from the Press were so vilely uncomfortable to me, that it's almost a relief. What I regret as much as anything is that I should have involved of all people you in a failure [. . .] doubly and trebly so since I so nakedly beseeched you into it against your better judgment.'

Work began within days on another Rogers film, *Carry On Spying*, and Williams should have loved it – for the first time in a film he was using the Snide voice, in a send-up of the 007 franchise. 'It's Double-o Oh!' promised the posters, with Williams in a Sean Connery pose, arms folded and flaunting a pistol. His gun barrel is bent. Hawtrey, Dale, Cribbins and Richard Wattis were his supporting cast, plus a newcomer, Barbara Windsor.

Each morning he woke in the silence of his new flat, his 'drawer in the sky', with the park and the steeples beyond his window; he had never felt a home to be such a haven. His finances were in good order, with £7,240 on deposit for his April tax bill – a constant preoccupation, since his father's bankruptcy – and enough besides to send his mother on holiday to Tenerife, even after he had paid £750 into his pension plan. Codron, Beaumont and Eade were making regular offers of work, from a bit part in Hollywood to a television series with Billy Cotton to an Anouilh double bill in the West End, which Williams, with mechanical disdain, turned down. Every aspect of his life was better than it had ever been, yet he was distracted and fragmented. The public rejection of the play was a blow that had concussed him, and the pain of it recurred like a headache.

Stanley Baxter took him for a Chinese meal one evening, before they headed on to a Schlesinger party. These riotous, boozy extravaganzas were peopled with film stars and theatre grandees, and the director was celebrated for them: 'Everybody was there. Fantasy', Williams confessed. In a blurred and blotted note, he recorded that he had lost sight of Baxter, and had spent the evening arguing about religion and getting very drunk. The next morning, the ink almost hisses on the paper. 'I haven't been to one of these theatrical parties for years: and I shall never go again. I must be mad. It is disgraceful to have to mix with people who are artistically so unequal to oneself.'

He dripped the vitriol nightly upon *Carry On Spying* – 'a soulless waste of time'. The worst days left him feeling physically injured, when he scraped his ankles crawling down a tunnel, or when 'they hung us upside down on some girders and the blood rushed to the head. I shouted when the pain was too intense and Charlie Hawtrey collapsed. It is an absolute disgrace.'

The film's salvation was Barbara Windsor, a star on television's *The Rag Trade* as well as in the West End hit *Fings Ain't Wot They Used t'Be*. When she arrived, Windsor was in awe of him: 'I was crazy about the theatre he'd done. He was this magnificent actor, he could take anything on. I was very fortunate as a young girl to see him as the Dauphin, and I was a huge fan of *Pieces of Eight*. I saw that so many times! So he was the only one I was absolutely scared of working with.'

On set, she mangled her first lines. Williams glared at her from behind his secret agent's black whiskers. 'Darrr-ling,' he sneered, 'do please get it right.' Windsor, a graduate of stage school and the Littlewood theatre, could deal with bullies. 'Don't you yell at me,' she snapped, 'not with Fenella Fielding's minge hair all round your chops!'

Williams leered. 'Oooh,' he said, 'ain't she wonderful!' He liked her better still when he discovered she never had bad breath, something he hated in other actors. 'I really love you, Bar,' he told her.

'You're the only person round here who cleans their teeth after lunch.'

Windsor had married her boyfriend of three years, Ronnie Knight, in a register office ceremony the day before filming started. When she told Williams she had postponed her honeymoon, he suggested they could take it in Madeira – if they flew via Lisbon, there was an evening ferry to Funchal. One hotel there was reputed to be wonderful, and the holiday would be the most romantic experience of her life. It was so idyllic, in fact, that he would come with her . . . and he'd bring his mother and his sister too.

Williams always liked to attach himself to couples, and there were strong similarities between Ronnie and Barbara and his own parents: she was small, lively, funny and fussed over him, and he was gruff, short-fused and occasionally revealed a disarming gentleness. He thought too that, with Pat and Louie for company, he would not be bored when the honeymooners wanted to be alone. His egocentric view of other people's relationships always had left him unable to know when he was being importunate; to bring along your mother on your wedding night is a bad omen for a marriage, but nothing could be more ill judged than to take your mum on someone else's honeymoon.

For all the obvious reasons and more, the holiday was a fiasco. They arrived early at the airport, left the lounge late and almost missed their flight; a second plane took them from Lisbon to Madeira, where they boarded a ferry. 'It sounds so romantic,' said Windsor, 'but it wasn't – it was one of these awful ferries with all the locals and all the cattle and all the chickens, and pigs and dogs. There was a hurricane, big, big waves, and Ronnie Knight was hanging over the sides, and I was hanging on to his legs, and he was saying, "Let me die," and Kenny was yelling out, "It's all in the mind, Ronnie, it's all in the mind!"'

The Savoy was a dump: their rooms had no baths, and the beds were cramped. Louie bickered with Barbara, and Pat rowed with Louie, while Knight and Williams avoided all of them and played cards amid the bar's 'dreary decor, arum lilies + general funeral parlour atmosphere [. . .] B said, "You're not very sociable are you?" and flounced out [. . .] The atmosphere has undoubtedly gone from cordial to loathing. This entire holiday is a disaster.'

'He was an absolute pain on holiday,' Windsor said. 'Oh God! It all had to be done round Kenny. He'd be sitting by the pool in a collar and tie, and a suit, with a towel pulled over him. And he hated it because there was all these Germans there, with their boobs hanging out. Of course, I rowed with him, and his mother rowed with me, saying, "Don't you have a go at my Kenny!"'

By the time the party flew back to Portugal, they were barely able to look at one other. In Lisbon they bumped into Lance Percival, who was working as a cruise ship entertainer; later, at a nightclub called Maxim, they almost got into a fight. As they flew home, Williams cursed himself for his stupidity, not in booking himself on a friend's honeymoon but in sharing a hotel with his mother and sister. He had been trying to take Charles's place, and it could not continue. In future, he resolved, he would holiday alone.

'It was Felicity's twenty-first!'
July 1964–December 1965

Maturity was poisonous to Kenneth Williams. His attempts at responsibility chafed him, until all his emotions became raw and infected. In the theatre, he needed to avoid not only the imposition of carrying a show but of all kinds of dramatic development. His talent was beyond improvement. 'Nobody can teach me anything,' he had snapped one night at Fenella Fielding, and it was true: everything he learned now was on the surface, like applications of polish, instead of stripping it away to reveal fresh and deeper layers.

Michael Codron, who had staged three revues and a fantasy with him, had not lost hope of casting Williams in a serious play. 'Still looking for IT (whenever and whatever it is) I promise you,' he wrote, and two weeks later he thought he had found it. 'I introduced him to Joe Orton, and they hit it off immensely: they came to dinner at my flat in Cambridge Gate, and I knew then that Joe was going to let Ken be in his next play.' This had the working title of *Funeral Games*, and it became *Loot*: a traditional farce with a woman's corpse in the cupboard instead of a meter-reader without his trousers, it was also a detective thriller where an inspector calls only to collect his pay-off. Orton took the plays that had constrained Williams, the *Sly Corner*s and *Paradiso*s, and scrawled sexual graffiti over them.

Orton and Codron had already scored a West End success with *Entertaining Mr Sloane*, a sex comedy about a teenage lodger who schemes to sleep with his landlady and her brother while he screws them for everything they've got. In his casting notes, Orton said the boy, Sloane, had to be 'someone you'd like to fuck silly', and one of his chat-up techniques was to tell young men that he wanted them to star in the Hollywood version. Williams had been reluctant to see

Sloane, but was agog at its daring and admired the sexual frankness of Orton's conversation.

'I warn you,' Codron had said, 'we'll have to have the friend, they're practically inseparable.' Kenneth Halliwell, taller and older than Orton, with sibilant, affected speech and a hairpiece, continually interrupted the conversation with small corrections, as though he was the writer's accountant rather than his lover. Williams was puzzled that Orton, so vital and energetic and amusing, could endure this constant dripping of banalities. Orton was fascinated by commonplace talk and its sententious, repetitious clichés. He listened to the mawkishness of lower-middle-class couples such as his parents in Leicester, and he felt no compassion, only a callous delight. With Halliwell, he played at being such a couple. If Williams had understood their dynamic, he would have grasped *Loot* as well – but he did not, and it would wreck his career in theatre.

His confidence had been seeping back since Madeira. There had been another attempt at a holiday, in Amsterdam, but he worked himself into a state of fright and fled after two days. Friends had urged him, since he was scared of sexual encounters in London, to go to a city where no one knew him, and Amsterdam offered anonymity to libertines. 'The story of my life,' he admitted, safely home at Farley Court. 'The run up and the run away.'

He was hesitant too about returning to the stage. Codron suggested several plays, including a Ray Cooney farce tailored for him, as well as the chance to take over as Robespierre from Donald Pleasence in *Poor Bitos* at the Duke of York's. That thought horrified him: 'It's all SUCH A JOKE. The very idea! And I have to sit and discuss it!!' He did accept a BBC television drama, with Simon Ward and Robert Helpmann: the casting was decidedly *Carry On*, with Williams as Napoleon, but the play was more subtle, a translation of Jean Anouilh's *La Foire d'Empoigne*. He wore a padded costume, and sulked when the director, David Benedictus, told him not to pose too often with his hand tucked in his tunic. In revenge, he refused to suck a liquorice stick, though Benedictus insisted it was the emperor's habit. 'I said I didn't give a damn and I wasn't going to,' Williams grumbled. But he realised, after two days' study and one of rehearsal, that he knew the part, and he began to remember that he did have some talent. 'I must be a v. good study,' he praised himself. 'There's no doubt about that.' The broadcast was beset with technical problems, which spooked him, and he muffed a cue; still, he was glad to do something that was mostly successful.

Carry On Cleopatra began filming in July 1964, a spoof of the Burton–Taylor epic. *Beyond Our Ken* had already parodied the most expensive movie in history, with Kenneth Horne as Caesar, Betty Marsden as the Queen and Williams as Nittius, a complaining senator, with lead-lined puns crashing around them.

Rothwell's script for the *Carry On* team was superb by contrast, probably the best in the series – Williams played Caesar, with Joan Sims as Calpurnia, Sid James as Mark Antony and Kenny Connor as an ancient Briton who has invented the square wheel. The best line was borrowed from Frank Muir and Denis Norden, and is often cited as the funniest joke in British cinema: fleeing from his treacherous bodyguards, Williams falls to his knees crying, 'Infamy! Infamy! They've all got it in for me!'

Williams found his toga awkward at first, but the thrill of parading with bare legs seduced him. He began leaving off his underwear, and would lift up the hem to flash his backside at the crew, 'and expose my cock and everything'. When that no longer provoked shouts of disgust, he invented the 'vadge trick', tucking his genitals between his legs and mincing along with his toga round his hips, mumbling like an old woman.

There had been enmity between him and Amanda Barrie, who played the vacuous Cleopatra, since they recorded a Peter Cook sketch for TV together, and Williams disliked her more when he saw the crew's reaction to her scenes bathing in milk. Dressing gowns were provided for all the cast, and while she was filming he switched the robes on their pegs. When Barrie flung one around her naked shoulders, Williams leaped up and started scolding her, accusing her of stealing his dressing gown. He demanded it back, knowing she was wearing nothing underneath. 'He was in a white rage, trembling, his lips pulled back in a kind of snarl, and there was real menace in his voice,' she wrote. Angry and embarrassed, Barrie rushed away, clutching another robe around her. 'Like many people who worked with him, I suspect, I was quite frankly terrified of him. You never knew what he was going to say or do, and he had a dreadful sourness about him.'

The malice in his laughter became so obvious that Gerry Thomas took revenge for Barrie: in a scene on the senate steps, where Caesar addresses the crowd in a long shot, the director told the extras to aim their tomatoes directly at Williams. 'A lot hit the back of my cloak – but I turned v. cleverly and they didn't succeed in getting my face. What a bunch of cretins these extras are.' This was more like the horseplay of the army, and by the end of the movie Williams had regained his swagger. He was recording his friends' conversation with relish again – what Stanley Baxter retorted to a rude head waiter, and who was at a dinner party in Peter Cook's flat ('All very malicious and pleasant'). When he was invited to contribute two songs to a Noël Coward compilation, he dared to insert an ad lib into 'Mrs Worthington' and performed 'Mad Dogs and Englishmen' too, racing through its hairpins with a superior gusto that excelled all the other contributions, even Joyce Grenfell's.

Orton's script was delivered in October. Williams had misgivings about its structure, since the central figure was the murderous nurse, Fay, until the policeman appeared. 'He did suddenly get fired with the idea of writing a zonking great part for me,' Williams told Orton's biographer. 'Instead of finishing his play and starting something else with me in mind, he dovetailed the two.' The playwright based his hopes on a skit he remembered from *Pieces of Eight*: 'Orton had seen me play a hen-pecked little bullying husband in a Pinter sketch I did, and became enamoured of the technique I used and said it would be perfect for Truscott. But it was in essence a caricature, all right for two minutes in a black-out sketch, but quite another thing to sustain for a whole play.'

Codron also felt doubtful. 'When the play arrived, I could not see Truscott and Ken at all. It needed a lugubriousness and dopiness. Ken is a bright person.' But Williams wanted to do the play. With his confidence renewed, he was facing 'an embarrassment of choices [. . .] (a) a revue thing on the telly, (b) a film about Poe's undersea myth, (c) the possible Joe Orton play. I know that it's the theatre that I want more than anything else. That much is definite. Out of the theatre, I am like some awful fish gasping for air, and become something without value and justification.' He had already rejected Binkie Beaumont's proposal of a Victorian farce, *The Private Secretary*, and he wanted to see Orton succeed. When he read that Jean Simmons was in London, he called Codron, urging him to cast her as Fay. The decision to take a role that suited him so badly seems to have been settled on the evening he first met Orton.

Truscott was written for Williams, as Jack o' the Green had been, but Jack was based on the writer's insight into his friend's puckish cruelty. Inspector Truscott of the Yard and the Water Board was inspired by a real policeman, Detective Sergeant Harold 'Tanky' Challenor, whose corrupt devotion to justice had been exposed by a Metropolitan Police inquiry. The former SAS commando had become a media figure celebrated for making swathes of arrests in Mayfair and Soho as he worked a hundred hours a week, and for the confessions his suspects made under interrogation. When it was revealed that prisoners were being beaten and convictions were obtained with planted evidence, a police psychiatrist examined Challenor and told the inquiry that the detective was 'quite mad indeed'.

In a post-war culture that revered the gruff decency of *Gideon of the Yard* and *Dixon of Dock Green*, it was incomprehensible to see a copper accused of beating up one suspect (a *Peace News* cartoonist) seven times before producing a brick and charging him with possession of an offensive weapon. 'Orton was obsessed with Challenor,' Williams said. 'He never stopped reading the reports and giggling uncontrollably.' Orton believed that all British institutions were hypocritical. Morality was as meaningless as small talk, and the reassuring catchphrases of law and order were revealed as obscene pantomime. 'You're fucking nicked, my old beauty,' Truscott says as he arrests *Loot*'s only innocent victim, and the line was nicked from Challenor himself.

Orton and Halliwell had also been arrested, in 1962, for stealing and damaging seventy-two books, smuggled out of Islington Library in a satchel and a gas-mask case. They removed hundreds of art plates to paper the walls of their Islington bedsit, and to create collages on the book jackets.

They were taken into custody by police who obtained a search warrant after a piece of entrapment: a council letter, requiring them to remove an abandoned vehicle, provoked an incensed response from Halliwell, who protested that neither he nor Orton had ever owned a car. It was typed on the same distinctive machine used to write the library blurbs and, with this as evidence, the police obtained permission to search the flat. Orton and Halliwell were sentenced at Old Street magistrates' court to six months, concurrently on each of five counts of theft and malicious damage to books, and fined 40 shillings each, with £262 17s 6d in damages and costs. Orton shrugged it off. 'I should probably have been birched. They won't ever do that so they just sent me to prison for six months.' The sentence shattered Halliwell, but Orton regarded it as an education and was more angry at the police deception and the council's insistence on claiming back the damages at 30 shillings a week.

When Williams visited the bedsit, he was fascinated by the collages – death masks and courtesans over the fireplace, ecstatic saints and Van Gogh landscapes around the bookcases, Monet nudes above the radio and Pompeii mosaic frescoes of male youths over the writing desk. The beds were unmade, with the blankets neatly folded on them in army dormitory style; St Francis stood guard over one, Michelangelo's Mary over the other. Orton claimed the pictures had been cut from magazines.

Delighted by his shameless and successful new friend, Williams began to show him off. He pretended to be aggrieved when Orton boasted of *Sloane*'s arrival on Broadway and of his plans for *Loot*, but mostly the writer sat in amused awe while Williams talked. 'Moira and I had invited Ken over to Islington, to our little house there, for lunch,' Baxter remembered. 'He had a very low threshold for boredom. And so after lunch, when he suddenly got bored, he said, "Let's go, let's walk round and see Joe. No distance, let's walk, lovely day." I asked if he knew the way – "Of course I know the way, I know the whole district very well, I was born here." And so we went round, and I was rather looking forward to hearing Orton speak. I'm still waiting to hear him. Ken just took over again. And the murderer [Halliwell] made a nice pot of tea and some biscuits, but otherwise there was no communication with either of them.'

Seeing the excitement that comic and playwright sparked in each other, Michael Codron decided to press ahead. He asked Peter Wood to direct, following his success with the Shaffer plays, and wrote to remind Williams of his own comment that when an actor signed to a play that, like *Loot*, would be gestating during a provincial tour, he should commit to it 'for the length of a normal pregnancy'. Williams, who had wriggled so long to avoid a contract longer than half a year for Codron's *One Over the Eight*, signed up for nine months.

Desmond Heeley, the designer on *Gentle Jack*, was brought in to create the set: Wood envisaged it as layers of white, in art nouveau patterns, with the actors silhouetted in dark costumes. 'We did it in black and white as a sort of Pop Art set,' Wood said. 'I was thinking of things like Tom and Jerry where [. . .] the essential violence has been stylised to the point where it's acceptable.' Orton lacked the confidence to tell this experienced director that his set revealed an utter lack of understanding. Codron felt he had to trust to the expertise of the man he had appointed, and Williams, though he knew the dialogue needed a realistic backdrop and not abstract cartoons, was struggling to find a voice for the policeman.

Challenor was heavy-set, brutal, addicted to doling out violence. Williams, slight and mercurial, fantasised about masochistic beatings. What Orton saw as similarities between their characters were really opposites: both men could be vicious, but one was physical, which the other could never be. Williams was narcissistic and fragile, where Challenor had invulnerable delusions of grandeur. There is nothing in all the pompous constables and pedantic council officials that Williams portrayed for Galton and Simpson, or the Blimps and bores he played for Cook, or the nervous, hungry private eye he created for Shaffer, that suggests he could ever have found a convincing mode for Truscott. Deadpan; obtuse; dully menacing; stupidly self-satisfied; soulless; a thug without wit or imagination or self-doubt: Harry H. Corbett could have played it, or even Sid James, but never Kenneth Williams.

Loot went into rehearsals at the beginning of 1965, though the Lord Chamberlain's office was protesting that the corpse had to be an obvious dummy and should never be undressed. Wood began to demand rewrites, including a new ending and an extra character, an assistant to Truscott. Williams was alarmed. Wood gave him a pipe to toy with, which left him almost unable to walk and talk.

He found it so difficult to act while handling props that, during the filming of *Twice Around the Daffodils*, when he had been required to deliver his lines while moving pieces on a chessboard, Gerry Thomas had resorted to filming the moves in long shot and cutting them into the dialogue. On stage, Williams disobeyed the director and dispensed with the pipe; within two weeks he was refusing to accept further changes to the script. 'If much more of this goes on, the cast will be nerve wracked. As it was, I watched them run through it, and felt the usual thing that I felt when watching sketches in the revue that I wasn't in – that feeling that everyone in the cast is better than I am.'

Though Williams's confidence was guttering, there was a thrill of media anticipation at the collaboration between radio's favourite anarchist and the latest bad boy of theatre. Predicting his arrival in the West End with *Loot*, *Plays and Players* published a full-page profile, calling him 'dangerously entertaining [. . .] behind those popular vocal effects a serious actor seems sometimes to be lurking: an actor of oddly sinister power'.

The piece emphasised his professionalism, and Williams was dedicated to making *Loot* a success: after one rehearsal, he invited Ian McShane, who was playing Hal, back to Farley Court so they could continue working. But all the cast knew the play was in fragments, and their tempers frayed; when McShane stumbled over one of the rewrites, Williams shouted at him, 'If you'd read the script properly, you wouldn't make such a mistake!' Later, when McShane seemed hurt, he apologised, but the episode was one in a catalogue of frustrations: 'One continually forgets how sensitive people are.' Wood insisted that the lines must be delivered with metronomic rhythm, and when the actors continued to vary the pace he threatened to install a real metronome. This time it was Duncan Macrae who rebelled, with Williams backing him up – 'I've never heard such an absurd idea.'

The company opened in Cambridge's Arts Theatre the following Monday, after a stand-up row during the dress rehearsal. Orton had written a prologue, where Truscott and his sidekick, Meadows, pushed a gramophone in a pram across the front of the stage. They were dressed as tramps, and debating whether their policemen's boots gave away their disguises; as the gramophone blared 'Abide with Me', the curtain went up on the first act. 'I suddenly realised that the first scene was totally alien in style to the first Act. Asked Wood to cut it. There was an appalling display of bad temper and pique in front of the entire cast in that awful green room. I said it embarrassed me [. . .] The only reason it is there is because of a fundamental attitude to the play which is WRONG – and a view held only by him – not the author.' Williams continued to defend Orton's vision, even if he could not make it out himself, and tried to convince himself that all that was missing was an audience's laughter.

On the morning before the play opened, the director phoned Williams at his hotel room and announced the front-cloth scene was reinstated. That night, after floundering through the performance, he had supper with Eade and dissected the problems. The cast was strong, and he thought Geraldine McEwan as Fay was excellent, but Wood was trying to force Restoration comedy manners on to a psychopathic farce, and the rewrites were full of contradictions. Eade shrugged and said he thought the make-up was wrong. According to the critics, all of it was wrong, everything. 'A particularly nauseating article', the *Cambridge Review* called it, 'an evening of very British rubbish'. Orton wrote to Halliwell: 'The play is a disaster. There were hardly any laughs for Truscott. The audience seems to take the most extraordinary lines with dead seriousness [. . .] I've already had two rows of nerve-wracking proportions.' Codron felt Williams was wearing his detective's raincoat like an SS uniform, and playing Truscott as Heinrich Himmler.

'It was a mistake not to have plumped for absolute realism,' Wood later said. 'I was kind of afraid of the play.' After the debacle of Cambridge, he decided the plot lacked the anarchic logic of the dialogue, and demanded more rewrites from Orton. During the six-week tour, 133 new sheets would be inserted into the 89-page script, and by the time they opened at Brighton's Theatre Royal the cast were performing one version to an audience while rehearsing another during the day. Reactions were dire: 'Near us in the dining room we heard a woman saying (about the play), "It's all disgusting – all about pregnancies," and another woman saying, "I left at the interval – I thought it was awful."' Friends who came backstage could say nothing to console the cast. Laurence Olivier commiserated, 'You haven't got a play here, that's your trouble.'

'It was the most painful period of my life,' Williams said, as he made his diaries available for research to Orton's biographer. 'We never did establish the confidence for the simple reason that we were in a terrible quandary ourselves, wondering which version was the right one.' He admired Orton's creative diligence, his determination to succeed, qualities which Wood saw too: 'They always looked like two delinquent schoolboys to me, both of them rejoicing in one another's schoolboy cleverness. And both needed success.' Wood exploited that by sending Orton back to the plot again and again. The playwright's agent, Peggy Ramsay, protested that his voice was being obliterated. So was Williams's voice, in a different way – he was chain-smoking to quell his nerves, and becoming hoarse. When they reached Oxford's New Theatre, the play had evolved again, and it died again.

Williams was so dejected that he was becoming humble. After hours of rehearsals in the theatre bar and on stage, and a post-mortem over dinner, he wrote: 'P.W. came out of it rather splendidly. I objected to a straight line in one part of his plotting and he blew up at me, but I was definitely in the wrong.' The opening night was grim, and after the second performance Geraldine McEwan came off stage in tears, saying that she couldn't go on any longer. 'She had to be taken home and given sedation,' Orton wrote to Halliwell. But he blamed Williams for the play's collapse. 'Everyone on the verge of a nervous breakdown. Kenneth Williams disastrous – just all his old performances from Beyond Our Ken. And then he wonders why he isn't getting laughs. "Ow many 'usbands 'ave you 'ad?" (Ugh).' Like Tony Hancock, Orton was reacting to the Snide voice; both felt it wrecked the realism of the dialogue.

Loot opened in Golders Green the following week, where Codron brought Donald Albery, his co-producer, to see the reshaped play. Fenella Fielding also came: '*Loot* was bad. It was really dreadful. Kenneth was so bad in it – he couldn't play it, and that's that. That part should have been played by somebody very ordinary, and he couldn't do that; he kept camping it up and taking it really so far. It had to be played straight as a die. The audience hadn't the slightest idea what hit them.'

It got worse at the Bournemouth Pavilion, where Orton commented that all he could hear was the banging of seats as people left: half the audience walked out one evening, and he overheard an usherette complain that it was 'unnecessarily filthy . . . as if there was a necessary amount of filth'. Peter Wood sat in the circle at the Opera House in Manchester, bellowing laughter but unable to start the audience laughing with him.

The mutilated script was further gouged and cut by the city's watch committee, a civic board of censors that was empowered to ban plays that had not been approved by the Lord Chamberlain's office: the cast performed in Manchester with a real policeman in the wings, ready to close the theatre if the actors dared speak lines that had been forbidden. Benedict Nightingale in the *Guardian* called the play 'incorrigibly flippant and pointless [. . .] so flat and heavy that it lays low even Mr Williams's bright antics'.

By the time they reached Wimbledon Theatre, the tour's last date, Codron knew *Loot* was unlikely to reach the West End. The cast and the director would be relieved to see it close, and the co-producer, Albery, detested it: 'He would pretend that he was trying to offer me a theatre and never did.' The management at the Phoenix in Charing Cross Road, a stage of last resort, announced they would rather stay dark than have Orton. Codron struggled to avoid defeat, and spent one of *Loot*'s last performances waiting by a phonebox outside, his last hopes pinned on an offer from the Garrick that never came.

Backstage, Geraldine McEwan was telling Williams that, even if Codron did prevail, he would have to find another actress for Fay. The disgust of the audience was summed up by a woman who strode across to Codron and Wood at the end of the night, pointed to her embarrassed daughter and declared, 'It was Felicity's twenty-first!' The following night, Codron told the cast that he might be able to persuade the Lyric Hammersmith to prolong the tour. Everyone declined.

Williams mourned *Loot*'s death: its run had been even shorter than *Gentle Jack*'s, just fifty-five performances. He knew that he had been as good as he could be as Jack, and that as Truscott he had failed. The knowledge was crippling. Three nights later, he woke from a nightmare that his hand had been sliced off; it was stitched back on but, despite the doctors' promises that he would recover, it hung there dead and grey.

'The end of *Loot* started my decline in being friendly with Kenneth,' Codron said. He tried to usher him straight into another revue, with Dora Bryan and Eleanor Bron, but Williams felt heartsick at the thought of it. His hopes fluttered at the thought of a play directed by John Osborne at the Royal Court, and of a two-hander by Charles Dyer, *Staircase*, but he turned down both scripts when he saw them. Osborne sent a telegram, asking him at least to discuss it; Williams wrote back to say he would not even talk about it over the phone. Persuasion, he explained, always preceded disaster. Undeterred, Osborne wrote to persuade him. Williams answered with a flat refusal.

He refused, too, to fly to Paris at Orson Welles's request for a voiceover, or to audition as Maxime once more for Peter Glenville's film of *Hotel Paradiso*, or to direct a Feydeau farce, *The Birdwatcher*, or to listen when Eade told him he should not accept £5,000 to make a *Carry On* when he was so much admired in Hollywood.

Williams was mortified rather than depressed. After a friend, Andrew Ray, attempted suicide, he visited him in hospital and wondered that anyone could care enough to kill themselves. 'He still wants to die,' Williams noted. 'Well, so do we all – or rather, so do I: but while we're in this suffering state it seems we have to make the best of it, and get on each other's nerves as little as possible.'

Orton and Halliwell told him, lounging in deckchairs in Regent's Park, that they were going to Tangier, and he began to think he needed a holiday – to set the pendulum swinging again, as he liked to say. Morocco with the rapacious Orton was too much swinging, though. Instead, he called Maggie Smith, to ask tentatively if Beverley Cross might be free for another Mediterranean cruise. Cross seized on the idea: he drove Williams out to their country cottage, gave him champagne on the lawn, and spread out the maps. Within two days they had plotted an itinerary from Athens to Istanbul and the Greek islands.

The days dragged before the holiday – after an afternoon of bickering and Scrabble with Louie and Pat, he wrote: 'I thought tonight, "There is no point in your living at all. You're just about getting

thro' the process of eating + drinking and earning money and occasionally talking a lot of drivel to some poor unfortunate you manage
to buttonhole, but you'd be better off dead and that's a fact".' On the
day they flew out, he woke with his spirits already lifting: Athens the
next day was beautiful, and the 'cascades of salmon pink blossoms'
took his breath away on the coastal road to the palace of Agamemnon
at Mycenae.

He allowed himself to be led by Cross, who possessed a sixth sense
for authentic cuisine, and by the time they boarded the *Marmara*,
Williams was cheerful. He was thrilled by Istanbul, exploring its
cathedrals and mosques, and fascinated by Islamic calligraphy in the
Hagia Sophia museum. Buttoned up to the collar in jacket and tie,
he managed to sunburn his nose so badly that it bled. They flew back
to Athens, and on to Heraklion in Crete where Williams found a
postcard waiting for him: Gordon Jackson had begun filming in Israel
as Williams started his holiday, and had timed his message to give his
friend a boost. The forethought and affection revealed in that gesture
explain why Williams regarded Jackson and his family as his most
supportive friends.

If he had felt relaxed in Istanbul, he was utterly abandoned in
Crete: 'We drove to Fedhele – birthplace of El Greco + had a picnic
lunch. (I am sitting in the hotel room at the Astir writing this –
completely naked and feeling half drunk with the wine and the
heat).' An English teacher persuaded him to talk about the theatre to
her pupils, a family gave them lunch at their farm, and Williams was
falling in love with the island until he found two travellers' cheques
had been stolen from his room. When he arrived in London, he took
his dirty laundry over to Kensington for his mother to wash, like a
boy home from a school trip.

With *Carry On Cowboy* due to start filming, Williams had a medical and took riding lessons – he played an old judge in a frontier
town who is taken hostage in his nightshirt by Sid James's outlaw,
the Rumpo Kid. Though he was famous for his decrepit old man
whose catchphrase on *Beyond Our Ken* was 'Thirty-five years!' this
was the first time he had portrayed an older character on film. He
gave Judge Burke his stock American bluster, based on a mumbling
impersonation of Hal Roach, which caused problems for the sound

recordists. When he saw the rushes, he was critical: 'The voice took a bit of getting used to [. . .] It's really too old + wheezy, for the face. The two things don't quite match.' The result was his least successful *Carry On*, a minor role with star billing. Jon Pertwee's myopic and short-lived sheriff earned more laughs.

He did a forty-minute TV comedy for ITA, *The Celebrity*, co-starring Hugh Paddick and written by Dave Freeman. *Film* magazine asked Williams to write 400 words about working with the designer Richard Williams. It was his first commission, so innocuous that he did not feel self-conscious, and he typed it in the conversational style of his letters. None of this soothed the bruises left by *Loot*. When he and Beverley Cross bumped into John Hurt in a theatre pub, the Salisbury, Williams made a point of calling Peter Wood 'a shit + a fraud', hoping the words would be relayed to the director.

Peter Eade had been pressing Williams to try a new tack. If he could not face filming in the States, he might direct that Feydeau in London – Binkie Beaumont would be delighted to back it. Williams did not want to try anything new. He wanted to relive his successes. The only play that had satisfied him for years was *The Public Eye*, and that had been perfection: he had supported a star he adored, in a small cast that did not rely on him for all the laughs, with a sparkling script and the critics scrambling over each other to offer bouquets. After the purgatory of *Gentle Jack* and *Loot*, he needed the safety of a hit play.

The Platinum Cat by Roger Longrigg had none of the hallmarks. The plot was thin and the style was old-fashioned, all one-liners and rising panic. Williams liked the play, which centred on a man besot-ted with his mistress, because he saw it as a perfect vehicle for Smith; she did not accept it, but Cross, whose relationship with Smith was falling apart, offered to direct. Richard Williams agreed to design the cartoons on the set. Surrounded by friends, Williams resolved to take the starring role as Bernard, a newspaper strip cartoonist, and accepted Caroline Mortimer as his foil.

He pretended that he expected a success, but anxiety about return-ing to the stage was making him ill: he had developed an obsession about dieting, and was barely eating. He was thirty-nine, and at his heaviest weighed less than ten stone; still, he was convinced his stom-ach was distended, and on days when he was not fasting he would eat only once. By the time of his costume fitting for *The Platinum Cat*, his waist was twenty-eight inches, his weight eight stones seven pounds in shirt and trousers. When Kenneth Horne threw a lunch, 'I only had the meat + some beans + cheese. They all said it was silly for me to diet and kept saying I looked haggard etc., but it's only because they were all overeating like mad and they've all got great paunches, and I don't want to get like that. I don't mind after I'm fifty, but not before.'

After the first rehearsal of *Platinum Cat*, he had a cup of lemon tea with Cross, and worried whether Mortimer could play comedy: 'If not, we're all going to be sunk without trace [. . .] he says the foundation is there, and that she has enormous sex appeal. Well of course I don't know anything about all that.' The next day he took her on one side and warned her to lose weight: ' "You're much too heavy," I said to her.'

Four weeks of rehearsals did not settle his nerves. He bickered with Cross, arguing about the moves, the pace and the delivery, issuing instructions to other actors that contradicted the direction, and refighting all his battles with Peter Wood. Cross was patient and professional, accustomed from their holidays together to these nervous outbursts. When Mortimer complained that he was continually telling her how to act, Williams called himself stupid and begged forgiveness. Contrition always calmed him.

He continued to diet, and became so thin that his clothes no longer fitted him: he noted happily that he owned only two suits, so it wasn't as if he was wasting a whole wardrobe. After a run-through for Albery, who was considering the play for Wyndham's Theatre, he began to feel resigned, and grateful for spiritual comforts: 'Played the Bach Double Violin, and the Vivaldi in the evening [. . .] it leads me to the inner quiet and that much nearer to my striving for God. My need is so great that sometimes I feel like some great dam waiting to burst – and my eyes start to fill with tears – so I just pray and pray. One thing is certain, HE is never far from my thoughts.'

They opened in Brighton, with Williams exercising as well as dieting – sit-ups, fifty press-ups and running on the spot, two or three times a day. If he ate two crispbreads, he noted the indulgence; two chocolates and he chastised himself; two glasses of wine and he embraced his hangover with self-loathing. On opening night, he rewarded himself with a slice of gateau, which he had been anticipating for days. Gordon Jackson and Bill Pertwee came backstage to offer praise, and Albery announced that Wyndham's would have the play. '1st house, very good. 2nd house, better still,' he noted on 30 October.

Peter Eade looked at the takings – £2,600 in one week at Brighton – and complained they should have demanded at least double the salary. Williams had seen Jackson's new Jaguar, and knew what his friends were making in movies and television, but insisted that he did not feel envious: 'My point is – there are two ways to negotiate a salary. 1) get as much as you can. 2) get what you need to live on. The second is the way I like to do business. It's quite enough for me.'

After a week in Oxford and another in Birmingham, where the reviews were indifferent, Williams was full of spite and dread at the opening night in London. He was suddenly certain the play would flop, and that all his technique could not compensate for a weak script and his co-star's inexperience. The first reviews were insipid, except for Ronald Bryden in the *New Statesman*: 'Mr Williams shows himself one of the most brilliantly accomplished comic actors extant, wrapping himself round the good lines like Edith Evans round Wilde's handbag, wading into the weaker ones, gobbling and preening like some exotic fowl at dust-bath, until they glitter in the air.' Other reviewers deplored the play's thin plot and superficial style, but audiences did not care: the box office predicted a hit.

Jeremy Rundall's review in *Plays and Players* the next month was a rave, calling Williams 'an electrically driven, life-sized model made of Potty Putty and endowed with one of the most off-beat voices in the theatre [. . .] Within his self-imposed limits his range is immense. He can be sardonic, self-deprecating, abusive, pathetic, triumphant, desolate, sexy or eremitic, changing mood with a single modulation of his voice, with a twist of his shoulders [. . .] He is one of the most articulate actors in the theatre, so that when silence does come it is devastating [. . .] Suddenly he stops talking, and it is as though the sun has gone out.'

By the time the piece appeared, silence had descended. Williams believed the play was a flop, a piece of dead theatre that he had to reanimate each night with the vitality of his performance. He dismissed the praise of friends as sympathetic embarrassment, and was even ashamed of himself for his prayers, for asking God to give him full houses instead of being thankful for the nightly strength to carry on.

At night he couldn't sleep, but when he went to his hairdresser's he dropped off in the chair; the barber, Henry Watson, who had been cutting his hair since Charlie retired, nudged him awake and remarked on the poor reviews he'd read for *Platinum Cat*. Williams left the shop with a sense of doom and, he suspected, a headful of flu germs: 'Henry had a cold there. I know. If it hits me badly I shall go to Patrick Woodcock and get a letter to be off,' he promised himself. Over the next three days he mapped the encroaching symptoms, and then cut his face when he stumbled and almost fainted on stage.

Despite his obsession with petty fluctuations in his health, Williams had rarely missed any performance in his career – he had postponed an operation until after the run of *Pieces of Eight*, for instance, and a heavy cold had kept him away from *Share My Lettuce* for just one night. This time, he seized the excuse. On Tuesday 7 December 1965 he phoned Woodcock, his doctor, and asked him to write to the producers at Wyndham's, David Conville and John Gale. Then he took to his bed. Louie brought him food the following day, and Williams lay under the blankets, aching and wretched.

The play was insured against early closure provoked by the indisposition of its star. With poor reviews, receding audiences and a struggling cast, Williams's withdrawal suited most people. The insurers sent a doctor, who heard his complaints and said, 'Frankly, I'm amazed you stuck it as long as you did.' The play was taken off, and Williams felt a cloud lift: 'No longer the fear of having to return and perform that vacuous rubbish every night, with a leading actress who couldn't get a laugh out of a backside.' He felt so restored that he called John Hussey, who brought round a fish-and-chip supper. They devoured it.

Williams knew he had not been too physically ill to continue. He had suffered a crisis of confidence, a mental collapse that he regarded as a breakdown. After *Gentle Jack*, he had feared his dramatic presence was not enough to sustain a weak play. After *Loot*, he had known that all his stagecraft and celebrity catchphrases could not shape difficult material to his mould. Now, in *Platinum Cat*, he was expected to carry a lightweight cast through a thin play. Everything depended on him. He could not bear it. A fear gripped him that suicide was the only cure for a breakdown, and the only course left to an actor unfit for the stage. Sheila Hancock, who had suffered a flop on Broadway with *Entertaining Mr Sloane*, called and listened to his worries for more than two hours; Michael Codron brought him a gangling pot plant, and Nora Stapleton came to cook for him.

His oldest friend was in Australia and due to return in the New Year. Moira Baxter came to lunch and suggested that if Williams needed a holiday, he might fly to Beirut; her husband could meet him there on his way back to Britain. Baxter, in fact, had hoped to return via Hong Kong, but he rearranged his plans so as to meet Williams at the airport in the Lebanon. 'Made me change all my arrangements so I could be with him on Christmas morning,' Baxter said. 'He rang me and he was in a pitiful state – "It's all just death, dear! Yesss, well, I've been alone all my life." All hearts and flowers . . . So I stepped off the plane and there was a bad face waiting for me. But I think he was pleased.'

Baxter was concerned that his friend's morbid tone hid more than the usual ennui and feels in retrospect that this crisis marked the beginning of a change in Williams's attitude to suicide, as it shifted from a dark temptation to a bleak destination. 'Whether he'd have taken the pills with him to Beirut if I hadn't been there . . . He might have done. He certainly had a strong suicidal tendency from halfway through his life.'

'You always talk to the one you *don't* like'
February 1965–August 1967

After the first night of *Loot* in Oxford, two undergradu-ates strolled back to their digs discussing Kenneth Williams's disjointed performance. One of them, an English student called David, wondered what the actor could be like in real life, a man who appeared to combine such intelligent wit with the bawdiest humour. The other, Tom Waine, a Christchurch scholar in the last year of his history degree, suggested they should each write a fan letter and ask to meet him. David's letter was 'long and boring, all about modern theatre and trends and actors'. Tom insisted they send his own letter instead. It read:

> Dear Mr Williams,
> There are amongst Oxford's dreaming spires two quite undreamed-of young men who have charm, elegance, poise and, how shall I say, a sort of quiet beauty. If you have had as much difficulty meeting them in the last two weeks as we have in the last two years, perhaps you would care to come round for a conciliatory cup of coffee to the above address.

The day after they sent it, a telegram arrived: 'UNABLE ATTEND YOU COFFEE IN LONDON FOR WORK RETURN OXFORD TONIGHT KENNETH WILLIAMS.' A note followed, in pencil: 'Dear Mr Waine – will eleven o'clock tomorrow suit you? I could call fr. this belated coffee then, if not convenient leave message by phone at the Mitre + I'll under-stand. Yrs Kenneth W.'

At 11 a.m. on Friday 19 February 1965, Williams knocked on the door of the Georgian house at 15 St John Street, and as he walked up to the first-floor apartment he was hiding his nervousness behind his *Carry On* persona. 'Yess, hellloooo, it was all that,' Waine said. 'I put some music on, light classics, and they just talked about theatre, especially Brecht. They went on and on, and then he suddenly turned round and said, "Do we have to have this bloody music on? I can't hear myself speak!" After about twenty minutes, I said, "Do you want a cup of coffee then?" and he said, "That's what I bleeding come up here for!" So I got the coffee, and I thought, he obviously doesn't like me, it's David he likes.'

Williams took them to lunch at his hotel, the Mitre, where most of the talk centred on trends in acting. As they were leaving, he suggested they meet for lunch again, before the next day's matinée. In that evening's diary, he wrote: 'Received this charming fan letter, + went this morning to meet Tom Waine and David [B]. They were quite delightful and made it a pleasant break in the tour [. . .] Both those boys thought it was a lousy play. I think it is rude of them to say so. I do.'

Saturday morning's rehearsals of the latest version of *Loot* were fraught: Duncan Macrae was drying up nightly on stage, unable to remember which lines had been replaced, and was hectoring the cast to compensate for his embarrassment. Tom and David waited for Williams at the stage door; lunch was a more muted and awkward occasion than the first, and Williams noted later that he had felt unreal, as though part of him was so shocked at his forwardness that it had stepped out of his body and was staring at him in amazement. After a glass of port, David left, saying he had a tutorial. Knowing that Williams had an afternoon performance, Waine made to leave too. 'Ken said, "No, dearie, sit down, have a brandy." So I said, "Well, you get on very well with David, don't you?"

'He said, "Mmm, well, you always talk to the one you *don't* like, don't you?"

'And that was the remark that really started a friendship. I said, "You seemed to be so engrossed."

'"Yes . . . boring queen, dear, boring Jewish queen."

'We chatted on for about an hour, until I said, "Do you want to give me your address?"

'He said, "Oh, I don't think so."

'I said, "Fine, OK, well, you know, be lovely to see you again."'

Though he had found a way to state, obliquely, his attraction to Waine, he was not brave enough to make a date to meet again, much less arrange to see him that night. Instead, he took a car back to Farley Court after the last performance, reaching home so late that the porter was asleep on the lobby sofa and he had to bang on the glass door to be let in. But the next morning he resolved to give Waine at least a hint of encouragement, and sent a note on headed paper: 'V. pleasant seeing you on Saturday. The matinee was foul but last house good: so it took the sting out of the week.'

Bouts of jaundice and flu prevented Waine from visiting London and, instead, a correspondence began, which for Williams was the most propitious way of developing a friendship. By March he was signing, 'love Kenyeth', and by 3 April his letters were full of the surreal innuendo he reserved for trusted friends.

This nascent friendship had become less alarming to him when Waine revealed he had a steady boyfriend, a young postman named Clive Dennis. They had met at a party the previous year: Dennis was engaged to be married, but Waine was smitten and tried to call him three times at the Post Office. 'That was embarrassing,' Dennis said. 'Postmen just were not gay in those days.' They met again, by chance, in August 1964, when Dennis was hitch-hiking, and a relationship began. 'It was fate. It had to happen,' Dennis said with conviction. Almost half a century later, they are still together, living in an elegant house, furnished with paintings and ornaments that are mementoes, not only of their friendships in the theatre world but of Transformation, the interior design business they ran in the early seventies.

Before agreeing to share their deep knowledge of Kenneth Williams for this biography, they had never spoken publicly about their friend: in scores of entries in the edited edition of the Williams diaries, and also in the published version of Joe Orton's diaries, they are identified only as 'Tom' and 'Clive'. Throughout their twelve-year friendship, a platonic relationship that nevertheless was the closest that Williams ever approached to a steady love affair, Waine kept all his handwritten notes and letters in careful order, almost 200 of them.

Williams was relieved to have an excuse for confining his sexual interest in Waine to his fantasies – there was 'the friend', even if he felt jealous that the undergraduate preferred a young man who was broad-shouldered and barrel-chested with a rakish grin. He wrote to Waine to tell him that John Schlesinger and Geoffrey Sharp were throwing one of their notorious parties: 'I could always take you along if you liked, but I think it might be a little wild + I don't know that Clive would care for that.' In another flash of confidence, he added his latest telephone number. Williams changed it regularly, because he hated to be phoned when he didn't feel like talking, especially when the call concerned work. He preferred all producers to contact his agent, and all acquaintances to write; only close friends should ring (and then never before 10 a.m.).

On the evening of the party, 8 April, Waine and Dennis arrived at Farley Court in a red MG Midget that Waine's father had given him when he threatened to buy a motorbike. Before going on to Schlesinger's house in Kensington, they had drinks in Williams's austere apartment above Baker Street tube.

'It was like a show flat,' Waine said. 'Dark green fitted carpet, no wallpaper, just white walls, absolutely empty kitchen units. There were a few pictures, original paintings, but G-Plan furniture in this little sitting-room; a bookcase with the diaries, and an Anglepoise lamp and this one chair, and that was it, that was the flat. The bedroom was very small and simple, a single bed and a boxlike bedside table with a lamp on it. Everything was absolutely minimal. When he gave you drinks he would produce a little bottle out of the kitchen cupboard.'

The newcomers caused a stir at the party: one theatre luminary appointed himself their guardian, and Williams enjoyed a frisson of notoriety as the corrupter of two innocents. He had discovered the ideal consorts: the young men were welcome guests, they reflected youth and glory upon him, they were light-hearted and, since they were a couple, he could slot into his favourite role, as the third wheel, the centre of all types of attention except sexual. During the next few months, Waine and Dennis found a flat in Highgate Village, on Shepherd's Hill, and Williams saw more of them, especially after his return from Beirut. As Dennis saw it, 'He was in love with Tom, in the only way that Ken could be.'

'I think it's a bit glib to say he was in love with me,' Waine said. 'Perhaps he was in one sense, but Ken's form of love wasn't like anybody else's and that's what people don't understand about him. He loved the idea of me, the idea that I was at Oxford, and tall and blond. He loved the ethos of me. I was something that Ken would like to have been. Ken was always very aware of his background, of coming from King's Cross, going to the local school. I seemed to be quite prosperous, and Ken liked people who were prosperous.'

For eight years, Tom Waine and Clive Dennis were Williams's closest companions, so much a part of him that he introduced them to most of his other friends – an unprecedented confidence. His relationships were generally sealed off from one another: Baxter, for instance, remembers dining at an Italian restaurant when Williams walked in with Maggie Smith, spotted his army friend and 'she was swirled round and taken out the door. He wanted to monopolise her, and he felt if she started getting interested in me, it would just detract from him.' Waine and Dennis were shared and shown off; they met his mother, and soon Louie was a regular at Shepherd's Hill too. They became good friends of Hattie Jacques and Joan Sims, and dined with the Baxters, the Jacksons and with Ronnie Knight and Barbara Windsor.

Partly this was forced on Williams by their confident, gregarious personalities: he could not wrap up their affection and confine them to a corner of his life, as he did with the diffident Nora Stapleton. Mainly, though, he shared his life with them because he wanted to – he loved the relief from loneliness and the obligation of yearning which that imposed. As long as he had Waine, he need not berate himself for living without a lover ... and as long as Waine had Dennis, he felt safe from any risk of a physical relationship.

Williams returned from the Lebanon at the start of 1966 determined to break with the stage. James Roose-Evans asked him to star in an adaptation of Dylan Thomas's *The Skin Game*: 'Replied saying I didn't want to do anything in the theatre fr. a long long time. This is true. I just can't risk getting tied-up in something that could cause me anxiety + pain + eventually drive me neurotic with worry.' A chance encounter confirmed his loathing for theatre life – a car hooted, and Williams turned to see the driver was an acquaintance from the doomed run of *Platinum Cat*. 'Suddenly I was plunged back into the meretricious atmosphere of that bloody play. I could have screamed [. . .] I *never* want to get mixed up in that world ever again.'

Freed from the burden of his ambitions, and buoyed up by friendship, between 1966 and 1973 Williams would achieve the greater part of his most famous work – the best of the *Carry On* films; his television breakthrough with *International Cabaret*; *Round the Horne* and *Just a Minute* on radio, and his first appearances in the role that would transform him into a national treasure, as a TV chat-show guest. He also poured out his life into his diary and his letters during these years, in a multimillion-word torrent.

It was the first episode of *Round the Horne* that had taken him to London on the day Waine proposed coffee. *Beyond Our Ken* had been wrecked by Eric Merriman's demands: by February 1964, after seven series, the show was attracting 10 million listeners a week, and Merriman became the first scriptwriter to be billed in *Radio Times* above the cast. Kenneth Horne found him 'more swollen-headed and difficult each day. I really don't know whether I can face another series with him at the helm.'

Horne, whose schedule across radio and both BBC and independent TV was frenetic, was booked to appear in a Light Programme show called *Down with Women*. Merriman issued an ultimatum: he had made Horne into a star, and he reserved the right to veto any broadcasts that featured him. *Down with Women* was too similar to *Beyond Our Ken*, he claimed – if the BBC didn't withdraw the programme, he would quit, and he would not allow anyone to take over the writing of *Beyond Our Ken*. On 24 September 1964, he carried out his threat. Hugh Paddick broke the news to Williams, who realised that, as much as the income, he would miss his status as national court jester.

Horne refused to see his team broken up. He pleaded with Roy Rich, the head of light entertainment, to commission a new series, and he took the cast for coffee and cakes at a pastry shop in Sloane Street to plot the future. Horne thought he could co-write the show with Barry Took, aided by a collaborator he had known for twenty years, a Salvation Army volunteer with three children and a grim determination with puns, named Mollie Millest. She had been contributing, uncredited, to *Beyond Our Ken* for years as the erratic Merriman delivered incomplete scripts long after deadline.

Horne's influence on the writing was also swelling: though no one could deliver a pun with more relish, what he really loved to slip in was a ripe innuendo. 'I'm all for censorship,' he liked to declare: 'if I ever see a double entendre, I whip it out!' The jokes had become saucier – in the penultimate *Beyond Our Ken*, Williams was rescued from an avalanche: 'Oh, I'm so cold,' Williams moaned. 'I keep rubbing my leg but it feels as if it doesn't belong to me.' 'It doesn't, but don't stop,' replied Betty Marsden.

Took convinced Roy Rich to let him co-write the series with Marty Feldman, a writer and stand-up whose comic imagination was not only fecund but randy. During the meeting, Rich's carnation fell out of his buttonhole; afterwards, Feldman and Took claimed they had deflowered the head of light entertainment. If the BBC did not know what sort of show they had commissioned, they had no excuse for naivety. During the opening trails in the first episode of *Round the Horne*, Williams announced that enthusiasts of flower arranging should stay tuned for a reading from *Lady Chatterley's Lover*. Louie Williams's laughter can be heard clearly on the recording, more like Sid James's dirty cackle than her son's whinny.

Round the Horne, broadcast as family listening at lunchtime on Sundays, acquired a reputation for loucheness. Every catchphrase, even the most innocent and meaningless, sounded saucy. A slew of complaints was provoked by a monologue that Horne wrote, celebrating a British delicacy relished by master bakers, the crumpet; with it brought a letter of disgust from a Member of Parliament, Sir Cyril Black, and a warning that the writers and cast must keep 'within reasonable bounds' or else face 'drastic steps to clean this show up'. Barry Took claimed that the BBC's director general, Hugh Greene, was *Round the Horne*'s greatest defender: when asked why, he replied, 'Well, I like dirty shows!'

All the dirtiest laughs fell to Kenneth Williams. As Horne told the audience, 'You can make anything sound as if it has a double meaning . . . if you know how.' And Williams knew how. Obvious innuendos were delivered straight, as though he were oblivious to the nuances. Everything else burst out in a crescendo of scandalised proprieties. When he interrupted Horne's monologues, he sounded like a hysterical landlady who has seen a chamber pot poking out beneath the bed – disgusted, and outraged, and terrified that her guests will see it too.

To his regular voices, Took and Feldman assigned names. He was J. Peasemold Gruntfuttock, a heavy-breathing cockney who harboured lewd fantasies about women TV presenters and complained about the lack of explicit sex on the BBC; Dr Chou En Ginsburg MA (failed), the fiendish mastermind who plotted to blackmail world governments by firing nuclear fireworks out of giant milk bottles; Spasm the butler, who felt a touch of the dooms coming on. Lecherous Arthur Fallowfield from *Beyond Our Ken* was reborn as a richer, funnier character, one that Williams grew to love playing – the incomprehensibly obscene folk singer, Ramblin' Syd Rumpo.

Fallowfield had ploughed his catchphrases into the ground: it was only the slyness in Williams's voice that made the repetition bearable as every week he murmured, 'I'll make no bones about it, I'm looking for love.' He got laughs with mild innuendo: 'Lorelei Nantucket . . . I can't think what it was I went out with her for, but whatever it was I didn't get it.' Syd Rumpo used the same West Country drawl to perform the Runcorn Splod Cobbler's Song, the Clacton Bogle Picker's Lament, and the Terrible Tale of the Somerset Nog.

What began as a one-note satire on folk revivalists became a tuneful, affectionate send-up of rural dialects and forgotten village customs. Ramblin' Syd became adored by the public, perhaps because his contempt for Kenneth Horne and the offhand disdain with which he pulled songs from his 'ganderbag' were balanced by his enthusiasm when he sang. Williams had a good, light singing voice, and he could fill a ballad with pathos as he told of a lovelorn orang-utan drowned at sea or a thieving cordwangler hanged by the postern for handling others' moulies.

The most celebrated characters on *Round the Horne* wrapped their subtexts in Polari, the slang of the gay world. Julian and Sandy, played by Paddick and Williams, were a pair of actors, 'just filling in between engagements' while they worked as cleaners or waiters. Jule and Sand didn't just speak Polari, they screamed it, throwing in the odd translation if they thought the audience needed help. They became so popular that protests arrived in sackloads if they were ever left out of the show. Most weeks they had the last sketch.

Sand liked to be sophisticated and slip in a bit of foreign tongue. 'We're entrepreneurs . . . That is your actual French,' he always boasted. The trade varied – one week they were film-makers, another restaurateurs, then wrestling promoters, guest-house proprietors, landscape gardeners, tattooists, pop-star managers and ticket touts.

Williams had reservations about the success of *Round the Horne*. In terms of ratings, its predecessor had been as successful, but *Beyond Our Ken* was regarded as mass entertainment and mostly ignored by critics. Those critics now embraced the new series and labelled it daring, ground-breaking, controversial: Williams was called outrageous, an epithet he had attracted for a decade and which he despised as lazy and meaningless.

In both shows he dominated by playing to the house, riding big laughs from the studio audience and baiting the rest of the cast. If his performances were now hailed as the best and boldest on radio, where two years earlier they had rarely been remarked, the difference had to be the material. And of course it was: Williams finally had revue sketches that were worthy of his talent. He had not worked with writers who were consistently this good since leaving *Hancock's Half Hour*. When he threw in an ad lib, Took and Feldman would seize it and turn a throwaway into the centrepiece of a sketch the following week, as if they were challenging Williams to heckle them. Early in the first series, Horne introduced a skit about the Boys in the BBC Backroom, and Williams halted the show with a snigger, a little squirt of toilet humour; the next week, the Backroom feature returned, with that snigger developed into a scripted gag: 'Are they *still* in there?' squealed Williams. The line got a roar of applause.

Competing with comic talent on level terms roused his jealousy: 'I'm sick of the self-important posturing of these people. I made material funny, whether it was by Galton + Simpson or Eric Merriman or Barry Took or Marty Feldman or Peter Cook or Harold Pinter.' In the cases of other actors, though, this rule was reversed. Harry H. Corbett, cast as the amorous detective in *Carry On Screaming*, was drawing television audiences of well over 20 million a week in *Steptoe and Son*. This success Williams attributed to the writers.

As he returned to Pinewood, he noted: 'Jim Dale I like, and Peter Butterworth, but Harry Corbett I'm afraid is a bore. The wavelength is earnest + serious without any profundity to justify either and the humour contrived and laboured. It makes one a little embarrassed. Another case (like Hancock) where a modicum of talent has been shown to great advantage by good scripts, and doesn't wear well, outside that sphere.'

Talbot Rothwell deserved credit for *Screaming*, the cleverest of the *Carry On*s – it cast Williams as a vampiric scientist, a synthesis of Dracula and Frankenstein, who can revive his own corpse with electricity, and regenerate Neanderthal monsters, and encase living women in plastic shells to be sold as shop dummies. The director of photography once again was Alan Hume, a veteran of Hammer horror films who understood how to light a set to create a chilling atmosphere. Fenella Fielding's smouldering vamp stole the picture, though; she played Williams's sister, and at first he had misgivings about working with her again. These soon dispersed: 'She was v. pleasant,' he wrote with surprise. 'Curiously enough, I find myself quite liking her these days.'

The difference in their relationship, Fielding believed, was really a difference in environment – in *Pieces of Eight*, they had been repeating the same material for months to unpredictable houses, while at Pinewood they were working among sympathetic colleagues, with a trusted director who rarely needed more than two takes.

Williams celebrated his fortieth birthday at Pinewood with champagne and a cake, followed by dinner with Tom and Clive, and Stanley Baxter. The next day he strolled through the St Pancras streets where he had grown up, and 'thought old thoughts', but he was not alarmed at becoming middle-aged. The obsessive dieting of the previous year was forgotten: now he would eat a pound of sausages for lunch and be pleased with his appetite, and when his doctor suggested low blood pressure might be causing his bouts of tiredness, the treatment was a whisky and soda before dinner with a half-bottle of wine to follow. 'I must start accepting myself,' he decided. 'Pot belly and all. Stop pretending I'm a perennial juvenile.'

To deter Peter Eade from sending him playscripts, he suggested he would like to play Algy in *The Importance of Being Earnest*, if Binkie

Beaumont could find the ideal cast. That assignment was nearly impossible, though Beaumont liked the idea. As a phantom project, it served to protect Williams from other productions. Even the concept of a revue by Took and Feldman, commissioned by Michael Codron, was not appealing. Beverley Cross offered him a part in his latest musical, *Jorrocks*, which he refused (though he worried he had turned down a hit).

He also rejected a pop movie that tried to cast the Spencer Davis Group as the new Beatles:

Peter E. sends me a script for a film called 'The Ghost Goes Gear' which is accompanied by a fulsome letter asking me to play the leader of a pop group – or manager rather – from the director Hugh Gladwish. I read it and I think it is indescribably bad. All the lines are would-be CAMP: every one of them seems to finish with the word 'ducky' and the director's letter says of me – 'Ever since I saw you in Share My Lettuce I have thought you were a MUST, and this isn't a load of toffee . . .' all v. pleasant, but that is neither here nor there. You can only do with any part, what you can see in yr. mind's eye, so to speak: and I can't see ANYTHING here, except a raving and rather posh poof.

Peter Bridge pleaded with him to play Freddie in a revival of Maugham's *Home and Beauty*, opposite Joan Greenwood: 'I beg you to reconsider [. . .] Why in heaven's name can't you see the enormous possibilities? [. . .] I do wish you'd trust me [. . .] you would be pulling off a tour de force.' Williams dismissed him with a note.

The dramas that intrigued him were playing at the Old Bailey. He treated trials as theatre, and had been watching criminal cases since the fifties, judging the lawyers like a drama critic. His verdicts, naturally, were harsh:

Walked to the Old Bailey [with Andrew Ray] . . . It was a gang of youths up for assault and battery. The judge was a coarse-looking, bovine creature, and his rudeness to counsel was sometimes contemptible. His frequent attempts at humour were Bathetic – viz – 'Have you been in the canteen again?' to late counsel, with sycophantic laughter from the bar. Disgusting, inept and stupid. It was disquieting to think of such people dispensing justice, and I was struck by the lack of reverence in the proceedings – the leaning over and whispering – the giggling behind hands – the undertones of shared jokes and rudeness. Little in the proceedings to remind one of the HIGH SERIOUSNESS.

Ray and Ned Sherrin were regular members of 'the O.B. Club' (President: K. Williams), though his first visits were with George Rose. In an uninterrupted monologue on *Just a Minute* two decades later, he explained:

> I've attended the Old Bailey very regularly. At one point I was a devotee in the Upper Gallery, and later on I had the honour, if you will, of being given a corporation seat, which is something of a privilege [. . .] I remember saying to the constable at the public entrance, 'What court has got the best one? I don't want all that summing up, I'm only interested in cross-examination.' That's where you get the thrust of the barrister and the question that might trap the witnesses . . .

He was becoming more comfortable with TV appearances. Dave Allen invited him to be interviewed, which he enjoyed, and by March he was guesting on *Juke Box Jury* with Millicent Martin and Pete Murray. The broadcast provoked a letter from Edna Welthorpe (Mrs), berating him: 'I regretted many of your remarks which, in my opinion, were quite uncalled-for and tasteless in the extreme. Especially offensive to me as a nursing mother was your attack on infants and their ways. My own baby, born recently, cried throughout the programme.' Edna Welthorpe was an Orton pseudonym.

Williams was back at television centre the following day for *Call My Bluff*, with Joan Sims also on his team. An executive named Barry Lupino buttonholed him afterwards, asking whether he'd like to present an hour-long show, in any comedy format he chose. Williams shrugged and said he'd consider it, if the script was good; he was more concerned with the buffet, which had been picked clean of sandwiches by Robert Morley and his guests. Huffing, Williams and Sims withdrew to the BBC restaurant.

The notion of his own television show seemed a pipe-dream,

and he was finding that impossibilities were much less stressful to contemplate than mundanities. His mother and Pat, who had been sharing the Kensington flat, made him despair with their bickering. His solution was to give the property to his sister and to buy another apartment, in a block on Osnaburgh Street opposite Great Portland Street tube station, for Louie. The lease on the flat, at 7 Marlborough House, cost him £6,000, with a further £1,000 in annual rents, a sum large enough to terrify him but small enough to be affordable. What he found exhausting was his mother's helplessness: he could not leave her to do anything by herself, even to shop for furniture or book a workman to fix the sash windows. His sister, he felt, was content to let him bear all the responsibility; perhaps she felt it would have been pointless to try to stop him.

Fanciful projects reassured him. He recorded several voiceovers for Richard Williams, who was planning an animation based on tales from *The Thousand and One Nights*, and they discussed how they might script and make a film together; the producer Wendy Toye suggested a tour of America, lecturing on Shaw as a dialogue between an actor and a director ('I think that could be done, and it could be attractive'); Peter Eade proposed to demand, if the BBC was serious about a series, £1,000 per television show, and Williams played along, insisting he ought not ask more than £500. In this mood, when George Borwick suggested a holiday in Tangier, he agreed immediately.

The Moroccan coast, which he had glimpsed from Gibraltar, held a particular attraction for many British men. Male prostitution was common in Tangier, and the behaviour of tourists tended to be overlooked. Gay bars were dotted along the waterfront, trade was plentiful and the concierges never objected when guests took young Arab men back to their hotel rooms. Orton and Halliwell had visited the city after the disastrous tour of *Loot*, and sent post-cards of a youth with a python to their friends. 'The snake is real,' Orton jotted on the back, 'but the boys are stuffed.' Williams was thrilled by 'fantasies about sexual licence in Morocco' and Orton's descriptions filled him with lascivious longing. To pique his excite-ment, Orton wrote from Tangier at the end of May 1966, promis-ing he and Halliwell would be there to greet Williams and show him the city.

He did not unbutton, of course, except for thirty-five minutes on the second day when he removed his shirt to sunbathe on the beach; nor did he flirt with Moroccan men. He did spend every day in the bars and pavement cafés, gossiping and denigrating and preening and insulting. His diary of the week, though slurred, is full of bitchy put-downs: of a would-be actor, 'He didn't want advice. He wanted a hospital for alcoholics,' and of a woman who made herself impor-tunate by gate-crashing the all-male company.

Back in England, and urged on by Peter Eade, he accepted an invitation in June from Eamonn Andrews to be interviewed, though the £250 fee shocked him – chat-show guests didn't merit a quarter of that. His co-stars were Shirley Bassey and James Garner, as well as Dora Bryan: there were histrionics backstage, which Williams observed with delight, and when he walked on to the set he was bubbling: witty, pithy, catty, he snatched up the audience and made them howl with laughter. All the next day there were phone calls and telegrams, including one that read, 'THOUGHT YOU WERE MARVELLOUS LAST NIGHT HAVEN'T LAUGHED SO MUCH SINCE HARRY CORBETT HURT HIS FOOT PETE BUTTERWORTH.'

That afternoon the BBC head of light entertainment, Tom Sloan, rang to offer him the compère's role in a seven-week run of a BBC2 variety bill called *International Cabaret*. After his domin-ation of the shambolic Eamonn Andrews show, Williams was so brimming with confidence that he accepted on the spot: 'I think it's high time I had a shot at this kind of thing,' he wrote. 'Other idiots have been getting away with it for years.' The light entertain-ment unit had been discussing for months how it could best engage Williams's talents on TV, and Sloan had chosen his moment well, with Peter Eade's guidance. When Williams began to have doubts, and complained he was being thrown 'into completely strange waters', his agent replied, 'I wouldn't throw you if I didn't think you could swim.'

A meeting with Sloan, Bill Cotton and Frank Muir confirmed that Williams would produce his own scripts, working with the writer John Law, a stocky, ebullient Scot, on monologues linking the caba-ret acts. By lunchtime they were already at a desk in a BBC office, and within twenty-four hours they had enough material for the first broadcast.

Press interviews and a BBC radio discussion programme helped to promote the launch of *International Cabaret*, just a week later. After such brief preparation, the first night was chaos – the invited audience didn't know what to expect, the singers, dancers and jugglers on the bill didn't know what to do, and the monologues didn't work. Striving in front of the cameras, Williams realised that this was not revue, and it was not acting: for the first time in his life he was working as a stand-up comedian. His routine went over like a third-rate comic's patter on an end-of-the-pier bill at a wet Tuesday matinée. He reeled off stage at the end, deaf to the assurances of Sloan and BBC2's controller, David Attenborough, that the show had been not too bad and that a dull audience could be fixed in the editing room.

Days of misery followed: 'The despair inside – I seem to be in an abyss. Keep saying to myself – "it's only another TV show – not the end of the world" but it's not true. When the thing doesn't work for an actor, it IS the end of the world.' The video playback left him partly reassured; the audience had seemed stilted, he decided, because he was delivering lines so fast, cutting off the laughter instead of milking it. But his confidence had been mauled: 'A lousy first night with all its accompanying feeling of unworthiness [. . .] I'm finding audience reaction v. hard to shake off these days. It obsesses me + fills the days. Must make them laugh or I'll go mad.'

At the next show, the backstage chaos continued – most of the acts were European, and the BBC had not provided interpreters, so that a cacophony of questions in Bulgarian and Italian were going unheeded. But Williams hit his pace from the start, playing much of his monologue to his sister Pat at a table close to the stage. Her booming laughter cued in the audience.

The pattern of the monologues varied little. Williams berated the acts, complained of his base treatment from the BBC, and blamed everything on 'that John Law'. He teased the audience with double entendres and then feigned embarrassment, chastising them for their filthy minds. Williams realised he could not be a stand-up, but he could play the part. He was acting, even though he was also writing the material. And the material, in its mixture of erudition, coarseness and hysteria, could only have been his:

> I shot in to that John Law – he's the one that writes all this rubbish, and all the time he's been posing as my friend, always saying, 'I'll see you're all right, ducky, I'll drop a word in the right ear – there's a lot coming up – they'll be knocking on your door and making you a very nice proposition.' Well, I haven't been spoken to like that for years. I said, you've got me going, you did. I've been sitting in the hall for months, waiting for the call. You told me you'd look after me . . . you said you'd put in a word for me. I got all worked up and I was crying hysterically and he bashed me right across the face and said, 'Pull yourself together. Remember where you are – the Corporation – do you want to be known as a cissy?' I said, 'Oh no.' He said, 'Well, put away that scented handkerchief and listen to me.'

International Cabaret proved so popular that the seven-week series was extended, eventually spanning eight months. Williams's success prompted Eade to demand more money for the next *Carry On*, a ploy Peter Rogers squashed easily: he offered an unprecedented £6,000 and pointed out that any actor without an international movie to his credit was hardly a star. This combination of flattery and derogation was nicely judged to manipulate Williams's need for constant re-assurance. 'When you're standing on a stage getting the laughs,' he reflected; 'when you come off afterwards and know that it's been effective – when the director says, "You were great", all these things add up to joy. Admittedly it all vanishes a few hours later, and you're suddenly walking around the streets with no identity save fr. an inferiority complex the size of a house, and wondering whether you can ever do it again.' Quibbles over money jeopardised the more important issue of whether Rogers and Thomas, and by extension the public, wanted Williams to return.

Carry On, Don't Lose Your Head was a French Revolution farce starring Williams as Citizen Camembert and Butterworth as Citizen Bidet. Sid James returned to the series, as the intrepid Black Fingernail. When Tom Waine spent a day at Pinewood, he was struck by the antipathy between Williams and James, despite an association that went back to the beginning of *Hancock's Half Hour*. 'Ken introduced me to everyone, and most of them were charming. But I got the feeling Sid didn't much like Ken, and he definitely didn't like me. That was clear. It was simply because I was gay – in that very brief exchange, I felt he didn't want anything to do with me, whether I was Ken's friend or not.' It was this intolerance and rudeness that Williams found objectionable.

Joe Orton's reaction to the 'Babes in the Wood', as Tom and Clive were nicknamed, was quite different: he mistrusted Waine, with his Oxford education and his job at *The Times*, but he was attracted to Dennis, as Williams had intended he should be. They met at Farley Court, where Williams had arranged for Orton and Halliwell to drop by when Dennis, now working as a telephone engineer, was mending a plug at the flat. In the months before the murder, the 'Babes' would visit Orton's house in Noel Road five or six times.

The friendship between Orton and Williams had cooled after the reworked *Loot* opened on London's fringe and then, garlanded by the critics, in the West End. When Eamonn Andrews invited him back to be interviewed with the playwright, Williams was scornful. Orton, who usually revelled in seeing how he hurt the feelings of others, tried to repair the friendship with a note: 'LOOT has had the most wonderful notices [. . .] I do hope this won't affect our friendship. Do give me a ring. I'd love to have your opinion on the play [. . .] I haven't rung you because Kenneth says you're working on a film and you learn lines on Sundays.' Sincerity was not one of Orton's qualities; still, if this was calculated, it was perfectly judged. Williams expected flattery and would have noticed if it were missing, but what he valued more was consideration.

They did not meet again, though, until February 1967, when Williams was a team captain on the BBC word game *Call My Bluff*; Orton was invited to join his panel, for a fee of £75. Orton sent Williams an Edna Welthorpe letter as a thank-you ('Mr Joe Horton must have taken some handling. But you showed you were a past master of the art of diplomacy') and a Dior tie that had been given to him by Peter Wood during the *Loot* fiasco.

They met again in March, when Orton wrote a long character sketch in his diary, dissecting the Williams persona in an effort to discover how the uninhibited performer could exist in the same skin as the timid bachelor. He was puzzled that, with the Carnaby Street fashion for outlandish clothes, Williams chose to dress in a 'dust-coloured mac [and] nondescript suit', with a tie that was 'mumbling', like a 'middle-range bank clerk'.

Orton, whose career sprang from his contempt for the lower middle class, did not believe that anyone could aspire to its respectability. He wrote out a long anecdote about Williams's holiday in Spain with Hugh Paddick, was impressed when the names of Maggie and Larry were dropped, and deplored the anticlimax in all the stories of flirtation: 'Sexually he really is a horrible mess. He mentions "guilt" a lot in conversation [. . .] Kenneth W. isn't able to have sex properly with man or woman. His only outlet is exhibiting his extremely funny personality in front of an audience and when he isn't doing this he's a very sad man indeed.' This was Orton being as egocentric as the people he despised and lampooned in *Loot*: he could not see that, when Williams encouraged him to brag about his pick-ups and hand-jobs, he was pitying this promiscuity as deeply as he envied it.

Williams tried to analyse the paradox when he was writing his autobiography: jotting pencil notes on the back of an envelope, postmarked July 1984, he sifted his feelings:

> When I related Joe's stories to others, there was the same mixed reception. [They] expressed surprise about my enthusiasm for such prurient details. I said that I derived vicarious pleasure from Orton's erotic dalliances. 'My own sex life is barren enough + I admire his capacity for vulnerability [. . .] The mixture of non-conformism + the puritan in me rules out immorality. [I fear] the recrimination of my own conscience [and] guilt is a healthy yardstick as far as I'm concerned. If I behave badly, I feel guilty + guilt is the reminder that I might do better [and] I try. I think it's all in the trying.

In the autobiography, he describes how he warned Orton against carnal addiction; when Orton recounts the same conversation, he is urging Williams to embrace promiscuity. Both men loved to talk about sex, and neither understood what the other was saying.

Williams also wrote to Orton about his desires; three years after the playwright's death, his solicitor returned the letters. 'When I re-read some of them,' he told Waine, 'I thought "just as well!!" cos they're v. blush-making to read at this stage, I can tell you. I suppose they'll have to be burned.'

The stories Williams liked best were brutish and never tender. In many, his friends were punished for their lust — beaten up by their trade, or robbed and threatened. That violence aroused his imagination, but he used it also as an excuse for sublimating his urges: 'All sexual depravity is largely the result of boredom. Viewed objectively, it can only be seen for what it is — childish, pitiful and utterly futile [. . .] If one has to face the unpleasant truth that one has desires which are abnormal etc: one's only hope lies in canalizing such desires + visions, into some sort of constructive work. Obviously the artist can be an excellent example of this.'

Orton met Louie, and was surprised that Williams swapped lewd chatter in front of her just as eagerly as he did when he was baiting BBC managers. He goaded Orton into recounting a story of sex in a Leicester doorway, and Louie scolded him, 'Joe! You might have caught your death of cold!' When Williams implied that she probably wished she was on holiday with Pat in the Aegean, chatting up Greek fishermen, Louie retorted, 'At my age it's nourishment I want, not punishment!'

Orton assumed son must be bullying mother, trying to embarrass her, but the reality was subtler: Williams wanted Louie to know that, though he indulged in homosexual fantasies, he was chaste, and he needed to be reassured that she always would be too. Her sexual history before he was born did not concern him, but the thought, for instance, of her remarrying and sharing a bed disgusted him. He expected her to have a saucy sense of humour, but never to have desires. Louie understood, and accepted that her relationship with her son imposed celibacy, a kind of asexual monogamy. She sometimes hinted that her marriage had long been sexless, and that if Charlie had ever seemed amorous a couple of bottles of brown ale would quell his ardour.

Waine and Dennis tried to discover what kind of men attracted Williams, introducing him to workmen and squaddies who were the antithesis of the theatre world. One Saturday, after an afternoon having tea at the Dorchester with Phil Silvers and Dick van Dyke, he arrived at the flat on Shepherd's Hill to find an Irish soldier called Dave was making up the foursome. 'I certainly DID NOT like yr. latest "offering" as you put it,' he warned afterwards. 'The unutterable commoness of it I found contemptible, and plus the effect of a barrack room mind [. . .] Let us get this offering business straight – I do like to meet the odd layman – yes – it makes a change and it is v. pleasant if it's dishy, but my interest is only social that's all. I'm too old, too tired and too talented to care about all that other frippery.'

Like most of Williams's friends, Tom and Clive were expected to share and embellish stories of sexual adventure. 'Ken was a prurient prude who lived vicariously on the sexual accounts of others. It was said of him that he was the only man in London who could *talk* himself off,' said Waine. Orton's obsessive talk of sex was different: he used erotic images not only to arouse himself but to torment his partner. His diary that year was filled with pornographic stories for Halliwell to see. Some were probably true and some improbably orgiastic, and at least one was flatly contradicted. 'He fantasised about me, but if he said he ever did anything with me, he lied,' said Dennis. 'We never, ever did.'

Williams engineered the meeting between Orton and Dennis with cunning; Clive must appear to have called in to fix a cracked phone socket. He sent a note: 'Listen ducky, if you're going to come straight from work to do my plug you must remember to take it with you when you go to work. Do you see? Otherwise all will be rendered pointless.' The note went on to thank Dennis and Waine for dinner – 'you're easily the best hosts in London there's no doubt of that' – and to describe his taxi journey home: 'I was v. piss elegant in the back – rigid with camp, restricting all to monosyllables.'

The ploy worked, and in his next note he wrote, 'Joe Orton rang and said how delightful to meet such charming fellows etc. etc and could he have the number cos "I'd like 'em to come up and taste my haddock . . ." it is a dish they do very well.' Haddock, like sliced white bread, was a staple at Noel Road, but Williams had not realised what else had gone into Orton's fish pie.

'We went round there for dinner one night,' Dennis remembered, 'and they served this pie, and it tasted very odd. He'd put bloody hash in it.' Orton had tried marijuana in Tangier, and by mid-1967 was using it regularly. Williams was tricked into trying it too, when Halliwell passed round slices of hash cake. 'We went up there with Ken, and ate this cake,' Waine said, 'and then I started feeling a bit odd. Ken started giggling. Joe started laughing, and Ken wanted to know what the joke was, and they admitted they'd put cannabis in the cake. Ken flung it down, he was furious, absolutely appalled, but because he adored Joe so much, he forgave him. He loved Joe's talent and he was in love with the ethos of Joe.' Williams was enthralled by the spectacle of a working-class man admired and fêted for his plays, who was fearless in his intellect and his sex life.

Others were disgusted: Gordon Jackson, the father of two boys, was revolted by Orton's boasts of sex with young teenagers. Williams seemed unaware of the cruelty behind Orton's vaunted callousness, just as he had been unable to grasp the sadistic violence of Truscott. He could not see, either, that Halliwell, in a sludge of tranquillisers, was close to a breakdown. Orton's empathy extended no further than experimenting with his partner's librium tablets. 'Their relationship was on the rocks,' Waine said, 'because Joe had become so successful. It was Halliwell who taught Joe how to write, so it was all a bit tempestuous, very near to the bone: he really wanted to offload Halliwell, so he was trying to set him up in a hotel in Tangier, or a guest-house somewhere else – anything to get him away.'

Halliwell murdered Orton with nine hammer blows to the head as he lay sleeping, on 8 August 1967, and then took a massive over-dose of barbiturates. Williams had been talking about them to George Borwick hours earlier: 'I said that all this promiscuity was dangerous + wrong.'

The following afternoon, within hours of the discovery of the bodies, Williams heard the news and was numbed. In one of fate's sarcastic symmetries, Clive Dennis was with him at the time, repairing the phone socket again. The BBC called to ask him to discuss Orton on television; Williams refused and went to the cinema instead, his standard escape – he had done the same when his father lay dying in hospital. It was months before the fact of Orton's death seemed real. A trivial incident unblocked his grief: he took a book from the shelf, and a piece of paper fluttered out. It was a note from Orton. In the guise of an agony aunt, he was proffering advice so banal and repressed it was hilarious. Willliams started to laugh at it, and then cried and cried.

13

'You can't be childish at 42 and get away with it but nonetheless, I shall try'

August 1967–August 1968

Two days after Orton's death, Williams flew to Morocco. It was his third visit: he had spent two weeks over Easter in Tangier with John Hussey, staying once more at the Rembrandt Hotel and talking Polari with the crowd. That visit had been so boozy and relaxed that the Jule-and-Sand slang seeped into the diary, 'filling Tangé with yr. actual silly queens and naf polones'. They spent several days with Lionel Bart, who had hired York Castle overlooking the city and was full of gossip about plans to film his musical, *Oliver!*

Bart, who met Williams on *Pieces of Eight*, shared his glee in tattle about friends: 'Lionelli told me that after remonstration with Rachel Roberts apropos drinking during *Maggie May*, he had the phone call fr. Rex Harrison about "What have you been saying to my wife? Now look here, you little pouf!" – Lionelli [said] "Not so much of the little . . .!!" which was quite fun I thought.'

Williams invited Waine and Dennis to join him in Morocco and hoped to surprise them at the airport; instead, they were forced to put up for a night in a resort outside the city when their flight was diverted. At breakfast the next day a waiter called them to the telephone, and a nettled voice said, 'Yeesss! Well, it's all fallen rather flat, hasn't it!'

Two cliques dominated the British expatriates in Tangier, clustered around a pair of minor aristocrats, Robert Eliot and David Herbert: the two 'Honourables' competed to throw the best parties. 'There was a lot of rivalry,' Waine said. 'On Sunday mornings they used to congregate on opposite sides of the church to see who could raise more for the collection. But this holiday was fantastic, it was all parties and restaurants, gay bars all along the front, such as George Hardy's Beach Bar.'

'Ken loved Hardy's,' Dennis agreed. 'He used to sit there, always in this blue jacket, with a white shirt and this little tie – no matter how hot, he seemed to wear it everywhere. He just wanted to be formal. He liked to be proper, although what was going on was improper in a way, but he wanted to have that façade of looking right.'

Williams needed a holiday after his most gruelling *Carry On* shoot, on *Follow That Camel*. This adventure-romance of Bedouin slavers and the French Foreign Legion was largely filmed on location, though on Peter Rogers's budget that meant Sussex, not the Sahara. Phil Silvers, star of the fifties TV comedy *Bilko*, had been drafted in after Sid James suffered a heart attack, and he was billeted with Williams, Gerald Thomas and Jim Dale at a clinker-clad motel called Rumpels, outside Rye.

To keep location expenses to a minimum, Rogers announced on the first day that the cast would have no time off over weekends, and that filming would continue on Sundays. As if to thwart him, the next morning a bitter rain started to pour, turning to sleet and hail after lunch. All the ingenuity of Alan Hume could not transform that into a heat haze on Camber Sands.

Williams, who had liked Silvers when they were introduced, realised over dinner that the man was desperate and sad, in full flight from loneliness – his wife had divorced him, taking their five daughters – and the collapse of his career. Williams's heart could ache, but only for friends, and he had no sympathy for anyone who hogged the talk at dinner. Silvers told dismal jokes and laboured his puns; he even stood up and sang to get attention. On the first night, Williams and Thomas escaped to the nearby pub where Angela Douglas and Peter Butterworth had rooms. The next morning on location, as snow fell and a freezing wind shook the marquee where the cast huddled, Silvers was at full tilt again, acting the big star and even ordering Williams to fetch him a Coke. 'Get fucked,' Williams told him, but that too provoked only another Hollywood anecdote.

If Phil Silvers had been funny, Williams would have hated him. As it was, he was pathetic: '[He] started another monologue and kept asking Gerald, "Am I boring you?" all interspersed with how he'd won endless awards for his acting . . . "I'll tell you this because you guys are in showbusiness and I think you'll be interested" [. . .] After a bit, we went in fr. dinner + Gerry + Peter carefully chose another table so of course I was stuck with him. He told me that he was in the depths of depression and didn't really know what he was doing.'

The weather cleared at last and, with Williams as the monocled commandant with an iron-grey crew-cut, they marched over the sands and defended the desert fort to the last man. When Thomas drove them to the cinema in Rye to watch the rushes, Silvers insisted on sitting in the front, because he was the star. Williams often claimed to have an inferiority complex, but it is a measure of his self-confidence that he rolled his eyes at Thomas and climbed into the back seat.

On Monday mornings Williams had to be back in London for *Round the Horne*, which had evolved from its smutty, anarchic beginnings. By the second series, it was untouchable, Took and Feldman smashing up the BBC policy guidelines like a couple of protection racketeers in an antiques shop. They named the stars they sent up, from Sean Connery and Zsa Zsa Gabor to Ken Dodd; they mocked the ban on advertising, giving Douglas Smith voiceovers and songs to promote horse purgatives called Dobbiroids; and they made the gay sexual innuendo more blatant than ever. When Kenneth Horne tried a little Polari, Williams snapped back, 'Ooo . . . wonder where he spends his evenings!' The BBC's censors could plead but they did not dare impose cuts – and this was the same light entertainment programme that had once imposed a five-year ban on the most popular comedian in Britain for a double entendre.

The third series achieved a surreal nirvana. Each week Horne announced some cause for celebration: it was Festoon a Gnome in Bacon Rind Day, or Smear a Goose with Camembert for International Motherhood Week. Jule and Sand set up in chambers, as barristers, and coined their most notorious gag: 'We've got a criminal practice that takes up most of our time.'

The series opened in February 1967 with Williams as a World War One German air ace in 'The Plastic Max' ('Ain't there anything about my appealing elfin face? My doe-like orbs? My fashionably flat figure? My coltish legs? Isn't there anything about that? I could've been another Twiggy!') and by May Horne was pretending despair and closing the programme with the words, 'I apologise for Kenneth Williams.'

That afternoon he returned to Rye, where filming had been cranked up to a breakneck pace. Rogers later commented he could have completed the picture a week earlier without Silvers, who constantly fluffed and forgot lines even when they were chalked up on a blackboard. Williams spent his evenings with Jim Dale, who shared his taste for serious conversation and escapist films. 'There's no question but what he's a v. good person,' Williams wrote. 'A man of conscience.' For the first time on a *Carry On* set, however, he was counting the days and his pay packet: eight weeks filming at £6,000 came to £675 a week after Eade's fee was deducted. He did not, of course, know that Silvers's salary was seven times more, at £40,000, with a first-class return from Los Angeles and a limousine to Pinewood. Eade had never been able to include a car in his client's contract: Williams had to book and pay for his cars himself.

As with many *Carry Ons*, his journal was a catalogue of scratches and bruises – a scraped knee, a splinter, a swollen foot where Jim Dale had dropped a rifle on his boot. 'If there is one thing to learn from this,' he resolved, 'it's as follows: 1) To remember that the whole experience has been a Nightmare. 2) Resolve NEVER to stay in the same hotel as those you work with. 3) Never sign a 7-day film contract again. 4) Don't go on location.'

Filming moved to Pinewood ten days later, in the cramped I Block where they had shot *Carry On Teacher*, and he was tired and low; a boil under his arm would not clear up, and a monotonous thumping was shaking the pipes of his flat. Depression wore him down until the film ended, when he began to write the scripts for the second series of *International Cabaret* – Eade had talked him out of ditching it. The work, and Law's kindly humour, began to lift him. Bill Cotton, now BBC head of variety, warned the monologues must be free from double entendres, but Williams took no notice. The night before, he had packed a year's supply into a return appearance on *The Eamonn Andrews Show*. Stanley Baxter phoned to scold him – how could a man who boasted of his virginal sex-life sit and flirt with Roger Moore on national television, and call him 'a great dish'?

Williams was defiant: 'Yess, I can do it, dear, cos I know I go home and *say my prayers*! I'm pure.'

His favourite segment on *Round the Horne*, because it showcased him and promised a deluge of laughs, was the dip into Ramblin' Syd's ganderbag. On Monday 3 July 1967 he recorded a concert of the nonsense songs at EMI's Abbey Road studios, in front of 200 people convulsed with laughter. The screams of hysteria during his introductions took him aback. There is a touch of Beatlemania about the recording, and songs like 'The Black Grunger of Hounslow' and 'The Pewter Woggler's Bangling Song' were greeted with a din that drowned the accompaniment.

This was not the first LP he released in 1967, but the other had been quite different: a collection of children's songs, with the only innuendo in its title: *Kenneth Williams on Pleasure Bent*. He had recorded it at the tail end of 1966, at his own expense, and his voice had not sounded so innocent since *The Buccaneer*. The opening number, 'Pardon Me, Sir Francis', is a treat: it displays his technical mastery as he takes the Snide character and makes him sing for the first time. His favourite track was 'A Boiled Egg', a poem by his friend Michael Hitchman. He often quoted the tagline, that a nicely boiled egg gave him as much satisfaction as the news that another nationalised industry had been restored to its rightful owners.

Other pieces, though, sound like third-rate imitations of Noël Coward, or Edward Lear, or Flanders and Swann. There was a song about Boadicea with a New Orleans jazz setting; numbers with names such as 'The Mesopotamia Tango' and 'The Itty Bitty Hitty Potamus'; a tale of a lovesick computer, and a satire on life peerages for Labour MPs. The lyricist was Myles Rudge, a BBC writer who persuaded Williams first to listen to the songs, then to meet the cost not only of the sessions at Ad Vision Studios in Bond Street, but of the pressings too.

The record failed to sell enough copies even to cover its costs. Though it was compared to Joyce Grenfell by *The Gramophone* ('sent this reviewer into transports of delight [. . .] please hear this') it completely ignored Britain's mood. Children in 1967 could listen to 'Penny Lane' and 'Strawberry Fields' on pirate radio, while much of *On Pleasure Bent* would have sounded old-fashioned on a forties broadcast of *Hello Children Everywhere*.

By the time Williams flew to Tangier, he and Law had completed twenty-six scripts, and Peter Rogers was badgering him to do another *Carry On*. He protested that Frankie Howerd, as a faith-healing charlatan, had a much funnier role, and that he didn't want to play the body-building wimp of a surgeon who inflames the lust of Matron Hattie Jacques. Three telegrams, promising that Howerd would be dropped from the film, arrived in Morocco and won him over: he did play Doctor Tinkle, and it gave him and Hattie one of their best-loved scenes. He's in a gym vest, she's in a fluffy negligee as she throws her arms round him. 'You may not believe this, but I was once a weak man,' he pleads. 'Once a week's enough for any man,' growls Matron.

A stint at Pinewood used to leave him too stretched to scribble more than 'Filming all day' in his diary, but his pride in the journals had been increasing throughout the sixties. No pages were blank, and most contained at least 250 words, usually in the flowing hand once reserved for mundanities. Impressions of each encounter or appointment were written up, sometimes in detail but without striving for literary effect. He wrote as he spoke; yet his awareness of his own shifting emotions, if not those of others, had an novelist's intensity.

After a wet Wednesday on the set, for instance, he dined with one acquaintance who told him about his schooling at a Catholic oratory: 'When I said goodbye to him I said, "Well we must meet again soon," lying in my teeth and he didn't reply, just did that smile with the lips and not the eyes, and leaves one ommelette sur le visage.' His aim was to record, rather than to reflect, though when he felt he had achieved a clearer understanding of some psychological detail, he set it down concisely: for one entry which begins, 'All criticism is a form of vanity,' he used red ink, which implies the observation was meant to stand out.

Another practical innovation influenced his writing: he gave his old typewriter away and bought a new model, 'fr. £15.19.6!! [. . .] I don't often use them, but it's useful fr. the scripts.' By November he was typing all his overseas correspondence, keeping carbon copies on foolscap sheets so light they are almost like tracing paper. The same compulsion that made him cram his A4 diaries now impelled him to pack the forms with single-spaced type, filling them to the last line and running on his paragraphs without breaks. The effect of this was to make each letter a headlong rush, a monologue with no space for breath or interruption.

Over the next decade he typed hundreds of them, always to friends abroad – his notes to friends in England were handwritten, and shorter. Over his lifetime Williams wrote in excess of 4 million words, with almost half this output achieved between 1966 and 1976. He wrote, too, for nothing, not simply to fill the silences when he was not talking but because he was possessed by the need to pour words on to paper. The Roman poet Juvenal knew this compulsion: he called it 'cacoethes scribendi', the all-consuming urge, simultaneously creative and self-destructive, to write.

Until Williams was forty, his style in letters was sometimes pretentious, striving to impress with its rectitude and learning. Though it emerged again in his autobiography, this tendency was dormant after 1966. His long airmails were raucous, confessional and coarse, racketing through the news. One of the earliest, to Noel Willman, gives the flavour of them all: it opens with greetings and commonplaces, shrieks off into a series of anecdotes, and collapses in a welter of innuendo. His urge to misbehave and then to seek absolution is also illustrated:

Mon cher Noel: It is nearly eleven o'clock in the morning, and I am sitting here in the study with the electric light on. Outside it is practically dark! Isn't it ludicrous? – the last four mornings have been the same. Dark and fog and completely mild. The atmosphere muggy, airless and full of germs. Well I have got nothing but disasters to tell you. Gordon Jackson asked me to have dinner with him and Alec Guiness after the show at Wyndham's last night and like a fool I went to these Americans in Chelsea for drinks first. Well of course they were giving me these great vodkas you see, and I started showing off, and doing the Barry Chats and the pirouettes, fell on this piano stool and broke it. They were obviously furious because it was quite a ritzy apartment and I said I was sorry goodness knows how many times and then I got a taxi and was talking to myself all the way to the theatre. When I got there Alec came to the dressing room door and I went in and there was that awful Redgrave and Sadoff. And something was said about working in the theatre and I said I couldn't do the eight a week any more, and AG said 'Well I have to' and I said 'Yes ducky but we all know you get the earliest release clause in any contract' (I was being terribly loud – bawling away and smirking at everyone, knowing it was all going wrong and unable to stop – catching sight of my face in the mirrors at odd angles, looking blotchy and slit eyed). And Redgrave pointedly turned away from me and said 'Well goodnight Alec – and thank you again' and they swept out and I said, still looking in the mirror, 'Oh! my hair is a mess – it's all over the place' and AG stroked the bald bit on his head and said, 'Oh I do understand – mine is the same – can't do a thing with it' but I was too far gone to acknowledge the joke and went on and on about this disgraceful hairdresser and then Gordon came and we all went to this restaurant and I had the drinks again and by this time the head was just swimming and I was getting more and more dictatorial – poking the finger at Alec and prefacing EVERYTHING with 'I'm here to tell you ducky . . .' and people at other tables were looking and he was embarrassed and I wished I was dead. I don't know how we all got through it. An experience so horrific. Bits of it keep coming back to me – shameful realisations of the crass stupidity of one's own banal remarks. When we had dropped Alec and Gordon was driving me home I said guiltily 'I'm afraid I wasn't much help tonight' and he said shortly 'I knew you were drunk when you came into the room' so this morning I was on the phone to John Law and he said 'Forget it – it is always far worse to remember and mull it all over – don't write apologies – just forget it' so I thought yes – I shall write and tell Noel all about it. Well of course you are quite right about Baxter. He is a very good person fundamentally – and his friendship matters to me. I go right off people every now and again and am capable of utter treachery [. . .] He told me, 'I was appalled to hear that you were going round calling me nasty names and attributing base motives to perfectly reasonable actions – after a friendship of 20 years – it seemed such a betrayal . . .' I said 'yes I know I'm very sorry'. It was all very lame and unpleasant I can tell you. Then on the Thursday you see, I went to the National with Maggie Smith and Bob Stephens [. . .] This play about Rosearse and Goldbum was TERRIBLE. Mags said in the interval 'Are you enjoying it?' and I said 'It's the most awful boring rubbish I've ever sat through' and she snapped back 'Well it's a free world why don't you leave right now?' Of course I said no and sat on to the end. So glad that you like using your key for number one. A lot of people don't realise that the small el serves for it. The margin setter is terribly easy to work. On the trough behind the roller you've got these two sliding nobs and if you depress them and slide they move to any position on the rod that you want. The left hand knob decides your margin [. . .] The best thing to do with the right hand knob is to depress it and slide it back towards the end of the roller as far as it will go.

The sudden switch from Stoppard at the National to typewriter knobs and rods is a good example of his grasshopper style. Williams, still proud of the clerical skills he had learned in the army, had given his old typewriter to Willman. The guilty cringe about Baxter stemmed from one of the messy, vindictive, petty spats that had started with someone else's best intentions.

The well-meaning fan this time was Bill Cotton, who believed Williams was wasted in a crummy nightclub show on a minority channel. Cotton knew that he and Stanley Baxter were old friends. Baxter was staging solo extravaganzas for the BBC, the antithesis of *International Cabaret*'s cheapskate acts, and the head of variety wanted Williams to match him, or perhaps work with him. An original concept, something that did not rely on revue skits and musical guests, was needed, and Baxter supplied it: a chat show where the guest never varied but the presenter changed in every show. 'That was the whole gimmick,' Baxter said. 'Because he had worked with so many famous people who were fascinated by him – the Burtons, Orson Welles, an awful lot of people – to have a different famous person each week as the host, announcing [Orson voice]: "My guest this week . . . Kenneth Williams!"'

Cotton loved the idea. Williams loathed it. Such an act of hubris, to make himself the focal point of shows that featured the biggest stars in film and television, was to invite a critical mauling that would not be confined to the telly section but plastered over the front pages. Furious with Baxter, he enquired whether his friend intended to present one of the editions – and then accused him of self-promotion. Taken aback, Baxter agreed not to appear and offered instead to produce the programme. 'He said, "No way! You're not going to ride on my back!" I had no intention of it. That's what he was like – not an easy friend.'

The rift worsened when Baxter threw an impersonation of him into a sketch show. 'I did a take-off of *International Cabaret*, just a version of him as I'd seen him in that show, but he said, "No-oo! You were into my soul, you knew things about me that nobody else knew and it was all in that performance." I told him this was rubbish, but "No-oo! I know what I'm talking about."'

Williams simmered in a foul mood for weeks. He tried to have one of his directors sacked, he announced he would take his script-writing fee just to spite John Law, and he seethed in judgement on his guests: 'Tops tonight [was] the Loathsome Sandy Shore [Sandie Shaw]. A really terrible singer with a nasty little cockney personality and a rude brashness to match.' The only friend to escape his flail was Tom Waine, who saw him often: he and Clive never missed a show and always went backstage to praise and reassure him. They cooked for each other, or dined out, several times a week, and Williams sent a stream of thank-you notes.

The rumbling noise above his apartment continued to torment him – he lay awake, listening to it and timing the intervals when the machinery fell silent, as it thrummed for thirty seconds and fell silent for forty more before starting again. If he walked up Marylebone Road, past Madame Tussaud's and Harley Street to Regent's Park and his mother's flat beyond, he was conscious of the stares and the pointing that television celebrity brought. Success had become a torture to him, he reflected as he totted up his accounts: of the £10,200 he earned between April and September 1967, he had paid £7,800 in tax. Above the tables, he noted bitterly: 'I hate figures, but ironically I am v. good at them – like everything else I set my hand to.' He told a journalist that he didn't want to earn large sums, because of the danger of spending too much and being unable to pay his taxes. 'If I earn £1000 I tend to think I can spend £500 of it. You bloody can't. If I earn £50 I know how to manage it.'

The fourth series of *Round the Horne* began, without Marty Feldman, Bill Pertwee or the Fraser Hayes Four, and with three new writers. The surreal edge was lost, but the innuendo was more brazen than ever, and the cast stoked the laughter by mugging to the audience. 'Williams was the worst (or best),' writer Brian Cooke said. 'He'd stick out his backside, roll his eyes, grimace outrageously and often cackle with laughter even when he was off stage [. . .] doing his donkey laugh in the background. All totally calculated, of course.'

In February 1968, the Variety Artists' Club voted him radio personality of the year. Williams refused the award. He knew he deserved it, but for fifteen years he had consoled himself that these accolades were spurious, dispensed on a rota – to accept one now would be to concede it had some merit. Worse, the theatre award went to Edith Evans, and to share a stage with her would be a reminder of the humiliation of *Gentle Jack*.

Piles were causing him constant irritation. When he 'stuck out his backside', he was exaggerating the pain that had troubled him for weeks. Walking, sitting and lying down all brought discomfort. Each day's diary began with a description of his bowel movement and the ointments that followed. There were jellies, creams, suppositories and washes, and then the diagnosis – the bum was screaming or it was quiet. Amid this, Rogers sent him the next *Carry On* script, for *Up the Khyber*. He was to play the Khasi.

His specialist, Desmond Mulvany, booked him into the St John and St Elizabeth Hospital where he had been treated after *Pieces of Eight*. An inflamed rectal fissure was stitched, and he was given an enema of barium in a white liquid before he was X-rayed. He did not seem embarrassed, even when he was shaved: the experience, in fact, was delicately civilised, something reflected in his choice of books for the weekend – he took Boswell's *Hebridean Journey* and *Sisyphus* by Camus.

On a folded insert at the front of his diary, he kept a 'chart showing progress of the bum from the 22nd February which was the first day out of hospital'. He graded it from 'bad' to 'marvellous', and between his birthday and the end of March the graph shows a week of pain, broken by two good days, followed by steady improvement, until he was able to chart two weeks of good behaviour. Red felt-tip highlighted his happiness on 13 March, when the bum achieved 'marvellous': 'First no pain day! [. . .] I did not experience any pain or irritation of any kind from the bum AT ALL. At first I was almost on tiptoe [. . .] but no, it continued to behave like a proper bum all the time.'

On his birthday, 22 February, he resolved: 'You can't be childish at 42 and get away with it but nonetheless, I shall try.' He was most like a schoolboy with Tom – the previous weekend they had driven down to Brighton and, in a deserted playground, larked about on the swings. He sent Waine silly letters: one was signed Beauregard Bumhole, on behalf of Secretary of State Williams, complaining of 'excessive familiarity' and warning that 'proper deference is due to the dignity of office, and that your habit of crying out "Whoops girl! – how's it going?" on the scrambler telephone is inappropriate, and could lead to impolitic conjecture.' At other times, the prankster of the third form could turn into a stuffy prefect. After an *International Cabaret* broadcast from the Talk of the Town, where Vera Lynn topped the bill, Williams reprimanded his friends: they had a midnight dinner date with the glamorous Rudolf Nureyev, and were planning to skip work the next day. Tom and Clive were ordered home to bed without their supper.

Up the Khyber started shooting in mid-April. Rogers, with one of those typically gracious gestures that sidestepped the need to pay better salaries, presented Williams with a bottle as big as a vase of his favourite scent, Les Plus Belles Lavandes by Caron. The film was a costume comedy of the Indian Raj, set in the Hindu Kush. Despite the vows Williams had made to himself, it meant location work again, this time in the Himalayas of north Wales.

Rogers scheduled the Pinewood scenes first, and the atmosphere was joyous. Williams slipped in and out of character easily, making his Rajah seem like an impostor as well as a villain. He bantered with the director, and tried to disrupt filming by making the crew laugh while maintaining the pretence of professionalism: 'On the set today Gerald said, "You've got to do that again," and I said, "That's all right, I can take it," and he said, "Yes I know you can take it, it's what you do with it that worries me . . ." and everyone hooted.' On chat shows he often told of swooping to kiss the governor's wife, Joan Sims, on a couch; as he lunged, he broke wind. The scene collapsed, and Williams defended himself – Valentino had farted on the set, he said. 'They were silent films,' Thomas retorted. For a dinner party with Angela Douglas and Kenneth More, he dressed as a twenties roué, with sunglasses and a soft felt hat, and was snapped on Polaroid. Joan Sims was draped over his shoulders in a fun fur, like a gangster's moll.

He went mad for holidays that year. Before the film, he had already visited Tangier twice, once at New Year with his show's musical director, Alyn Ainsworth, and once in March. As soon as the last episode of *Round the Horne* was recorded (Kenneth Horne urging him at the party afterwards to visit Cyprus) and he had guested again with Sims on *The Eamonn Andrews Show* (where the Farting Valentino story had its first airing), he flew to Morocco. 'I'm off again + not sorry,' he wrote to Waine. 'My life has been deeply disturbed and restless for some time now – perhaps it's the change in life. Something must have dropped somewhere and it certainly wasn't a penny.'

The decision to take frequent breaks abroad was deliberate, an attempt to find a real substitute for theatre work. To be happy, he needed to be performing, and television and radio did not sustain him: the shows were over too quickly. Stage work, though, was relentless, and he could not face the danger of nightly failures in front of paying audiences. Films were a good compromise, but even the *Carry On* conveyor belt could bring round only two movies a year – and he was now so strongly identified with the series that other casting directors never called.

He thought he would like to have been a teacher: the pupils would be his audience, and education was worthwhile and lasting, unlike entertainment. Stanley Baxter agreed: 'He was highly literate and enormously knowledgeable. He would have been happy if he could have had an education that took him to Oxbridge, because he'd have been a great don. He'd have been superb. Wildly attracted to all those youngsters, but he would never have got into trouble. And he'd have loved having them around him.'

When he arrived home, his apartment had been redecorated. The walls were bare, and he liked them that way – he gave his paintings to Waine and Dennis. They joined him for his fourth Moroccan holiday that year, two months later in August 1968. He adored their company, and filled pages with stories of their days together.

233

One Saturday before they flew out to Tangier, he spent the day with Tom, having lunch at a Steak House before driving out to Beverley Cross's country home for tea on the lawn, and going back to Highgate to watch TV and play Scrabble. The affection with which it is set down reveals Williams as he rarely could be, neither alone nor performing, but relaxed. It was how he longed always to be, and he said so: 'I told Tom in the car that the two of them had become a v. important friendship to me + quite unlike any other relationships I've got. The thing is – they're never boring to me: always interesting + lively and attractive.' Even this relationship suffered from the paradox that had destroyed his vocation: if he did something he loved every day, he started to hate it. They spent two weeks in Tangier, and by the end he was barely speaking to them.

'When Ken had his rows they were over absolutely nothing,' Waine said. 'Clive was wearing sandals, and he didn't want to get them shined by the shoeshine boy – and that caused a row.' Williams, who had been itching with boredom all day, asked him to do it as a favour, then ordered him. The boy needed to make a living, he said. Clive offered to give the boy money; Williams got angrier and called him patronising. Clive walked away, but the row kept stewing, until by the end of the fortnight they were raking up slights and insults that went back months.

'Ken was always like a naughty child,' Waine said. 'A child gets bored. Even having the ice cream, they get bored suddenly – they don't want to be on the pier, and you see them crying. Ken was like that in life.'

14

'It's all whoops and bonnet over the windmill!'
September 1968–December 1969

Williams tired of everything, and now he was tired of constantly masculine company. Brought up in such a matriarchal family, dominated not only by his mother and aunties but by his grandmothers, his big sister and his cousin, he began looking to women for friendship.

Nora Stapleton, still at Endsleigh Court and working as a stage manager, joined him on a string of outings. In Brighton he almost broke her heart, telling her they should have got married ten years earlier and adopted children: 'We've both of us wasted our lives and the days have run thro' our fingers like bathwater.' Nora worshipped him. On polling days, she would ring him to ask whom she should vote for. She signed her letters, 'All my dearest love dearest heart', and, 'Having come to terms with your greatness, eg the simple fact, I do love you, in fact, could not love you (or anyone) MORE. Nor X.' Sometimes she seemed to be begging for a rebuff, and Williams could be heartless enough to supply it.

In 1966 she was attacked at the Theatre Royal, Drury Lane, by robbers who tied her up and stole the takings. She ran to him after the ordeal and broke down in tears as she described it. He could not comfort her; his emotions were too tightly repressed. Instead, he laughed.

She still clutched for encouragement, and after an afternoon together she sent him an overnight telegram. It simply said, 'I LOVE YOU KENNETH WILLIAMS – NORA.' She got a scolding for her thoughtlessness: he did not wish to be startled by delivery boys on Saturdays. Mortified, she risked a letter: 'Kenneth Heart – Tried to 'phone just now [. . .] re the telegram, sorry to give you a fright, nothing could be further from the intention – which was a feeling which simply has to be expressed.'

Richard Williams saw how attractive the actor was to women. 'He didn't seem gay to me, I didn't have that sense of him. I told him, "You should get married – you aren't really gay." He said in his clipped way, "I am *mentally* homosexual." But I could see there were women who were dying to fall in love with him. I asked him what it was he found so unattractive. "Their shape," he said. "Their glands. In front."'

He took his mother on his next holiday. It was the first time he had used her as his sole companion, someone who would be deferential and submit to his arrangements, but would not make embarrassing protestations of love. Louie was stilted when she tried to state her emotions – her thank-you notes, for birthday presents and meals, are all schoolgirl formality – but she proved her loving loyalty all the time. She never held a grudge for his moods nor minded his antics, and he heard her laughter at all his performances. This was love that he controlled: she would obey him even if her life were in danger.

On the second day of their cruise to the Canaries, he tested it. During lunch in the Bay of Biscay, their ship, the *Monte Anaga*, lurched and, as the crockery slid off the tables, the officers hurried out of the restaurant. Many passengers followed, but Williams ordered his mother to stay seated. Their dessert had just arrived. 'Let's have this baked apple,' he told her. 'It's got all those raisins and brown sugar in the middle.' Louie hesitated. The ship might have been sinking, and the dining-room was almost empty. She tucked into her apple: it was very nice, she agreed. Later they heard the ship had hit a fishing boat, killing five fishermen.

Williams was a confident sailor. On the return journey the ship hit a heavy swell, and he scoffed at the passengers who stayed in their cabins. They had no business being on a cruise if they got seasick. He was enjoying himself: 'This voyage is curious because, just at the period when you anticipate acute boredom, you are surprised to find yourself quite buoyant [. . .] With a heterosexual crowd, everyone is infinitely more attractive than all those silly queens.' His mood was crushed two days later, on 15 February 1969, on hearing that Kenneth Horne had died. He had suffered a heart attack while presenting tele-vision awards at the Dorchester: seconds earlier, he had announced

Marty Feldman and Barry Took as the winners for the Best Comedy Script. They helped to carry his body from the room.

The news floored Williams. He had admired Horne more than any comic he had worked with. When he arrived home, after a grinding train journey from Liverpool, a letter waited, on Horne's familiar notepaper headed Albert Hall Mansions, Knightsbridge; it asked him to contribute to a publicity feature for the next series of *Round the Horne*. Instead, he found himself scribbling a tribute, in a taxi on the way to the Ministry of Defence studios in Dean Stanley Street, for a Forces Radio broadcast in Germany. The cadences of his brief eulogy reveal that Williams was emerging as a writer with the power to make his listeners swallow hard, as well as laugh, as he recalled Horne's 'particular brand of humour – something essentially English and decent – and that is probably the thing that will be most preciously remembered by all those who worked with him – laughed with him – and loved him'.

The BBC proposed a replacement serial, retaining Williams, Paddick and Smith, to be called *Stop Messin' About*. Joan Sims, who was to have taken over from Betty Marsden in *Round the Horne*, joined the cast. Williams felt unsure. He did not want the sketch show to end – he had been starring in it for eleven years, and the recordings were now the closest he came to live theatre work. But he was not happy at heading the bill.

He wanted to appear on other people's shows, under their names, and steal their thunder. Chat shows let him do that. It was not only Eamonn Andrews who kept inviting him back; Simon Dee interviewed him three times and laughed off Williams's impersonations of him on radio ('And now, Simon Dee . . . praved! Dee . . . cayed! Dee . . . ceased!'). David Frost also made him a guest three times in 1968, as Williams discovered he could slip snatches from sketches – Snide the bullfighter, Mr Grole and his asp, the thinnest fattest man in the world – into his anecdotes. His range of impersonations, and the speed of his delivery, made it seem as if a crowd of guests had burst on to the show. 'You were sensational,' Michael Codron wrote after one appearance. 'What about *An Evening with KW*? The plays all seem to be rubbish, so why not concoct something of our own? Is it too atheatrical? Have I gone mad? Think it could be marvellous, though.'

There were other TV slots – on ATV's *Stars*, and *The Wednesday Show* with David Jacobs and Sheila Hancock, and a panel game called *Tennis Elbow Foot* with Paddick. On radio there were two guest spots on the *Late Night Extra* chat show, and Joan Sims joined him for a one-off comedy, *A Bannister Called Freda*, with script and songs by the writers of *On Pleasure Bent*.

He recorded his first *Jackanory* story in December, reading 'The Land of Green Ginger' by Noel Langley, for an audience he knew he could enthrall. 'Done by you, it will be extremely funny,' the producer, Anna Home, promised. The serial ran in fifteen-minute segments on weekday afternoons, with footage of the narrator interspersed with illustrated stills. Williams loved talking to children, and he performed a cavalcade of voices while dressed in a gold-embroidered kaftan of blue silk.

Though he had decided not to present a third season of *International Cabaret*, a run of repeats was scheduled, and Bill Cotton was urging him to find a format for a *Kenneth Williams Spectacular*. And to fill in, to do a little broadcasting on a radio panel game that required no learning of lines, he recorded half a dozen episodes of a show chaired by Nicholas Parsons. It was such a frivolous business that he didn't even trouble to get the name right: at the front of his diary, he noted the dates under the heading *Wait a Minute*.

Just a Minute, as it was really called, was a parlour game devised by Ian Messiter, who had also brought the *Twenty Questions* format to radio. The first series had launched in December 1967, with Clement Freud and Derek Nimmo as regular players: the challenge was to talk for one minute on a given subject, without straying from the topic, repeating words or pausing. Opponents challenged and won points by claiming deviation, repetition or hesitation. Parsons was an enthusiastic chairman, geeing up the audience like a boisterous uncle at a Christmas party, but the players, even the effervescent Nimmo, seemed unable to avoid two pitfalls – either they were entertaining and ignored the subject, or they stuck to the topic and were dull.

The show seemed doomed, but its producer, David Hatch, threatened to resign unless a second series was aired. As he cast round for a brilliant radio wit who could improvise, ad lib and be simultaneously competitive and silly, one name stood out. Kenneth

Williams recorded his debut on 13 September 1968, still bristling from days of bickering with Tom and Clive in Tangier, and he was ready for a screaming argument. Seconds after Freud began to lecture on 'Learning to Fly', Williams tore into him: 'Well, I challenge that. It's a disgrace, it's deviation, isn't it! He was deviating! I could see him deviating! His eyes were deviating too!' Minutes later he was talking about 'Friendship' with barbed candour: 'Some friendships can become a *great bore*. This is largely because you overdo it from the start. It should be rationed, you see. Friendship should be rationed . . .'

When he was challenged, he started to bawl, and when Williams lit a cigarette the chairman asked whether he was feeling the pressure. 'Oh yes! I'm throbbing here, I really am!' he gasped, and it became a catchphrase: 'When I get going, I often throb a bit!' 'Kenneth Williams, will you stop throbbing!' snapped Freud.

The programe was recorded at the Playhouse Theatre on Northumberland Avenue; afterwards, Williams caught a bus home ('the 505 Express red Bus, 6d everywhere'). He had rescued the format, and *Just a Minute* was to give him a starring vehicle for twenty years, a run as long as the *Carry On*s.

'Once he'd found his feet after that first show,' Parsons said, 'we always had him in every recording. The audience loved Kenneth and that's why he was so successful. For all the edge that came out in some of his humour, he was extraordinarily lovable. That's the most important thing, charm: it's an old-fashioned word now, but if an actor or a performer lacks charm they'll never have the big success. It may be an individual charm, something you don't want to analyse, but the audience warm to them. And Kenneth Williams, he had such charm, basically a lovable quality.'

By the end of the series, the producer was his devoted fan. 'I must just write and say how absolutely brilliant I thought you were on Friday. They were two excellent programmes, and this was very largely due to you [. . .] you did it without seeming acquisitive for points, and at the same time being funny all the way. It was absolutely masterly.'

Williams insisted that a West End theatre run was too exhausting to sustain, and the energy he would burn during a play or revue, with six nights and two matinées each week, can be gauged by how much work he crammed now around his four holidays.

That autumn, aside from six chat shows, and *Just a Minute*, and *Jackanory*, he filmed one of the best-loved *Carry On*s. Shot in a muddy field at Pinewood with the bare trees sprayed green and massive arc lamps to simulate summer sunshine, *Carry On Camping* updated the series' original theme of working-class larks. There was Sid James and Bernie Bresslaw, trying to lure their girlfriends into a bit of topless sunbathing, and Terry Scott and Betty Marsden bickering on a tandem, and Hattie Jacques as a headmistress with the name of her gals' school, Chayste Place, emblazoned across her bosom. Williams celebrated the start of filming by pasting a publicity photo of himself on to a full page of his journal, in his striped blazer, with a side-parting in his schoolboy cut (starting to grey but not receding) and his grin revealing English dentistry.

The shooting schedule, as always, was just six weeks, and the director ran the set like an assembly line. When Peter Rogers invited Williams to join him at a party, Thomas forbade him to leave early: 'You are here to work until 5.20.' Actors had little time to chat. 'It was like being at school,' Barbara Windsor said.

Rain had left the campsite waterlogged, and Williams tricked her into moaning about the cold and wet while he was wearing a throat mike, knowing her complaints would be heard by the director. He was rapped over the knuckles, and then called to stay behind after class – Thomas and Rogers felt that he was drifting out of character and playing his lines for laughs from the crew. The criticism buckled his self-confidence, which was probably the point: he had been chafing too much about the hours and the conditions.

The cost of his car to the studios each day was a point of contention, though it was the principle and not the cost that irked him. When his chauffeur, newly married and with a baby on the way, confided that he was struggling to pay his mortgage, Williams gave him £200 and told him it was payment for comedy ideas.

In this flurry of work, he was busily turning down offers too. Baxter wanted them to star together in Orton's *What the Butler Saw* but Williams did not fancy working with Sir Ralph 'Face Like A Bumhole' Richardson; Peter Eade suggested a Feydeau farce, again, and a two-hander opposite Joan Greenwood; Bill Cotton invited him and John Law to write six episodes of a TV series for BBC1, *Kenneth Williams at Random*. Cotton favoured a twenty-five minute format that was similar to a Saturday night revue that would become one of the biggest family entertainment successes of the seventies, *The Two Ronnies* – opening patter, followed by musical guest, and another stand-up routine, leading into a situation sketch, patter, another song, and the closing gags. 'I'd like you to break out of those Carry Ons where you're just ONE of a team, and come to television and be a STAR,' Cotton told him. 'I think he's a good man and I think he genuinely likes me,' Williams mused, but two weeks later he managed to be talked out of it.

Over lunch with Beverley Cross, they discussed his options: 'He said, "What's the point of knocking yourself out, doing all that work like Stanley Baxter? – you can get laughs just by sitting chatting in the Frost Show or something! – no, if you want to do television it would be better for you to find a good situation comedy series . . ." He is a good objective critic for me.' Instead, he wrote a pilot episode consisting of only a monologue to camera, misleadingly titled *The Kenneth Williams Spectacular*. The recording flopped. Rather than learn his lines, he resorted to autocue, which caused three false starts. The scripts were heavy attempts at whimsy, and the only big laugh came in the interval, when he tried to warm the audience up with a vulgar joke about dentists' drills.

The first episode of *Stop Messin' About* was recorded the day before shooting started at Pinewood on *Carry On Again Doctor*. Myles Rudge, Johnnie Mortimer and Brian Cooke collaborated on the radio scripts, and it sounds like comedy written by committee – jokes are clambering over each other to get in, and the routines lack shape. Some new ideas were funny: Meg and Tone, two pensioners having a furtive affair, deserved a series ('If you can't come to the boil after fifty-nine years, either your gas has gone out or you've got fur in your kettle'). But the folksinging trio Peter, Paul and Mrs Nosepoultice were a poor substitute for Ramblin' Syd Rumpo, and skits such as Williams's Wartime Memoirs were laboured.

Because Took and Feldman claimed copyright on their characters' names, 'Jule' and 'Sand' cropped up anonymously as racing drivers, or astronauts, or oil executives, and to hear the familiar voices underlines what was lost when Kenneth Horne died.

The knowledge for Williams that he was the star made him so anxious he was hardly able to get his words out. Self-consciousness had become a dizzying paralysis, like vertigo. The producer, John Simmonds, made it worse when he warned against letting the series become *The Kenneth Williams Cult Show*. 'A little of you,' Simmonds said, 'is a very rich diet.'

Every opportunity for a headlining role on stage or television seemed a threat to his sanity now. When Michael Mills, the head of comedy at the BBC, tried to bounce him into a one-off *Comedy Playhouse* sitcom, Williams retreated in panic: 'I could not attempt this script at the moment, let alone work with an actor I don't even know. I am too vulnerable. I have hardly slept during the last week with worry about it.' Mills offered £600 and every concession: he could delay production until Richard Pearson, an actor Williams liked and admired, was available; he could have the script reworked; and he could shuffle the whole series around this one episode. 'I quite understand your worries,' he promised, 'and have moved heaven and earth and certain parts of the Television Centre today to put this right.' To Williams, this persuasive flattery felt like harassment. 'I told you in my letter,' he insisted. 'I am not going to do it.'

When he felt no pressure, though, he was capable of unscripted, impromptu performances that delivered everything Bill Cotton or Michael Codron were desperate to see in his one-man shows. Invited to give a talk on his life in the theatre, at the '84 Club' in Margaret Street, he scribbled some general headings when he woke from an afternoon nap, strolled to the venue, walked on to the stage and held a packed room spellbound. Almost his only preparation was to leave his trousers open, so that he could say, ''Ere! You might have told me . . .' and launch into Guinness's advice during *Hotel Paradiso* – 'Always wipe your nose and check your flies.' After two hours of stories, the audience applauded so hard that they seemed determined never to stop.

Peter Rogers too was trying to persuade him on to television, for a Christmas show and a series of shorts called *Carry On Laughing, or How Stupid Can You Get?* That insulted him too – here were the

BBC heads of variety and comedy, trying to tempt him into prestigious series, and Rogers seemed to think he could be treated like a
bit-part comic.

He made *Carry On Again Doctor*, happy to be working with his
favourite co-stars, Barbara Windsor, Hattie Jacques and Jim Dale,
but he had been nursing a grudge since the muddy fields of *Camping*.
When the script arrived for *Carry On Jungle Boy* and he turned it
down, Gerald Thomas assumed this was the usual bout of coyness
that preceded every film. He sent a bantering note, with an invitation
to lunch and signed off, 'Hope you are keeping well both "top and
bottom".' For once, Thomas had misjudged his tone.

When he saw Williams was earnest in his refusal, he sent a long
and formal apology. 'I am sorry you have apparently been brooding
[. . .] I wish you had talked about it before because I am sure it must
have built up in your mind [. . .] I personally apologise if I have ever
treated you like a crowd artiste, but I am sure this is not so as I hold
you in high personal regard.' When this tack failed, he tried to play
on Williams's insecurities, hinting that to miss one film was to walk
out on the whole series: 'I feel this is probably the parting of the ways
[. . .] How unhappy I am that after so many years we have had to part
company.' Williams took a dramatic step to register his hurt. Rather
than risk being available for the film or for *Carry On Laughing*, he
agreed to Cotton's incessant requests for a six-part variety series on
television.

The title *At Random* was dropped. This would be simply *The
Kenneth Williams Show*, and he started work on it with John Law in
June 1969. The scripts did not flow easily, and Law seemed fractious
and unable to concentrate. Williams trusted him to deliver sketches
and situations that he could work into his own style, and their slow
progress did not worry him. He guested twice on David Frost's show
and made an unscripted appearance on *The Jim Dale Show*.

At weekends he let Waine and Dennis entertain him with outings
and meals. 'They were fun days, brilliant days, glorious,' Waine said.
'It was terribly funny to be with him.' Williams had planned to visit
Italy with them that summer, but decided he couldn't spare the time.
'Pesaro was Ken's idea,' said Waine. 'At the last minute, he cancelled,
said he couldn't face it, and we were left in the lurch.' Instead, he sent

long letters to them in Italy, cramming seventy lines of handwriting on to a page, so that a single airmail form contained 1,000 words.

'This was only intended to be a little note, you see,' he concluded the first letter, 'and you know I am no scholar – not for me the niceties of language and the veiled subtleties of attenuated violins.' The letters were mostly frivolous: he wrote of seeing the Rolling Stones' free concert in Hyde Park, and the bitchiness of BBC writers ('he said of Barry Took, "He finds his talent very difficult to live with. It's so small" ').

His correspondence, like his conversation, could suddenly digress into serious themes, and the first airmail included a confession of his motives for staying single:

> Living with someone always means a denial of self in SOME way and I suppose I have always known it was something I couldn't accomplish. So I've always stayed on the sidelines. Getting the pleasure vicariously. It's not wholly satisfactory but then of course no lives are, and you know what I think about indiscriminate sex and promiscuous trade. I think it's the beginning of a long, long road to despair. Only in the channelling of energy into construction – in career or in private life – does there lay the seed of hopefulness. And we can't live without hope [. . .] All problems have to be solved eventually by ONESELF and that's where all your lovely John Donne stuff turns out to be a load of crap because, in the last analysis A MAN IS AN ISLAND. He may like to communicate but if he CANNOT it doesn't kill him. But enough of seriousness, you are on holiday and it's all whoops and bonnet over the windmill!

Six weeks later, at Waine's urging and in need of some 'whoops and bonnet over the windmill' himself, Williams walked to a travel agent and booked a flight to Tangier, via Gibraltar, for the following morning. This unplanned escape was an attempt to give his whole life the slip, to take the anarchist on holiday without the chaperone.

He was greeted at the Rembrandt Hotel by the hall porter, Hamadi, who always took care of him; in return, Williams would send Hamadi books, clothes and shoes from Britain. He unpacked in his room overlooking the Boulevard Pasteur, where the queens were 'all having the stroll-ette', and dashed off a letter to Waine and Dennis: 'John M[aynard] is coming round at 7.30 for the drink-ettes and the chat + then we'll have dinner somewhere exotic – with a touch of Les Plus Belles Lavandes behind the lughole and your actual hydrocortisone up the arse so keep your fingers crossed for your loving chum.'

After a week, he worked up the courage to meet a male prostitute, called Jafa, in a Kasbah club, and was taken to a seedy apartment block in an alley off the Medina. In thrilled phrases, he wrote to Waine of 'brown and white limbs locked in a curious kind of poetry. O! What a night it was.' Waine believes the whole episode might have been a fantasy: 'He was prone to elaborate. I'm pretty sure there would have been more money, laughs and fumbles than sex.'

Self-disgust caught up with him. Two nights later,

instead of going home at 1.30, I foolishly went into El Piano. There was a group of English hearties – one v. drunk who said, 'I used to admire you until I saw you in this bar with all these queens – are you a poof?' I said, 'It's none of your business,' rather lamely, but he insisted – repeating it louder and louder, 'Are you a poof?' It was endless. Eventually Sid [the bar's owner] said, 'That's enough from you – you've gone too far' and they went [. . .] The entire incident served to make me feel inferior and depressed . . . I got to bed about 4 o'c. Quite sober, but the inside full of shame and misery over the incident with the drunk fellow. Oh! the paradox of a nature that wants so much to be respected, but is continually at the mercy of the disrespectful. I know the fellow wasn't THAT drunk. He would have thought those thoughts if he'd been sober. He voiced the prejudice of bigotry and conformity and is probably an unfulfilled and unhappy creature, but it still happened and it still disturbs and rankles. I was a fool. At the start of his question I should simply have said 'yes'.

Before Tangier he had recorded another *Jackanory*; now he returned to London, expecting to continue writing his television series and to maintain a hectic schedule of radio and chat shows. Instead, the tide had turned and his career was beached. He had rejected so much work – everything the theatre offered, most of the television work and two of his established series, in the *Carry Ons* and *International Cabaret* – that producers had ceased to ask. His TV pilot for the monologue *Spectacular* had been rejected, and plans for a second series of *Stop Messin' About* were on hold. John Law was too ill to work; Williams, who hated his friends to be sick, dismissed his bronchitis as a bout of self-pity and asthma. He did two episodes of Rudge's cod biographies for Radio 3, *Tribute to Greatness*, with Joan Sims, and tried to work by himself on the last two scripts for *The Kenneth Williams Show*.

It was not only producers who had grown fed up with him. His friends were frustrated too. Juliet Mills, who had patiently supported him during the agonised rehearsals for *Gentle Jack*, was hurt by his abrupt refusal when she invited him to a party. 'I hope you have a lot of new and loving friends,' she told him, 'because you certainly never bother about your old and loving ones.'

Peter Eade wrote the same day, after a severe scene in his office. Eade, who detested confrontation, tried to warn him that people read his constant rejections as bitterness, and that his determination to stay away from the stage had metastased into a phobia. All Williams could hear was criticism. His handwriting, which had been chatty and untidy for weeks, became a tiny, cramped print. After a second talk with Eade, he was miserable: 'I longed just to stop and break down. Give way to the waves of despair and LET them engulf me.' Eade would not let up: 'People for whom you have been working in films, radio and television [. . .] have all been distressed by your attitude and behaviour,' he wrote. To make matters worse, John Law was now in hospital: that night he suffered a heart attack and was taken into intensive care. His wife, Beryl, phoned and asked him to pray for John.

Williams took refuge in meditation – not the transcendental form of self-hypnosis, which was the fad of London in the late sixties, but a deep spiritual reflection. He listened to Schubert, read Isaiah Berlin, and wrote a letter to *The Spectator* dissecting 'our current moral malaise', quoting a long and complex passage from Erich Heller's *The Disinherited Mind*. 'What Blake called the "mental fight" has been going on with me, since 1946,' he concluded. The magazine's sub-editors did not take him wholly seriously: the letter was headlined, 'Let's All Swing Together'.

To prove to Eade that he was willing to work, he appeared on Radio 2's *Pete Murray Show*, and flew to Dublin for *The Late Show* with Gay Byrne. He stayed at the Montrose Hotel, where his room was equipped with an electric 'automatic massage boy', which he eyed with distaste. That evening, at a party in the home of the actress and director Shelah Richards, he met Siobhàn McKenna again and wrote a delighted pen portrait of her: 'Easily the loveliest and most talented actress in Ireland today – looking radiantly youthful, the hair streaming and sparkling, with those great eyes wide above the high cheekbones, and the generous lips smiling in welcome. She has a distinctive trait of giving you a look of fleeting apprehension before she bursts into laughter. It's the thing I always remember about her.'

Just a Minute had returned with four players and a new producer, Simon Brett. Williams always sat beside Clement Freud, and instead of challenging on technical points, which tended to slow the show down, he would distract his opponents, by pulling faces, sticking out his tongue, raising his legs and pulling his trousers up to his knees, or nibbling Freud's ear. These antics convulsed the studio audience, so that whoever was speaking seemed to be hilarious. Brett wrote to praise his 'infinite variety' and added, 'I am grateful not only for your beautifully timed anecdotes and changes of moods, but also for your hard work as a censor, immediately cleaning up the programme when it threatened to go over the top.' When the series ended in November 1969, Williams decided to return to Tangier, with Tom Waine.

The holiday collapsed. At Gibraltar, the onward flights were fully booked for a week, and the ferry was in dry dock. They spent the day in a series of bars with a group of officers from HMS *Blake*. After his humiliation in August, Williams seemed intent on outing himself and by midnight, 'in the bar with the sailors, I was shouting, "Of course I'm queer – what d'you think I'm in here for?" and these officers were obviously embarrassed.' They didn't return to their hotel until 5 a.m., when Williams was so drunk that the porter had to unlock his door for him.

The next day, hungover and fed up, he booked the midnight flight back to London, and picked up two ratings from another British ship, HMS *Hermes*. By the evening, they were staggering through a party, where Williams was being shown off as the prize guest. He was introduced to the captain of the *Hermes*: when he realised who this officer was, he adopted a grand voice and, dragging the two sailors over, declared, 'I believe you know Daniel and Sylvester – they're on your boat.' The captain bridled. The *Hermes* was a ship, not a boat, and it was the size of a small town, he said. He could not be expected to recognise all his crew.

'Of course Ken knew it was a ship,' Waine said. 'He just couldn't resist baiting figures of authority. And he used outrageous comments or downright rudeness to cover, I always thought, his discomfiture with larger groups of people.'

They returned to sub-zero temperatures and heavy snow, and went up to Highgate Ponds to throw snowballs and take photographs, breathing plumes of frozen mist in the clear air. Williams quizzed Tom and Clive about their sex life, and confessed that his own libido was more immature than ever. He had developed a crush on an American actor, Scott Hylands, and wanted to see him again and again in the movie *Daddy's Gone A-Hunting*. He had even sent a fan letter. If the actor had materialised in his bedroom, though, he would not want sex – only 'schoolboy cuddles'.

'His answer to all the normal urges was to live vicariously through the lives of others who were less afraid of commitment, and to fantasise,' Waine said. 'That's why he loved the cinema where the fantasies could not impinge on his life. Ken raved about Scott Hylands for days and days . . . just another fantasy, a way of letting off steam, of letting out basic urges. I don't think it was a fear of rejection. He wouldn't have been rejected anyway by any one of a number of people he met. There was a garage mechanic in Tangier and a number of other attempted liaisons, all abortive. When we'd ask how it went, he would say bleakly, "You know me. When it came to it, I started telling the jokes and humour is death to sex." The problem was that the people he fancied had by definition "the commonness" factor and "the barrack room mind". He liked the frame but couldn't cope with the picture inside it. He liked minds, humour, intellect and not bodies.'

In mid-December he recorded *Christmas Night with the Stars* at Shepherd's Bush, and was humiliated to discover his dressing-room was a hole in the wall on the third floor. The other celebrities – Harry

Secombe, Roy Castle, Val Doonican – had star treatment; even the dancers were not exiled to the third tier. Bill Cotton claimed it was an oversight, but Williams knew how television's hierarchies of prestige were structured. He had treated their blandishments with contempt, instead of accepting them as the polite mandates they really were. Now he was paying for it.

As rehearsals for his TV shows approached, he felt he was splitting into pieces. The noise from the overhead fans, which ventilated the bathrooms at Farley Court, was 'getting beyond sanity' and on the first day of run-throughs he overslept: trying to escape the machinery's stop-start clatter, he had taken two Mogadons and dragged his bed away from the wall. By the end of the week, he was shivering in the parks and streets, afraid to go home and face the noise. He resolved to move out, and asked Noel Willman if he could hole up in the basement of his Chelsea home. Willman had misgivings – the room was not really fit to be lived in. They went to the cinema, and Williams started to cry; he kept sobbing as they walked back to Baker Street to collect an overnight bag. It was Louie's birthday, and he pulled himself together to take her to dinner with the Jacksons, before he spent the night in Chelsea. The next day he moved back into the flat, promising himself that he would sell it as soon as the TV series was over. If necessary, he could move in with his sister.

The first episode of *The Kenneth Williams Show* was taped on 22 December 1969, in front of an audience so grudging, 'I think they combed the geriatric wards of London for them'. His tension subsided, though the second recording was worse still. During his warm-up he criticised the audience for being lifeless, and Bill Cotton warned him, in the viewing-room later, not to do it again.

The following day, after he and his co-star Joan Sims had watched the rough edit, a script editor came over to break bad news. After four months in a coma, John Law had died. He was forty. Williams was stunned. During the next month, he rehearsed and performed material they had written together, and brooded on how, when the sessions were going badly, he would wail, 'Oh what's the point? We're all just waiting for death anyhow!' And Law would shrug and say, 'There are one or two things you could do while you're waiting.'

15

'I adore this woman and will forgive everything from someone who has her sweetness, radiance and generosity of spirit'

February 1970–June 1973

The *Kenneth Williams Show* flopped. Because he refused to own a television, Williams watched the first broadcast at Peter Eade's home and tried to convince himself the show was nothing to be ashamed of. He knew, though, that the material was tepid and the audience stone cold, and he had paced it all too fast.

The next day his hopes disintegrated in stages, like stop-motion footage of an exploding balloon. The *Daily Mail* liked the show, and he cut out the review, which compared him to Hancock and called it 'a particularly amusing, witty and intellectually stimulating perform-ance'. Friends offered faint praise – Tom said it wasn't really at all bad, and Clive added it might have gone better on BBC2. When Williams went out, though, a man at the news-stand told him the show was 'a load of shit'. At the supermarket, the man on the bacon counter called it 'rotten'. Peter Blenkinsop, his driver, thought Marty Feldman was funnier. Noel Willman called to warn he needed better material, the type of sketches that Cook and Pinter had once writ-ten for him. Stanley Baxter made him laugh, saying they should pool their earnings and flee to Australia without paying income tax – but even that joke had a bitter twist, for Australia was a byword among British comics for washed-up talent.

He felt happier about a poetry reading for Radio 4. The fee was just £20, which matched his current valuation of himself, and he was allowed to make his own selection: he opened with a verse Baxter had written in CSE, 'Berlin in the Twenties', and flew into 'Bagpipe Music' by MacNeice and Tennyson's 'The Lady of Shalott'. Waine felt the choices reflected the 'fundamental bleakness' his friend was feeling: 'I wouldn't put it as strongly as despair. It was more an inevitability, a vague feeling of foreboding, of the pointlessness of life.' A broad streak of mischief cut through the programme too. One listener wrote to complain that Williams should not have announced he was dying for a pee.

He watched the second show with Tom and Clive, and realised he had to get out of the country while the rest of the series was shown. The following afternoon he flew to Paris and boarded an evening flight for Tangier. This time, he embraced the city's excesses. He wanted to blot out the past few months. 'There is no doubt about it, it's a really v. good resort for the gay,' he wrote to Tom. 'Because there's an essential air of utter TAT about everything. Apart from the English expatriates there is nothing piss-elegant about the place or the people + they give you a good romp for your money AND out of season like this it is PERFECT cos the idiots are not here from your Lyons Tours + your Gibraltar Silver Wing shit.'

He celebrated his birthday with defiant abandon – the streets were so warm that he took off his jacket, and later there was 'the tradeola, 20D[inar] all in', with two Moroccans, Omar and Mohammed. 'The vada on the terrazo with the lemon tea is my latest affectation, and then a stroll up to the socco for the encore. I think I sat *too* long in the solay today cos me ecaf [face] is BURNING. So are the balls + I suppose you can guess why? Yes – I caught them again!! That was the result of the threesome. Found 'em crawling next morning so rush off to get the stuff at the chemist who remembered me for the same thing last year and asked if it was my "speciality" – I think he imagines I'm cultivating them or something.'

Whispers brought the BBC's verdict on his TV series when he returned. Bill Cotton told the producer, Roger Ordish, who told Eade, who told Williams: it had been disastrous. Peter Rogers, judging his moment as always, invited him to return to the fold, with a supporting role in *Carry On Loving*. He played an unmarried marriage guidance counsellor called Percy Snooper, and rewrote the part to suit himself better ('Much funnier,' Thomas told him. 'Clever boy, I'll buy you a lettuce leaf'). When Williams walked on to the set, the cast and crew broke into applause. Even Sid James seemed glad to see him. The thought that he might quit the series had dismayed everyone. 'Who,' demanded Charles Hawtrey, 'is to silence Connor by telling him to shut his cakehole – who is to insult Joan Sims and then steal a kiss – who is to expose themselves in the corridor?'

He returned also to an invitation from Harold Wilson, to a reception at 10 Downing Street for the Swedish prime minister, Olof Palme. He told none of his friends, fearing they would try to persuade him to go, and instead wrote immediately to the private secretary: 'I have to decline because these grand functions fill me with awe and I become hopelessly inhibited.'

His instinct too was to reject all official honours as hypocrisies: he had sneered at Noël Coward's knighthood in the New Years honours lists. Perhaps if the invitation had come from a Tory PM, he might have felt differently. 'When offered something which obviously isn't worth the price – like cinema ice-cream and Labour governments – we still have the right to say "no thank you",' he had written to *The Times*, five months earlier. During the fifties he had voted Labour, like his parents. Devaluation in 1968 snapped his last ties to the Left. By the time he began airing his political views on chat shows and panel games, he believed capitalism was the only just system of economics, though he still disliked apartheid and colonialism.

Stop Messin' About was revived for a thirteen-part series, and after the first recording he felt happier than he had for months. He bumped into Lord Snowdon at a Viennese restaurant in Swiss Cottage, and they shared two bottles of wine with Tom and Clive before going to the Spartan Club. Hugh Paddick was there, and Williams was gratified to hear him remark, 'Let's face it, we all know it's YOUR show.'

That was his last night at Farley Court – he had bought a bigger flat in Queen Alexandra Mansions, where both he and his parents had lived before. The apartment was being soundproofed with lead lining, so Baxter, who owned a property in the same block, offered to let him borrow it until his own place was ready. Williams was delighted to realise he could hear the children in the playground of his primary school, across the road.

Other noises and interruptions were less welcome. There were no fan motors, but the neighbours upstairs were walking on bare boards, and he had forgotten to make his telephone number ex-directory.

Only close friends knew the code, though – three rings, then stop and dial again – so mostly he ignored the phone and answered letters. After his poetry broadcast there had been hundreds, many from fans asking him to read their own poems, and he replied to them all. When the correspondents caught his interest, especially servicemen and admirers who sensed his depressive moods, he would write affectionate, newsy replies. Some fans treated him as a gay agony uncle: he told them that homosexuality was normal and its suppression unhealthy, but that promiscuity was poison to the soul.

He was cramming every page of his diary. At the top of each entry he noted the weather, sometimes recording the room temperature and barometric pressure too, and listed his ailments, his medications and the time of his bowel movement.

That summer, with only his weekly radio show to do, all his anxieties were focused on moving into 80 Queen Alexandra Mansions: his post was already delivered there, and each day when he collected his letters he inspected the work. His nerves were strained:

> T+C arrived at 6oc and I gave them tea. Tom started pouring it and I suddenly screamed out, 'I never gave you permission to pour out the tea! – this is my house you know – you can't do as you like here . . .' and when he + Clive protested I said, 'Perhaps you'd better just go, and we can forget the whole bloody evening . . .' and eventually I calmed down. It was disgraceful behaviour, but I know it's the result of TURMOIL inside – the build-up due to the utter frustration of WAIT-ING, WAITING, WAITING for somewhere to LIVE.

When he did move in, he was obsessed with finding fault. There was a loose floorboard under the fitted carpet, which he was not supposed to vacuum for at least six weeks, and the sink leaked, as did the cistern. His mother had gone on holiday, to the Scottish islands. He felt overwhelmed: he would beg workmen to make urgent repairs and then fret at the intrusion.

These problems were dwarfed when a new neighbour arrived downstairs. 'A dreadful looking woman moving into the flat directly underneath me. She's got a PIANO! Even while they're shoving her furniture in, she's rushing to the keyboard and doing mad trills up and down the ivories and the noise is as if she was in the SAME ROOM. It is death.'

He was eating in restaurants more than ever, and 'having the drinks rather than the drinkettes'. Eade warned that gossips said he was becoming a drunk. Williams used alcohol as social fuel and, because he never spent an entire day alone, he did drink daily. He could get 'high' on half a bottle of wine, but no matter how much he consumed he never blacked out. He never missed a show or gave a bad performance through drinking. Alcohol made him noisier, and cruder, and more abrasive, and sentimental, and reckless – all the things he wanted to be. It probably worsened his depressions: sometimes, when he was dieting, his moods would stabilise after a few days' abstinence. While his diets could become obsessive, his drinking never did. In the mornings, when he was alone, he drank coffee; at night, when he couldn't sleep, he used tablets.

The clubs and parties masked his boredom. Aside from the TV series, and the radio, and the films, chat shows and voiceovers – none of which really counted – he felt he hadn't done any work for years. He booked a holiday, cruising to Istanbul, with Waine and Dennis: it started badly and got worse. Four days before they left, Williams had guested on Simon Brett's *Highlight* programme, and after the interview John Simmonds buttonholed him to say *Stop Messin' About* had been cancelled. The scripts had sagged, and there were too many complaints about the crudity. Williams packed his suitcase, knowing that his career had dwindled to the annual run of *Just a Minute* and six-week bursts of filming on the *Carry Ons*. The only extra that summer had been a voiceover for a Dixcel toilet tissue advert, though he had also turned down *No Sex Please – We're British*.

After a ten-hour delay at Gatwick they joined the *Fiesta* cruise ship, which was crowded and claustrophobic. Games were compulsory: they were given numbers and ushered on to the catwalk to parade in the Mr Fiesta contest. Williams won, which meant he had to dance with Miss Fiesta. 'There is no gaiety on a cruise,' he wrote to Paul Florance. 'In fact cruises are about the heartiest kinds of holiday one can have. They are awful. This ship was like a sort of floating holiday camp without the camp and the sight of all these bodies lying about the deck getting suntanned was revolting to say the least. And of course, on a ship, you can't just get up and walk away. Otherwise you drown. All you can do is to go and skulk in your cabin and write rude things in your diary and that's what I did. A lot of the time.'

Within a week, Williams was seething at his companions, furious that they had gone on a tour of Santorini, by donkey, when he hadn't fancied it. He took revenge by going on an excursion himself, without them. 'The first week was all right,' Dennis said, 'but the second week was just murder, because we fell out with him. He made our lives very difficult.'

Williams was scathing and spiteful when they came home. 'Mon cher Tom, your letter sounded like Queen Victoria,' he sneered. The row bubbled for weeks and erupted after a walk round Kensington Gardens. Williams felt he was being chivvied to go to a café when he preferred to go home.

'Ken was like a child,' Waine said. 'We'd been crossing Bayswater Road to get back to the car, and Clive and I nipped across just as the light was changing, and he hadn't, and out of that came a huge row, like a tantrum. He was sitting in the back of the car, and his whole face was tight and thin. I said, "It's no good sulking in the back there." He said nothing, didn't say a thing until we were driving round the one-way system at Marble Arch. Then he started: "I'd just like to get out of this car, *please*." Clive stopped right in the middle of the road, and said, "Well, get out then, you fucking queen." And he got out in the middle of the road, and all the cars were going round him.'

Williams complained to Baxter that he couldn't help his moods. He was beset by illness and constant din, and his soul was suffering a crisis. 'Spiritual malaise my arse!' said Baxter. 'You want to get on the box, mate, and do some work! – that's half your trouble! – sitting around feeling sorry for yourself and moaning about the ontological creed!' Williams would take advice from almost nobody – certainly not from his agent, nor any producer – but he trusted Baxter's guidance. The next script he received came from Binkie Beaumont. It was Shaw, an obscure early play called *Captain Brassbound's Conversion*, and Ingrid Bergman was to star, with Frith Banbury directing. Williams knew he should take it. Bergman's name would ensure a hit, and if the production was bad she would be blamed. Her role demanded presence, but little comedy. He could turn up every night and steal the laughs.

After a day at Pinewood – he was Thomas Cromwell in *Carry On Henry*, in costumes filched from the Tudor epic, *Anne of the Thousand Days* – Williams went to Beaumont's home in Lord North Street. He met Bergman and Joss Ackland, who would play Brassbound, and liked them. His character, a rattish sailor called Drinkwater, was a bit-part after the second act: 'it rather fizzles out,' he wrote to Beverley Cross, 'but they all said that I would be very telling in the role and so on, and I said all right because I thought it would be a way of filling in the evenings.' Beaumont, who had been trying to lure him back to the theatre since *Gentle Jack*, could not have guessed how much Williams secretly wanted to do the play.

Rehearsals began in the New Year, and provided an excuse for avoiding jury service. Shaw's 1899 description of Drinkwater seems almost a premonition:

> His frame and flesh are those of an ill-nourished lad of seventeen; but his age is inscrutable [. . .] A Londoner would recognise him at once as an extreme but hardy specimen of [. . .] nurture in a city slum. His utterance, affectedly pumped and hearty, and naturally vulgar and nasal, is ready and fluent [. . .] not unlike that of smart London society in its tendency to replace diphthongs by vowels (sometimes rather prettily) and to shuffle all the traditional vowel pronunciations.

That suggests the slippage in Williams's accent, from gentry to gutter, might not have seemed unusual in Victorian London. Shaw's attempts to render the language phonetically make the part almost unreadable, though. Drinkwater's first lines are, 'Awtenoon, Mr Renkin. Yr honor's eolth. Youre not best pleased to be hinterrapted in yr bit o gawdnin baw the lawk o me, gavner.'

The shock of rehearsing after six years almost sent Williams into the state of funk that killed *The Platinum Cat*. He picked holes, and did his 'spectre at the feast bit, going around spreading despondency like there is no tomorrow'. To Banbury, he complained that Ackland was underplaying and that James Gibson, as the missionary, Renkin, was deaf and decrepit; to everyone else he moaned that Banbury was stale and that the play needed a young, zestful director such as Franco Zeffirelli. When his victims turned on him, he was shocked. Banbury accused him one afternoon of playing a speech all on one note and losing the audience's interest. Williams protested that he kept the house hanging on every word he spoke, and Ackland said, 'You want to bet?'

Williams was on the brink of quitting. The thought of taking direction, and facing criticism, and sustaining feuds, and opening to a flop, was hateful. He had a blocked-up nose and asked his GP to sign him off for two weeks. Stuffed with medicine, his body reacted: he had been suffering intermittent stomach cramps for months, and an attack now made him bring up bile. After a miserable weekend, Williams decided he didn't want to be ill. He would rather do the play.

They opened in Brighton, with Williams in such a raw state of anxiety that he was making mistakes – coming in too early on one cue at the dress rehearsal, in front of Beaumont, and missing another altogether on the first night. Bergman chided him, but he felt no anger. She was the one member of the cast whom he liked without reservation. Her fame was so much greater than his that they could never be rivals, and she was earthy and charming. He preserved the card she left in his dressing-room before the first night at the Cambridge Theatre in Earlham Street: 'Be my next director! Feed out of your hand I would.'

The reviews were mixed in the best possible way – most critics dismissed the play but admitted that Williams got the laughs. The *Mirror* called it 'the nearest Shaw got to writing panto', and added, 'Williams cavorts in outrageous fashion and brings every drop of fun from his cheerful Cockney sparrow role'; he was 'rampant carry-on just in control and very funny', said the *Evening News*; Shaw had hoped, said the *Telegraph*, to see Drinkwater 'played by a comedian rather than an actor – he [Shaw] mentioned Dan Leno – and Kenneth Williams plays him to the hilt in his familiar but endearingly idiosyncratic manner'.

A few had forgotten Williams as a West End actor, and regarded him as an intruder from television. 'Another piece of odd casting,' huffed *Plays and Players*. 'He plays him very much a la "Round The Horne" (as Julian, or was it Sandy?). He goes too far by half; it's not so much a performance as a turn, and also largely inaudible. That particular camp twang comes off into a microphone, but reverberates unintelligibly round an auditorium.' The audience knew what they wanted – they applauded the slight figure in a sailor's jersey and belt, with a woollen hat like a stevedore, when he walked on, and they cheered in Act Two when he was dragged offstage to be bathed 'in cold water'.

Williams was not at ease among the cast. He had lunch with Ackland and others at Colosseo, and began gossiping about absent colleagues. Jimmy Gibson, he said, was stuck together with stamp paper and would probably drop dead on stage one night. He was told to be quiet and sulked for the rest of the meal: 'To them, all wit is really unacceptable because they pretend not to accept malice + malice is an essential part of wit.'

The next night, despite a trying day and a 'nightmare' performance in the evening, 'I came out of the stage door and the night air was mild and there was a light rain falling + I suddenly realised how utterly beautiful it all was. In our moments of anguish and mental turmoil we completely forget that sudden surge of joy which really good things bring to you.'

The difference was Ingrid Bergman. She had the gift to make him feel, with a look or a few words, as if he was her cornerstone, the true friend whose talent kept her world intact. She was never precious, and she did not pretend to be a great actress, but her sincerity made a word of praise seem worth more than all the critics' specious columns. Everyone felt that magic. One evening, Bergman invited Williams to supper, with Binkie Beaumont and Clive Dennis, whose pop-star looks pleased the impresario. She served vodka and Swedish meat-balls. 'I ADORE this woman,' wrote Williams, despite her stumbles and lack of stagecraft, 'and will forgive everything from someone who has her sweetness, radiance and generosity of spirit AND who PACKS the house as she does.'

Brassbound was profiled in a BBC2 arts programme, *Aquarius*, with Humphrey Burton. Williams was booked to compère another show on that channel, a revamp of *International Cabaret*, called *Meanwhile on BBC2*. In need of a writing partner he turned to Myles Rudge, though their friendship had not survived his rejection of Rudge's

Comedy Playhouse script. 'I actually don't LIKE Rudge,' Williams muttered in his diary, 'he's the nearest thing to a mean-spirited spinster in pants that I know.' He tried writing with the actor Hilary Minster but much of the time he was compiling the material for his three-minute links himself, working in longhand and giving the pages to a BBC assistant for typing. The shows featured the old mix of stars, has-beens and novelty acts, all incidental to his stand-up routines.

He also recorded a series written by Rodney Wingfield, featuring as a spy in *The Secret Life of Kenneth Williams* – a series of eight half-hour productions for Radio 4 from the drama department, rather than light entertainment. His fee on radio was £70 a show, far less than the £400 he received for *Meanwhile*, but the money was an irrelevance. He was glad for the chippings of stardom the BBC scattered on him, which set him apart from Bergman's other co-stars.

He was also filming *Carry On*s. *At Your Convenience* was his twenty-first – this time he was W.C. Boggs, managing director of a firm making lavatories, fighting the European regulations that could put bidets in every British bathroom. It was the first in the series not to make a profit, and the cast thought it might be the last one ever: Rogers had always said he would keep producing films until one lost money, and then he would quit. Cinema was dying, he insisted, and the only way he could *Carry On* would be on television.

At Your Convenience flopped because it broke the first law of *Carry On*s: although it had bawdy gags and a seaside pier, and Charlie Hawtrey got drunk, and Kenneth Williams was chased round the desk by his secretary, and Hattie Jacques and Sid James were locked to the death in marriage . . . in the end the bosses won. In the story Williams humiliated the unions. His son, Lew Boggs, was a smarmy nob in a sports car who got the girl. Sid the foreman was an ex-worker who had turned middle class. It all seemed fraudulent and sour, an old friend who was becoming bitter in his middle age.

Later that year Rogers returned to his failsafe, the hospital formula, in *Carry On Matron*: Williams played Sir Bernard Cutting, a hypochondriac surrounded by medical textbooks, who believes he is turning into a woman. It was *Carry On Abroad* the following year that brought the series back to its concept, a blend of workers' playtime and Blitz spirit, with Williams as a travel agent taking a raucous crowd of Brits on a package holiday to a half-built hotel in Spain.

At some point during this rapid succession of shoots, Williams must have asked Joan Sims to marry him. By the time she wrote her autobiography, thirty years later, she could not be sure when the proposal came, but it was probably the early seventies, between *Loving* and *Behind*: the most likely date is August 1973, when they spent a desolate evening at 'a lousy restaurant [. . .] In the middle of the meal (half of which was uneaten) Joan burst into tears and said, "I need somebody in my life, Kenny!" [. . .] I gave her my handkerchief and she kept squashing it into a sodden ball and crying convulsively.'

Sims, who had been through two broken affairs, was drinking hard, and had lost hope of ever having a husband and children. Though she was flattered and glad to be asked, she turned Williams down. Everyone on the films heard the story, and it became one of the *Carry On* legends – how Kenny had once wooed Joanie with the promise, 'You don't have to worry, there won't be any hanky-panky, none of that saucy stuff,' and how she had replied, 'But Ken . . . I rather like the saucy stuff!'

Williams did not record the rebuff in his diary. He had given up fantasies of fatherhood a decade ago, though he was a favourite of other people's children. Yet Sims could not have invented his declaration – rumours like that, if they were lies, would wreck a friendship.

Sims regarded that proposal as light-hearted but sincere. Williams cannot have attached any importance to it, or her rejection would have wounded him. Barbara Windsor, his closest friend on the set, explained the offer was made to cheer Sims up: she knew, because he had once asked her to marry him too.

'He said to me one day – we were walking along the corridor, going to lunch – he said, "Would you ever leave Ronnie?" I said, "No!" He said, "Well, if you did, would you marry me?" I told him not to be so silly. He said, "Oh, I do like you – but mind you, Bar, there'd be no sex." So he'd say things like that. I've got a feeling Joan took it a bit more seriously than he meant it, but that was Kenny, making her feel wanted. She always felt very unwanted, cos out of all of them, Hattie had her great family, and Sid did, and Butterworth, and me, and Joanie didn't. Kenny could be terribly sweet, very harsh and very sweet.' Sims had sometimes seemed pitifully unhappy, she added, and Williams would try to help by telling filthy stories, very loudly, about mutual friends such as Peter Eade, until Joan could not cry for laughing.

Williams had been taking Sims to lunch since 1958. He thought she was hopelessly suburban – so morally conventional that she was neutered. He appreciated her ability to halt his bad behaviour before he caused irrevocable offence, however. When, during *Carry On Camping*, he had refused to let a young actress named Liz Knight join the 'regulars' in the canteen, Sims called him 'a demonic little sod' and pointedly led the newcomer away to sit with her at another table. That sort of reproach – direct, rude, practical – was the sort Williams appreciated best, and he never resented it.

She was his co-star on *The Kenneth Williams Show*, when he coined a wordy catchphrase to announce her: 'With a great deal of respect and not a little warmth . . . Joan Sims!' At the series' end, he presented her with a plate, inscribed, 'With a great deal of respect and not a little warmth to a very nice person'. Two months later, she received a card, in an envelope addressed to Miss Joan Sims (née Bagwash). The card was a printed note of refusal, the kind Williams dispatched to fête committees and businessmen's conventions, but with a hand-written amendment. It read, '*Mr Kenneth Williams thanks you for your suggestion, but regrets that because of other engagements he is unable to accept your invitation* to a cheap lunch next Wednesday & says you can stick it up your arse. Love, K.'

Sims and Jacques were among the guests at the opening of Transformation, a furniture and interior design shop in Muswell Hill launched by Tom Waine and Clive Dennis. Their relationship with Williams did not follow a trajectory – it was more of a ricochet, sometimes explosively close, sometimes whining and distant. When he needed their company, he expected to be collected and returned home, and to be cooked his favourite meals, especially omelettes and apple pies, and above all to have their full attention. Dennis said, 'All our friends would complain, "We never see you because you're always with him."'

'The truth was that friendship with Ken was very difficult,' Waine said. 'He was incredibly demanding and at his insistence you ended up seeing far too much of him. Then periodically he'd go off the rails and have one of these eruptions.'

They joined him in Tangier after *Brassbound* ended its six-month run, having broken West End box-office records. That autumn, with no work planned before the next *Carry On* (apart from five recordings of *Just a Minute*), he saw them often. They continued to be the only friends he permitted to breeze through the divisions in his life; theatre colleagues, the Tangier set, *Carry On* pals, his family, all were arranged in slices, as if his social world was a pie chart. Partly this protected him against himself: he would gossip about each of his friends to all of the others. He also recognised that he was often a poor judge of character. At a dinner on his mother's sixty-ninth birthday, he sat her next to an entertaining and bitchy actor who was nick-named Poison Ivy. Like all Williams's friends, Ivy knew the secret of Pat's illegitimate birth – it was too late to intervene when Williams heard him say to Louie, 'Your daughter and Ken look nothing alike . . . but then, of course, they had different fathers, didn't they?'

Tom and Clive accompanied him everywhere. Williams thanked them continually, in a stream of notelets. One which began, 'Ah! Gracious sir, your kind remarks / Have quite transformed our evening larks,' became an ode to sleepless nights, the nuisance of nocturnal trips to the lavatory and British Rail's prohibition on flush-ing: 'Which when the train is in the station / Doth yet encourage constipation.' The three spent Christmas together, struggling with *The Times*'s jumbo crossword, and had Boxing Day with Pat, and the following day with Clive's parents, and the next watching *The Great Escape* on television – and, like a leaf under a magnifying glass, the friendship shrivelled. Williams could not share his life at that sustained pitch. He began phoning at one or two in the morning, wanting to talk about his health. Then he refused to go to a New Year's Eve party, deciding instead to spend it without Tom and Clive, at the Jacksons' home.

'We were miffed,' Waine said. 'But of course, Ken could never be wrong so, as was the pattern in these rifts, we were painted as the villains. We had a letter from him talking of "snubs to me" and "a desire for vengeance" and concluding as these things always did with, "I don't want to put myself in that kind of jeopardy ever again so let's just leave it alone." All very precious. If anybody else had reacted in that way, he'd have said deprecatingly, "Ummm! Silly queen!"'

Williams broadcast versions of that row to all of his friends, and dwelt on it for weeks in his diary. Gentle encouragement from Baxter and Jackson, who both saw how much the triangular relationship protected him from loneliness, did not persuade him. He wanted to hear that Tom and Clive weren't worthy of his talent or his sensitive soul.

Beverley Cross, who was living in the South of France, heard out this querulous litany and invited him to stay. Williams was so pleased at the thought of joining another couple that he rejected a three-page telegram from Richard Burton, who was celebrating his fortieth birthday with Elizabeth Taylor in Budapest. Williams suspected the wire was a hoax and, even when he discovered it wasn't, he preferred a country retreat with familiar friends to a strange city and a crowd of hangers-on. As he boarded the plane for Nice, he did not seem pleased to be travelling. 'Do you not like to be recognised?' asked the woman in the next seat. 'I'd never have thought you could have looked so solemn!' Though he always protested he was uncomfortable with strangers, he was soon deep in conversation with the woman and her husband, and, when the cabin crew offered to upgrade him to first class, he insisted on remaining with his new friends.

The hilltop farmhouse in Seillans was not what Williams had imagined. The steep path from his hotel was very dark after sunset and, as he stumbled back with a torch each night after dinner, to a room with a portable shower and corridors that stank of bicyclists' embrocation, he was glad to think he lived in London. Listening to Beverley and Gayden, he was alert for clues that they envied him his mansion flat in an English city. When the row with Waine and Dennis had died down, though, he visited Seillans again, and brought Tom. 'Beverley was the sort of man Ken would like to have been,' Waine said, 'mannish, intelligent, solid and a great gourmand.'

Williams spent three weeks in Morocco that summer too, and returned with a resolve to leave Queen Alexandra Mansions. The problem of the pianist had been solved: one evening he had gone downstairs to complain and realised the woman was half mad with loneliness. Now when he heard her singing, he felt pity, not anger.

A flood from upstairs, when another tenant let a bath overflow, did upset him, and he wanted to escape; he was looking at Highgate and Hampstead and Kent, but when the perfect property came along he knew at once. It was next door to his mother's rented flat. Better still, he was able to buy both properties, for £24,500.

On 3 August 1972, he moved into 8 Marlborough House in Osnaburgh Street, opposite Sir John Soane's Holy Trinity church and a minute's walk from Regent's Park. Great Portland Street tube station stood on the other side of the Euston Road. Peter Eade dropped by at lunchtime with champagne; Tom and Clive brought six bottles of Chablis, and took Williams and his mother out to dinner. Late that evening, he sat with Louie, drinking coffee at No. 7. Saying goodnight to her at half past midnight, he walked along the hallway to his own apartment. He had found a home.

In this contented mood, Williams was ready to work again. With Ted Ray, he had already recorded a pilot for radio, *The Betty Witherspoon Show*, and the BBC had commissioned a thirteen-part series for the autumn. When the youth theatre in Hillingdon, Middlesex, which was about to stage *Entertaining Mr Sloane*, invited him to lecture about working with Orton, he stood and talked until his feet ached, describing the disastrous *Loot* tour and explaining the history behind some of the lines. Michael Codron offered a script a fortnight later. He read it that afternoon and wrote a note, in time for the last post, to accept it. The play was called *The Fat Dress*, by Charles Laurence, a TV sitcom writer and first-time playwright. It would become *My Fat Friend*, Williams's biggest West End play in more than a decade and the play that wiped out his stage career.

'The whole thing started in such high hopes that it was a wonderful part for Ken, and he would shine in it,' Codron said. The director was Eric Thompson, and Williams decided he disliked him before they ever met. Peter Eade took him to the Cambridge to see Robert Sherriff's *Journey's End*, directed by Thompson, and before they set out he warned that Williams would have to shed his layers of stifling cynicism. He had to trust Thompson, the way he had as a young actor when John Fernald directed *Saint Joan*. Laurence's play was delicate: if it was camped up like a *Carry On*, it would come apart.

By the time they reached the theatre Williams was ready to hate everything Thompson said and did, and he came out complaining that *Journey's End* was 'reppy, uninspired pedestrian muck'. He was happier after the director promised he would restrict himself to telling the cast when to speed up or slow down.

When rehearsals began a month later, he realised Thompson wanted to muffle many of the laughs, playing for emotional depth instead: 'The play is light enough,' he said. 'We have got to make it dark.' Williams saw it as a farce, a fat suit crammed with gags. He was Henry, an aggressive, bitchy tax inspector, who bullies his obese landlady into slimming down. His first line, as he dashed on stage clutching his flies and hammered on the bathroom door, was, 'I'm a queen, dear, not a camel!' Then he relieved himself in the bird bath. It was the crudity, the ribald camp, that made him love the script. There were more puns than an episode of *Beyond Our Ken*, and Thompson scraped them off as if the play were a slice of burnt toast.

Williams watched in disbelief. His punchlines were being squashed and any hint of his vocal repertoire brought a rebuke. These were the restrictions that had driven him out of *Hancock's Half Hour*, and made miseries of *Gentle Jack* and *Loot*. In a three-page letter to Codron, which he never sent, he dissected every slight.

On the third day, I was subjected to this – 'You have been acting. It has all been very clever and very interesting and very lovely, and I don't want to see it EVER AGAIN . . .' This was addressed to the whole company [. . .] I began to wonder why I had ever been cast. Every tentative attempt I made at a comedy effect was rejected with smiling assertions like, 'Stop it. It doesn't need it. Just [. . .] speak the lines naturally' – how can you speak 'naturally' lines like, 'Don't you want to see his legs buckle and his eyes reel from their sockets when he beholds her new-found loveliness?' Is this the language of everyday conversation? As far as I was concerned it needed every kind of verbal panache and vocal pyrotechnics [. . .] I got more and more inhibited. Some days when I arrived at the rehearsal room I didn't actually go in. I walked around for a bit while my stomach churned over. Eventually I entered on my hands and knees.

Williams knew plenty of Henrys. As he told Codron, he knew the pubs where they drank, their hissy fits and amateur dramatics, and he knew Henry could never be overplayed. At the first reading, Codron told him sharply to stop sniping. For two weeks he struggled to submit to the direction and, when he found he could not, he took the only possible path. He stirred up trouble.

Codron had to support his director. The alternative was to sack him. Williams focused on the writer, Laurence, wailing over every change to his script and warning that the play was being destroyed. When it opened at the Theatre Royal in Brighton on 6 November 1972, changes were still being enforced.

Once the tour began, Williams started to discard the restrictions. He talked to the audience, echoed his own lines, started to mince and scream, uncorked his voices and wrung the laughs out of every line. His spirits rose and the curtain calls were ecstatic. The houses were packed all week, as Williams waved away the director's protests. By the time they opened at the former cinema hall in Wilmslow the following week, the queening had gone too far and the play was becoming a cheap sitcom. Codron, fighting to keep a balance between show and star, told him to rein it in and revealed a secret: *My Fat Friend* was opening in December at the Globe.

Peter Eade tried to warn him against sending the play up too high: he called it 'Sticking your bum out'. When Tom Waine remarked that it was funniest if the pace wasn't always frantic, Williams began to see what Thompson wanted. There were undercurrents in *My Fat Friend*, moments of shadow that could be poignant but not sentimental, if the cast trod delicately.

Two weeks of rehearsals were interrupted by bouts of dentistry, as he had a molar pulled and a bridge inserted to support a false tooth. Metal caps were fitted to protect the teeth but Williams, who looked like an eight-year-old with braces, found he kept biting his cheeks and tongue till they bled. The caps were replaced with plastic and, on the day the play opened, his dentist fitted a new bridge. 'It feels WONDERFUL! I wanted to shout and sing in the streets!'

When he arrived at the Globe, his dressing-room looked 'like Christmas', stacked with bottles of champagne and festooned with telegrams. The play was a triumph and Codron told him so afterwards.

Williams forgot the rows: 'He is a darling boy + it's OUR success I care about, since we've a special association from those early early days of youthful aspiration when he first had faith in my kind of performing.' After a dinner for thirty at Hostaria Romana, Waine drove him to Fleet Street, where they picked up a first edition of *The Times* to read Irving Wardle's review: 'It is hard to believe in Mr Williams as a tax inspector but I have never seen him draw more resourcefully on his special range of outraged squawks, nasal chortle, rabbit-like gloats and flared-nostril postures of mock reproof.' He was thrilled, almost in tears, to be vindicated, and waving a copy of the paper he ran to the bays where the lorries were being loaded with bundles of papers, and earned one more burst of applause, singing 'Everything's Coming Up Roses' to the drivers.

Friends crowded his dressing-room all week, as Ingrid, Barbara, Maggie and more squeezed in. The reviewers lauded him. 'What a performance!' said the *Mirror*. 'There is none funnier to be seen in London.' 'Highly gifted [. . .] tenaciously well-disciplined,' declared the *Financial Times*. 'A somewhat soiled garden pixie, outrageously queer, adenoidal and insolent [. . .] Williams has never been better,' ruled the *Sunday Telegraph*. 'At last he has transcended the campness of his stand-up comic and proved himself an actor of substance,' agreed *Plays and Players*. The rest of the cast were 'dwarfed by the memory of the whinnying, head-tossing, outrageous Mr Williams', the *Evening News* said. 'This actor can also switch in a moment to seriousness – as he did last night when alone at the final curtain, the comic mask came down and he gave us a momentary glimpse of a lonely, middle-aged man yearning for normality.'

He spent Christmas with Hattie Jacques, whose invitation arrived in verse ('We start Christmas Day around about noon / And continue 'til roughly the next full moon'). 'Hattie was a fabulous cook,' said Waine, 'wonderful English cooking. Mouth-watering. She did this fantastic Christmas dinner for about twenty people.' That party became another *Carry On* legend, where Joan Sims played the Christmas Fairy and brought presents to everyone, especially Hattie, until she was surrounded by a mound of gifts with a bird in a cage on top.

My Fat Friend repaid its production costs before the end of January, packing the theatre for eight shows a week and taking over £1,000 a night. The houses never flagged, even during train strikes and an IRA bombing campaign. His euphoria faded quickly, though. If a line faltered, or a laugh didn't come, Williams was convinced the play was unravelling. Now that he was free to parade all his vocal contortions, he appreciated the importance of keeping them in check. There was not a word of the script he did not weigh, and he tried to read each audience, varying his delivery according to their reactions – he could be knowing, or crude, or emphatic. And when the other actors were less responsive, he began to fret. It was already intolerable that he was the only big draw, the sole famous name in a play by an unknown. Must he carry every performance on his own?

The landlady, his fat friend, was played by Jennie Linden. She was an adept, quick-witted actress and he admired her at first, but she had little patience for his needling and his neediness, and he began to feel a kind of sibling rivalry towards her. When his leading ladies petted him – as Bergman and Barbara Windsor did – he adored them. When he thought them clever – as Sheila Hancock and Siobhàn McKenna were – he felt a spiteful regard. But if he ever suspected them of indifference, he could be hateful.

The first complaint to Codron seared off his typewriter on the first Sunday of the year: Linden had said a line with a giggle instead of a sigh, and when he upbraided her in the dressing-room, she brushed him aside and said she had to catch a train. 'It represents an appalling betrayal,' he wrote. 'We will be left in Gagsville.' He took a taxi to Eric Thompson's house and poured out his worries. When he confronted Linden the following day, she burst into tears and he was contrite, but he still had Peter Eade stationed in the audience, taking notes on her performance. The diplomatic Eade produced a pad of scribbles at supper and said, 'I'm afraid I can't read my own writing.'

Thompson asked him to report back if he thought performances were slipping, and he did – long, angry pages of recrimination, all of it directed at Linden. He kept a crime sheet, 'listing all the idiot tricks which this bitch Linden has played'. He followed that with three pages of notes to Codron, castigating her for moving or not moving; ad libbing or reciting; playing to the house or ignoring the reactions. He attacked her diction and then he accused her of laying too much emphasis on words. 'This sort of mad drawing out of vowels ruins credibility,' he glowered, and did not seem aware that the same criticisms from Peter Wood and Noel Willman had once driven him to hysterics.

Codron did not know how to appease his star. The proximity of Williams's favourite actress made his difficulties worse: Maggie Smith was at the Queen's Theatre next door in *Private Lives*. 'She said, "It must have been PLANNED . . . you being next door," and I said, ' "God arranges these things".'

'I think they drilled a hole between their dressing-rooms,' Codron remarked. Williams felt such intense affection for Smith that he was afraid of seeing her too much. She would look in at the Globe, and they would go to supper and sit till midnight, and then carry on talking over coffee at Marlborough House until 3 a.m. When he did not hear from her, he fretted about her emotional state until his stomach churned.

Smith was starring with her husband, Robert Stephens, who was recovering from a breakdown; their marriage was disintegrating. Stephens moved out of their home, first staying with Jeremy Brett and then going to Chichester to play Chekhov. This tension seemed intolerable to Williams, and he compared it to his mother's grief when her husband died: 'I had to go on and get laughs! In the same theatre where I played comedy in '62 while Louie went through all that anguish with Charles and the death by poison.' When he complained about his co-star, he ached to be starring with Smith instead: 'MAGGIE came in at 70c [. . .] she told me how lines which Linden has in this play COULD be delivered . . . phew! What an eye-opener it was! [. . .] If I'd been acting this piece with Maggie it could have been MAGICAL.'

He started to criticise Linden's performance, in whispers, on stage. When he muttered that she was being rotten tonight, he could see her falter. He told himself that a real actress could take the criticism and use it to produce a greater performance, but his secret hope was that Linden would withdraw and that either the understudy, Jenny Robbins, would step in (he liked her; she gave him lifts) or the play would be off.

Stressed and frenzied, he was attracting trouble. A group of youths barracked him at the pictures; he went over and told them to be quiet, but they taunted him so much that he was driven in tears from the cinema. A few days later, another gang yelled at him as he left the Globe. Frightened, he started to run, slipped in the gutter and sprained his hand.

He began to find any company intolerable. He refused to see Joss Ackland backstage, and barred Peter O'Toole. When Paul Florance visited from Australia, Williams hectored him to agree he had no more loving, constant friend in the world; two days later he was writing that Paul was a 'dreary philistine [. . .] I think it's for the chop'. Every twinge became an agony – a bout of wind doubled him over, cramp in the neck prevented him from standing, and when he woke on 1 May with a swelling on his abdomen he remembered a strain he had felt one night and was sure he had suffered a hernia. Desmond Mulvany, the Harley Street specialist who had first treated him during *Pieces of Eight*, diagnosed an ulcer in the rectum and booked him into hospital.

Codron felt betrayed, thinking that this illness must be an excuse, because he wanted to leave the play. They confronted each other backstage that night and the discussion became so heated that the curtain went up five minutes late. The following day, Williams and Eade sat down with the producer and Toby Rowland, who was leasing the theatre. A compromise was reached: Williams would check into the St John and St Elizabeth Hospital for a week's treatment, and a car would bring him to the Globe for each performance. After three months the play would be withdrawn, and he could then have surgery if it was still needed. Codron had misgivings, but Rowland assured him, 'Ken's your friend. He won't let you down.'

Williams easily met his radio commitments, recording thirteen episodes of *More Secret Life* and half a dozen *Just a Minute*s; he had already appeared on *Woman's Hour* and been interviewed by Richard Baker and Pete Murray that year. Broadcasting House was a haven. The Globe was an inner circle of hell. As *My Fat Friend* dragged on for a nightmarish month, he charted the declining houses – a graph at the back of his diary showed a fall-off from 8,000 a week to 6,000 – and hid from friends. Even when the audience applauded, he wondered whether they were mocking him. When Smith announced she would be leaving *Private Lives* in July, his last consolation was gone. He brooded over every show he had ever done with Codron, and as he nursed the pains in his stomach, his diary became inflamed with entries in red biro.

By the end of May, he had a new diagnosis: proctitis, or irritation of the rectal lining. His sinuses were blocked, his mouth full of ulcers and a blood vessel had burst in his right eye. On 4 June 1973, he wrote: 'I suddenly realised in the middle of the first scene – "Why are you sitting here night after night trying to make a go of it? Why are you flogging this dead horse? Nothing will bring it back to life."' That was his last night in the play. He booked himself into hospital the next morning; the following day, Eade formally withdrew him from *My Fat Friend*.

For three weeks, friends came to smoke, gossip and tell jokes at his bedside in the private hospital room. Williams was grateful, but the Mandrax and Valium he took at night left him groggy all through the day. When Louie visited, he could do nothing but find fault – the pyjamas she brought from Selfridges 'felt like cardboard [. . .] cheap and nasty and an absolute swindle at 5 pounds' – and her martyred look made him snarl when he asked her to leave. When reporters asked how he was, the official line was 'mild colitis' but what Williams described, as flatly and clearly as if he was pinned under glass, was depression: 'The letters pour in with every quack's idea of how to cure colitis if you please. Perhaps, somewhere, someday, I shall get over all this and start to laugh again, but at the moment, all I want to do is weep. More and more I begin to see the reason for so many suicides among the people I have known. There DOES come a point at which you can't continue.' When he left hospital, he did not have the energy to go to Tangier, and asked Clive Dennis to hire a car and take him on a driving holiday in the West Country.

On the first day he did not want to stop anywhere – they raced through Sidmouth, Exmouth and Exeter, and on to Taunton, where they checked into rooms at the Castle Hotel and Williams, miserable at being recognised, ground his teeth at the waiter's jokes. When they visited Wells, the streets were thronged for a royal visit. Theirs was the last car to pass the police outriders before the road was closed for Princess Anne's motorcade. 'We were crawling along,' Dennis said. 'Ken wound the window down and started waving to the crowds, calling out "Hello, hello, my dears," and of course they recognised him and started cheering. Bizarre, but he loved it.' They drove on, with Williams unwilling to stop anywhere for longer than half an hour, through Cheddar, Axbridge and Bristol and into Bath, where he lay on a hotel bed and decided he had to go home. The story he told Louie later was that Dennis offered to take him to the station, but not back to London.

Clive Dennis remembers it differently: 'We'd checked into this hotel to see a friend of ours called Leslie. When I came downstairs, I'd left Ken in his room, and he was supposed to meet me in the bar for drinks. Leslie said, "Oh, he's left in a taxi." I didn't believe he'd just leave me like that, but Leslie said, "He's paid the bill, and he's paid for your room." So I flew down to the station, and it was pouring with rain, and he was standing on the edge of the platform, with his cap on and his collar up and round his face tightly. I looked at him and said, "Are you all right?" and he said, "Oh I've had it, I've got to get back." I told him I didn't have enough money on me even to pay for petrol to get the car back to London, and he got very odd. He said, "Somebody will film this, they'll film me giving you money here, won't they?" '

Dennis kept his temper and pointed out that no one was watching. He asked Williams to come back to the hotel. Williams refused. He thrust out £30, and turned away. When Dennis asked again if he was all right, he said nothing and walked further up the platform, with his coat turned up against the rain.

16

'Critics will say "tired, laboured, unfunny", etc, but it don't matter and I do need the money'

December 1972–August 1977

Kenneth Williams made his first appearance on the *Parkinson* show in December 1972. He had turned down an invitation a year earlier, labelling the presenter a 'North Country nit', but at that time the chat show was on Thames TV. Michael Parkinson was king-pin of Saturday nights on BBC1 now, and Williams was flattered to be asked. His analysis of the show filled a page, counting off his anec-dotes – the army audition, and doing *Moby Dick* with Orson Welles, and how Dame Edith had accused him of having a peculiar voice, winding up with the story of Grandma Williams and her incontinent neighbour who kept a pair of mildewed boots in the piano.

His mistake, he thought, was to share his airtime with his fellow guests, Frank Muir and Patrick Campbell: 'If you are on stage with a couple of duds the best and most practical thing is to ignore them and help yourself.' Viewers and reviewers loved him: one critic claimed his stories 'touched greatness [. . .] His incredible voice caught with grotesque accuracy the plaintive aggressiveness of that aged woman's voice – her dialect, her age, her class and her defiant pathos.' Though Williams worried he might have seemed vulgar, the BBC was delighted with him and with the viewing figures, and a return was inevitable.

For his second visit, he was persuaded by Maggie Smith to join her in a doleful reading of John Betjeman's 'Death in Leamington', while the poet sat facing them and simpered. Apart from the recital, Williams was unprepared. Instead of telling stories, he gave in to an urge to needle the host. Parkinson, with his Yorkshire accent and his grammar school education, seemed the epitome of the socialist thinker – a unionist, not a tradesman. Williams detested organised labour: a foreman who coerced his boss into raising wages was as much a thief, he believed, as a businessman who didn't pay his bills. Strikers were threatening to halt the trains that spring, which would hurt the theatres: 'They all get worked up about a couple of pounds in their pay packet,' he declared, waving aside Maggie Smith's attempt to speak. 'Why can't they care – if unions are really socialistic and say they care about our fellow man, why can't they march about [. . .] a few pounds for somebody else who's really hard up? What is the statue outside the TUC? [It] depicts a man helping up another man who's on the ground [. . .] If you stop trains, people can't get to work [. . .] Why do you have to do something which endangers the livelihood of your fellow men, when that statue represents helping, not hindering?'

'Ken went into some tirade,' Parkinson said. 'There was a lot of industrial unrest in Britain at the time. And he started going on about strikes and the workers, and I suggested that he didn't know what he was talking about. I told him he was talking crap – I shouldn't have done that but I did, because he angered me. And he reacted wonderfully, "Oooh! I've never been so insulted in all my life!"'

Williams, while he insisted that he made each performance as good as he could, refused to admit there was glamour or creative satisfaction on the stage. He was a worker, he said, every bit as much as a fitter on a car assembly line. The show's producers wanted him back within three weeks, hoping to capture the national political debate on a chat show. This time, his opponent was a real trades union leader, the shipyard orator Jimmy Reid.

'Reid was one of the bêtes noires of the time, a formidable debater,' said Parkinson, 'and it became quite apparent that Kenneth was out of his league. They first met on stage, twenty minutes prior to the programme, when we brought them on to have a sound test. Kenneth tried this wonderful pro's trick, because he reckoned he was at home and Jimmy wasn't. Just to check the sound levels, I asked, as I usually do, "What did you have for breakfast?" and Kenneth said, "I don't want to talk about that! I have a poem that's relevant to the occasion, I think." And he spouted that, and Reid's looking at Kenneth, smiling. At the end, I said, "That was quite beautiful," and I was about to ask who wrote it, when Jimmy Reid said, "Aye, that was Yeats, wasn't it?" Kenneth, flustered, said yes, as a matter of fact it was. Whereupon I said to Jimmy, "What did you have for breakfast?" And he said, "Ach, I'll read a poem for you too." And he did this wonderful poem, to camera, and he turned to Kenneth and looked at him quizzically. Kenneth said, "I don't know, who wrote it?" And Jimmy said, "I did!" In that moment Kenneth realised that he had lost, because he had underrated the opposition.'

In his diary, and later in his autobiography, Williams seethed against Reid, calling him a rabid communist and a spokesman for 'the illiterate mind with a grudge'. He was crushed in the debate, trying to fend off Reid's pounding rhetoric with flippancies. The union man declared a rich man's luxuries meant a poor man's children starved. The actor retorted limply that the wealthy had a right to wear mink-lined jockstraps if they wanted. BBC1's controller, Paul Fox, watched grimly and ordered Parkinson never to attempt celebrity politics again.

His friends winced too. 'I hated that interview,' Barbara Windsor said. 'He was out of his depth. I think some producers used him too much – it was, "When in doubt, let's get Kenny on".'

Williams had not featured in *Carry On Girls*: he turned down a weak script in early 1973, claiming he needed all his energy for *My Fat Friend*, and became too despondent even to accept Gerald Thomas's invitation to come to lunch at Pinewood during the shoot. He returned to the series after the regulars were treated to a meal at Mirabelle in Curzon Street, where 'I behaved atrociously. Getting up and making speeches and shouting and bawling obscenities (once, Gerald asked me to lower my voice) and Peter Rogers observed, "I was wise to order a private room for this event" [. . .] Sims was doing all the "give it a rest dear!" etc etc. Eventually came home in Peter's Rolls.' Mollified and guilty, he came back to play Captain Desmond Fancey in *Carry On Dick*, after turning down the highwayman's role. Instead, Sid James played Big Dick Turpin.

'There was something a bit rough and ready that Kenny didn't like about Sid,' said Windsor. 'And Sid didn't like him but it didn't matter, they never showed it. When I was having an affair with Sid, though, he was awful.' On set, Williams asked her suddenly, 'You having it off with Sid James?' Windsor, hoping that no one could have

guessed, denied it: 'I said, "Don't be so bloody daft, I'm married."
He said, "You are, aren't you? I know, because Sid's joining us for
lunch now! Never done that in all the years he's been here. And the
way he comes over and helps you into your seat – he's a much nicer
man. I quite like him now."' Windsor pretended James was simply
being chivalrous. Williams was not fooled.

'He was wicked. One day he went and sat with Sid. Most days,
Kenny would do the *Telegraph* crossword, Bernie would do the *Times*
crossword, Sid would get out his cards and play poker with anyone
who wanted to, and Charlie would go and sit far away and smoke
the Woodbines. Usually, I'd sit with Kenny, hanging on his every
word, cos you heard all these silly jokes you'd heard time and time
again. Anyway, this one particular day, I wasn't there and he sat with
Sid. And he said, "Nnn-yess, have you heard all those stories about
Barbara Windsor? Do you know what she does? She has a bag of
wigs, and every time she goes out to see one fella she puts a black wig
on. Another week, a red wig for somebody else. That poor husband
of hers." Of course Sid didn't like it. It made me laugh, but I told
Kenny he was terrible, wicked to mix it like that. He said, "No, it's
only a joke, he's got to take it." But he was quite pleased with the
way Sid was reacting.'

The *Carry On*s were a vestige of a career that had died at the
Globe. Williams was no longer an actor; he was a television personality. His new identity had been established in that trio of chat shows.
Compared to the tens of thousands who saw him as Henry, the queen
from the Inland Revenue, tens of millions watched him being himself
on *Parkinson*. They saw a man who could underscore every argument
with lines of poetry, contort his face and voice to bring to life the
characters in his anecdotes, and convulse an audience with vulgar
wit. It was a persona he had developed for David Frost and Simon
Dee, and nourished on *Just a Minute* – he had invented himself, and
now he became famous for being himself. As he recovered from his
collapse, he accepted more television work without understanding
what had changed.

Michael Parkinson believed celebrity demanded its own price: 'Of
course he wanted to be a serious actor, but when you start to perform
for the public a serious actor is the last thing that you are. What

you always got with Kenneth, even in the serious moments, was the clown breaking through, that inability to be serious for too long. He would always break the spell for one reason or another.'

He made his debut on *What's My Line*, another of the BBC's parlour games, being chauffeured to Birmingham and back to join the panel. He flew to the Isle of Man for a live broadcast on *The Pete Murray Show* from the Gaiety Theatre in Douglas, and tried out a music quiz called *Pop Score* with Tim Rice and Terry Wogan. 'Tim Rice was altogether charming,' he wrote, 'though of course I deplore his show Superstar etc. + cannot bring myself to use the name of Jesus in the title.'

Williams kept working. Ad agencies hired him to record voice-overs for Cadbury's and Pomagne cider; Chris Serle, one of his favourite interviewers, talked to him about Hancock; Melvyn Bragg asked him about his heroes. On Russell Harty's chat show – more arch and mischievous than Parkinson's – he proclaimed the impossibility of a sexual relationship: 'My world revolves around me . . . First thing in the morning I look in the mirror and think, Oh! What a dish! Wonderful figure . . . I spend hours, looking in the mirror, thinking of all this beauty, and I wouldn't want to share it.' As if forced to contradict himself, he got drunk over dinner at Peter Mario's that evening and went to another flat in Marlborough House with two young Kuwaiti men. The assignation ended in farce when he fell off the bed, scratching his arm, and hurried back to his own flat to put ointment on the wound.

Helen Fry, the radio producer who had recorded his readings of Tennyson and MacNeice, invited him to discuss his favourite music, and asked him to compile another selection of poetry. His choices – Clough and Chesterton, as well as Pope, Chaucer, Wordsworth and Gray – were less well known than his previous anthology, and he chose a phrase from an obscure poem by George Orwell as his theme: 'The Crystal Spirit'. When it was broadcast six months later, dozens of listeners wrote to thank him, and he spent six hours one day answering their letters.

He was disappointed, though, at a review in *The Times*, which likened Williams to a court jester who slipped morsels of philosophy into his capers: 'Surely nothing that voice says can possibly be serious?' In fact, the programme was an attempt to express his religious beliefs and explain his certainty that an incorruptible force of goodness existed, almost outside the range of our perceptions. This perfection of truth and beauty was an ideal for which we must strive. It was the pole star of the moral universe. Rituals of worship and the hierarchies of organised religion were impediments; dishonesty and sexual incontinence and greed could blot out the soul, but never extinguish the guiding light.

This idea was hard to express simply. Searching for precise definitions that would give the weight of words to faith, he would become stranded in long, obscure passages from Erich Heller's philosophy. When he let others argue against him, though, he knew by instinct where their theories ran hollow. Robert Bolt invited him to his home and declared that death was no solution to suffering. 'When I said, "The spirit is inviolate," he said, "Don't talk CRAP . . . when you die you DIE mate . . . there's nothing left hovering around . . . you're dead as mutton".' One of Bolt's daughters heard him and burst into tears. Williams did not need to refute Bolt's atheism in his diary: he only had to show the helplessness of a father whose intellect was no match for his child's emotions.

Williams, whose mind was a compendium of verses and tag lines, speeches and quotations, felt his thoughts were clearest when told in other people's words. Wilfred Owen, Roy Fuller, A.E. Housman, John Milton and T.S. Eliot all left deep grooves to which he returned for handholds, proving the truth of an argument by showing that the thought had been beautifully phrased by a better mind.

His letters fell back on catchphrases from favourite sketches: 'deep joy in the eyebold', a favourite greeting, was one of Stanley Unwin's manglings from *Carry On Regardless*, and many of his notes concluded with a lament supplied by Peter Cook, 'I'd have been all right if only I'd have stayed off the milk!' The quote that most often closed his letters (sometimes in full, sometimes indicated with just the words 'chaff & grain') was from a forgotten Victorian novelist, Mrs Craik: 'Oh, the comfort, the inexpressible comfort of feeling safe with a person, having neither to weigh thoughts nor measure words, but pouring them all out, just as they are, chaff and grain together, certain that a faithful hand will take and sift them, keep

With Joe Orton and Geraldine McEwan during rehearsals for *Loot*, 1965.
'I've always wanted to do a film called "Carry On, Jesus" . . . one could cast
Kenneth Williams as Simon Peter,' Orton said

1969: 'Me and Stanley [Baxter] in front of Tom's Corsair motor car, in the drive at
Dale Lodge, Highgate – taken by Clive, with my Kodak Brownie'

Carry On Spying, 1964: 'I was astonished at the excellence of Charlie Hawtrey. He was superb. So was [Bernard] Cribbins. The rest awful. Including me'

Williams as Dr Tinkle, Hattie Jacques as the rapacious Matron, in *Carry On Doctor*

With Julian Holloway and Barbara Windsor, on set early at Pinewood in *Carry On Camping*: 'Up at 6. Have the coffee, go to the loo and bath and shave etc all in a miasma of madness'

Williams was pictured in *Radio Times* in December 1967,
to promote *International Cabaret* on BBC2

After a dinner party:
'Joan [Sims] was
wearing Angela's fun
fur. What a gas!
Angela [Douglas]
wrote on the back
– "Where is your
other hand?" '

Williams as Jack o' the Green in Robert Bolt's *Gentle Jack* – 'a vast mosaic of shapeless pieces, each one of which contradicts and refutes the others,' complained *Plays and Players*

Williams as Drinkwater, in *Captain Brassbound's Conversion* by George Bernard Shaw, at the Cambridge Theatre in 1970. The play marked his return to the theatre after five years' absence

With the playwright Beverley Cross, Seillans, August 1972. 'Ken was different with Bev, more deferential, more eager to impress,' said Tom Waine

A schoolboyish Williams with Louie aboard the *Monte Umbe*, coming home from a cruise in Las Palmas, February 1969

Williams on the sea wall at Asilha, Morocco, August 1967

With George Borwick, 1971: 'Taken . . . in Asilha, on the walls of the old fortress. You can certainly see the grey hairs appearing on my head now! I look every bit of forty-five'

With Tom Waine and Clive Dennis at Highgate Ponds on 30 November 1969,
a couple of days after a disastrous excursion to Gibraltar

Williams's calligraphy at its most
exuberant: a decorated envelope,
from October 1967, bearing the
motto 'It's an absolute disgrace.
No, it really is, ducky'

With Tom Waine, near the end of their
friendship, 1976

With Lorraine Chase in *The Undertaking*, August 1979. 'He really was terribly cheeky,' Chase said. 'You'd be hurt. Then he'd wrinkle his nose and do that lovely laugh, and you'd just know he was pulling your leg'

The first series of *Countdown* on Channel 4, 1982, with Richard Whiteley, Ted Moult and Carol Vorderman

An Audience With Kenneth Williams, on 1 December 1982, the only time he gave a full performance of songs and anecdotes in a one-man show

With Louie on holiday at the Plaza, Tenerife: 'Walked back to the hotel. Sat in one of those mournful Spanish lounges which look like a crematorium waiting room. Oh! Dear'

In Leeds, signing copies of his second book, *Back Drops*, on 9 March 1983

Williams's face in this Polaroid, taken on 28 March 1985 during the photo-session for the cover of his autobiography, reflects the pain that he charted day by day in his final journals

what is worth keeping, and with a breath of kindness blow the rest away.'

He quoted Mrs Craik to Mavis Nicholson as he tried to explain his reliance on friends. An actor needed privacy, he insisted, to learn his lines, and a family was a constant intrusion. 'The paradox of it all is that one does need people, and anyone pretending that they don't is lying to themselves – either that or they're something of a saint, and I'm neither,' he said. Rona and Gordon Jackson were his dearest, most dependable companions, who would know from his voice when he was desperate for company. His worst depressions, he confided, were rooted not in loneliness but in the fear that he would never again act in anything worthwhile. Without the sustenance of friends, he would wither.

To reciprocate was more difficult. Even when he heard that Transformation had gone out of business, he did not dare approach Tom and Clive. He was not afraid of making an apology, providing it was a magnanimous gesture that proved him right; what scared him was rejection. Depression frightened him, too, when he encountered it in others, as though he might be infected. After Andrew Ray's suicide attempt, for instance, the two saw little of one another.

'Depression was too close to his own feelings,' said Stanley Baxter, 'and he would say, "You're no fun any more." We'd sometimes go to dinner, and I'd pick him up at that little flat of his, and this manic face would be looking out of the window. And he rushed down, because he didn't want you to go up to his place. And then when he got in the car, I'd find out what kind of evening we'd be in for. If he was rather ebullient and said: "*Do you know* what you SAID to me? Twenty-four years ago today?" I'd say, "No, I obviously don't have that kind of memory." "Well, I'll tell you, it's all in me diary," and you'd know it was going to be quite fun that night. Other times, he'd have his collar turned up in that way of his which he thought – quite wrongly – disguised him and I'd ask how he was . . . "Well, it's just waiting for death, isn't it?" And you'd know it was going to be *that* kind of evening. And if you were low, if you said you'd had an awful few weeks, you got no sympathy at all.'

On a wet February evening they went to Lariana's, where Williams was in a sarcastic temper: he had been invited on to a cookery programme with Fanny Cradock, which seemed 'all so barmy you begin to doubt your sanity'. Baxter was tired and nursing a cold. In the middle of the meal, Williams announced, 'I've very little time for illness,' stood up and went to sit at another table. He phoned Baxter the next morning to brush off the incident and found his friend had taken the phone off the hook. 'Obviously he is FURIOUS about last night and is refusing to talk to me. Oh dear oh dear. It is all so STUPID and fatuous. Well I don't care. I don't see that much of him anyway, so perhaps that is the end of another beautiful relationship. It don't signify. I've still got Gordon and Rona.'

His emotional behaviour had become more puerile in the months since he moved in next door to his mother. Two days into the sulk over Stanley, Louie cooked lunch for him – 'certainly better than anything I've ever eaten in a restaurant. As far as English cooking is concerned, she is superb.' They spent most of their free time together, and Williams felt twinges of jealousy on evenings when she visited her sister Edie, or on the days when she helped out at hospitals for the WRVS. They walked through London together, sometimes as far as Parliament Square, before catching the bus home.

Her sense of humour delighted him. It was coarse, prudish and disapproving, much like his own: one of her favourite expressions, applied to any woman dressed or acting in a sexually provocative way, was, 'Gawd help us! She must want a job!' His friends were always shocked by how uninhibited Williams was around his mother.

David Hatch, the producer, joined the pair of them for dinner after a *Just a Minute* recording, and realised his star trouble-maker treated restaurants as an extension of the radio stage. Williams's diary entry is unrepentant: 'I foolishly shouted to some people at another table and though they were kind they obviously didn't want to know, but I couldn't leave it alone and cried out, "You have a retarded sense of humour!" and other rude remarks which they wearily ignored. Got a taxi [. . .] and fell on the floor laughing with Louie. Got to the flat about 10c in the morning . . . reeling and laughing and bawling in the hallway with Louie saying, "Oh! Do be quiet!"'

Again and again that year, as he settled into the flat next to hers, he thanked God for the love and forbearance of his mother, and he prayed that she would always be there. Once a week she went dancing, and he would let himself into her apartment to watch television and make little repairs around the place. She mended clothes for him – when he split his trousers, striding away from an admirer in the street who called out for his autograph, it was Louie who sewed up his seat.

The thanks became an incantation: 'One thing I have learned since I came to live here: the irreplaceable and invaluable nature of LOUIE – all through every crisis she is the one who is consistent and sustaining: there will never be anyone like her in my life.' 'There is no way to show this lady how much I care for her and what a mainstay she's been to me thro' thick and thin.'

When she was away, on holiday, he was bereft. Anyone who treated her kindly earned his automatic friendship. One neighbour, Paul Richardson at No. 29, got to know Louie when he carried her shopping up the stairs. His fondness for Louie sustained the friendship. 'She was a great character. I used to have Sunday nights off [from his work in the theatre] and we'd play Scrabble, just the three of us. And it was a riot.'

His gentle demeanour and broad general knowledge both soothed and stimulated Williams. 'He used to spend a lot of time in my flat, just talking. We went out quite a lot together, to the park, or shopping. He came to the old theatre [Sadler's Wells] a few times, to sit in the canteen and have lunch. And everybody used to be sitting around, dancers and technicians, taking no notice of him, and he liked that. Not being gawped at. In some ways he should have been a family man. I was never his partner but he once said to me, "What we should do is get a house in Brighton." I said, "I don't think I could live with you any more than you could live with me."'

Radio work had become as fragmented as the television bookings. *The Betty Witherspoon Show* was broadcast more than a year after it was recorded, the original thirteen episodes condensed to ten. It was woefully unfunny, perhaps the least entertaining comedy Williams ever made. His supercilous wit, and Ted Ray's bluster and decency, had combined in *Carry On Teacher* to reflect the team ethic of austerity Britain, where everyone worked together and differences were disguised. In the seventies, they repelled one another like magnets. Williams appeared each week as Inspector Spules of Scotland Yard, presenting a public information slot called Narks Five. Spules was a bent copper – he started with gruff jargon, 'appre'ending a verhiacule proceding in an heasterly direcshon', and interrupted his broadcast to chat up Ted Ray: 'Mon cheri, petit lily of the valley.' If Ray had overreacted, the way Eric Morecambe did when he thought his masculinity was being questioned, the gag might have worked. Ray just sounded bemused. The only noise from the audience was the whispered squirming of embarrassment.

Convinced that Williams could succeed in his own series, instead of dominating other people's shows, the *Witherspoon* producer Simon Brett tried a quartet of *Playhouses*, as he searched for the right format. These one-offs, recorded in late 1974 and broadcast eight months later, cast Williams in three situation comedies and a revue. He was a liverish Blimp in *The General*, recounting his war exploits to reporter June Whitfield; a private detective who traps a bank robber on a train in *The Lying Scotsman*; an accident-prone bore undergoing psychiatric therapy in *The Analysis*; and everyone from Mr Justice Fizzwhackett, to Sherlock Holmes, to private eye Grit Gritstone (played as Snide) in *Get On With It*. The first three episodes were lacklustre: he needed better writers when he was trying to carry a show rather than disrupting it. The fourth pilot was good enough to become a series, with Miriam Margolyes and Lance Percival, but when Ramblin' Syd Rumpo sang a ballad about a fisherman and a mermaid the show was exposed as a limp echo of past triumphs.

'Williams is the funniest man I have ever met,' Brett said. 'The fact is that his talent is anarchic – he is the force that deflates the structures of pomposity. His performances actually tend to diminish the show he is in; their very strength weakens the structure of the entire vehicle.'

His best radio work for years came after he travelled to Bristol to record a discussion for a book show, *Can't Put It Down*, with Arthur Marshall and a BBC presenter, Amanda Theunissen. They discussed *Cold Comfort Farm* by Stella Gibbons, and the producer, Pamela Howe, invited him back to read a six-part adaptation. The overwrought language of the tale and its caged, brooding characters suited his precise delivery and vocal exaggerations. His heroine, Flora Poste, was sentimental but brisk about it, his Old Adam Lambsbreath querulous, rustic and very, very old, and his Seth moody and masculine enough to make the sukebind bloom. When his Aunt Ada Doom declared she had 'seen something nasty in the woodshed', his pitiful wail implied he must once have seen something very like it himself.

The recordings were spread over three days, and on both evenings Williams visited the Theunissens' home. Seeing the mesmeric effect he had on her children, she suggested he might read them a tale of King Arthur as a bedtime story. Williams, resenting any hint of being asked to sing for his supper, hid his indignation: the children were 'heavenly', he admitted, and he was flattered when the boy, Richard, told him, 'You're better than Mummy.'

Williams was a regular guest on bookish programmes on both television and radio in the mid-seventies. These included a edition in June 1974 of the BBC's *Read All About It*, chaired by Melvyn Bragg, whose novels he admired so much that he had bought two as a present for Maggie Smith. The show was a disappointment to Williams, who felt he wasn't given the opportunity to shine. 'I think,' Bragg said, 'he'd expected to be able to talk about books and at great length, when in fact it was quite a tightly organised programme, and you had to get a move on. I may well have chivvied him, indicated that there wasn't time for these great expositions which I suspect he wanted to make.'

One day in March 1975, on his way to the Paris Studios, Williams passed Michael Codron and walked on without saying anything. Three days later he received a postcard: ' "That was spooky . . . keep well, M" and I wrote back: "Not spooky at all: simply the product of despair; since I haven't heard from you since '73 I thought you didn't want to know me + thought I was saving you from embarrassment. Love Kenneth".' Williams still writhed with guilt at his behaviour in *My Fat Friend*: he was certain Codron would never employ him again and thought there was nothing they could say to each other. The loss of the friendship saddened him, but worse, since Codron was estranged and Beaumont had died in March 1973, he was stranded on a shore with television and radio, and no way to get back across to the theatre.

Louie saw how much he needed the stage. He was back at the Talk of the Town, writing and hosting another series of *International*

Cabaret for Bill Cotton on BBC2, but it didn't satisfy him. They took a cruise, his first holiday abroad in more than two years, and he was tormented by the constant stares and pointing. Since *Hancock*, his voice had been one of best known in Britain, but chat shows and panel games had inflicted fame of a grosser kind. When his CSE comrade Peter Nichols joined him for a walk around Greenwich Park, to discuss memories of Singapore for his play *Privates on Parade*, the constant shouts and catcalls were more intimidating than intrusive. Nichols thought he himself would lose his temper if he were subjected to so much ceaseless banter.

Tom Waine believed there were days when he enjoyed the attention and even courted it: 'If we were walking in Regent's Park with Ken and no one recognised him, the voice would get louder and louder, until eventually someone would say, "Oh look, it's that one off the films," and he'd say, "Oh God, isn't it dreadful? One can't go anywhere!"'

Too much attention – 'the moron's wink and the cretin's nudge' – would drive him indoors, and though he told himself it was irrational to care about insults from people whose names he did not know, he was sometimes wounded by homophobic sneers, the 'poof off the telly' and 'little queer' remarks. To prove to himself how unimportant it all was, both the celebrity and the insults, he would sometimes refuse to sign autographs or even speak to admirers who had waited patiently to see him. 'He would be very dismissive of fans,' Baxter said. 'If anyone approached Ken – "No, I don't do them!" They'd say, "Oh please . . ." "I don't do them!" Gordon Jackson told him, "You're an absolute bastard, you know – these people simply worship you, and you won't—" "Oh fuck 'em, dear, I couldn't care – they're not going to pay my rent!"'

Williams and Baxter had turned their backs on each other for more than a year. When the reconciliation came, it began with long phone calls, as though they were on separate continents instead of in different postal zones of north London. They met for coffee in a hotel lounge overlooking the city skyline, with 'the worst staff (and they're ALL on the ugly pill)'. When Baxter caught his eye as a palsied waiter poured coffee over the saucers, Williams had to double up to suppress his giggles. It was as if they were back in Nee Soon, sending up the officers.

Baxter urged him to revive his career and suggested an American adventure. Revue, drama, farce, stand-up – whatever he tried was bound to succeed and, even if it didn't, he would have lost nothing. 'You'd go like a bomb,' Baxter promised. Brooding later, Williams decided that a bomb was bound to come back in fragments.

'What frightened him,' Baxter reflected, 'was the feeling of being totally unknown there ... though he wouldn't have remained unknown for long.' Williams needed familiarity. He wanted to do what had worked before, even though he had seen so often, with *One Over the Eight* and *Stop Messin' About* and *International Cabaret*, that he could not repeat his successes. He turned down a detective series on TV, the sort of opportunity that, if he had seized it, might have changed his life. Williams instead fell back on routines he had adopted thirty years earlier: he toured the provinces in a ninetenth-century farce.

The play was *Signed and Sealed*, adapted from Feydeau by Christopher Hampton, and was offered by Helen Montagu at H.M. Tennent's. Montagu shared the faith of Binkie Beaumont before her: at the first casting meeting, she told Williams, 'We don't need names ... people will come to see you ... Everyone adores you.' Williams was flattered but doubtful.

The play was a comedy of accidental bigamy – Barillon, a middle-aged bachelor, is supposed to marry a well-off heiress but, owing to a registrar's mix-up, finds himself hitched to her fat, moustached mother instead. When the girl's long-lost father turns up, scandal sweeps the town. Williams was ideal for Barillon, but at the heart of the play was the matron, and her casting would be crucial. Hattie Jacques was the first choice and she refused: 'I would have adored to have been in something with you because I love working with you, but I quite honestly can't stand Feydeau, it's just not for me.' Joan Sims turned it down too; at last Peggy Mount was hired. Other friends avoided his invitations, aware that he could become impossible in a long run. Bryan Pringle and Jane Carr were eventually cast as the father and daughter.

The director, Patrick Garland, tried to give the play a Caribbean setting, to distinguish it from the run of Feydeau farces being staged that year: Williams detested this, and unleashed all his anger at past productions on this one. After the play opened in Bristol, he and Garland had a shouting match in the dressing-room: '[Patrick] said, "They didn't understand because it was too fast for them to take in . . ." (RUBBISH) I said, "No, they didn't understand your terrible set or where the place is supposed to BE".' Two days later, Williams began giving different moves to the cast and rearranged the set. Garland was at a loss; he decided to let Williams try his own interpretation.

They travelled to Nottingham (where the stage door was half blocked by rubble), Glasgow (where the box office was padlocked, and a handwritten notice invited theatregoers to try at the town hall for tickets) and Edinburgh. By the time they reached Newcastle, Garland had retreated. Alternately thrilled and overwhelmed by his dual role as leading man and director, Williams was pleading with Montagu to withdraw the show on one day and could not wait to bring it into town the next.

Scribbling a note on hotel paper in the spare minutes before an interview for Tyne TV, he wrote: 'It has been like a Siberian exile. The audiences non-existent, the notices terrible, the towns like piston blocks. Sometimes I've thought of suicide. It has been horrific in every sense [. . .] The director is the biggest con you've ever come upon. Prevailed on the management to get the twit out of my hair + effected improvements while it was away.' Two days later he bragged, 'It's a question of trying to put right a mass of things that are wrong. I am the only one with any ability, + it all gets flung on to me [. . .] Who is there to do the teaching? Exactly. It's your Aunt Ada every time.'

They opened during the heatwave of 1976, at the Comedy Theatre where he had starred in *Share My Lettuce*. On the first night, Thames TV broadcast an Eamonn Andrews interview to promote it.

He confided in Sheridan Morley that he wasn't looking forward to the opening. 'Everything depends on a couple of hours when you might not be feeling like being funny at all. You have none of the safety valves in the theatre that you have in radio or television, where you can say to a studio audience: "Look, I am terribly sorry, that bit was not really quite right, let us go back and try it again." I often wonder how I dare go through with it.'

In the oppressive heat of the theatre, the reception was languid, and Williams was despondent: 'I said "it will get SLATED by the press . . ." and said they'd all mention my peculiar voice or facial gestures etc etc.' *The Times* that next morning obliged: 'We get large doses of "Carry On Barillon" in that familiar frenetic manner [. . .] with flustered movements and his constantly changing voice.' Other reviewers were less charitable. After a week, he was so downcast that he sat down sobbing at his desk and wrote farewells to his mother and his agent. He intended to kill himself after the Saturday performance: he could not do it sooner, because the miserable play was his punishment for walking out on *My Fat Friend*. When he reached the theatre, he was told the production was being withdrawn; instead of suicide the next day, he took Louie out for a champagne lunch.

The failure of the play and the absence of steady work on a film or a radio series left Williams feeling redundant. He worried that he would be unable to keep himself and his mother, and cut back on every expense, cancelling the daily paper and taking the bus instead of phoning for a car when he visited friends. He sat for a portrait by John Bratby but declared he could not afford £350 to buy it; he did not even buy a present for Louie's seventy-fifth birthday.

In fact, television appearances and adverts generated a good income. His voice became ubiquitous; he could even be heard warning workmen to wear steel-toed boots, on a corporate safety film. Any work was acceptable, as long as he didn't have to leave the country. John Hussey rang out of the blue to offer eight weeks in South Africa: 'Financially I'm aware that I SHOULD do this job but oh! the wrench of working outside England.' When a Canadian channel offered to fly him to Toronto for a chat show, he was horrified.

One-offs worked well, but his final attempt to star in a television series flopped. Bill Cotton invited him to try *The Kenneth Williams Show* once more. This time he agonised over the material and strived to obey all the advice at rehearsals. The pilot ended strongly, with 'Crêpe Suzette', a collection of French phrases sung with a Gallic throb to the tune of 'Auld Lang Syne':

Double entendre, restaurant,
Jacques Cousteau, Yves St Laurent,
Où est la plume de ma tante?
C'est la vie, ma crêpe Suzette.
Faux pas, grand prix, espionage,
Brie et camembert fromage,
Mayonnaise, all-night garage,
RSVP ma crêpe Suzette.

The song was glorious, and would remain a Williams party piece; the whole show was good, but the response was not, and the BBC did not commission a series.

Tom Waine and Clive Dennis were in the audience. Their friendship with Williams had been revived after they ran into each other at a party: it was 'like a new-found old key turning the same lock'. With Louie too, the four spent a week's holiday in Malta.

Williams had started to take his mother to dinner parties and official functions, as his partner, and he was indignant when people patronised her. The faces of mother and son had grown more alike as they aged. 'We adored Louie,' Waine said. They'd have dinner with her, and after the meal they would watch television: 'Ken wouldn't have a set in his flat, but he liked watching television, and he'd be saying, "Come on, what's on then?" And she'd say, "I don't know why you don't bloody get one." He would sit there watching, absolutely quiet, and at the end he'd say, "Mmmm, load of rubbish".'

It was a perceived insult to Louie that ended the friendship. In retrospect, Waine felt the break was inevitable: they had never really recovered from the row after *My Fat Friend*. 'There was a phrase Ken used a lot: I'd say, "How's so-and-so?" And he'd say, "Well, she doesn't know it, dear, but she's for the chop." He used to truly decide that a friendship was going to end. And we were for the chop.'

The axe fell after a Sunday lunch in late April 1977, when celebration was in the air: Clive had just passed his bus driver's test, Tom was training to be a probation officer, and they had a ten-week-old labrador puppy called Max – 'the most adorable thing you'd ever seen. Ken came up and he was just in a dreadful mood. This was one of the "waiting for death" days. He was brittle, so I invited him to walk Max with me in the park. It was a brilliantly sunny day, and we bumped into a friend, Little Albert, a very likeable, chirpy Scot. Albert had polio badly as a child, and his leg had been in callipers. He asked how Clive got on in his bus test, and I said, "He passed – go over and congratulate him, we'll join you for a coffee in a minute." We walked on, and I have to tell you, Ken couldn't stand any kind of disability, in adults or children. And after a minute, he said, "What did you have to ask him for coffee for?" I said I didn't think it made any difference. Albert wouldn't stay long anyhow. He said, "Yes . . . cripple, dear. I don't want him there. I don't want to meet strange people. You've no regard for me at all, have you? No regard. You've no respect." I said, "Oh come on, Ken, you're upset. We see you two or three times a week. You and Louie come up almost every Sunday." He said, "Oh! Ohhh! Now you're insulting my mother." I said, "I'm not insulting her, I'm just saying we have that much regard for you that your life is our life." He said, "Yes! Insulting my mother!" He just kept repeating the phrase. And he walked across the park and we scarcely ever saw him again. Got in a taxi and that was it.'

Waine made several attempts to revive the friendship. If there had been another long sulk, fresh warmth might have thawed the silence, but this time Williams was worse than silent: he was perfunctory. Two days later there was a grudging apology – 'Sorry about the outburst. Thought it was going to be the usual cosy trio and was quite put out to find people who were strange to me. Put it down to old age.' He admitted his insincerity in his diary: it was 'only in the cause of social harmony. I won't be taking Louie to that house again.'

'To start with,' Waine said, 'I was devastated. I couldn't get over it. It took me years to understand that Ken got to a point in his life lots of times when something just went. It was a bit like a spaceship sending off an engine into space. Something was jettisoned.'

He could break with friends, but not with patterns of work. Sid was dead, and Hattie, Charlie and Jim had bowed out of the *Carry Ons*, but while Williams had avoided the stage and television versions he continued to star in the films. He was an archaeologist, Professor Roland Crump, in *Carry On Behind*, sharing a caravan with Elke Sommer. His twenty-fifth appearance was as the compère of *That's*

Carry On, introducing clips from the series with Barbara Windsor and paying tribute to cinema's comic tradition in a Churchillian speech.

That's Carry On was the last in the series to be distributed by Rank, and it wasn't even a main feature, merely the support to a Richard Harris thriller. The slap-and-tickle, whelks-and-eels humour was part of the national heritage, and cinema-goers cringed when Rogers tried to wheel it out one more time, in a parody of the soft-porn romps that had followed the slackening of censorship. *Carry On Emmannuelle* was dire. Dreadful editing, a witless plot, arthritic jokes and queasy racism are the worst of the problems, but that does not explain why *Emmannuelle* is horrible while *Carry On Up the Khyber*, ten years earlier, had been sublime.

In *Khyber*, the wicked Khasi leads a Burpa uprising to overthrow the British when he discovers that the Highland troops wear woolly drawers under their kilts; in *Emmannuelle*, the French ambassador is unable to satisfy his wife after an accident with a church steeple while he is skydiving nude. Both starred Kenneth Williams doing a silly accent. Both had strong supporting casts. One, though, is a fantasy celebrating the crude pleasures of schoolboy humour. The other is an envious sneer at the permissive society. *Khyber* is joyous; *Emmannuelle* is sour, and most of its cruelty is inflicted on the actors. In his first scene, Williams has to stand with his back to camera, lifting dumb-bells. His shorts fall down, exposing his backside. In his next scene, he is face down on a bed, miserably impotent, wearing only socks and trainers. It is a pitiful episode.

He should not have made the film. Bresslaw and Windsor, his closest friends in the team, turned it down, and Williams had no shortage of television jobs. This was Rogers and Thomas, though, and he was a loyal workman. 'All my life,' he wrote to Thomas, 'I am conscious of how much I owe, both to you and to Peter.'

A simliar loyalty had impelled him the year before, when he made a film for his first new director in decades. The movie was *Hound of the Baskervilles*, starring and scripted by Peter Cook and Dudley Moore; the director was Paul Morrissey. Williams looked at the script and knew it was shabby, but Cook had given him two West End hits. He wanted to repay that, and he knew Cook would be good company. Friendship was a fine motive, but work without payment was amateur and almost dishonest, so he convinced himself that his bank manager demanded it. 'Critics will say "tired, laboured, unfunny", etc,' he wrote after viewing the first rushes, 'but it don't matter and I do need the money.' He earned his biggest fee for any film, £7,500 plus a chauffeured car, but this was poor recompense compared to the fees being mooted for television adverts.

He enjoyed the filming; though it was slapdash, confused, frequently drunken and rarely coherent, Cook's deranged wit made up for it all. Williams was swept away: 'My conversation is endlessly repetitive and obscene . . . worse than barrack-room rubbish. There's a note of sheer desperation. PC + DM talk a lot of juvenile filth which is v. infectious to me.'

An account in the *Evening Standard* of a day on the set describes that manic atmosphere – Williams at lunch, topping everyone's anecdotes with stories of Burton and Hancock and Welles, and leaping up to perform a vigorous arabesque that almost knocked Cook out of his chair. Later, he claimed the movie, which also starred Irene Handl and Max Wall, was an authentic Sherlock Holmes: 'It's being played for absolute reality. It's not a Carry On. Everything has to be sincere and every reaction has to be honest. That's what makes it so screamingly funny.' At lunch a few weeks later, he got so drunk that Cook dragged him into the stable yard, half undressed him and ordered him to play a love scene to Hamish, the Baskerville hound.

The film flopped. Like everything Cook wrote, the jokes had been funniest the first time they left his mouth. When that spontaneity could be captured, he was peerless. Between takes one day, Cook conjured a surreal picture of the Sitwell family at home, with Sacheverell scrawling poetry over his sister – 'Edith Sitwell became an enormous CULT [. . .] She wasn't aware of the size of her cult cos she was absorbed by her Art. She didn't notice the cult at all.' Within days, Williams was using the line, in a letter to George Borwick. He started to say it on *Just a Minute* and, with such clear diction that the double entendre was barely audible, on chat shows. 'I wield my mighty sway,' he declared, 'over millions who rush to do my bidding and obey my slightest whim. I've become a cult! An enormous great cult figure!'

17

'The tide is receding and leaving some incongruous wrecks exposed'

October 1969–December 1983

Williams began compiling notes for his autobiography in the late sixties. He had material enough for a shelf of books but, before he could begin to write them, he had to learn the trade. His thousands of letters and decades of diaries did not qualify him; nor did the dozens of scripts he had co-written, for no fee, with John Law. Real writers saw their work published, and he dared not aspire to seeing his name on a book. He had contributed a piece on the animator Richard Williams to *Film* magazine, but that didn't count either: he had been writing 'just as I speak'. His self-conscious attempts to write began four years later, in 1969, with a letter to a magazine, *The Spectator*.

By then, it should have been evident to any editor that Williams, who could extemporise so fluently on chat shows and panel games, must be a natural writer. It could not have been guessed, though, from his letter: he sounded as dull as a sociology lecturer at a new-town polytechnic. The magazine printed his name and address in full, which suggests the letters editor did not connect the writer with the entertainer.

A few weeks later he contributed, without payment, a full page to Durham University's rag mag. This time he was funny, though all the anecdotes were true: how Joan Sims locked herself out of her house in a housecoat and no drawers, and what a woman in Portland Place had shouted when he would not give her his autograph, and why dining out was dangerous. Williams was pleased with the piece. 'I feel like Lytton Strachey today,' he noted after posting it. 'There is some satisfaction to be got from setting things down on paper . . . (I think what I would really like to do is WRITE and live in a cottage in some lonely place).'

When Leicester's rag mag invited him to contribute the following year (they couldn't get the Queen, the editor explained, so they were asking him), Williams described how his literary career had been stymied, after initial success: 'I remember the shock of seeing my name on the printed page and shuddering with surprise; I never dreamed that they would give it space. [Then] I tried it on twice with the Times and nothing happened so I stopped taking the paper and now I do not care whether it flourishes or not. I am not going to stand about risking further snubs from them. Rejection of any kind incurs feelings of inferiority and I've got enough of that to cope with as it is.'

After the debacle of *My Fat Friend*, he hinted to Eade that he would consider occasional journalism. *Radio Times* proposed a monthly column, looking ahead to choice programmes. Their commissioning editor, Sonya Shepherd, called at Osnaburgh Street to explain what was wanted, and staged an accidental demonstration of everything that most infuriated Williams: 'Sonya came + made about SIX phone calls (this job is going to cost ME money) and used my lavatory without even asking, smoked endless cigarettes + spilled ash on my table + carpet + irritated me beyond measure.'

Despite this, he tackled the column and began with a declaration: 'It is the capacity for taking pains which I admire.' He was a conscientious and diligent reporter, sitting through advance screenings with a notebook and cramming nine or ten previews into his 800 words. As well as wide-ranging choices – *Panorama*'s profile of Richard Nixon, the Wimbledon championships, and the poetry of Stevie Smith, all in his first column – he included interviews with actors and producers. Asking the questions, he discovered, could be as frustrating as answering them: 'Tried doing the rest of the PREVIEW article. Phoned Ronnie Barker. He said, "I haven't anything to say about the show really . . . I loved doing it . . . but I'm not much good at off the cuff remarks . . ." Tom Conti rang about his play and said "I can't think of ANYTHING I'm afraid." Thank goodness I'm not a journalist.'

As well as a selection of Christmas poetry for *Woman's Hour* in 1975, he recorded a collection of 'comic, patriotic and improving Victorian verse', called *Parlour Poetry*, including 'Jabberwocky' and 'The Walrus and the Carpenter' by Carroll, Longfellow's 'Wreck of the Hesperus', and 'The Dong with the Luminous Nose' by Lear. The nonsense verse is a delight; even more wonderful are the melodramas, which he reads without irony or mockery. He shared the morality of the music hall, its reverence for working-class hardships as well as its coarseness, and his sincerity is an evocation of camp sensibility at its most pure. When he brings the bereaved miner home to his hovel in 'Little Jim', and describes the death of a girl in rags at the frozen roadside as she clutches a rose for her brother, his voice breaks with tears. Other performers would be knowing, or pompous; only Williams, with his nineteenth-century strains of repression and chastity, could restore the emotion to 'In the Workhouse: Christmas Day'.

The combination of poetry readings, literary debates, discussions on current affairs, book adaptations, television reviews and opinion columns began to create a new perception of Williams, as a disciplined anarchist with a subtle appreciation of the rules he shattered: smutty, puerile, dirty-minded but literate with it. Always popular with students, he now received letters from debating societies as well as rag mags. The president of the Oxford Union Society, Benazir Bhutto, invited him to argue the motions that 'This House Would Rather Rock Than Roll' and 'This House Likes Dominating Women'. He turned her down, but accepted a commission for £110 from *Radio Times* to write a portrait of Peter Jones, his colleague on *Just a Minute*. The article had to be 'analytical and perceptive and entertaining and anecdotal', and Williams took him out to dinner for the interview, before filing a politely insightful piece.

Punch tried to poach him from *Tatler*, for which he was engaged to write a monthly column, and agents and publishers began, at last, to make approaches. Anne Powys-Lybbe, a literary agent in Sussex, wrote: 'If you ever thought of doing a sort of "Kenneth Williams Talking" a book with some of your gorgeous stories, with some chapters perhaps on your philosophy [. . .] I do know that at least five top publishers would leap at it.' After a burglary at Williams's flat, where thieves took mostly cash – they ignored his watch, but grabbed four pairs of shoes – Gordon Jackson proposed a motive: 'Obviously the burglar was a man from Macmillan's the publishers! You can see him getting back to head office, & them screaming at him, "Not the *shoes*, you fool! The DIARIES – the DIARIES!!!"'

Those diaries now included political and social commentary, not with the intention of compiling a record of contemporary Britain, but as indications of how society intruded on his life. As a young man he had been oblivious even to great events – the death of King George was significant only in that it meant the cancellation of a television appearance, and the Suez crisis merely because it had sparked a running debate with Hancock. Now he felt twinges of emotion at all sorts of headlines that harked at injustice: the aftermath of dictatorship in Uganda, the strangulation of the Labour government by its union allies, the rising price of petrol in the wake of Iran's revolution, the assassination of the British ambassador to Holland by the IRA. None of these things affected him directly – he had never been to east Africa, nor met Sir Richard Sykes, and he did not drive a car or vote Labour. These events cast shadows on his landscape, though, in a way that much darker clouds had once failed to do.

Political consciousness had nudged him on to the council of Equity, the actors' union. A left-wing faction, aligned with the Workers' Revolutionary Party, had been trying to exert pressure on the economy and even engineer a general strike through the entertainment industry – it was a hopeless plot, though its figureheads were well-known actors. The threat of a communist junta controlling Britain's sitcoms and West End farces caused consternation. Williams was invited in February 1976 to stand for the council: his sponsors reasoned that his fame, and the prospect of dirty jokes under Any Other Business, would ensure his election, a docile right-winger plugging a hole in the great dyke of the theatre. He was hesitant at first, but the twin appeals of duty and an audience of his peers won him over, and he served on the council until his death.

Publishers still plied for his autobiography. Weidenfeld & Nicolson came closest to persuading him: he would not sign a contract but, after two years of flattery and encouragement, he sat down to draft the story of his life up to demob. The editor, John Curtis, was enthusiastic: 'You've really done it! As I always imagined you would, you write with consummate skill.' Williams replied that the work was insupportable, and that if Weidenfeld wanted to kill him they were going the right way about it. Curtis, aghast, offered to provide a ghost writer, and the last glimmer of Williams's confidence was snuffed out. Conveniently, he now had an excuse to fend off other publishers: he already had a verbal contract with Curtis, though the thought of writing an autobiography turned his stomach. 'I found it all appallingly depressing,' he admitted. 'Going back over the past, dredging up all the sludge of the almost forgotten sea bed.'

The manuscript of his life story was written in cramped copperplate, in light pencil, the strokes almost too faint and too constricted to be legible. His diary, by contrast, was almost always in ink (though occasionally, on holiday, he had to resort to a ballpoint pen) and if a word was smudged or scrawled, he would write it again, above the line, in small block capitals. For dramatic and significant events – a burglary, a reassuring phone call, a blister – he used thick felt-tip to print his words.

On Thursday 26 April 1979, he entered a whole paragraph in blue felt-tip. 'LAURENA telephoned at 9.55 in a terrible state: "PETER [Eade] DIED LAST NIGHT . . . A SUDDEN HEART ATTACK . . ." + I mouthed some sympathetic platitudes but the enormity of his loss hasn't really hit me yet . . . Peter dead! the only + the best agent I EVER HAD . . . dear God . . . it is appalling.' The death devastated him. For days afterwards, he would be on the verge of tears if he tried to speak about it.

Laurena Dewar, Peter Eade's assistant, asked him to read the eulogy at the memorial service, and Annette Kerr drove him to the church at Ropley, the Hampshire village where Eade's father still lived. It had taken him a day to write the speech: 'Every time I turn to it I start crying + I fear I'll not be over this by the time it comes to speak the words.' Dewar continued to run the agency for several months, fielding chat-show requests and forwarding fan letters, and it was through her, combined with his penchant for Equity politics and the intuition of one of his neighbours, that Williams returned to the stage for his final play.

Bill Kenwright, a former *Carry On* extra who had elbowed his way into theatre production with a revival of *Billy Liar*, lived near Osnaburgh Street. 'I had a play by an old and dear friend, Trevor Baxter, and the leading character was an undertaker. I love adventurous casting. I said to Trevor, "Kenneth Williams is a superb straight actor." And he said, "Yeah – give it a go." I sent it to Ken's agent, and less than twenty-four hours later, which never happens, I got a phone call: he wants to do it.'

Kenwright was taken aback. Williams had walked to his agent's offices as soon as he'd been told the script was waiting, read his part and accepted it immediately. Baxter was prominent in Equity and renowned for a 1973 speech that ridiculed the revolutionaries: Williams had admired it so much that he had sent a note of praise. After agreeing to a short run in south London, at the Greenwich Theare, followed by a provincial tour and then the West End, if the play proved successful, Williams bumped into Kenwright outside an Equity meeting. Explaining his haste to take the part, he said, 'I'd read anything that man has written.'

The Undertaking was a surreal sitcom, as if Orton had written an episode of *One Foot in the Grave*. Two brothers and their wives arrive at a family funeral, not knowing who has died. The undertaker provides a special service: he robs the grave and embalms the corpse in some fetishistic pose, but his job is complicated when he discovers that the deceased – a young woman, played by Lorraine Chase – is not dead, but comatose. To make the farce still darker, the undertaker had no pratfalls, no puns, no innuendo. His sincerity was deadly. 'There was not a laugh line in it for Kenneth,' Kenwright said. 'But he just loved it. And when Kenneth loves something he gives his all to it.'

The opening and the subsequent tour were sold out on the strength of the names. Gerald Flood and John Barron were the brothers, both well known from television comedies, as was Miriam Karlin. Chase was famous for three words, in a Campari advert, and for the bathetic contrast between her classical profile and Estuarine accent. Williams knew that audiences would be baffled by the play, and that all their expectations of him would be confounded, but he was indifferent to that. Partly this was a reaction to Eade's death. Without an agent, he felt no obligation to succeed: he was working on no one's behalf but his own. Professionally, he was a widower. His enthusiasm for *The Undertaking* was not a negative whim, however: the play fascinated him. Bolt and Orton had written parts around him, but it was Trevor Baxter who, without knowing him, had preserved slivers of his personality in aspic.

The nameless Undertaker knew the importance of embellishing anecdotes: 'I always think it is somewhat lazy to just tell the truth; the additional effort required by fiction is invariably worth it.' He appreciated that honesty was both essential and impractical: 'The truth is not unlike gold; necessary to give backing to the currency but hardly convenient for day-to-day transactions.' And he understood the urge for a celebrity to feed the ghouls who want to devour him: 'When we die the microbial population to whom our body has been as a continent starts to devour the land. Embalming swiftly arrests this. But there are other predators; friends, relatives who eat their way through papers, letters, diaries, bills, scavenging in drawers and peering under beds, searching for the core, that essence of personality which made the deceased, while they were alive, peculiarly themselves. Many people have no objection to this and leave well-indexed diaries.'

He set to learning his part, weeks before rehearsals began. He dispensed with the script after the first read-through; the director, Donald MacKechnie, commented that Williams and Olivier were the only actors he knew who could do this. For three weeks he was obsessed by the preparations, so absorbed that whole days were written up without a reference to his health, and all his criticisms were constructive – either he saw improvements in the other actors and encouraged them, or he was grateful for hints that made him conscious of his own failings.

Chase had not acted in theatre before, knew no one and was apprehensive at rehearsals. On the first day, she ate her lunch in a corner, afraid to speak, and that became a routine: downstairs at lunchtime to buy a sandwich at the bar, along the street to the grocer's for salad and crisps, and back to the corner of the rehearsal room. 'I was getting really quite unhappy. I was sat there one day and Kenneth Williams was with Miriam Karlin, and I heard him say, "Look at her over there! Every day with her little cheese sandwich and her watercress and her crisps, all on her own. Come over here, you silly cow, and sit with us!" He was so kind to me, but he wouldn't do it in a way that was obvious. One of the kindest men I ever knew. I loved his company.'

The Undertaking opened in Greenwich to bad notices. The Mail called it 'metaphysical tosh', and even Louie struggled to hide her disappointment. 'I didn't understand much of that play,' she said. 'Haven't you got long words to say?' The audiences wanted to see a *Carry On*, and the critics tried to help them find it. 'No one arches an eyebrow quite so superciliously as Williams, nor elongates a vowel to such devastating effect,' said one; 'not his usual comic self,' complained another – 'he plays the repellent character with a clammy calm which made me shudder'; 'one wonders why an actor of his eminence should have accepted a part so small,' said a third.

His detachment, the sense that he had become invisible in the role, was wrecked. By the end of the week he was ready to walk out. 'Bill rang me,' Trevor Baxter remembered, 'and said, "You'd better get down to Greenwich, Kenneth wants to leave".' When he arrived, the male actors were in the communal dressing-room.

'Kenneth said, "I'm not happy! It's the laughs, they all get laughs, they've got funny lines and I get jealous. I don't like it."' Baxter pointed out that the attraction of the role had been its chilling absence of humour. 'He said, "I know, but I get jealous. I'm not a nice person." And he went into this extraordinary tirade that lasted quite ten minutes, which involved a physical transformation: at one moment he was like a little, quiet boy, and at others he was like a horrible, bitter old man. He was quite extraordinary. This absolute rant about what he was like as a person, what he felt about the play, how he hated them all getting laughs, and at the end of it I said, "All I can do is argue for my play. If you come out of it now, it can't transfer – we can't replace you because the critics would smell a rat. Please, just stay with it." Kenneth just stood there and suddenly said, "Oh all right." And that was it. In the diaries, this comes out as "If you really believe I'm essential to your production, I will not let you down," but he didn't say that. He just said, "Oh all right," and we all fell into the bar with relief afterwards.'

Baxter could not know that this was a reprise of the scene Williams had played with Codron in Brighton, during the tour of *One Over the Eight*. He suspected it was attention-seeking, a star's tantrum staged to remind the other actors of who commanded their fates. In fact, Williams was establishing an alibi for himself. He had seen the notices. When the play flopped, he could console himself that he had wanted to leave and had stuck with it out of altruism. 'A compulsive entertainer, and he needed desperately to be the centre of attention,' Trevor Baxter said. 'He was lovely one to one, but add two other people and he had to perform. Absolutely compulsive. One's company and two's an audience. He could be very sweet and unassuming when he dropped all the act.'

The Undertaking did reach the West End, struggling into the Fortune after traipsing through Poole, Brighton, Wilmslow and Welwyn Garden City. 'People went to see Kenneth the comedian,' Trevor Baxter said. 'They wanted *Carry On*, or anecdotes, and it looked as though the whole thing was going to be a bundle of laughs, and I'm afraid it wasn't. In Wilmslow you could hear the seats banging up as the audience walked out, they were so angry.' In the diary, red Biro started to appear – back pain, swollen gums, a cold, itching in one eye.

'In Brighton we stayed in the same hotel,' Chase said, 'and we used sit on a bench on the promenade – he'd say, "Even if it's cold, you have to have the sun on your face." People would go by and they'd say, "Oh! Oh my God, it's Kenneth Williams. Oh Kenneth, how wonderful, oh Mr Williams." And he would do that terribly posh voice, and I'm afraid he used to tell them to fuck off. And they went, "Oh! Oh Kenneth, how could you!" He could never offend them, people would take anything from him. He could get away with anything.'

Poor reviews killed *The Undertaking* and by January the cast were playing to audiences of a few dozen. Tickets were given away to nurses at nearby hospitals to make the stalls less empty. 'John Barron used to whisper in the wings: "What few there were is diminishing! you can see people leaving! this management must be mad!"' Williams wrote. 'I told him, "We must have been mad as well, doing it in the first place!"'

Like the tour of *Loot*, *The Undertaking* was billed as an adult comedy. Children's drama was proving more successful. After the play closed, Williams took a train to Wales and spent four days at the recording studios of Nimbus Records, at Wyastone Leys outside Monmouth; in a series of exhausting sessions he read the whole of the Chinese fable, *Monkey*, which had inspired a popular children's serial on television. The recordings, supervised by Numa Labin, were issued as a fourteen-hour collection of LPs. Labin had a reputation for perfectionism, but he was staggered by the precision and invention of Williams's reading. Monkey was effervescent and irrepressible, the supreme deity was an echo of Noël Coward and the slow-witted Pigsy sounded as though he was always half a page behind.

His impeccable sight-reading made him a favourite on *Jackanory*, the storytime slot that screened on BBC1 after the nursery programme *Play School*. Watched by around 2.5 million children, many too young to know him through repeats of the *Carry On* films in the evening schedules, he made sixty-nine appearances. His readings included three stories featuring Agaton Sax, and others such as 'Tales of Incrediblania', 'The Dribblesome Teapots', and 'Count Backwerdz'. He also recorded an abridged *Wind in the Willows* and a selection of *Just William* stories, though as commercial releases and not a BBC broadcast.

His last *Jackanory*, in 1986, was Roald Dahl's *James and the Giant Peach*, which he had first admired when the author asked him to read a film adaptation twelve years earlier. He also read *The Rose and the Ring*, playing Princess Angelica much as he had in the Manchester Street Junior School play, 'bawling and stomping around the stage and generally receiving a lot of attention'.

Befitting his cult status, he was the voice of *Willo the Wisp*, in the five-minute animation slot before the evening news. *Willo* had begun in 1975 as an educational short for British Gas, by Nick Spargo, who drew a pilot flame with twinkling eyes and a two-tier nose. He spent years developing the concept, until Willo lived in a magical wood with his friends: a dumpy fairy called Mavis Cruet who was searching for romance, and Arthur the Cockney caterpillar, and Carwash, a cat in spectacles who thought he to was Noël Coward. The Doyley Woods were haunted by Evil Edna, a wicked witch imprisoned in a broken television. Williams supplied all the voices, with hints of repressed innuendo – tut-tutting about silly fat fairies, and pronouncing 'Doyley' with just enough distaste to invoke the rhyming slang, D'Oyly Carte. Younger children would never guess at the double meanings; that was what made Williams such an artful cult.

All his restraint was ditched for *Just a Minute*. A dozen times a year, the recordings at the Paris Cinema enabled him to parade his erudition and exercise his despite. Ian Messiter would set him questions that pandered to his historical tastes, for classical philosophers, medieval painters and post-Renaissance monarchs. Giotto, palaeontology, Spenser, sigillography, clerihews and the *Marie Celeste* were just a few of the recherché topics he was invited to discourse upon in the early eighties.

The show had become a ritual, no longer a game but a catechism of beloved phrases and jokes, as comforting and predictable as a church service. Freud would recite the days of the week or parts of the body, Nimmo would refer to recent travels in China or the Persian Gulf, and Williams would shriek that he hadn't come all the way from Great Portland Street to be insulted. Within the confines of these traditions, he managed to advertise his breadth of learning, his memory for lines and his penchant for scatology. Asked, for instance, to define the Theatre of the Absurd, he cited the playwright Artaud, whose surreal symbol of colonial rule in Algeria was, 'the French soldier crying out, "Oh would that could I smell the air of France," and his comrades breaking wind over him!'

Nicholas Parsons tried to protect Williams from cavils by other players. 'He would go into a sulk. I knew him extremely well, and knew when this had happened. It's such a difficult game to play that, however experienced you are, it is so easy to pause. So there were occasions when he'd be challenged for hesitation, and he would dramatise it, to get a laugh, but it came from the heart – "Oh well, you have it . . . oohh, you missed a very good story there!" I could sense his mood, and when he next got a subject I'd build his confidence up: "Now, Kenny, this audience have come because they love you, they're just waiting to hear from you, with your flamboyance, all that wonderful panache, you can give them so much!" And I could see him pull himself up.'

Williams repaid his consideration with cruelty, both on stage and behind the scenes. During the game, he berated Parsons for his decisions or applauded sarcastically – 'Ooh, you're a very good chairman. I've always said so!' During a TV pilot, Parsons struck back, asking whether he'd brought his fan club with him after a couple of weak jokes raised laughter. Williams boiled with spite: 'PARSONS was death. He is an awful chairman + he dithered + dithered so much that the programme never got under way [. . .] We dribbled to a wet conclusion. I told the director + Roger Ordish (producer) that the programme needed a lively, genial and competent chairman and that without that, the format was a dead duck.' The next morning he phoned Ordish and announced that he would never appear on television with Parsons. After those blisters of malice had burst, he forgot them, and Nicholas forgave them: 'I just think of Kenneth making me laugh, playing to the audience, slipping from one voice to another. This is why he was a unique performer. None of us could suddenly slip into different modes of voice that are akin to our personality and yet not quite our true voice.'

Williams, though sensitive to slights, lacked that self-awareness to know what others felt about him, when their feelings were disguised. He described his friendships in his diaries with such clarity that he could give a sense of discussions that lasted hours, just by recounting a few essential comments – yet he did not often reflect on what was unsaid. He could give offence, and be told later that he was forgiven, and would be honestly surprised to realise years later that his friend had never forgotten the hurt.

His erudition was in demand, from silly panel games such as *Opinions Unlimited* on Southern TV, to Radio 4's *Bookshelf*, to a dissertation for the World Service on calligraphy, which he listed as his primary recreation in *Who's Who*. It also found an outlet in a frivolous genre of writing that suited his façade – the literary joke book. Gyles Brandreth, a colleague on *Just a Minute* and a prolific writer and editor, knew what an eager market existed for a book by Kenneth Williams; he saw too that, despite the constant glimpses of autobiography in his anecdotes, Williams detested intrusions into his life. His best stories, though they seemed to be about himself, actually focused on other people. His wit presented a paradox: he had no enemies, because he inspired such pity and patience in his friends – and yet the public loved him best when he was being vicious, sarcastic, wounding, lacerating.

Brandreth's solution was a book of scathing stories, told by Williams about people whom, by and large, he had never met. They compiled *Acid Drops* on to tape recorder in early 1980: Brandreth's transcriptions retained the wordiness of Williams's style, with every punchline honed. His theme was 'the cruel bon mot [. . .] its sting drawn by the laughter that ensues', and to justify that he quoted Oscar Wilde: 'no comment was in bad taste if it was amusing.' Groucho was in there, of course, and Churchill, and Beecham, and Margot Asquith's putdown to Jean Harlow ('the "t" is silent, as in Harlow'), and Denis Healey's 'savaged by a dead sheep', and many that were not especially acidic but funny nonetheless, such as the tale of the African diplomat who was sharing an open carriage with Queen Elizabeth, when one of the horses broke wind; 'Oh dear, I am sorry,' said the Queen, and the ambassador reassured her gallantly, 'That's quite all right, Your Majesty . . . if you hadn't spoken, I'd have thought it was the horse.'

The book sold strongly, helped by Williams's vigorous promotion on chat shows and at book signings in shops from Bristol to Manchester. By mid-September it topped the best-seller lists, and in reviews of the year it was a favourite choice for Christmas stockings. He was encouraged to try a sequel, *Back Drops*, based on selections from his diaries: published three years later, it was neither autobiography nor acid. The excerpts were so bowdlerised that they were meaningless, and the ones that were not invented had been culled from such a range of dates that there was no sense or continuity. *Back Drops* sold weakly and was remaindered.

Williams took two holidays after *The Undertaking*. The first was to Cyprus, with his mother; they stayed in Limassol, chatting to families at the hotel poolside. That summer he visited Tangier for the last time, in almost the final attempt of his life to escape from his prim conscience. The gay cliques had dissipated, back to Britain or far away to Thailand, and the remnant of Morocco's sex tourism was worse than seedy now. Williams spent most days drinking coffee at the hotel, grumbling about the raucous Germans by the pool. He was tempted into one assignation, with a man called Hassan, who relieved him of 70 dinar, took him to a guest house and, to Williams's relief, slipped away to book a room and never came back.

Back in England he needed a new agent. Dewar was leaving the business, and Peter Eade Ltd was to close. Gordon Jackson suggested ICM, where his own agent, Ronnie Waters, worked, but Williams was uneasy about throwing in his lot with a friend who commanded high fees for Hollywood movies and blockbuster TV series. He had known another ICM agent since his rep days, though – Michael Anderson, who had once played a servant in a Maugham play at Eastbourne in 1950 with a cushion tied round his middle.

'I remember walking along Albemarle Street where our offices were,' Anderson said; 'it was lunchtime and Kenneth was on the other side of the road. He just pointed at me and said, "Oh, you'll do!" I said, "What do you mean, I'll do?" He said, "I think I need an agent. Laurena's giving it up, getting married." And that's how we got together. It was a very happy association. People ask about that all the time, because he could have a reputation for being difficult, but I found him very easy to get on with. He used to turn up at the office, hardly ever made an appointment, but I could hear this bray-ing voice down the other end of the corridor. He'd come and see the secretaries and make them laugh, and then he'd bowl into my office and chat. I don't know how much work I generated for him, because he was getting his own work. I did the contractual work, getting the right fees and so on.'

That transition began in January 1980, and took more than a year to effect. He felt weightless again, as though nothing he attempted in the theatre could have consequences, and when David Porter, the associate director at the Lyric Hammersmith, invited him to direct Orton's *Loot* for their Studio Theatre, he accepted immediately. His enthusiasm took Porter aback – the Studio's remit was to take risks, but Williams had never directed.

The first crisis was opposition from Peggy Ramsay, agent for the Orton estate and a strident personality capable of forbidding the production. 'When I first approached her about it,' Porter said, 'she thought I was completely mad.' He turned for advice to Michael Codron, a champion of the Lyric Hammersmith, who once more gave Williams his protection and suggested to Ramsay that she should put aside her objections.

Porter hoped the intimacy of the Studio, with just 120 seats, would draw out the dark domestic humour of *Loot*. He met Williams and was relieved that his hyperactive public rudeness was not evident in private. The urgent intensity, though, was more heightened even than it appeared on television: casting was a matter of two half-day sessions, for instance, where ten candidates were seen for each role and nine summarily dismissed. Maureen Lipman was asked to audition as Fay, which Porter worried was tactless for such an established sitcom star. More tactlessly still, she was rejected. 'If I'd had more confidence I would have said we should cast her,' Porter admitted. 'But that's probably why I got on so well with him – I was deferential, and he was able to get his way, whereas a more experienced producer might have challenged him and had problems later on.'

The casting of Truscott was problematic – Williams considered David Ryall, but settled on John Malcolm, who played the policeman at first like a sergeant-major. Afraid of repeating Peter Woods's mistakes, Williams was insistent that *Loot* must be neither mannered not self-consciously comic: the characters had to behave as though everything was real to them. That dragged him into arguments with actors about 'motivation', the theatrical conceit that exasperated Williams more than any other. Now he was the director, he had less than no patience: 'Your world is entirely *real* to you,' he snapped at Joan Blackham, who played Fay. 'That's all that matters.'

After a lifetime of disparaging his directors, he could not take criticism from actors. 'I asked Philip Martin Brown "What is the trouble? Why are you cross?" + he said "Well I've been trying my best + it doesn't help when you keep faulting the way I deliver each line . . ." So I said, "Then ignore it: do what you want to do."' He admired Malcolm's energy, and felt he carried the play at moments where the action dragged, but when the actor asked him to make a celebrity appearance at his wife's theatre, Williams refused: 'His cheek is breath-taking.' He was no more conciliatory to the press – the *Guardian*'s interviewer was a 'prize bore' and the *Telegraph*'s an 'unctuous creep'.

Within two weeks, rehearsals were over. Williams directed with the practical approach that he took to washing the walls or buying a raincoat. He remembered Orton's intentions for the set and followed them; he expected moves to be crisp, lines to be audible and actors to be natural. 'There wasn't any kind of directorial spin, and that was the strength of the production,' Porter said. 'It allowed the true voice of Orton to come through, and the play was incredibly funny.' Their sole disagreement was over the poster: the first version featured two young men, shimmering with erotic suggestion. Williams insisted it did not reflect his production and, with only a few days to go, a new design featuring only the play's title above a banknote was commissioned.

The run was sold out, and the notices were excellent: 'Instead of instructing the actors to roll the lines round their tongues,' Michael Billington wrote in the *Guardian*, 'Williams gets them to play the situation [. . .] instead of imposing a style, [he] extracts a dotty kind of truth.' 'Williams The Conquerer', declared Jack Tinker in the *Mail*; 'Mr Williams has done a largely successful balancing act,' said Ned Chaillet in *The Times*. 'Each elaborately phrased joke has a chance to be heard.'

After the tension of the first night, Williams was jolted to receive a call from Porter, warning that Malcolm had been in 'an altercation' and, with sixteen stitches in his face, would not be able to perform. There was no understudy, so Williams picked up the inscribed copy of the play that Orton had given him, and ordered a 2 p.m. rehearsal. 'Kenneth came in, visibly excited by the whole thing,' Porter said. 'He was going to do the whole part reading from a clipboard, which would suit the character. The excitement within the building was absolutely immense. Within half an hour of us making that decision the phones just never stopped. It was sold out, there weren't any tickets to be had, and the box office were under siege.

'Mick Jagger and Jerry Hall turned up. I remember thinking, I'm the director of the theatre and I do not understand how they have got tickets. It was an outrageous evening. Kenneth's performance was camp. He just could not play it straight: it was very over-the-top, and he milked everything. It was completely different to how he'd directed the show. Of course the audience loved it. It was almost impossible for the cast, because they were being upstaged and corpsed, but it was very, very funny. One extraordinary night, and I was lucky to be there.'

Williams was elated. As he received congratulations from the cast afterwards, he knew that he had laid the ghost of his shattering failure fifteen years earlier. He had finally delivered his Truscott, to an ecstatic house, in a production he had cast and directed. This was a triumph. It was also his last appearance on a theatre stage: Malcolm returned the next night. Williams never acted again. 'When John came back, Kenneth was very upset – he'd tasted a thing that he loved,' Porter saw. 'But if Kenneth had gone on doing it, the play could never have come back to the style he'd directed it in. It would have gone through the roof in a different way.'

Bill Kenwright saw the production's success, and transferred it to the Arts Theatre, though Williams refused his pleas to take over Truscott. 'He was a smashing director. But it stopped with *Loot* and *Sloane* – he never took anything to fruition. And you think, Why did you put in all that hard work? But he wanted control of his life and maybe taking that next step up was out of his comfort zone. Starring in a West End play, like having a relationship, was putting your head above the parapet, exposing yourself to critics and he didn't want to expose himself ever – physically, mentally. The public adored him but he never believed it completely. "They'll never come," he'd say to me. You just want to grab him and give him a hug, but you couldn't ever go anywhere near him. He hated being touched. I loved him, simple as that. You meet so many people in your life, but how often can you say, "I loved him, I would have done anything for him"? We could sit and say nothing, or just read together . . . although he used to make me cry with laughter. He was my idol.'

Loot opened at the Arts on the day of Hattie Jacques's memorial service. She had died from a heart attack, which left Williams sad and shocked: 'All the chums have died [. . .] one is left marooned on the shore . . . the tide is receding and leaving some incongruous wrecks exposed . . . I fear I am one of them.' He read lines from Clemence Dane's 'The Welcoming Land' – 'Sweet as a kiss on a summer day' – and told the congregation at St Paul's in Covent Garden that when Hattie had learned his treasured 78rpm recording by Noël Coward of the poem had been lost, she had scoured junk shops to replace it for him.

That night's opening was 'a juddering mess . . . it just SCRAPED through'. By then he had already agreed to direct *Entertaining Mr Sloane*, again at the Lyric, and was fretting over something Orton had said about a failed production – audiences would like the play only if Kath, the landlady, had sex appeal. He considered asking Fenella Fielding and then, inspired, turned to Barbara Windsor. She had not forgotten a conversation on a sixties *Carry On* set: 'He said to me, "Joe's been moaning about the actress. He said, 'Who'd want to fuck her? The thing about Kath is, Sloane has got to want her.'" Kenny always said to me, "You should play Kath when you're older."' Once Windsor was signed, he cast Dave King as Ed, and Glyn Grimstead as the boy. Windsor had worked in panto with King, and on television when he had his own show, and she knew he could be difficult – 'talented but hard, not a very nice man'.

When rehearsals started in February 1981, King and Williams clashed immediately. When Grimstead stumbled on his lines, Williams snapped: 'Just slow down and make a point of the line instead of gabbling! I can't have that kind of amateurism.' The bickering went on till the dress rehearsal and Williams was furious to discover that, even after the play opened, King was holding post-mortems on stage when the audience had gone home.

'There was very bad feeling,' Windsor said. 'The thing about Kenny is, he wants to do it himself. He was getting up and saying, "Now, this is what I want." Of course that caused quite a few arguments – not with me, cos I knew what Kenny was like, but Dave was saying, "Why don't you do it all yourself?" We opened, and it was a success – we ran for four weeks. But he wasn't what I would call a good director. He wanted you to do it the way he would. It wasn't easy.'

Bill Kenwright had urged him to present a one-man show in the West End, and he was vacillating – Eade had always liked the idea, as had Codron, and he had spent a couple of days in 1977 roughing out a programme with the writer and director James Roose-Evans. He was almost ready to take a professional step that all his friends had advocated for years. But none of them could have predicted the step, when it came. Williams decided to try working abroad.

Michael Parkinson was hosting his chat show in Sydney. Williams had been his guest six times, most recently with Tom Lehrer, and Australian audiences had heard none of his stories. The producers offered £2,000 plus first-class flights and accommodation. Williams agreed on the spot; his only condition was that the return flight had to be pre-booked, so that he could be certain of his itinerary. 'I don't seem to have anything else to do,' he shrugged.

He flew out on 15 June 1981, so apprehensive that he could barely write, and remembering how he had flown to Beirut alone after fleeing *The Platinum Cat*. His first two days in Sydney were fraught; he was staring about him as if he had never been in a big city before. 'He didn't travel well,' Parkinson said. 'I remember him walking round in the height of the Australian summer, in a Burton's mac and a belt, and a sensible suit. I was with him more than I had ever been before, living in the same hotel. I'd have dinner with him, and "uncomfortable" is the word. Sydney had a huge gay scene, but he seemed to be uneasy with that too, unable to embrace in the social sense those people who were determined and delighted to meet him. He was just this little island of discomfort.'

The first show was a triumph, with all his favourite stories – the army medical, and Barri Chatt in Singapore, and how Orson Welles dismissed him from the stage, all topped with 'The Ballad of the Woggler's Moulie'. Bill Kerr was also staying in the same hotel, and the two *Hancock* veterans recorded an interview for a Perth radio station. Kerr remembered the light tone of the meeting was darkened by a question about Tony's suicide. 'I said, "My God, I hope that never happens to me." And do you know what Kenneth said? "If you ever feel like topping yourself, phone me and I'll talk you out of it." ' It was the last time the two spoke.

Williams spent his second weekend in Sydney with Paul Florance, the lawyer and old flame he had known almost as long as Kerr. He recorded another show with Parkinson and anaesthetised himself with brandy for the long haul home. During the flight he fell asleep and woke with a cricked neck – 'I asked the steward for an osteopath to fix it + he told me "We don't carry one, I'm afraid". Lousy service.' Back in London, when friends asked what Australia was like, he told them, 'Death . . . it's what happens when the working class take over.'

He came home to a minor crisis: there was a crack in his lavatory pan. Housework had become an obsession, and he would be disgusted with himself if he failed to clean Louie's windows every six weeks. When visitors came to the flat, he played up to his reputation for neurotic hygiene and sometimes sent friends across the road to use the tube station toilets. This was a pose, of course, though it was also a convenient way of dismissing people who were boring him. 'He didn't like anyone using his loo,' Tom Waine said. 'If it was one of us, he'd say with a wry smile, "Yes, dearie, well, I suppose you'll have to . . . but just the pee."'

The saga of the cracked pan filled almost two days, after a plumber agreed to fit a new unit for £90. Williams was bereft, as though he was parting with an old friend: 'Washed and shaved and waited in trepidation [. . .] Will today be the last time I sit on this loo? Yes, it will.' When the plumber arrived, Williams put his celebrity to work: 'By 100c the old one was OUT + deposited in his van, with me squaring the Traffic Warden: "Oh all right Ken . . . just put a ticket up saying it's an emergency."' He usually baulked at demanding special treatment from officialdom; the next day, for instance, when a bus conductor refused to take his fare, he grumbled that the bus company and his fellow passengers were being cheated.

Parkinson invited him back to his BBC show twice more in the months that followed, interviewing him ten times in all, and he summed up Williams's contradictions: 'One of the most extraordinary guys I ever met. He was a gossip, and he was frank, and he was brutal. He was a brilliant anecdotalist, a wonderful, entertaining, charming man when he wanted to be. Then the other extreme was this unhappy, wizened soul, he was disenchanted, he was bitter – about what?'

During the early eighties he earned more money than he had ever banked before, with work that was often desultory. A BP commercial, encouraging customers to save energy, had him dressed up as a devil in horns and a velvet cape, and performing on demand, but a day's work earned him more than five weeks' filming at Pinewood.

He presented a show on Radio London for three weeks, talking to callers and interviewing showbiz friends, including Nicholas Parsons and Morecambe and Wise. There were television quizzes such as *Give Us a Clue*, voiceovers for Supersoft Nappies and Quaker Oats and Temik pesticides, book signings from Ealing to Dublin, after-dinner speeches, and a children's sketch show called *Whizzkids Guide*, where he starred with Arthur Mullard and Rita Webb as overgrown schoolchildren. He was interviewed about the career of Barbara Windsor, diaries, his religious beliefs (though the producer cut everything bar his reading of a poem) and the history of radio comedy. Every week brought new distractions, demanding enough to absorb him and insignificant enough that, whether they went wonderfully or dismally, they were easily dismissed.

His handwriting had settled into a constant form. He still used red ink to highlight all his twinges, and capitals to emphasise stray words; each entry still began with a verdict on his morning bowel movement. His old joy in calligraphy, and all the variety of styles that expressed his cartwheeling personalities, had been forgotten, though. The days were written up in a uniform, schoolboy script, and when he didn't feel like saying much he let the margins expand, so that the entry became a wedge of blue down the middle of the page.

Established now as a television personality and voiceover artiste, he had fewer offers for the theatre. Peter Nichols invited him to play Lady Dodo in a pantomime satire on the Chinese opium wars, at the RSC, directed by Terry Hands. Williams thumbed through the script, 'noting with dismay that it's a DRAG role', and went next door to his mother's flat: 'Told her about the play offer + she said, "Why do you have to dress up as a woman?" Which puts the whole dilemma in a nutshell.'

With so much TV work, he felt confident enough to agree to a one-man show for London Weekend. The producers promised an audience of his friends and tame celebrities, and he decided that the spontaneous air could best be achieved if he planned and rehearsed as little as possible. The studio was booked for 1 December 1982, and with less than two weeks to go Williams was refusing to enter a rehearsal room, even to practise his songs with the accompanists: 'I said it could be left till the last minute.' He talked through the running order with the director just twenty-four hours before the show, and rehearsed the musical spots – Ramblin' Syd and the 'Crêpe Suzette' number – the next afternoon. At 6 p.m. he roughed out a couple of pages of notes, which he took on stage two hours later.

The show was called *An Audience With*, and they were with him, from his first remark – he hushed their applause and drawled, 'May I say what an honour it is for you to have me . . .' The camera lingered on old friends convulsed with laughter as Williams etched scenes from his career like a draughtsman working with acid. He described

Stanley Baxter's efforts to avoid cemetery duties as a coffin-bearer in CSE ('och no, sir . . . Church of Scotland'); how an angry Siobhàn McKenna burst into Frank Royde's dressing-room during *Saint Joan* when the elderly actor had his feet up and his archbishop's robes hitched around his waist ('I said, "Did you have it out with him?" . . . she said, "He had it out already!"'); what Sheila Hancock called his grandmother on the stage at a CND benefit ('silly old cow!'); why he left *Hancock's Half Hour* ('he didn't really like my kind of comedy, said it was a bit cardboardy and stereotyped . . . a lot of people think that too, I don't mind'); what Noël Coward told him about piles ('papilli are islands in the South Seas'); and how Joan Plowright came to bash Orson Welles in the testicles. The response was rapturous, and he was moved and grateful: 'They were all very encouraging. The sheer loyalty of so many people was very heartwarming.'

The show was first broadcast almost a year later, on Channel 4, after the main commercial network, ITV, passed it up. Reviews were bright: 'A brilliant and sustained performance,' said the *Mail*. 'The fellow is a genius.'

Bill Kenwright had coaxed him over and over to stage a show like this on the West End. Williams had refused; the audiences would never come, he said. After thirty years of excuses, he had finally given in to every plea . . . not only to perform a one-man show, but to direct in the theatre, to write a book, to work abroad. If he had summoned his courage decades earlier, his career would have been quite different. By the eighties, the public just wanted to see him do his turn on panel shows and TV ads. And for the rest of his life, that's what he did.

18

'Nobody should live past sixty-five, because nobody should have to face deterioration'

January 1984–*April* 1988

> This is our real damnation,
> This thin drizzling rain.
> Not the perilous east ascent,
> Or the desert's fiery pain.
> It's not the great big kick-up-the-arse things
> That finally get you down.
> It's the steady drip of suburban leaves
> That are not in, and not out, of town.

Over dinner in an Italian restaurant in Soho, Williams quoted that verse at its author, one night in 1977. The poem was titled 'Eight Lines on a Small Point', and it was not the only composition from Stanley Baxter's army days that he remembered: he had included a burlesque called 'Berlin in the Twenties' for a selection on Radio 4. This poem had a particular resonance, though. He asked Baxter to write it out for him, and that night he pasted it in his diary.

Williams liked rain. Sunny afternoons on a deckchair in Regent's Park could be pleasant when he felt like nattering with admirers, but it was rain that he associated with poetry: 'Caught in a shower of light rain: it was like a mountain mist descending.' It pleased him that other people were deterred by wet weather, and that the pavements were cleared by a downpour, and that car headlights glittered and were refracted in the puddles, and that afterwards the streets seemed cleansed. Rain was London's benison, the absolution for its grit and dust.

The steady drip in his life eroded him, though he was fascinated by the drizzle of ill health as well. Like droplets on leaves, the details of his ailments and medicines pattered into his diary. He could not take a pill, for a headache or indigestion or insomnia, without recording it and commenting on the effect. He never suffered a major illness, though he consulted some medic or specialist almost every week of his adult life; at times during his last years, he saw doctors daily. He did not have a heart attack, a cancer or a stroke, yet when he saw friends disabled by illness – Bob Bolt in a wheelchair, unable to hold his pen, or Ken Tynan taking oxygen to combat emphysema – Williams seemed to view them as fellow sufferers.

The one person whose frailty was beyond his endurance was Louie. He felt her illnesses as vividly as he did his own, and with the terror of death that most people experience only on their own account. Cuts, blisters, rashes, the type of irritations that Louie might have thought too trivial to notice, fretted her son to distraction. He counted the days it took for a bruise to subside if she banged her arm, or a scab to heal if she knocked her ankle. When she saw a doctor, he would try to snatch a few words in private, to press for a deeper diagnosis. The thought that she could die was too awful to contemplate. Even a light-hearted remark – 'You'd soon miss me if I wasn't here' – could turn his stomach over. If she was tired, he blamed himself and fussed around her flat in search of anything that would make her life easier. He fitted rubber stoppers to her letterbox, to stop it rattling when the post arrived, and washed her dishes before she could rise from the table, and if he saw her from his window, setting off for the bus stop, he would hurry down into the street to carry her shopping bag.

Louie had suffered fainting fits since her husband's final illness. Unable to predict or prevent them, Williams tried to dismiss their significance: after one bout, when she blacked out in front of the television and could not be roused for several minutes, he persuaded himself it was only wind. Louie reassured him with white lies, and in her eighties would tell him that she'd brought on a funny turn by giving up smoking or missing a meal. Usually, her lapses were followed by confusion, which she would try to cover up. Sometimes, the effects could not be hidden – she passed out at the tea table in front of Edie's daughter, Joy, who thought her aunt was dying; at home, she burned a dress when she collapsed at the ironing board, and spilled a teapot over the carpet, and dropped a lit cigarette.

Williams watched her closely as they sat together in the evenings, chastising her if she fidgeted – Louie swung her legs like a child when she was bored – and worrying when she was sluggish. He could not be there every night, though, and at the beginning of June 1984 he was shuttling to Manchester for a game show called *Some You Win*. There were friends on the teams but Williams could not enjoy it: Louie had been complaining of stomach pains and tiredness. When he returned to London, clutching a present from the producer – 'BOOKS!! Which weigh a ton and add to my burdens. Oh!' – he was horrified to see his mother had fallen and bruised her face. The next day Louie failed to recognise her daughter in the street. Her speech was affected, 'not so much impaired as SLOWED . . . words formed laboriously as opposed to her old style of rapid delivery'.

Two months later, Pat had a stroke that paralysed her right side. Williams was close, though not devoted, to his sister; her disability and the deaths of his aunts, Edie and Alice, reduced the women in his family, once a regiment, to a lone sentry. He believed his mother was sliding into senescence, 'fighting the shadows that are closing in round her', and that he would have not only to watch but to cope as well, as she died one day at a time. It was an intolerable duty: 'God! I'd like to be miles away from ALL KIN at the moment. Why the hell was I burdened with it? The millstone which Charlie left goes on clogging my life.'

On 21 February 1986, a day before his sixtieth birthday, he went into Louie's flat after breakfast and discovered her collapsed and shivering on the floor, with both legs gashed from her fall. Metallic noise squealed from her deaf aid. Williams helped her into a chair, and washed and bandaged her cuts, before leaving her in bed: he had a voiceover booked, for British Telecom, and to miss it would be unprofessional. He called his sister and asked her to sit with Louie; before lunch, he was back in the flat, discussing the crisis with Pat.

Since 1963 he had been warning her that he couldn't be relied on to cope for ever, that he wasn't cut out to be anybody's nursemaid, that he was too busy and too successful to sacrifice his career and become a carer. Pat, now retired and more cantankerous since her stroke, insisted that it was too late to hand Louie over to her care. Williams wrote an angry letter to her GP, complaining that she had not received the care she needed and that she should be in hospital. He dropped it off by hand; the GP came out, and called for an ambulance. That evening, as his mother was treated in a casualty ward at University College Hospital five minutes' walk from her flat, Williams had to make an appearance with Michael Aspel on LWT's *The Six O'Clock Show*.

The next day, he convinced Pat that their mother would have to go into a nursing home. It wasn't only the physical infirmities and the blackouts that made Williams fear for her; she often seemed bewildered, unsure what time it was or what she had been doing. He sat beside her bed and explained firmly to Louie that she could not go home to Osnaburgh Street. She was not safe. He couldn't be with her every minute of the day. He'd be a rotten nurse, she ought to know that by now. He had to find a home for her. Louie listened to him, and surprised him when she said, 'Yes, as long as it isn't somewhere posh.'

It should not have been a shock: she always did agree with her Kenny – and if he had been able to see beyond his own fears of change and loneliness, he would have known that Louisa was well suited to life in a nursing home. She was sociable, amiable, chatty, in need of constant distraction. Her solitary life in Marlborough House was a pale reflection of her son's existence: she did not have a career, or a love of literature and music, to occupy her. She watched the television, and kept herself busy with the WRVS and her dance nights, but more company would be a blessing.

Williams spoke to Social Services and within a week a place had been found for Louie at a home in Hampstead. She was looking forward to the move – she didn't care what happened to her flat and her furniture, as long as she could get out of hospital and rejoin the living. The fees were high, at £150 a week, but Williams knew he could afford them, even before he thought of selling No. 7. What he could less well afford was the separation. Where would he go in the evenings? Who would let him pick out the programmes to watch on their television? Whom else could he bear to see day after day? To exile his mother to a home would be to inflict both a bereavement and a divorce on himself.

He began to seek out opinions that would let him delay the separation. After Louie had been in hospital for a week, he was living in a daze, forgetting to take his own medicine or losing the pill bottles, and weeping whenever he was alone, even in the street. A doctor at UCH agreed that Louie was capable of returning to Marlborough House, if she had plenty of care; medication for a thyroid deficiency might prevent the fainting fits. That was all the permission he needed. He made up her bed in the flat, arranged for a taxi to collect them from UCH, and prepared a ham salad for their lunch, with a bottle of champagne from Stanley Baxter to celebrate Louie's homecoming.

During all of this, one figure provided constant, almost invisible support, as he had for more than a decade. Michael Whittaker was a senior director at an employment agency, an untheatrical business-man who happened to meet Williams at the moment, after *My Fat Friend*, when he most wanted to leave the stage. Urbane, well-heeled and educated, Whittaker shared his love of English architecture and music, and his fondness for Soho's Italian restaurants. He was an endlessly appreciative audience, a fan who relished the anecdotes and the performances, and one who never bored Williams by trying to top his jokes. Most of all, he had an instinctive understanding of the relationship between son and mother: he treated Louie both as her son's partner and his responsibility. Williams began to rely on him, for conversation, for reassurance, for transport and for company, and by the eighties they were dining together almost every Sunday, usually at Joe Allen's basement restaurant in Covent Garden, as well as one or two evenings a week. They also took regular jaunts into the countryside, to visit churches and to indulge Williams's fantasy of a rural retirement by inspecting estate agents' windows.

'In the week, we would often go to run-of-the-mill Italian restau-rants,' Whittaker said. 'He was very keen that you look at him the whole time. Somebody could die at the next table, or throw a plate, and God help you if looked in that direction. "You're supposed to be with *me*, you know, *me*, I'm the object of the evening." It was quite wearing, one-to-one. On Sundays, we'd get to Joe Allen's at about twelve so the waiters were attentive because it hadn't started filling up. I remember one occasion when Louie looked at the menu and said, "I haven't had a bit of pork for ages. That'd be lovely." And Kenneth said, "No! We are enjoined by both Deuteronomy and Leviticus not to consume the flesh of non-ruminant ungulates." To which Louie's response was, "Oh Gawd blimey! Gawd help us!" And the waiter of course was absolutely stumped. Kenneth said, "Oh, she'll have an omelette." She didn't really mind.

'Louie doted on Ken, he was her little boy. In many ways they were like a married couple. He'd say things to her that a son would never normally say to his mother: he'd accuse her of looking at a waiter's crotch and wondering if he'd got a big one. She was used to this sort of rudery – because Kenneth of course was very rude and scatalogical, but also very moral. I once said to him, "You'd be less lonely in a relationship, if you could sustain it," and he said, "No, certainly not. Homosexuality is a cul-de-sac and its pathology must be resisted."'

Williams no longer insisted on using notes for communication. After Eade died, he stopped screening his phone calls, and if he did not want to speak with anyone he simply unplugged the jack. 'When I phoned Kenneth, there was no code,' Michael Anderson, his new agent, said. 'He just picked up when I rang.' The typewritten screeds on airmail forms had started to tail off after 1976, and in the last decade of his life he preserved few carbons. The diary entries were attenuated too. Some were shorter than half a page now, and he rarely wrote more than a couple of sentences about anything.

'There weren't many letters to me,' Whittaker said. 'But he was in contact with me all the time, calling me at the office twice or three times a week. I think he liked to talk with my secretaries; they were thrilled it was Kenneth Williams. We visited churches together – Peterborough was a favourite place because it wasn't too far by car and it had a cathedral – then we'd go to a hotel and have lunch. He was like a Dalmatian: he travelled in my car with his paws on the dashboard. And he insisted the car must have been polished and cleaned first. When we were driving, of course his view would be obscured from time to time by vans or other traffic. And he'd say, "Oh I can't see . . . overtake immediately!" I'd say, "I can't do that, Kenneth. I can't tell what's coming round the corner. We might be killed." He'd say, "Oh, it doesn't matter, we've lived too long anyway. Overtake now, I can't stand this!"'

One day in the late summer of 1986, Williams demanded to stop before Peterborough, in St Neots. Whittaker asked what the interest was, and was told to mind his own business – 'bit of a cheek, seeing as I was driving'. In the town's high street, Williams bought a map and navigated to a run-down house on an estate, where 'the gate had lost its catch, the paint was peeling off the windows, the little garden was overgrown, the curtains were filthy . . . and he made a note of all these things'. Whittaker was intrigued, but knew better than to probe again. Days later, Williams explained that occasionally he received hate letters from religious fanatics, condemning him as a pervert. These were almost never signed, but one man in St Neots had given his address and said he prayed the comedian would be 'struck down by the Lord Jesus for the filthy practice of sodomy'.

Williams had written back. He did not keep a copy, but Whittaker remembered the gist – ' "Your mind is as filthy as your house. The front door wants painting, the windows are filthy, the curtain in the right window is ripped – on receipt of this letter I hope you have the most terrible illness, with excruciating agony for days, and eventually die a terrible death." I said, "God, what about the headlines? Kenneth Williams threatens death to pensioner!" He didn't care. And of course this man knew Kenneth must have been to his address, and he wrote an abject letter of apology. All Kenneth wrote back was, "I'm amazed you're not dead yet. And I still hope you will roll around in deepest agony and be afflicted with the worst possible suppurating boils." Kenneth didn't forgive people. He felt everything must be atoned for.'

Just Williams, his autobiography, was published in hardback in 1985, and appeared in paperback eighteen months later. The story followed his stage career and ended before he was fifty. He launched the book with an abridged reading on Radio 4's *Story Time*, and appeared on Terry Wogan's early-evening chat show to tell stories of his army days. As the book topped non-fiction lists, Williams flew to Edinburgh for a book signing, before touring the south coast and then taking a train to Newcastle, with another Wogan show squeezed into the schedule.

The book incorporated the chapters he had written years earlier, and the whole manuscript was completed in pencil. Orton's biographer offered loyal praise, while noting that 'Williams is a complex and tormented man whose façade of high spirits at once masks and admits his sharp intelligence and poignant loneliness'. George Melly was less equivocal: Williams, he said, 'either refuses or is unable to lie about himself. He makes no attempt to win us over. Someone who disliked him intensely couldn't have done a better hatchet job [. . .] He is not without self-knowledge, but his ingrown narcissism is astounding even in a profession not given to self-effacement [. . .] He is the original cat who walks by himself.'

Whittaker brought that review when he took his friend to lunch on the day it appeared. Williams recognised its truths: 'It is not flattering but it isn't NASTY which is OK.' His enthusiasm for writing was almost spent. He still composed verses, as he once had for troop shows with CSE: they were doggerel, with forced metre and a payoff in the last line, made to be recited.

His last book was published in a limited edition, a collection of children's verse, just thirty pages or so, with drawings by Beverlie Manson. It was titled *I Only Have to Close My Eyes*. His editor at Dent urged him to work at the poems, but his delight in the sound of words and the patterns of their echoes when he read poetry was absent in his own compositions.

Commercial voiceovers, dozens of them, were his chief source of income. Ad agencies played on public affection for his radio series, so that he was sometimes reunited with Hugh Paddick and Bill Pertwee, or with Miriam Margolyes. His voice was instantly identifiable, in its varied incarnations, and listeners associated it with a well-loved persona. He was coarse enough to be believable as any kind of animal – there were parrots, monkeys, pigs – and yet sound cultured, as though anything he endorsed ought to be good quality. He promoted everything from cream crackers to sheepskin coats and kitchen paper to boardgames, with such professional skill that he could arrive at the studio, record three flawless takes and be gone within twenty minutes. He did not object when directors cheated: one claimed, after Williams had polished off an ad before 3.30 p.m., that the artiste was booked for the afternoon and had time to record three more voiceovers. He could have walked out, or phoned his agent to renegotiate the fee; instead, he rattled through the scripts.

There were fistfuls of confectionary television – *Child's Play*, *All-Star Secrets*, *Through the Keyhole*, *Looks Familiar*, *Did You See?* and

Whose Baby? as well as the voice of SID the computer in *Galloping Galaxies*. On radio he did *Give Us a Clue* and returned to *Start the Week*. When Channel 4 launched, the game show *Countdown* opened the schedules and Williams quickly established himself as the judge in *Dictionary Corner*: he appeared from Episode eight to the end of the first series, and throughout most of the second season, recording forty-eight episodes during 1982 and 1983.

He returned to Shepperton to shoot a film short, for a four-part training video titled *So You Want Your Shop to be a Success*. Williams played the Genie of the Green Peas, offering tips to shopkeepers on advertising, promotions and dealing with customers. Once he had been the incorrigible spirit of England's film studios, exposing himself in the corridors, and making starlets cry by spreading whispers of sexual indiscretions, and offering boozy propositions to the grips and gaffers' boys. When other actors wasted time or larked around now, he scolded them. He wanted to get the work finished as quickly as he could.

The chat-show sofas, from *Breakfast Time* till *Newsnight*, continued to welcome him. On TV-am he discussed the morning's headlines with David Frost and Selina Scott; six weeks later he was back, with three other veteran comics, for a show that 'went like a bomb' and was followed by a champagne breakfast. Tipsy by 10.30 a.m., Williams went home to bed. On a late-night news discussion with Joan Bakewell, he argued against a ban on tobacco sponsorship, claiming that prohibition might as well be applied to cars, or pubs, or dairies.

When he declined to be a guest on Joan Rivers's show, the producers doubled his fee to lure him. His appearance, with Peter Cook and Dudley Moore howling with laughter at his side, was a triumph: Rivers adored him, and seemed able to mouth the words to her favourite stories as he remembered farting during *The Public Eye* ('Front row 'eard that,' remarked Maggie Smith) and what Coral Browne said when confronted by a nineteen-foot gold-plated phallus ('Well, it's no one I know'). Rivers urged him to fly to the States for a return date. Even the offer of Concorde tickets could not tempt him.

He had made a second trip to Australia in the summer of 1983, to record five appearances on *The Mike Walsh Show* – he loved the

VIP treatment, the luxury hotels and the way his name appeared on guest lists as Sir Kenneth Williams. It was a pleasure to recycle all the anecdotes he had used up on British television, and to get laughs with toilet humour and revue sketches. In Australia even more than Britain, though, he knew his life was being diced and served like junk food. He was a TV dinner, to be washed down with a can of beer and, before he flew home, his leftovers were picked clean in a succession of radio interviews from his hotel room. He accepted an invitation to return, but it preyed on his mind: 'I keep thinking about this job in Australia [. . .] I hate the idea of the ENDLESS plane journey. When you are companionless it is a nightmare.' One Sunday morning he woke with a resolution that he would not fly around the world again. He wrote to Anderson, cancelling the job, and walked over to Albemarle Street to drop the letter through his agent's door. He did an interview with Walsh the next year via satellite link.

Wogan, without its eponymous host, gave him his best showcase, when he presented a week of programmes in 1986. He had become a favourite on the series, which went out at 7 p.m. on Mondays, Wednesdays and Fridays, and when Terry Wogan took a fortnight's holiday Williams was invited to stand in. The show's producer, Peter Estall, had grown to rely on him as a perfect guest – fluent, funny, outgoing and available at short notice.

When he rang on 1 April 1986, Wogan's departure was just four shows away. Williams accepted immediately. His only misgiving was over the size of the fee, which would cover in one week about half of what he felt he needed to earn in a year: 'Michael Anderson phoned and said I'm to get about 10 thousand for the three Wogan shows! So Heaven knows what Wogan must be paid!' The prospect thrilled him more than any work he'd taken in years, and when he was called in to the studio at four hours' notice to discuss the format he became the hopeful enthusiast of his rep days again: 'Everyone there was v. nice [. . .] Peter v. enthusiastic, "You will be great on this show" + his producer, "You'll go marvellously". There's going to be a lot to live up to!'

The stint began with a handover sketch, at a whelk stall in the studio, followed by a chat with Sue Lawley, the newsreader who was to cover the first week. He urged Estall to find him a crew of sewer workers, to get off the celebrity interview treadmill, and fretted when none could be found – Williams wished he had asked for an actor in waders instead. Frank Bruno and the left-leaning Tory MP Julian Critchley turned him down too, but the first show went off well, with Derek Nimmo, the singer Elaine Paige, the impressionist (and widow of Peter Butterworth) Janet Brown, and photographer Norman Parkinson. 'Derek was sweet: O! he's a lovely bloke. Janet was a stalwart . . . Oh, everyone was kind, but it was a LOUSY house . . . only interested in the OBVIOUS and the dirty.' On Wednesday he welcomed Barbara Windsor like a puppy, cavorting around her. Stephen Fry was as nervous as he was, and Michael Palin gamely filled in with limericks when his interview underran. 'Got home + told Lou I was dissatisfied with it. "Oh! you always say that," she told me. "Never satisfied, that's your trouble . . . it looked fine to me".'

The Friday show featured Nicholas Parsons, who had already sat for a dummy interview the week before during rehearsals. Paul Richardson came backstage before the broadcast to watch the preparations: in the dressing-room Williams was marvelling at the array of ties in Wogan's wardrobe and snapping at Estall when he brought a last-minute suggestion.

Richardson marvelled at his friend's ability to introduce the interviews without notes; Fry had been equally struck that Williams disregarded the autocue. 'He went on, and he was absolutely perfect,' Richardson said. 'When he'd finished, he said to me, "I don't want to go into the hospitality room, I want to get out of here. I have a plan – we'll say we're meeting Louie at this restaurant at half past eight."' They went up to the green room and within minutes Williams pressed the escape button: 'He said, "Oh Paul, what's the time?" I looked at my watch and said, "I thought we were meeting Louie." He said, "We should have been there five minutes ago!" We were straight out of there and got in a BBC car that took us to a Greek restaurant in Cleveland Street. He'd been on a high, because it was all live. You could still see the tension, when we got to the restaurant; then there was a big sigh, you saw it all drain out of him, and he was totally relaxed.'

When Williams reflected on the experience, it seemed unreal: 'Must say, if anyone had told me, at the beginning of the year:

"You will have a show on TV for 3 nights in April" I would not have believed them. I would have thought I was a write-off as far as BBC TV is concerned. It is still something of a surprise to me that it happened at all!'

He returned four more times to the show: the last was in November 1987, when he and Hugh Paddick performed a Jule and Sand sketch. Williams had spent the previous day with Louie, looking out at the rain and worrying that the blithe campery of *Round the Horne* struck the wrong note in eighties Britain, where homosexuals were blamed for an Aids pandemic and prominent gay performers made strident and litigious denials of rumours about their sexuality. After the first rehearsal, with Wogan playing Kenneth Horne's role, Paddick murmured, 'I think this is all going to be a bit HAIRY . . .' They watched Irene Handl and Beryl Reid do the first spot – 'Beryl Reid pissed! Irene forgot her lines and Beryl couldn't string a sentence together. Oh! it was ghastly.' When Bob Monkhouse appeared on the monitor screen, 'Harry Secombe muttered "These you have loathed" and Paddick + me fell about [. . .] Barbara Kelly shouted at me, "Now just sit down and shut up". I think she was annoyed with me cos I'd said of her polo necked pullover, "You look as though you're wearing a surgical appliance." Learned later that it was cover for scar from cancer operation.'

The day-to-day planner at the front of his diaries was filled now with more red ink (for medical appointments and illnesses) than pencil notes (for engagements). He had been in pain since the beginning of 1986, when an ulcer had flared up behind his ribs. His GP looked at the catalogue of over-the-counter antacids that Williams had self-prescribed and referred him for an internal examination. He saw the specialist, Iain Murray-Lyon in Devonshire Place, for the first time on the day that he did the Joan Rivers show; three days later he was in the St John and St Elizabeth for a barium X-ray. The rest of the month's diary was filled with analysis of his gripes and spasms, and detailed accounts of every bowel movement. Murray-Lyon suggested a sonar scan to check for kidney stones and found diverticula instead, infected nodules on the intestine. They were not bad enough to cause the intense back pain that Williams was suffering, or the bouts of foul wind and cramps that doubled him over. At the end of January 1987 he went into Charing Cross Hospital for a gastroscopy, and a gastric ulcer was diagnosed.

The pain abated with treatment, but other complaints spattered the day-planner: a rash on his leg, aching molars, sinus pain, a sprained hand, nausea, lumps on his tongue, sore thighs, bleeding gums, a cricked neck, irritated eyes. He complained incessantly, until he began to tire even good friends. His illnesses had always been a favourite topic for him, but the people who loved him best had been able to make a joke of it once. Just before his fiftieth birthday, he had a fibroid neuroma removed from his left hand, under a general anaesthetic. Williams was left-handed, and for several days, while it was in bandages, he wrote with difficulty. Friends sympathised, but ribbed him too – his left hand was one of his best appendages, sighed Hattie Jacques, and it had so often proved useful.

Now in his sixties, he found he was turning down dinner invitations, because his diet was so limited, and he was seeing less of his friends. Months passed between visits to the Jacksons; he wrote to Baxter, saying he was an old army buddy and asking whether Stanley remembered him.

Barbara Windsor heard his voice as she was hurrying down Marylebone High Street, about to go on holiday: 'I was trying to run around and get things done, and I looked across, and I thought, Oh shit, I haven't got time to talk to him. Oh, I'll just run across and say I'm in a hurry. I'd promised him dinner, and he said, "I haven't had that grilled liver yet, darling," so I said, "I'm going on my holiday but directly I get back, honestly, we'll do it. But I'm not a great cook" He said, "I know that!" And that was the last time I saw him. Kenny did know how much people loved him, they all loved him. The thing that upsets me more than anything is whether he thought that, when he did wake up in the middle of the night, he couldn't phone anyone. Which he could have done, he could have phoned anyone. I was round the corner, I'd have gone and sat with him.'

His GP was Carlos 'Bertie' Clarke in Upper Tachbrook Street, a West Indian former test cricketer from Barbados, who had studied medicine at Guy's during the war. Clarke had been his doctor since the sixties, and he was a good friend and confidant. Nowhere in the diary did Williams use racist language about his doctor; that would have been hypocritical and a betrayal of trust. His misanthropy certainly found vent in racism when he was condemning strangers – the 'negroes' who called out 'Carry On Kenneth' in the street, for instance, or the 'load of blacks' who became MPs in the general election: one of them was a 'chimp called Boateng' and another 'celebrated with black tribal dancers!' Dr Clarke was a good-humoured man, who enjoyed Williams's diatribes and prescribed stomach powders and sleeping pills while trying to curb the worst of his patient's hypochondria.

Before the ulcer Williams had thought little of walking across the West End and Green Park to Pimlico, but now he often took a cab to the surgery. Taxi driver Dennis Parkinson regularly took him from the rank outside the White House Hotel, opposite his flat: 'He always used to sit behind you and pull down the seat and talk. The old glass divider in those days used to open pretty wide and we used to laugh, laugh, laugh . . . it was hard to drive, especially when he started telling jokes.'

Williams told both Clarke and Murray-Lyon that the pain of his ulcer and the strain of seeing his mother decline into senescence was making him suicidal. During many episodes of depression throughout his adult life, he had been morbidly and sometimes romantically eager for death. When he first left Stanford's to apply for theatre work in 1948, he felt a longing to achieve the immortality of tragic poetry, by plunging into the Thames from Westminster Bridge. After his father's apparent suicide, Williams was afflicted by loneliness and began to feel that it would be better not to exist, and better still never to have lived. His crises in the theatre made him despair and twice drove him to breakdowns, but it was when he was gnawed by pain, or the fear of it, that his spirits were lowest. During the last two years of his life, there was no respite, either from the pain and worry, or from the depression.

'Nobody should live past sixty-five,' he told Whittaker, 'because nobody should have to face deterioration.' His friend was alarmed. 'He showed me the pills, some years before he died; there was a jar, in the kitchen – like Smarties, all different colours. He said they were "exit pills, I've been collecting them for fifteen years".' Whittaker warned him that pills might lose their potency and urged him to do nothing stupid: 'I said, "You wouldn't like to be half dead." He said, "Oh fuck off, I've got enough to kill sixteen people."'

The pills were sedatives, synthetic barbiturates such as Mandrax. The existence of this stash since around 1970 suggests paradoxically that Williams was not at risk of harming himself. Nowhere in the diary does he muse seriously about the mechanics of suicide, of how many pills he would need to swallow and how fast they would act. He was never tempted to lean out of his second-storey flat while he was cleaning the windows and 'accidentally' fall to the pavement. He was not afraid, when he used the tube, of standing so close to the edge that he might step on to the rails, or of diving under the wheels at a bus stop. When he stood on a high balcony, or ate in a restaurant at the top of a hotel, he did not have to fight an urge to leap. He was not haunted by the self-inflicted deaths of his friends; he did not compare the methods they used, or imagine what they felt and suffered. The efficiency of Kenneth Halliwell's ruthless suicide – he had died within seconds – did not seem to impress him. Williams lived for a decade and a half with a jar of sedatives in his kitchen, and never once did he feel that this jar was like a live bomb that had to be flung out of his home. It was there for safety, not self-harm – insurance against intolerable pain or, worse, the death of his mother.

Williams did not expect Louie to outlive him, nor did he imagine he would live long after her. In such a close filial relationship, it is not unusual for the son to commit suicide within days or hours of the mother's death. Williams never stated that intention, but his mental decline during Louie's illness in 1986, when he thought she would have to move into a nursing home, suggests he would have coped badly, however well his friends supported him. There was no provision for Louie in his last will, because by the time he made it she was frail and could not be expected to manage money herself. Williams feared that anything she had would be stripped away by nursing-home managers. He left everything instead to his friends and trusted them to look after Louie if, by mischance, he died first.

'I was with him in Marylebone Road,' Whittaker said, 'and he suddenly told me, "You know who I'm leaving my money to? I've been to the bank this morning and you're going to have it." I was

NOBODY SHOULD LIVE PAST SIXTY-FIVE

stunned, and I said it might poison our relationship. He said, "Don't be so bloody middle class. How fucking bourgeois. You ought to say, 'Hope you die soon! Good!'" He really got quite annoyed, and marched off.' Williams made it clear that Whittaker would also inherit the responsibility for Louie with the flats and his investments; Michael Anderson was to have the income from royalties, since he would have the trouble of collecting them; Paul Richardson and Williams's youngest godchild, Robert Chiddell (the great-nephew of John Vere), would share his personal effects, including his papers and diaries.

The ulcer flared up in August 1987. He told chat-show audiences that it was a 'spastic colon': 'Woke conscious of secum [caecum] moaning [. . .] by 10c there was the usual pain above secum as the stuff encountered blockage. The colon groaning and gurgling with effort to get through.' Dr Clarke prescribed Zantac, which inhibited stomach acid, but by the autumn he was miserable with a pain like needles in his abdomen, and 'churning + gurgling [. . .] the agony seems endless. The secum blown up + the swelling even causing backache'. A gastroscopy at the end of October showed the ulcer had receded; it left him listless and humdrum.

He recorded his last television appearance on *Did You See?*: 'It was rather dreary cos we had to sit there for LOADS of clips before we started!! [. . .] I praised Hi Di Hi and said that Patrick Pearson was superb in When We Are Married. *Hope* it isn't cut out!!' On Christmas Eve he made his final chat-show appearance, on radio with Gloria Hunniford. That winter he did less work than at any time in his life, and he did not seem to notice the lack of it – three recordings of *Just a Minute*; an interview at the Egton wing of Broadcasting House, about funny voices; a voiceover for Pallasades shopping centre in Birmingham, where 'the girl made me go back on it loads of times to get timing exact. Three 30 second commercials. All the time the ULCER was playing up! Stabbing as far as the mid-breastbone.' He appeared before a BBC radio audience for the last time to sing a couple of Ramblin' Syd songs with Terry Walsh, his guitarist from *Round the Horne*: 'Oh! it was a delight to see him again. Alas! we have both grown old.' His final appearance on *Just a Minute* had been recorded on 6 March 1988, the day before.

He no longer had any desire even to visit the theatre. It was a toy whose make-believe belonged to his departed youth, a world that was walled up like the childhood fantasies of Our Game. He had arranged to see Maggie Smith, on the opening night of Peter Shaffer's *Lettice and Lovage* at the Globe, the previous October, but handed back the tickets after a phone conversation with the producer, Robert Fox: to Fox's deep embarrassment, Williams decided to infer that Smith did not want him in the audience. Fox wrote, pleading that he 'would love you to see the play, if you want to, at any time [. . .] I will of course be delighted for you to be my guest.' The misunderstanding gave him a convenient excuse, though his health was the only alibi he needed. When Bertice Reading greeted him in Joe Allen's and invited him to see her in the revival of *South Pacific*, he retorted that he had a spastic colon, as though it was a restraining order.

By mid-March the ulcer tormented him every hour of the day. He could hardly speak, or bear to be with anyone, and he was frightened to eat. His diary was written in dribbles: 'Awake since six [. . .] This is the first time I've ever had PAIN first thing in the morning! Went to the shops and to the post feeling suicidal [. . .] Had the cornflakes and the Boots drink after. Lots of groaning + squelching but no PAIN! [. . .] Went in to Lou [. . .] I ate 4 fish fingers. After, there was the usual pain + by 8.45 I could stand no more so I returned to flat and went to bed. Woken by phone at 11.15! [. . .] I pulled plug out but the ringing unexpectedly gave me a headache.'

Whittaker urged him to go back to the specialist, but he was afraid: this time, hospital would mean an operation. He liked the thought of an autopsy better – the surgeon could discover the cause of his pain and there would be no danger of a recurrence. He made half a resolution to kill himself: there was no need to write farewell letters, since his friends would find out soon enough from newspaper reports. He thought he hadn't the energy to keep on living but, as he sat in the barber's chair for a trim and then walked in the spring sunshine, he worried that he would miss so much when he was dead. On Monday 21 March he watched a *Horizon* documentary with Louie and, when he returned to his flat, took down the jar of barbiturates. He took two and lay on the bed, wondering what would happen. The next morning, he woke with a thunderous headache.

By the end of the week, he was in the Cromwell Hospital for another internal examination. Stanley Baxter visited: 'It was the last time I saw him. He kept saying, "Oh the pain," every time he ate anything. Pretty miserable. I asked what the doctors wanted to do – "Yesss, well, they want to operate. I don't think I'll go through with it. The surgeon said, 'We're going to have to cut a lot out, chum. It's an arsehole to break-fast operation.' I thought, fuck that!" So that doomed him. Arsehole to breakfast, he was not about to put up with. It was not so much fear of the knife, because he had great, great physical courage. And moral courage. Anyone who can face an audience like he did, with every-body barracking, has proved great courage. No, it was the indignity of hospitalisation, that's what was really worrying him.'

He decided to stop smoking and threw away his cigarettes when he went home. He ordered Louie to give up too and even scrubbed her walls to remove the nicotine stains. The day before his gastroscopy, he had recorded his last voiceover, an AA advert with Brian Blessed and Bryan Pringle: 'It was LOVELY being with actors again. Oh! I do enjoy their company.' He cancelled an interview on HTV about *The Buccaneer* and withdrew from the next recording of *Just a Minute*.

'I remember thinking it must be something very serious for him to miss it,' said Nicholas Parsons. 'So I wrote him a little note, saying it wasn't the same without him, and wishing him a speedy recovery. And he was very punctilious with his letters, so I got a friendly reply within a few days – "Dear mate, Yes it is the stomach and if the pills don't work I think it could be" – and I remember the phrase – "the dreaded surgeon's knife, and I don't know if I could face that." The phrase stuck because I thought that it showed an absolute fear of going into hospital. I just think he had no physical relationship with anyone and he couldn't therefore bear the thought of anyone invad-ing his body. The idea of being put to sleep and someone cutting him open was just too horrifying to contemplate. And I remem-bered something else he said to me once, just in casual conversation: "Sixty's a good age. I mean, if you've done something with your life, why bother to stay any longer?"'

His last professional engagement was a photo session, for the cover of the reprint of *Acid Drops*. He posed with a sweet, about to drop it into his mouth. Michael Whittaker took him and Louie to Sunday lunch, and warned that he would be going away for a fortnight's holiday. 'Every year I used to go away, and he'd say, "Oh yes, fuck off, I hope it rains, I hope the car breaks down, leaving me and Lou behind." It was half joke, half meant, but it was a ritual. But this time he said, "I'll be thinking of you." I said, "What, Kenneth? What about the car breaking down?" He said, "Oh no . . . well, you just think about me." I puzzled over this change of attitude all the way to Italy. Had I really thought he was on the verge, I wouldn't have gone.'

Desperate for relief from pain and dreading an operation, Williams booked several sessions with his osteopath to ease the spasms in his back. After the second session, the osteo urged him to go to hospital and have another X-ray. Instead, Williams cancelled his next appointment. He tried to keep himself occupied, meeting his bank manager to reorganise his deposit accounts, and walking to Paddington to book train tickets for an in-house video shoot in Swindon the following week. He was still not smoking, counting off the days of abstinence with a joyless determination: '18th day of NO SMOKING and NOTHING to show for it! Not even a teeny weeny symptom.' He had given up cigarettes before, usually with fanfare and fuss, but he had never managed to persevere for more than a week. This time he had cut back on coffee too, and when he did drink it, he took honey instead of sugar.

On Thursday 14 April the pain in his bowel was 'like rats gnawing at your belly' and he could not eat in the morning; hunger left him tired and faint. He forced himself to swallow some lunch but, while his mother went out to see friends at her club, he had no energy. The waves of nausea and the ache in his back prevented him from resting. In despair, he rang Murray-Lyon to ask whether he could be booked in for an operation and was told he would have to wait until the end of the month at least. He went to Louie's flat for tea and they watched television until 8.45 p.m., when he told her he was in pain and wanted an early night. His last words were to remind her that they both had appointments at the chiropodist's the next morning, and that she had to be ready to go out at 10.30 a.m. He had arranged to meet Richardson later, for lunch at the BBC in Portland Place.

He made his final entry in his diary that night: 'Pain in the BACK was pulsating as it's never done before . . . so THIS, plus the stomach trouble combines to torture me – oh – what's the bloody point?'

Going to the kitchen, he took several sleeping tablets from his jar of 'exit pills', with a glass of wine or gin, and went to bed. The tablets were sodium amobarbital sedatives, for insomnia. Williams was meticulous in charting his use of prescription medicine, and it is clear that the barbiturates were not his usual sleeping aids.

During the early hours of the morning he suffered a cardiac arrest, brought on by the levels of barbiturate and other drug traces in his blood, and died. His pathologist later suggested there was not enough of any substance to kill him on its own, but in combination the drugs had proved fatal: he identified barbiturates and amphetamines.

Williams did not use 'uppers'. He relied on adrenalin for his performances, and in a restaurant or at a party two glasses of wine were an ample stimulant. He never took medication for his depressions. It seems impossible for amphetamines to have been part of his exit stash; there is no record that he had ever bought them, and no suggestion that he knew they might prove deadly when taken with barbiturates.

He did rely on drugs to calm his ulcer, and within the previous three weeks he had started taking two Zantac pills where Dr Clarke had prescribed only one. The relief this effected from pain had surprised him. Zantac is the brand name for ranitidine hydrocholoride, which inhibits stomach acid. In tests for amphetamine, it can produce a false positive; it was this drug that apparently showed up as a stimulant in the pathologist's examination. The findings imply strongly that Williams had not swallowed enough sleeping tablets for the barbiturates alone to kill him. They reacted with the stomach medicine he habitually used, and which he had recently taken in greater quantities; this accidental combination provoked his fatal heart attack.

The last words he wrote were not a suicide note. He had written almost exactly the same forty years earlier: 'Oh! what the hell, what's the good? What's the bloody use of it all?' He had not said goodbye to Louie, and he did not treat himself, as a condemned man, to a last cigarette. His final actions, though reckless, were not clear-cut. If he had been entirely set on killing himself, he could have swallowed many more pills. The most likely explanation is that he was making another trial, to see whether he would wake up, as he had done in March. As with so much in his life, this was an indecisive act that produced a definite result.

During the night, Paul Richardson awoke in his flat upstairs, disturbed by a dream. 'I thought I actually saw him in my bedroom, in the early hours of the morning,' he said, 'but all I could see was his face, grinning. This is absolutely true. I said, "Go away, go away," and I didn't think anything else of it.'

The following morning, Richardson left the block and noticed that Williams's curtains were still drawn at 9 a.m., though his habit was to go out for the newspapers two hours before that. 'I was walking down Great Portland Street and I thought there was something definitely wrong. A couple of hours later, I was walking back, and outside the flats I saw this mass of people. With cameras. I thought, My God. Kenneth's dead.'

AFTERWORD

'It's fascinating, it's a little defeat of death'

In a high-ceilinged room on the first floor of a house in Albemarle Street that was once home to the publisher John Murray, the attention of guests is always drawn to the fireplace. It was in this grate that Lord Byron's diaries were burned. The temptation to poke around in the hearth, to see whether some scrap has survived the blazes of two centuries, is almost irresistible.

If Kenneth Williams's diaries had been destroyed after his death, no one would have imagined their loss to be a Byronic tragedy. Nothing he had published hinted at their scope or depth; no one would have guessed that they comprised the most exhaustive and meticulous flaying of any recorded human life. From the evidence of *Back Drops* and *Just Williams*, most people would have supposed his writing lacked introspection and focus. Admirers might have hoped that, at best, they documented amusing trivia about the *Carry Ons* – and there never was supposed to be any permanence about that series.

The existence of the diaries was widely known: Williams was photographed with them for the cover of his autobiography, and he would sometimes give readings for friends. Many people were uneasy about their contents and would have been happy if (perhaps following Dirk Bogarde's example) he had thrown them on a bonfire. He made no specific provision for their survival or publication: on the day Williams was found dead in bed by his mother, Paul Richardson gathered up the forty-three volumes and took them upstairs to his flat, to ensure they could not be stolen by reporters. The 1988 journal was borrowed, inspected and returned by the coroner.

After the will was read, it was agreed that Richardson would keep most of the archive. Because Pat and Louie were not named as beneficiaries, they had no say over the fate of the diaries – they would probably have destroyed the papers if they could, to eradicate any references to Pat's illegitimate birth and Charlie's bankruptcy. After her mother died, Pat did rip up the family photo collection, claiming that it contained lewd snaps. She might have objected to photos of Williams in his jacket and tie in the Moroccan sunshine, while friends in bathing trunks showed off their tans, but it is more likely that she wanted to get rid of every photograph of her with Charlie Williams, whom she detested.

Pat Williams gave an interview to BBC radio a few months before she died, and also provided much of the material for Michael Freedland's biography, published two years after her brother's death. So much of what she said was contradicted by her cousin Joan Carlin's account – and so much more was at odds with what Williams recorded in his journals – that it has not been possible to use any of her testimony in this book. Her hatred of her stepfather was transferred to Kenneth, implying that he went to sleep every night cursing Charlie's name; in fact, as I hope this biography makes clear, Williams respected his father and wanted his regard, and though he revelled in the differences between their personalities, they did share many traits, even down to their handwriting. It was only in Charlie's last years that his son found him impossible. It should be said that, although Kenneth was sometimes rigid with jealousy over her demands on Louie, Pat was well liked by friends and family before her stroke in the mid-eighties. In her final years, she was difficult and initially opposed publication of any part of the archive.

In his own diary, in September 1993, Alan Bennett commented: 'If you want the nation's press camped on your doorstep, say you once had a wank in 1947.' A few weeks later, a massive book comprising thousands of extracts from Kenneth Williams's diaries was published. The entry for 1 January 1947 revealed exactly what Bennett cautioned against; Williams referred to 'traditional worries', which was one of his coded innuendos.

The extracts had been compiled with great sensitivity and skill by the broadcaster Russell Davies, who achieved a balance between the obsessive meditations on health, worries about accommodation and fluctuating friendships, and the blossoming and stagnation of each play. Inevitably, the subtleties of this 800-page edition were largely overlooked by readers who flicked through it like the lady who searched Dr Johnson's first dictionary for obscenities. The diaries appeared during a vogue for 'Victorian values' alongside a moral panic about homosexual promiscuity. The facts that Williams was a champion of Victorian sentimentality, and that 'safe sex' was a euphemism for masturbation, were added to the heap of subtleties ignored. What stood out was the depression and the wanking, because to speak of either was to defy taboos.

Williams loved to talk about them both, of course. The playwright Trevor Baxter recalled a dinner in Whitehall where the actor cleared the restaurant with stories of his adventures in masturbation: 'He said, "I do it on the lavatory, and I do it so hard I break the lavatory seat! I get me legs up and I go WANK-WANK-WANK-WANK-WANK!" I couldn't believe my ears . . . this terrible word – "WAAANNNKK!" You know how a mosquito has a terrible whine? "*Waaannnkkkkiiinnnggg!*" '

The status of 'national treasure' was temporarily revoked. The nation wasn't sure it wanted to inherit an heirloom like that, especially one with such a miserable expression on its face. Williams was portrayed in television documentaries as morbid, lonely, socially inadequate and consumed by guilt. A trend for TV dramas that depicted Britain's post-war comedians as drunks, perverts and lechers threw up a play titled *Fantabulosa!*, which proved the single biggest obstacle in the writing of this book. Williams's friends agreed that the actor who played him, Michael Sheen, was very clever, but the script was a travesty. No one wanted to see anything more like that.

The scale of the diaries' importance will only be understood gradually. Full publication is difficult, for several reasons: Williams had no regard for other people's privacy, and he often issued moral judgements that were thoroughly libellous. The sheer bulk of the archive is also difficult – to read all of it takes months, though Williams's handwriting is as legible as print – and to publish it all would require ten fat volumes at least. No doubt it will one day be available online, probably through the British Library: when that happens, everyone will be able to taste the extraordinary privilege I have enjoyed, of tracing the whole of his life, a day at a time, being simultaneously inside his skin and at his shoulder, experiencing and observing at the same time. It is a voyeuristic voyage like nothing else in literature. When it is finally published, not only as a text but as a handwritten manuscript, Williams will be appreciated as a combination of flamboyant diarist and ascetic scribe, part Pepys and part monk – in short, one of England's outstanding writers.

He continues to be one of the best-loved comedians Britain ever saw, and thanks to the vigorous marketing of the *Carry On* films – once staples of Bank Holiday television, now screening on rotation via cable TV, and regularly repackaged on video and DVD – he remains instantly recognisable. The films flattered him, because he was able to demonstrate a range so much broader than the actors around him, while never seeming to stretch himself. Peter Cook once remarked that Williams could be the funniest man in the business, if only he would work a little harder: the *Carry On* movies seem proof of it. He could be suffocatingly hilarious in the best of them, and with scripts by Galton and Simpson or Took and Feldman. But he could also be sublimely amusing without any script, spouting fragments from plays and poems, or unleashing his voice across its registers.

He died shortly after video recorders became common in homes, so much of his later television work has survived, along with well over half of his radio output. Too much has been lost: twenty-two editions of *Hancock's Half Hour* that featured him, twenty-four of *Beyond Our Ken*, the unedited footage of *Moby Dick Rehearsed*, and almost all of his television before 1970. There are studio recordings of the revues, but no footage from the plays; it is as pleasantly pointless to wish that a reel-to-reel recording of *The Public Eye*, or *Saint Joan*, or *Loot* existed, as it is to wonder what Williams might not have achieved if he had dared. If he had gone to New York to play the Fool to Orson Welles's King Lear; if he had taken *Pieces of Eight* to Broadway and bewitched America; if he had flown to Hollywood with Richard Burton; if he had agreed to be the perpetual guest in Stanley Baxter's A-list chat show; if he had tried a sitcom or a detective series; if he had directed on the West End . . .

Williams knew what he was denying himself. He never wished to consummate his success. One night in 1967 at the height of *Round the Horne*, his friends tried to persuade him to be bold. 'Stanley started on about America + what I ought to do with my career. Then Tom started telling me too – everyone so keen on telling me what to do with my life. They're really telling me what THEY WOULD LIKE ME TO DO [. . .] The impertinence of the whole thing is really quite amazingly shameless.'

The frustration this caused to his friends and fans is mingled with the affection and pity that it also provoked. What is common to almost everyone who loved him is awe and regret at how wonderfully ephemeral his talent could be. 'You've got such rich veins of gold to explore. You'll be inundated,' predicted the actor Robert Hardy, during one of the first interviews for this biography. 'You'll be able to build a great picture of him, I think. It's fascinating, it's a little defeat of death.'

More than two decades after he died, Kenneth Williams is still making us cry with laughter. The tears and the laughs are another little defeat of death.

Acknowledgements

S o many people have contributed so much to this biography that it is impossible to thank them all enough. Paul Richardson, who oversees the Estate of Kenneth Williams Archive, has been immensely supportive and without his faith in me this book simply would not have been written. I will always be grateful to him. Michael Whittaker, another of Williams's legatees, has been unstintingly kind and helpful, and this has made my work much easier.

I can never express my gratitude adequately to Tom Waine and Clive Dennis, for their colossal assistance – their hospitality, the many hours of interviews, the long phone conversations, the countless emails, the painstaking care with which they provided access to their collection of photographs, letters and personal diaries.

My work relied every day on the support of Bristol Central Library's staff, who provided a secure place to store and consult the Williams Archive in privacy: the frontline manager Robert Harrison, the local studies librarian Jane Bradley, the tireless Dawn Dyer, and their endlessly helpful colleagues. It has been a privilege to work with them for so long.

Very special thanks are due to Stanley Baxter, for his hospitality and his poetry; to Nicholas Parsons, for the impetus his faith gave to this project; to Ray Galton and Alan Simpson, for the unprecedented access they offered to their script archive; to Michael Codron, for his meticulous attention to accuracy; to Trevor Baxter, for providing a copy of his extraordinary playscript, *The Undertaking*; to Fenella Fielding, for her kindness; to Bill Kenwright, for his support; to Barbara Windsor, for her patient help; to Bill Kerr, for the title; to Peter Cadley, for his enthusiasm; to Michael Parkinson, for his backing; to Thelma Ruby, for her technical assistance; to Tony Walton, for making me laugh until I couldn't breathe; to Michael Anderson, for his courtesy; to Robin

ACKNOWLEDGEMENTS

Sebastian, for the rare recordings; to Joan Carlin, for her hospitality; to Richard Tay of Sepia Records for his generosity (www.sepiarecords.com); to Nicolas Barker for his astonishing erudition.

My deep thanks are due to: Rona Anderson, Sally Bazely, Melvyn Bragg, Gyles Brandreth, Ian Broderick at CV Hair and Beauty (57 Marchmont St), Sybil Burton Christopher, Richard Caswell, the historian of British comedy Malcolm Chapman, Peter Charlesworth, Lorraine Chase, Brian Cooke, Bernadette Dunbar and her daughter, Sacha, Freddie Hancock, Robert Hardy, Norman Hudis, Alan Hume, the late Nora Stapleton's neighbour Miss C. Jenkins, Keith Mason of the Tony Hancock Appreciation Society, Andrée Melly, Diana Melly, the late Angela Morley, Leonie Orton Bennett, Dennis Parkinson, Bill Pertwee, David Porter, the late Peter Rogers, Gilly Sanguinetti, Ben Summerskill, Amanda Theunissen, Claire Tomalin, Richard Williams and Sandy Wilson.

Invaluable research was provided by: Ruth Allen and Shannon Aldridge of the Metropolitan Police, Dan Carrier at the *Camden New Journal*, Alison Fortythe at Joe Orton online, the London Western District coroner's clerk Louise Hall, insurance specialist John Hughes, the supervisor at Endsleigh Court Jim O'Brien, Lauren O'Hara at the National Archives at Kew, Jenny Paton at the Lyric Hammersmith, Vivienne Roberts of the John Bratby Archive, Allan Watson at the Hackney Empire, Zoe Wilcox at the British Library's Peggy Ramsay Archive, and Sally Winter and Robin Prior at Video Arts.

I am constantly glad of the indefatigable support and enthusiasm of my agent, Heather Holden Brown, and her assistant, Elly Cornwall (who delivered before I did . . . welcome to Lara Cornwall).

My grateful thanks as well to: Caroline Dawnay at United Agents, who acts for the Estate of Kenneth Wiliams, and her assistant, Olivia Hunt; the managing director of John Murray, Roland Philipps, and his team including Victoria Murray-Browne, James Spackman, Anna Kenny-Ginard and Polly Ho-Yen; the good-humoured help of many agents and assistants, including Carol Kenyon, Tessa Le Bars, Scott Mitchell, Tony Nunn, Sandi Pescod, Teresa Rudge and Chloe Saxby.

Most of all, my greatest love and gratitude to my family, who have supported me at every step. This book was made possible by my wonderful wife, Nicky, and our sons, James and David.

Illustration Credits

Allstar Picture Library: 10 above and below left. Alpha Press: 6 left. Courtesy Clive Dennis: 9 below, 14 below right. © ITV/Rex Features: 15 below left and right. Photograph by Douglas H. Jeffery © V&A Images: 15 above left. Photograph by Angus McBean © Harvard Theatre Collection, Houghton Library, Harvard University: 12 above left. Photograph by Houston Rogers © V&A Images: 4 below right, 5 above right. Courtesy Thelma Ruby: 6 below right. David Sim/*Plays And Players*: 7 above left and below right. Photograph by Snowdon, Camera Press London: 8 above. © Donald Southern/ Courtesy The Orton Estate: 9 above. Courtesy Tom Waine: 12 below, 13 above left, 14 above and below left. The Estate of Kenneth Williams: 1, 2, 3, 4 above and below left, 5 above and below right, 5 below left courtesy Stanley Baxter, 7 below left, 7 above right courtesy Gordon Jackson, 8 below left and right, 10 below right courtesy Harry Gillard, 11 below courtesy Angela Douglas, 13 below, 13 above right courtesy Alfred Haigh, 16 above and below left, 16 below right courtesy Oliver Hatch.

Every reasonable effort has been made to trace copyright holders, but if there are any errors or omissions, John Murray Publishers will be pleased to insert the appropriate acknowledgement in any subsequent edition.

Notes

PREFACE

1 'I was more pleased than I ever dreamed I would be': Kenneth Williams, diary, 12 October 1983.

CHAPTER 1
FEBRUARY 1926–FEBRUARY 1944

5 'Brushed over with false gaiety': KW, diary, 1 January 1942.
'It was a slum': letter, 8 October 1976, to Frances Meredith of Yorkshire, 'a very aged fan' who had written to Williams.

6 'Tin was slang': *Just Williams: An Autobiography* by Kenneth Williams (J.M. Dent, 1985), p. 206.
'I told her I didn't like her': letter to Frances Meredith, ibid.
in one of her favourites: 'Me and my Mum' by Kenneth Williams, published in *Sunday Magazine*, 1985.
the Oxford Music Hall: the Oxford was the West End's first music hall, at 14–16 Oxford Street, launched by Charles Morton in 1861 on the site of a former coaching inn called the Boar and Castle.
Daisy Dormer, born Kezia Beatrice Stockwell (1883–1947). 'After the Ball' by Charles K. Harris was the hit that established Tin Pan Alley as the heart of American musicland in the 1890s; the sheet music sold more than 2 million copies in 1892 alone, and 5 million during the decade.

7 punishments for abortion: Section 58 of the Offences Against the Person Act, 1861, made abortion a criminal offence. In 1929 the law was changed, to permit a termination, up to twenty-eight weeks, if the pregnancy threatened the life of the mother.
'In those days, it was a disgrace': interview with Joan Carlin, Kenneth

Williams's cousin, at her home on 14 July 2008, two days before her eighty-sixth birthday. Also present and contributing were her daughter Bernadette Dunbar and granddaughter Sacha.

8 'That was the phrase': interview with Tom Waine and Clive Dennis at their home, 28 April 2009.

'three pennorth of stale bread': KW, diary, 25 December 1968.

Family myth about Louisa's meeting Charlie Williams: 'Me and my Mum', by Kenneth Williams.

'In little dark houses': from *The Children's Newspaper*, edited by Arthur Mee, 12 February 1938. Sidney Street was torn down in the late twenties by the St Pancras House Improvement Society.

John Williams sometimes worked: John Williams's father, Henry (Kenneth's great-grandfather), had been an electrician during the late nineteenth century, working on the lights outside the Coliseum Theatre, which had an illuminated dome.

Princess Charlotte of Wales's (Royal Berkshire Regiment): later part of the Duke of Edinburgh's Royal Regiment (Berkshire and Wiltshire), now part of the Royal Gloucestershire, Berkshire and Wiltshire Regiment.

9 trench fever: spread by lice, this typically caused severe headaches, pain in the legs and a high fever that lasted five days. Recovery took at least a month, with feverish relapses. It was endemic in both the British and the German armies.

'I found this old snapshot': KW, diary, 6 July 1968.

'Of course there were no bathrooms': from notes for a talk on the architecture of Bloomsbury and St Pancras, which Williams wrote on 13 May 1975 for BBC Television. The programme was not recorded.

10 'Louie was very fussy': quoted in *Desperately Funny/Seriously Outrageous* (1998), a two-part BBC2 documentary on Williams, produced by Liz Hartford.

'sceptical and puritanical': 'Me and my Mum' by Kenneth Williams.

11 'something that was paramount': Williams and his Christian beliefs were the subject of a profile in the *Evening Standard*, by Mary Kenny, to mark the beginning of Lent, on 15 February 1978.

'My mother was a great one': *Good Afternoon, with Mavis Nicholson*: Thames TV, first transmitted 1 August 1974; part of a series, under the banner 'Is It Fun to be Funny?' with other interviewees including Peter Cook, Dudley Moore, and Eric Morecambe and Ernie Wise.

'Rodomontade', meaning 'extravagant, vainglorious bragging or boasting', from Rodomonte, the name of a boastful Saracen in poems by Boiardo and Ariosto; Williams took delight in archaic words that expressed his meaning while demonstrating his erudition.

12 his friend Wreyford: Wreyford Palmer (1926–2002).

13 'caught the infection of romantic poetry': note for BBC, 13 May 1975.

The Rose and the Ring: by William Makepeace Thackeray (1855). The *Radio Times* interview in January 1975 coincided with his reading of *The Rose and the Ring* on BBC1's *Jackanory*.

the salon in Marchmont Street: the shop, now called CV Hair and Beauty, is still at 57 Marchmont St, managed by Ian Broderick.

14 'He was very burdened': interview with Melvyn Bragg, Baron of Wigton, at the House of Lords, Monday 14 July 2008.

'I always remember being very young': KW, diary, 22 December 1971.

15 'with a gin and tonic': *Good Afternoon with Mavis Nicholson*: Thames TV, first transmitted 1 August 1974.

'Anyone who threatened': *Good Afternoon with Mavis Nicholson*.

'sort of phase I went thro': KW, diary, 1 September 1966.

'My father was a cockney': chat show with Russell Harty, recorded 31 October 1973.

16 'I was still there': preview, *Radio Times*, 12 April 1975.

'a magical abode': *Just Williams*, p. 14.

'The Charge of the Light Brigade' and 'The Yarn of the Loch Achray': narrative poems by Alfred Lord Tennyson (1854) and John Masefield (1918) respectively.

17 duties as a firewatcher: volunteer firewatchers earned 3s 6d for each stint of night-time duty, keeping watch for fires started by incendiary bombs during the Blitz.

'I've been pissed on!': 'Me and my Mum' by Kenneth Williams. The original text substituted 'peed' as a euphemism.

'almost melancholy, and brushed over': KW, diary, 1 January 1942.

18 'It seems rather dashed hard': KW, diary, 15 January 1942.

Jew Süss . . . 'very good': KW, diary, 29–30 August 1942.

She . . . 'balderdash! tripe! eyewash! blah!': KW, diary, 9 August 1942.

'all clumsy, furtive fumblings and really very innocent': *Just Williams*.

he had been infatuated with . . . James: KW, diary, 27 July 1971.

he 'went to Alan's': KW, diary, 21 June 1942.

'keeping a diary': KW, diary, 24–26 November 1942.

19 'patriotic windbag': KW, diary, 14 February 1942.

'jealous as hell!!': KW, diary, 8 October 1942.

'terrible!!!': KW, diary, 15 September 1942.

'Do hope I will be successful': KW, diary, 31 March 1942.

20 an Ordnance Survey cartographer: Valentine Orford (1906–93) remained a lifelong friend.

'I was entranced and fascinated': *Just Williams*, p. 16.

Sacha Guitry (1885–1957) was born in St Petersburg. *Villa for Sale* is a one-act play, which in 1938 starred Rex Harrison when it was first presented on television in English.

'Where will I be': KW, diary, 7–10 December 1942.

CHAPTER 2
FEBRUARY 1944–DECEMBER 1947

21 'Happy days, what a laugh!': KW, diary, 23 April 1947.

'I won't bore you': *Punch*, 1 December 1976.

22 'I'd always had my own room': *Wogan*, BBC1, 13 September 1985.

'my first real mentor': profile by Mary Kenny, *Evening Standard*, 15 February 1978.

he claimed on *Just a Minute* that he was punched: *Just a Minute*, 4 November 1968.

'with a pathetic group', 'You scrawny horrible creatures': *Just Williams*, p. 19.

23 his squad took the prize: this improbable victory was reprised fourteen years later in the plot of the first *Carry On* film, in which Williams plays a disdainful National Service conscript who torments his sergeant (William Hartnell) with his indolence and incompetence, before helping to inspire his comrades to a prize-winning display on the parade ground.

'even brass buttons': *Just Williams*, p. 25.

'Pity I didn't keep a record': KW, diary, 5 April 1976.

25 'The clouds hung like great golden peaches': the description of dusk in India is taken from a letter to Valentine Orford, quoted by Michael Freedland in *Kenneth Williams: A Biography* (Weidenfeld & Nicolson, 1990), p. 32. Williams used the phrase 'photo writer' to describe his duties, in his two-paragraph biography for Combined Services Entertainment's *High and Low* programme notes.

'dark curly hair': letter to a former RE sapper, Frank Wilson, 4 April 1976. Wilson said that, when he first saw Williams in *Carry On Sergeant*, he stood up in the cinema and shouted, 'I was in the army with him!'

a tentative experiment in masturbation: briefly described in a letter to Jeffrey Kemp, 12 January 1988.

26 'I spent a lot of time': letter to Frank Wilson, 4 April 1976.

the shooting of the snake: an incident related in November 1970 on *Just a Minute*. Williams believed the snake was poisonous; it might have been. Sri Lanka has one of the most copious snake populations in the world, but of its ninety-eight species, only five are venomous.

'Subadar Sahib'; 'Isn't it written in your book': *Just Williams*, p. 36.

27 'When I was in the Army': interview in London *Evening Standard* , 10 August 1968.

28 a NAAFI show: NAAFI, or, in full, the Navy, Army and Air Force Institutes, the trading arm of HM Forces. Combined Services Entertainment, or CSE, was the successor to ENSA, the Entertainments National Service Association, created by Basil Dean.

the Map Reproduction Section was disbanded: Williams had transferred to 66 MRS after 62 MRS was disbanded in December 1945.

Hardman's recommendation to CSE: letter to Frank Wilson, 4 April 1976.

'He said, "What do you do?"': letter to Rae Hammond, 5 March 1975. Hammond did a conjuring act in CSE and later became theatre manager at the Cheltenham Playhouse. Captain Olm (born 4 April 1923) changed his name to Peter Vaughan after the war and for more than sixty years worked as a character actor in theatre, film and television, ranging from *Straw Dogs* and *The Remains of the Day* to gangland boss Harry Grout in the BBC sitcom *Porridge*.

29 No. 1 British Transit Camp, Nee Soon: Nee Soon, now Yishun, was named after the banker, rubber magnate and 'pineapple king', Lim Nee Soon (1879–1936).

'conjurors, tap dancers, singers': *Just Williams*, p. 38.

'a melodramatic farce': *Seven Keys to Baldpate*, by George M. Cohan, is based on a novel by American writer Earl Derr Biggers.

Albert Arlen (1905–93) was an Australian, born Albert Aarons to Turkish immigrant parents. He served as a pilot in the RAF from 1939. He married the actress and playwright Nancy Brown in 1949, and together they had a major success with a musical, *The Sentimental Bloke*, in 1961.

30 'If in doubt you always go': interview with Stanley Baxter at his north London home, 18 December 2008.

31 'her bit of rough!': quoted by Peter Nichols in his autobiography, *Feeling You're Behind* (Weidenfeld & Nicolson, 1984). This is also the source of the descriptions of Nee Soon barracks and the hill station in the Cameron Highlands, and the facts behind CSM Marriott's suicide.

Williams made his first entries: the 1947 diary begins with an entry for Christmas Eve 1946, which was written with the same pen and in the same handwriting as the lines for Christmas Day; it seems very likely that they were made at the same time, and that the pocket book, an A6 Letts, had been a Christmas present.

32 'Traditional worries': KW, diary, 1 January 1947.
'Solitary coffees predominant': KW, diary, 3 January 1947.
'Shocking American type': KW, diary, 15 January 1947.
'Tandy extremely rude': KW, diary, 2 February 1947.
Babette O'Deal: 'Dominating personality of the Company and main-spring of the show is Babette O'Deal. Miss O'Deal is an experienced musical comedy artiste and the very presence of her very blonde hair, her full figure and her great ability adds enormously to the success of the production' (from an undated newspaper cutting in the Williams archive.

33 'Terrific reception – wonderful applause': KW, diary, 23 January 1947.
'Special mention should be made': undated newspaper cutting in the Williams archive.
'not only because of the nature': letter to Rae Hammond, 5 March 1975.
'These wogs are a filthy lot': KW, diary, 19 February 1947.
'This ship is bloody awful': KW, diary, 20 February 1947.

34 'Happy days, what a laugh!': KW, diary, 24 March 1947.
'we had left them all off': letter to Rae Hammond, 5 March 1975.
'good experience!': KW, diary, 12 April 1947.
'Met John Schlesinger': KW, diary, 30 April 1947. John Schlesinger (1926–2003) won acclaim as a director in the early sixties with *A Kind of Loving* and *Billy Liar*. He collected two Oscars for *Midnight Cowboy*.

35 Peter Nichols abandoned acting to become a playwright, partly at the urging of Williams. His successes include *A Day in the Death of Joe Egg* and *Privates on Parade*.

'the impeccable diction': quoted by Peter Nichols in his autobiography, *Feeling You're Behind* (Weidenfeld & Nicolson, 1984).

'There was all this anger': *An Audience with Kenneth Williams*, first broadcast 23 December 1983 on Channel 4.

37 Barri Chatt, who died in 1971, age unknown, came from County Durham. He became a female impersonator after the war, when he teamed up with Terry Gardener to become the Pin-up Girls of Comedy; they regularly played the Ugly Sisters in pantomime.

'had the most extraordinary effect': *An Audience with Kenneth Williams*, first broadcast on 23 December 1983 on Channel 4.

Arthur Marshall (1910–89), raconteur and broadcaster.

Black Amati: now known as Sentosa, a tourist resort.

38 'Really disheartening': KW, diary, 8 August 1947.

'Tandy became quite drunk': KW, diary, 3 September 1947.

39 'How curious it is': KW, diary, 26 May 1966.

'So gay it wasn't true': KW, diary, 3 September 1947.

David Whitfield (1925–80), an operatic tenor, earned a gold disc for his No. 1 hit 'Cara Mia' in 1954. He is perhaps best remembered for the theme song to television's *The Adventures of William Tell*.

'interesting opportunity?': KW, diary, 22 October 1947.

40 The Western Brothers' polished music hall and radio act (a pair of toffs with a piano) was popular in the thirties and forties. Kenneth (1899–1963) and George (1895–1969) Western were actually second cousins, not brothers.

Ted Durante (1926–2009) worked with Williams again in *Cinderella* at the Coliseum theatre in 1958: they were the Ugly Sisters. With his wife Hilda (1922–2006) Durante became a popular star of BBC1's music-hall series, *The Good Old Days*.

41 'you could hardly hear any clapping': *An Audience With Kenneth Williams*.

CHAPTER 3
DECEMBER 1947–FEBRUARY 1950

42 'The dream from which there is no awakening': KW, diary, 31 January 1950.

'Oxford . . . was actually a clever move': Robert Hardy was at Oxford with John Schlesinger. After training as an RAF pilot, he spent three years with the RSC at Stratford's Memorial Theatre, before going to the West End, the Old Vic and America. Phone interview, Monday 14 April 2008.

43 Nicky (or Vicki): Nicky/Vicki's surname is not known. Williams seems unsure even of her first name.

'conversation was light': KW, diary, 11 January 1948.

'I'm C.C.L.': KW, diary, 14 January 1948.

'this Hetero Goldwyn Mayer stuff': KW, diary, 24 January 1948.

'I came out of the cinema': KW, diary, 22 January 1948.

44 'I feel somehow nervous': KW, diary, 1 February 1948.

'He is home again in England', 'He makes me feel': KW, diary, 19 February 1948.

'I nearly died of cold': KW, diary, 19 February 1948.

45 Alan 'Jock' Dent was theatre critic at the *News Chronicle*; Basil Dean was not only the former head of ENSA but a film producer who founded what would become Ealing Studios; the critic and actor Peter Cotes was born Sydney Boulting, sibling to the Boulting Brothers, John and Roy; he became celebrated as the director of *The Mousetrap*.

'long shots, but they might strike': KW, diary, 4 March 1948.

'so I packs me bag': KW, diary, 22 March 1948.

46 'a massive, fat Jew': KW, diary, 23 March 1948.

'I am madly hoping': KW, diary, 24 March 1948.

'This is no calling for the faint-hearted': KW, diary, 30 March 1948.

'According to the stars': KW, diary, 11 April 1948.

48 'Told her I'd a part to learn!': KW, diary, 12 May 1948.

'playing the records': KW, diary, 12 July 1948.

'All our notices have been handed in': KW, diary, 9 July 1948.

'very charming': KW, diary, 1 May 1948.

49 'a complete waste of time': KW, diary, 10 May 1948.

'Went out for supper': KW, diary, 6 June 1948.

'Shall be sorry to see her go': KW, diary, 1 August 1948.

50 'God! This woman continually talks down': KW, diary, 12 August 1948.
after one final production: this was *The Importance of Being Earnest* by
Oscar Wilde, in which Williams played Algernon Moncrieff for six
nights from Monday 13 September 1948. 'At 22, Kenneth Williams
is one of the youngest members of the company, yet he has played
through the season many different roles, varying in age from 12 to 70
with complete success. If it were not for his keen sense of team work,
he would have "stolen" the show with his performance in this week's
play,' reported the local paper.
the Dolphin Players: Richard West's parents, Algernon West and
Gladys Young, were successful and influential actors, and he enlisted
the aid of both in the Dolphin Players. They in turn prevailed on
numerous well-known friends to join the board of advisory directors. Their other autumn productions were *Goodness, How Sad* by
Robert Morley ('Goodness, how bad'), and Emlyn Williams's ghost
story *Trespass*, directed by Michael Harald.
'Sonia rang up': KW, diary, 11 December 1948.
Oliver Ford (1925–92), 'the doyen of the traditional decorators [. . .]
recognised nationally and internationally for his impeccable taste'
(obituary by George Levy, *Independent*, 21 October 1992).
'tight, tired, but elated': KW, diary, 18 December 1948.

51 'Suddenly I looked across the dance floor': KW, diary, 22 November
1971.
'We said goodbye at the bus stop': KW, diary, 22 June 1987.

52 a courtroom serial, *Gordon Grantley KC*: this went out on the Light
Programme on Mondays at 10.15 p.m., starring Francis de Wolff.
Fly Away Peter, by Peter Dearsley; *Ten Little Niggers* – later retitled *Ten
Little Indians* and then, since that alteration seemed to miss the point,
changed to *And Then There Were None* – by Agatha Christie.
Nicholas Parsons was to be the chairman of BBC Radio's *Just a Minute*,
the panel show that for twenty years Williams treated as a playground,
a grandstand and a soapbox.
'He was difficult to cast': interview with Nicholas Parsons, 20 January
2008.
'It was absolutely bloody': KW, diary, 9 March 1949.
'Obviously clever': KW, diary, 7 March 1949.

53 'The part is very good': KW, diary, 18 March 1949.
'His is an odious part': reviews from the *Bromley and Kentish Times* and
the *Croydon Advertiser*; the reviewers were 'H.B.H.' and 'T.H.T.'

walk-ons in two BBC features: *Mannequin for Murder*, by Howard Bygrave and Trevor Ross, a thriller on the Light Programme, and *Virtue*, the Wednesday matinée.

Chekhov's *The Proposal* and Shaw's *The Man of Destiny*: in the first, Williams played Ivan Vassilyevitch Lomov, 'a healthy but hypochondriacal landowner', and in the second, Napoleon Bonaparte, 'youngest General of the French Republic'.

Williams took top billing: alongside Annette Kerr, whom he would select as his friend, confidante and, later, long-time correspondent.

54 'A ghastly day': KW, diary, 17 July 1949.

'Annette Kerr simply superb': KW, diary, 10 June 1949.

the rest of the season's plays: These included *Mrs Moonlight* by Benn Levy ('a dreary bit of sentimental slush': KW, diary, 14 July 1949) and *It's a Boy*, by Austin Melfford, Ernst Bach and Franz Arnold ('Dudley is a whopping part!! – I'll never know it!! – ye gods!! – how I deplore weekly rep': KW, diary, 20 June 1949). Their last production was *The Father* by August Strindberg. Richard West's ambition to stage Sophocles' *Antigone* was not achieved.

'Rehearsals – bloody': KW, diary, 29 June 1949.

'Naylin spends the entire day sulking': KW, diary, 8 July 1949.

'Pinched Joan Dale's bot': KW, diary, 9 July 1949.

'R. didn't speak to me at all': KW, diary, 15 July 1949.

'I must get out of this weekly rep': KW, diary, 22 July 1949.

'A tat town of the West Country': KW, diary, 29 July 1949.

55 So were the productions: They included *A Hundred Years Old* by Helen and Harley Granville-Barker ('My performance as "Trino" is lousy. I just can't get any feeling about this play at all!': KW, diary, 7 November 1949); *Treasure Island*, adapted by Georg Sheldon from R.L. Stevenson's story, with Williams as Dick Trym and Donald O'Malley as Billy Bones ('Appalling. CHAOS. Drear. Bad': KW, diary, 19 December 1949); *Eliza Comes to Stay* by H.V. Esmond ('No one seemed sorry to see me go!': KW, diary, 21 January 1950).

'I am so happy playing "Lachie"': KW, diary, 26 October 1949.

'Petty-farting little notes': KW, diary, 23 December 1949.

playing Reed in *The Guinea Pig*: by Preston Sturges, with Richard West directing.

'Ghastly contretemps': KW, diary, 28 January 1950.

56 'sweet'; 'having a vague sort of thing': KW, diary, 1 February 1950.

'This is the dream from which': KW, diary, 31 January 1950.
'like a rainbow!': KW, diary, 3 February 1950.

CHAPTER 4
FEBRUARY 1950–OCTOBER 1954

57 'What is right in this haphazard career?': KW, diary, 8 May 1951.
58 'freezing cold and miserable': KW, diary, 26 February 1950.
putting 'a great deal of action': from the *Eastbourne Gazette*. Admiring the easy relationship between the American Easterbrooks and their maid, the *Margate Chronicle* reviewer P.K. lamented, 'If British girls believed they could get away with such familiarity, employment exchanges would not have so many unfilled vacancies for domestics.'
Fools Rush in: As he had in his first season at Newquay, Williams played Joe, the bridegroom, in this Kenneth Horne comedy. The dramatist Kenneth Horne (1900–75) had a West End hit with *Love In A Mist* at St Martin's Theatre in 1942, the year that Squadron Leader Kenneth Horne (1907–69) made his radio debut, presenting *Ack-Ack Beer-Beer* on the Forces Programme; it was the latter Horne who would later be the ringmaster of *Beyond Our Ken*.
'The Welsh were trying to start': phone conversation with Sybil Burton Christopher, 22 April 2009, who was speaking from the Bay Street Theatre, which she founded in 1991, in Sag Harbor, New York.
59 a single word of instruction to one actor: 'The others naturally made way, and by the time he arrived centre stage there was a clear lane behind him, like a swathe cut through a field of ripened corn' (*Just Williams*, p. 55).
the first production was: *Family Portrait* by Lenore Coffee and William Joyce Cowen, set in biblical Nazareth, with Judith Fellows as Mary, David Morrell as Joseph and Kenneth Williams as Judah.
'At last I seem to be getting somewhere': KW, diary, 14 July 1950.
'Awful shock': KW, diary, 30 August 1950.
60 Rachel Roberts (1927–80) later married the actor Alan Dobie: they met in the 1953 Old Vic company, of which Williams was briefly a member. Roberts killed herself some years after the collapse of her second marriage, to Rex Harrison. Ray Galton and Alan Simpson attested to her ferocious appetite for an argument (interview, 21 April

2008). On the final transatlantic voyage of the *Queen Mary* in 1968, the writers witnessed several drunken rows between Harrison and Roberts, who were bellowing obscenities in front of all the passengers in the dining room. 'Top of their voices, they didn't care. We might as well not have existed.'

'madly sexually analytical': KW, diary, 15 November 1950.

he 'tried to make her see': KW, diary, 16 November 1950.

a lightweight double bill: *Hello Out There* by William Saroyan, and *Harlequinade* by Terence Rattigan, featuring Williams in a bit-part only.

'A great pity that the place': letter from Richard Burton, 5 December 1950, from the Royale Theater, West 45th Street, New York. It goes on to describe 'a cocktail party [where] I met people so legendary in our business that I naturally supposed them dead. Mary Pickford, Lilian Gish – the lot! [. . .] Pickford, who looks, conservatively, about ten days older than the sea.'

61 'No news of any work': KW, diary, 10 January 1951.

'Each week drags itself by': KW, diary, 8 February 1951.

'I become increasingly obsessed': KW, diary, 2–7 February 1951.

62 Joan Littlewood (1914–2002) and her company lived and slept in the Theatre Royal while they restored it. Productions of Jonson's *The Alchemist*, and *Richard II* starring Harry H. Corbett as the King, established the group's reputation.

in Worthing Rep for *Mrs Inspector Jones*: the play, by James Parish, was later a television series.

after failing an audition for Alec Guinness: Williams does not specify the production, but this must have been for Guinness's second attempt at *Hamlet*, which he starred in and directed, at the New Theatre. Ken Tynan commented that it was cast with 'exuberant oddness' (the critic was part of the company, as the Player King). It was not a success; Williams's long run of bad luck might have been doing him a favour here. He saw the play with his sister Pat, and noted: 'Very poor cast [. . .] Guinness fascinating. Interesting evening. Half empty house': KW, diary 5 July 1951.

Random Harvest had been filmed with Ronald Colman and Greer Garson, from the novel by James Hilton.

'Awful truth comes out': KW, diary, 2 April 1951.

63 'Peter quickly became very respected': interview with Norman Hudis, 4 May 2009.

The Immortal Lady: by Clifford Bax.

'tat of the most menacing order': KW, diary, 30 April 1951.

'I have a terrible feeling': KW, diary, 8 May 1951.

Two Dozen Red Roses, translated by Kenneth Horne from Aldo Di Benedetti's Italian play. 'Williams makes a very playful amorist of the florist,' said the *Surrey Times*.

'Like a skin rash': letter to Annette Kerr, May 1951, quoted by Michael Freedland in *Kenneth Williams: A Biography* (Weidenfeld & Nicolson, 1990), p. 55.

'Breakfast at 6.30': KW, diary, 9 June 1951.

64 'It will at least be a break': KW to Stanley Baxter, 29 May 1951.

'The show is in a shocking state': KW, diary, 27 September 1951.

Annette Kerr . . . 'wrote me a beautiful autumnal nocturne': KW, diary, 11 November 1951.

Donald Wolfit (1902–68), a grand Shakespearean actor who inspired Ronald Harwood's play, *The Dresser*.

'so unutterably common': KW, diary, 3 January 1952.

'I hardly sat down once': KW, diary, 12 January 1952.

'a success entirely due': KW, diary, 13 January 1952.

65 'a terrible play': KW, diary, 12 February 1952.

he had painted 'the downstairs lav': letter to John Hussey, 5 September 1952.

'Beloved . . . Do you like this paper?': letter from John Hussey, 1 December 1950.

66 'Really see no point in going': KW, diary, 2 April 1952.

'Bet the actress I have to play with': 18 April 1952.

'a negligible lot of creatures': KW, diary, 22 April 1952.

'with this awful Scot': KW, diary, 23 April 1952.

By Candle Light opened on a short tour: Chippenham on 5 May, then Newbury, Basingstoke, Frome and Weymouth: 'This is all so CSE it isn't true' (KW, diary, 8 May 1952).

'Bastien popped and bubbled'; 'grimy, slimy, nasal-toned': *Salisbury Journal*, 16 May 1952, and *Daily Echo*, undated, respectively. Williams played Backbite, a role he was offered again in 1961, for John Gielgud's production, starring Ralph Richardson and Margaret Rutherford. Williams turned it down: 'Rotten part, rotten play and rotten cast' (KW, diary, 6 October 1961).

'You must believe': letter to Terence Tiller, 21 June 1952.

67 'N.G.': KW, diary, 24 July 1952.

'unspeakably depressed and melancholy': KW, diary, 23 August 1952. The doodle is about an inch across, like a blurred fingerprint or eyelashes around an empty socket, with the tiny letters MO to one side.

'to seek work in snack bar': KW, diary, 2 September 1952.

The Beggar's Opera, directed by Peter Brook, co-produced by Herbert Wilcox. During the shooting, Williams also had a single line in *Valley of Song*, directed by Gilbert Gunn and filmed at Elstree, on Friday 24 October, and a BBC radio broadcast of *Buds of Sadness* on Sunday 2 November.

as Slightly in *Peter Pan*: for the entertainment of those few who have not heard it, readers may wish to insert here the comment of Kenneth Tynan on Noël Coward: 'In 1913 he was Slightly in *Peter Pan*, and you might say that he has been wholly in Peter Pan ever since.'

'I tried to make some kind of a stand': letter to Annette Kerr, 2 December 1952.

'I feel perfectly bloody': KW, diary, 1 December 1952.

68 'Kenneth Williams is an excellent Slightly': *The Stage*, 31 December 1952.

the Craig and Bentley murder trial: Derek Bentley was hanged in 1953, aged nineteen, for the murder of a policeman, though it was his friend, Christopher Craig, who fired the gun. Craig was too young to be executed. The jury heard that Bentley had shouted, 'Let him have it,' and decided that he was urging Craig to shoot the revolver, not hand it over. Bentley received a posthumous pardon in 1998.

'Can't relax at all': KW, diary, 13 May 1953.

69 'Birmingham is a filthy town': KW, diary, 17 May 1953.

'Norman Pitt is a great bulbous creature': KW, diary, 22 June 1953.

the artistic director: Michael Benthall (1919–74) first directed the Old Vic company in 1944, in *Hamlet*. His partner was Robert Helpmann.

'[Benthall] stood on the stairs of the Vic': letter to Rae Hammond, 5 March 1975.

70 Peter Eade was dismayed at the thought of upsetting Benthall: Williams claimed in his autobiography that he had written in his diary: 'Can't help wondering if I have done the right thing; my savings don't amount to much and I've given up a year's security.' In fact, these words do not appear. By the time *Just Williams* was published in 1985, though, he had already published *Back Drops* (1983), which consisted mostly of fictitious diary entries, and he probably felt no compunction at inventing another one.

Robert Hardy, who was also in the company: Hardy played Ariel in a production of *The Tempest*, directed by Robert Helpmann. *King John* was directed by George Devine; Hardy was the Earl of Salisbury, 'who was an aged knight of great repute'.

'Richard Burton could be absolutely wicked': Robert Hardy, phone interview, Monday 14 April 2008.

'That company was a very intimidating bunch': interview with Melvyn Bragg, Baron of Wigton, at the House of Lords, Monday 14 July 2008.

71 'a sort of psycho neurotic coward': letter to John Hussey, 14 October 1953.

'deplorable', 'utterly mediocre': KW, diary, 20 October 1953.

'because I suddenly felt very bored': KW, diary, 16 January 1954.

'decided not to do so': KW, diary, 26 January 1954.

Peter Brook auditioned and rejected him at the Aldwych: for *The Dark is Light Enough* by Christopher Fry.

72 at the Globe . . . he looked wrong for the part: in *Marching Song* by John Whiting.

'I think John Warrington is pure crap': KW, diary, 15 March 1954.

'He was very kind': KW, diary, 30 March 1954.

'As an actor, poor Alfred [Burke]': KW, diary, 18 March 1954.

a list of reasons to accept: KW, diary, 22 March 1954.

plays by 'Agatha Christie and that tribe': KW, diary, 23 April 1954.

73 he liked the idea less than he had pretended: he continued to be tempted, writing to Peter Nichols on 10 August 1954: 'Of course I like the idea of going out to Durban – all those beaches and sunshine – but all that racial discrimination frightens me soppy. I remember the terrible feeling of guilt which that kind of thing engendered in India.' Years later, he watched a documentary about the interrogation of journalist Ruth First and wrote, 'The sheer police state kind of Nazism in South Africa is something so horrifying that it makes one sick to learn about' (KW, diary, 23 June 1966).

'the usual sort of well-bred, drawing-room nitwit stuff': KW, diary, 3 May 1954.

Traveller's Joy, by Arthur Macrae, was followed by *Suspect*, by Edward Percy and Reginald Denham; Guy Paxton's *Painted Sparrows* ('the dialogue is such filth that I feel like vomiting continually': KW, diary, 24 May 1954); *Give Me Yesterday*, also by Percy and Denham; *Maiden Ladies* by Guy Paxton and Edward Hoile ('never been in such a dreadfully tatty farce before in my life': KW, diary, 7 June 1954), and Emlyn Williams's *A Murder Has Been Arranged*.

It was not the only time he would destroy his correspondence: the other chief instances of damage to the archive were: the destruction of his letters to Joe Orton, after Orton's death; the loss of his files from 1957 to 1963, which probably occurred during a move; the disappearance of his file of carbon copies and letters for 1974, after his death.

critics had been in raptures over Williams in *The Wonderful Visit*: 'Whoever found Kenneth Williams has the touch of genius' (*Evening News*); 'grace and much skill' (*Evening Standard*); 'a real find' (*Sunday Times*).

74 John Fernald (1905–85), former principal of RADA.
'I am amazed to find': KW, diary, 30 August 1954.
Siobhán McKenna (1923–86) died from lung cancer, aged sixty-three.
'I was horrified at being complimented': KW, diary, 28 August 1954.
'The part is not madly easy': KW, diary, 31 August 1954.

75 'Of all the shows I must have seen': Norman Hudis, speaking by phone from his home near Malibu, California, 4 May 2009.
'The Dauphin is written': interview with Nicholas Parsons, 20 January 2008.

76 'business of religion': letter to Annette Kerr, 1 October 1954.

CHAPTER 5
SEPTEMBER 1954–JUNE 1959

77 'Too popular. Quite so. Reely': KW, diary, 1 January 1956.
'rapturously received': KW, diary, 30 September 1954.

78 'Dennis used to bring us food': interview at Ray Galton's home, London, 2 June 2008.
'The comedy style will be purely situation': BBC WAC (Written Archives Centre), Caversham; memo from Dennis Main Wilson, dated 12 February 1954, headed 'Tony Hancock Series – starting in week 43'.

79 'tremendously dramatic, but funny': Dennis Main Wilson (1924–97), interview with Malcolm Chapman for the Tony Hancock Appreciation Society, 1996.
'this elegant, Irving-Garrick-type actor laddie': Dennis Main Wilson, interview with Roger Wilmut, quoted in *Tony Hancock 'Artiste'* (Methuen, 1978).

'Dennis came to us and said': Galton and Simpson interview, Ray Galton's home, London, 21 April 2008.

'I knew I could make this funny': *Just Williams*, p. 78.

80 'With the pudding still to come': *The First Night Party*, first broadcast 2 November 1954.

it 'went very well really': KW, diary, 30 October 1954.

he'd played a judge and a policeman, 'both badly': KW, diary, 6 November 1954.

'He took to it like a wasp': Galton and Simpson interview, Ray Galton's home, London, 21 April 2008.

81 'I sang old cockney songs': KW, diary, 18 December 1954.

'Ken would love to sing': phone interview with Bill Kerr, 14 May 2008. Bill was not expecting the call, but his memories of Williams were fresh and immediate. He had an unfeigned admiration for Williams's brilliance; his own deadpan timing was so automatic, and so marvellous, that he delivered his reminiscences almost as a comic monologue, fifty minutes long, completely unprepared.

the star was 'v. good': KW, diary, 22 December 1954.

82 'the true "lunatic grotesque" tradition': KW, diary, 17 April 1955.

'We wanted to get the show with no jokes': Galton and Simpson interview, 21 April 2008.

83 ''Ere, I'm a commercial traveller': *The Rail Strike*, first broadcast 7 June 1955.

'It brought the house down': Galton and Simpson interview, 21 April 2008.

'like a little dog with his tail between his legs': Dennis Main Wilson, interview with Roger Wilmut, quoted in *Tony Hancock 'Artiste'* (London: Methuen, 1978).

the idea was 'really absurd': KW, diary, 8 May 1955.

'Any old bits'll do': *The Television Set*, first broadcast 14 June 1955.

84 'He was that kind of a mischievous character': phone interview with Freddie Ross Hancock, 10 June 2008.

'Hancock felt slightly threatened': phone interview with Andrée Melly, 18 April 2008.

85 'They used to make each other laugh': Galton and Simpson interview, 21 April 2008.

'fabulous, terribly fun': interview with Fenella Fielding, Russell Hotel, London, 8 May 2008.

86 'He didn't act': phone interview with Andrée Melly, 18 April 2008.

'It was like the end of term': interview with Freddie Hancock, 10 June 2008.

87 'There is simply no point of contact': KW, diary, 7 June 1956.

'He was very obviously camp': interview with Freddie Hancock, 10 June 2008.

'We talked at length about theories': *Just Williams*, p. 92.

88 '"What's life about, Kenny?"': the witticism originated with George Bernard Shaw, in correspondence with Henrik Ibsen. Williams knew this (and cited it in a letter, 30 July 1975). Perhaps a comment by Hancock gave Williams the chance to claim the line for his own; perhaps he simply told the story to Tony. It was certainly apt.

'Went back with Tony Hancock': KW, diary, 29 October 1956.

89 'I had to come on and say': *An Audience With Kenneth Williams*, first broadcast 23 December 1983, on Channel 4.

'If we kept the whole cast': Galton and Simpson interview, 21 April 2008.

90 'They're cutting down': KW, diary, 1 January 1956.

'What's this button?': *The Diary*, first broadcast 30 December 1956.

he had 'hardly any part at all': KW, diary, 21 February 1957.

'I've got the legs for it': KW, diary, 19 March 1957.

two men sharing a room with one bed was 'poofy': *Just Williams*, p. 94.

91 '[Hancock] thinks that set characters': KW, diary, 10 June 1957.

'When Tony arrived': KW, diary, 10 February 1958.

'Tony thought Kenneth': phone interview with Freddie Hancock, 10 June 2008.

92 'Did the Hancock show': KW, diary, 4 May 1958. This entry refers to *The Junk Man*, first broadcast on 6 May 1958 and, as it happens, my favourite *Hancock* episode.

'Did the Hancock show from the Piccadilly': KW, diary 23 November 1958. This entry refers to re-recordings of *The Thirteenth of the Month* and *The New Secretary* for the London Transcription Services for overseas syndication.

'It came as a complete revelation': Galton and Simpson interview, 21 April 2008.

93 'I think that I am quite superfluous now': KW, diary, 7 June 1959.

'Lovely to work with this team': KW, diary, 10 June 1959.

'Hancock doing his pompous bit': KW, diary, 26 April, 1967.

CHAPTER 6
NOVEMBER 1954–JUNE 1957

94 'I could no more share a flat': KW, diary, 5 March 1956.
'Invited to Geoffrey Sharp's party': KW, diary, 27 November 1954.
congenial BBC producers . . . who wanted to cast him: Williams
recorded *The Silver King*, by Henry A. Jones and Henry Herman, for
radio, produced by Archie Campbell, in December 1954. The following month he turned down 'a vague offer' from producer Harold
Clayton, to play Marchbanks in a production of Shaw's *Candida*, as
part of BBC Television's *Sunday Night Theatre* series.
at a leading West End theatre: St Martin's, in West Street, took over
Agatha Christie's *The Mousetrap* in 1974; the play, which had been
showing at the next-door Ambassadors Theatre since 1952, has run at
St Martin's ever since.
(Jules) Henry Sherek (1900–1967) was an innovative producer who
championed T.S. Eliot and Dylan Thomas in the West End.
Beatrice Lillie (1894–1989) comedian and singer, was a film and radio
star, best loved for her anarchic improvisations onstage. Sheridan
Morley's entry on her in the *Oxford Dictionary of National Biography*
observes: 'Lillie's great talents were the arched eyebrow, the curled lip,
the fluttering eyelid, the tilted chin, the ability to suggest, even in apparently innocent material, the possible *double entendre*.' Kenneth Tynan,
reviewing *Share My Lettuce* in the *Observer*, remarked on the likeness
with Kenneth Williams: 'His concentration (which amounts almost to
a squint), coupled with his leer, his bleat and his fanatical resentment of
interruption, suggests a genuine affinity with Beatrice Lillie.'
'As I suspected': KW, diary, 20 January 1955.
95 'a creature called Grey': KW, diary, 25 January 1955.
'a coarse featured actor': KW, diary 25 January 1955.
'The same old Fernald': KW, diary, 3 February 1955.
'There are two main tasks': KW, diary, 15 February 1955.
96 'Lots of giggling': KW, diary, 10 March 1955.
'It would be wholly undignified': KW, diary, 6 April 1955.
97 Orson Welles (1915–85) actor, writer, director, producer and a human
parable on the destructive power of genius without focus.
Peter Sallis became famous three years later in BBC TV's serial *The
Diary of Samuel Pepys*. In 1972, *Last of the Summer Wine* began and
would become Britain's longest-running sitcom, with Sallis as the

put-upon Norman Clegg. His voice is now world-famous from the Oscar-winning Wallace and Gromit animated films. In his autobiography, *Fading into the Limelight*, Sallis writes at length about *Moby Dick Rehearsed*, but Kenneth Williams is given only a fleeting mention. 'Peter Sallis never changes,' Williams wrote after a dinner party given by Gordon and Rona Jackson (KW, diary, 1 December 1972). 'Still smiling like the sphinx and volunteering no information whatsoever.' *Moby Dick Rehearsed* is the play's title in most reference books and biographies, and it is by this name that the cast usually referred to it later. The title on the programme, however, was simply *Moby Dick*.

the story of Ahab and the *Pequod*: Welles played Father Mapple, as he did in the 1956 movie with Gregory Peck, and Ahab; Plowright, in her first West End role, also played Pip the cabin boy. Gordon Jackson was Ishmael, Patrick McGoohan, Starbuck.

98 the effect . . . won critical adulation: 'It is absurd,' wrote Kenneth Tynan in his *Observer* review, 'to expect Orson Welles to attempt anything less than the impossible [. . .] a piece of pure theatrical megalomania – a sustained assault on the sense which dwarfs anything London has seen since, perhaps, the Great Fire.' Milton Shulman in the *Evening Standard* described Welles as 'a black-cloaked wrestler . . . an aggressive organ . . . an artillery barrage caught on a rising and falling wind. He is virtue, evil and ham in about equal quantities.'

Tony Walton . . . saw all but three or four of the performances: 'It was such a dazzling show,' Walton said. He restaged it in New York in 1992: 'I called it *Orson Welles' Moby Dick Rehearsed Remembered* [at East Hampton's John Drew Theatre]. Joan Plowright, Peter Sallis and the few living ones talked to me about it [. . .] Richard Pilbrow, who was lighting designer on both those [*Pieces of/One Over the Eight*] revues – coincidentally, we didn't go together but he saw most performances of *Moby Dick* too. It was staggering.'

began calling him 'Miss Bankhead': a reference to Tallulah Bankhead, who was all sorts of queen in Hollywood.

99 'Kenneth, you bore me': Williams told forms of this anecdote on television and in his autobiography; this particularly wounding version was recalled by Peter Charlesworth, phone interview, 23 April 2009.

'I said, "That's very perspicacious"': from a handwritten script for a recording of BBC Radio 3's *Man of Action*, in which Williams discussed his record collection, 21 December 1976.

The Boy Friend . . . in the West End and on Broadway: at Wyndham's

Theatre (2,082 performances), and the Royale (485 performances), where it made a star of Julie Andrews.

'The problem was to find someone': Sandy Wilson, interviewed from his London home by phone, 15 May 2008.

Welles asked Williams to make films: Welles's plans were constantly in flux, and it is unlikely he had specific cinema projects in mind for Williams. His next two movies as a director, apart from the abortive attempt at *Moby Dick Rehearsed*, were *Touch of Evil* and *Don Quixote*.

in *King Lear*: Welles played Lear, in a wheelchair, at the City Center Theater, with Geraldine Fitzgerald as Goneril and Alvin Epstein as the Fool. It is tempting to imagine Williams, sidling and ingratiating, speaking the Fool's lines in his Snide voice.

100 'it was sheer agony': KW, diary, 18 June 1955.

'but they acted disinterestedly': KW, diary, 26 June 1955.

the star was distracted by his television series: *Around the World with Orson Welles*. Enthusiasts have uncovered miles of incomplete footage that Welles abandoned during his career but no remnant of *Moby Dick* has so far been found.

101 'This week has been sheer disaster': KW, diary, 6 August 1955.

'This show is really frightful': KW, diary, 11 August 1955.

'He was depressed, but we didn't know it': Sally Bazely, phone interview, 19 May 2008.

102 'It is difficult to sustain a standard': KW, diary, 26 October 1955.

'It went well': KW, diary, 2 December 1955.

'At the curtain of one act': Thelma Ruby, phone interview, 26 May 2008.

103 'Woke feeling utterly jaded': KW, diary, 28 November 1955.

'Betty Warren came in': KW, diary, 14 February 1956.

104 'My work suffers': KW, diary, 5 February 1956.

'I could no more share a flat': KW, diary, 5 March 1956.

105 *Hotel Paradiso*: Glenville directed a film of his production, in 1966, with many of the same cast. Derek Fowlds, later known as the junior civil servant in *Yes Minister*, played Maxime. Georges Feydeau (1862–1921) was the author of sixty plays, mainly farces, and the forerunner of absurdist theatre.

Bill Kerr was also in the city: Kerr was appearing in *Teahouse of the August Moon*, adapted by John Patrick from the novel by Vern Sneider, at the Alhambra.

a telegram . . . signed 'Binkie and John': Binkie Beaumont (1908–73) was the *éminence grise* of British producers. His assistant producer was John Perry, who had handled *The Buccaneer*. Williams relished the story that, when Betty Warren had demanded enhanced billing, with the word 'and' in front of her name, Perry had retorted: 'If she's not very careful, it will be "*But* Betty Warren"!'

a Rambler radio: the Rambler portable had a slatted wooden façade and dials on the top. Williams was delighted that there was no interference on the signal; being seven storeys up might have helped, of course.

106 Dennis Main Wilson suggested a radio panel game: he did record a 'test transmission' of an unspecified show for Main Wilson; it was broadcast at 9 p.m. on 4 June 1957.

'Guinness suddenly hissed at me': *Just Williams*, p. 89.

Gabor was the only woman he had ever tried to sleep with: Peter Charlesworth recalled in an interview on 23 April 2009: 'We one night challenged him, we'd all had too much to drink, and we got round to the subject of women. I think it was Ned Sherrin who said, "Kenneth, did you ever go out with a woman?" And he said, "Yes, I did one night, actually." We said, "What? Who?" He said, "Well, it was Zsa Zsa Gabor." And there was a sudden silence. Everybody looked at each other as if to say, "Yeesss . . ." We said, "What happened?" and he said, "Well, we got into bed and she said, 'Kenneth, hit me!' I said, 'What?' She said, 'Hit me! Spit on me! Swear at me!' I said, 'Just a minute, I'm going to write all this down,' so I got up and went home." *We don't believe that's true, do we?*' Charlesworth added with heavy emphasis. 'He was a great fabricator.'

107 'O! for the real courage': KW, diary, 30 July 1956.

'I was X Ray'd and blood tested': KW, diary, 8 August 1956.

Eden was weak, Macmillan a 'mediocre fossil': KW, diary, 10 January 1957.

'The atmosphere is incredibly real': KW, diary, 1 November 1956.

'It was all terribly Victorian': KW, diary, 1 December 1956.

108 'the looking glass world': KW, diary, 11 January 1957.

'a character performance I could easily sustain': KW, diary, 3 January 1957.

Venus Observed: by Christopher Fry. Williams would have played Dominic.

he 'was struck by the nature': letter to John Batchelor, 27 November

1971. Mervyn Peake (1911–68), the author of the *Titus Groan* trilogy, is barely remembered as a playwright; as another biographer, Malcolm Yorke, remarks, *The Wit to Woo* was obscured by the emergence of Osborne, Bolt, Delaney, Pinter, Behan and more.

109 Peter Wood, who had been resident director at the Oxford Playhouse and now held the same post at the Arts, staged Pinter's debut, *The Birthday Party*, at the Lyric Hammersmith in May 1958 and would later direct the disastrous try-outs of Joe Orton's *Loot*.

It was 'wonderfully wonderful': KW, diary, 19 February 1957.

'I *KNOW* it's no good to me': KW, diary, 24 February 1957.

'This is going to be murder': KW, diary, 10 March 1957.

good notices: despite the critics' approval, *The Wit to Woo* ran for just four weeks.

Gordon Jackson (1923–90). His films included *Whisky Galore!* and *The Great Escape*; he became a television star as the butler, Hudson, in *Upstairs Downstairs* and then as the spy chief Cowley in *The Professionals*. He met Rona Anderson on the set of the film *Floodtide*, and they later worked together in *The Prime of Miss Jean Brodie*. They had two sons.

'saw Stanley and Moira off': KW, diary, 7 May 1957.

110 'The more I visit home nowadays': KW, diary, 23 February 1957.

'seems lackadaisical, but he is kind': KW, diary, 10 April 1957.

a treatment: sexual activity: Dr Newman, the diary noted, was 'dying to be gay' (8 January 1957) so it is possible that this treatment could have been provided on the NHS.

'David – a charming fellow': KW, diary, 22–23 June 1957.

'There was a fight': interview with Stanley Baxter, 18 December 2008.

CHAPTER 7
MAY 1957–APRIL 1959

111 'Lots of old pals. It was all delightful': KW, diary, 5 November 1958.

'I must have prevailed on my father': interview with Michael Codron, 21 October 2009. Codron had also staged *Ring for Catty*, and *A Month of Sundays* – 'a desperately old fashioned piece of superficial "comedy" eked out by a mediocre cast with AE Matthews gagging and fluffing through, to the obvious delight of the first night audience. Age is obviously a substitute for talent here' (KW, diary, 28 May 1958).

Bamber Gascoigne: in 1957 a Cambridge graduate, later well known as the presenter of *University Challenge*.

Lyons Corner House was on the corner of Coventry Street and Rupert Street.

112 'all this talk about it being built round me': KW, diary, 13 July 1957.

'Very worried': KW, diary, 21 July 1957.

'Now it is bitterly apparent': KW, diary, 29 July 1957.

113 'Evening papers are excellent': KW, diary, 22 August 1957.

'Schulman is quite a rave': Milton Shulman (1913–2004) was the *Evening Standard*'s theatre critic from 1953 to 1991, and had a reputation for vicious judgments – *Look Back in Anger* was 'self-pitying snivel'.

114 'Mr Williams, dressed in Lettuce green': *Plays and Players*, October 1957, review by Peter Roberts.

Terence Rattigan (1911–77), playwright: Williams had a cameo in his *Harlequinade* at Swansea.

'the funniest man in England': KW, diary, 6 September 1957.

a sketch with Alan Young: Alan Young had his own show on US television in the early fifties, and was later famous as Wilbur Post in *Mr Ed*. A prolific voiceover artist, he is Disney's Scrooge McDuck.

Dick and the Duchess: an American comedy starring Patrick O'Neal and Hazel Court; Ronnie Stevens and Richard Wattis, both friends of Williams, also featured.

Kenneth Horne (1907–69) had presented *Much Binding in the Marsh* with Richard Murdoch from 1944 to 1953.

115 'Fabulous publicity': KW, diary, 24 October 1957.

Ned Sherrin (1931–2007) had qualified as a barrister before he became a broadcaster. He and Williams became friends, and watched trials together from the gallery at the Old Bailey.

'Share My Pisspot' and 'a ghastly TV excerpt': KW, diary, 15 December 1957.

'This time I obeyed him': KW, diary, 21 January 1958.

116 Peter Rogers (1914–2009). His previous credits included *Appointment with Venus*, starring David Niven, and *Time Lock*, in which Sean Connery made one of his first appearances.

a succession of writers: Eric Sykes, who mistrusted film producers, told Rogers to stick his script up his arse; Spike Milligan was on the edge of a breakdown and, so Rogers always claimed, was waving a revolver around when they visited his office at Associated London

Scripts; another ALS writer, John Antrobus, who had worked on *The Army Game*, produced a surreal story that could only have been done on radio.

'The script had been left hanging': Norman Hudis, by phone, 4 May 2009.

the fee 'seemed astronomical': *Just Williams*, p. 100.

'It is wrong that artists be worried': KW, diary, 5 March 1958.

'Bob Monkhouse is sensitive and kind': KW, diary, 9 April 1958.

Gerald Thomas (1921–93) directed all thirty-one of the *Carry On* cinema releases, as well as the television specials.

117 the producer . . . was able to make the film for under £80,000: in fact, for £77,956.

starting rehearsals on *Hancock's Half Hour*: this episode, *The Prize Money*, features Williams as a game-show host. Recording started at 8 p.m.

The Birthday Party: Harold Pinter's first major play, at the Lyric Hammersmith, produced by Michael Codron.

'it was an awful rubbishy play': KW, diary, 19 May 1958.

Michael Bentine (1922–96) was a founder member of the Goons. Kenneth Connor (1918–93) would remain one of Williams's favourite comics all his life, though they had little contact outside the *Carry Ons*; his turn as a quivering hypochondriac was the highlight of *Carry On Sergeant*. Bernard Bresslaw (1934–93) joined the *Carry Ons* for *Cowboy* and went on to make fourteen in the series.

118 an 'interview about "The Army Game" . . . epic banality': KW, diary, 2 August 1958.

'a crock of shit': KW, diary, 2 September 1958.

'daft Victorian comedy': Adrian Brown was speaking to Andy Merriman, in *Margaret Rutherford: Dreadnought with Good Manners* (Aurum, London: 2009). Rutherford (1892–1972) had starred in Ealing comedies such as *Passport to Pimlico*, and later epitomised Agatha Christie's detective, Miss Marple.

the Actors' Orphanage: now the Actors' Charitable Trust; its president is Richard Attenborough.

119 'It seems to me . . . the title': memo, BBC archives, dated 22 August 1957.

Jacques (pronounced 'Jakes') Brown, born Solomon Jacob Brown (1900–75), had produced Horne in *Much Binding in the Marsh*, as well as a number of *Goon Shows*.

Barry Took (1928–2002) became well known to TV audiences in the seventies with the BBC segment *Points of View*, presenting viewers' letters. He contributed the resumé of Kenneth Williams's life, published in the *Oxford Dictionary of National Biography* in 1996.

Hugh Paddick (1915–2000) was an experienced radio, TV and theatre actor who had enjoyed particular success in *The Boy Friend*.

120 Betty Marsden (1919–98), born in Liverpool and brought up in near poverty in Somerset, became an entertainer after her music teacher recognised her talent at the age of six and became her guardian.

Douglas Smith (c.1910–72) joined the BBC in 1955, and was a newsreader on the World Service, the Home Service and the Third Programme.

Ron Moody is best known for his role as Fagin in *Oliver!* though had he accepted the offer to succeed William Hartnell in *Dr Who* in 1969, he might have been equally famous as the second Doctor.

Bill Pertwee became a national treasure for his part in *Dad's Army*, as the ARP warden Hodges.

'Ken Horne took us all to lunch': KW, diary, 2 September 1958.

'Living with J.H. is torture': KW, diary, 30 September 1958.

'Went in to see Frank Jackson': KW, diary, 25 October 1958.

121 'it is perfectly foul rubbish': KW, diary, 26 October 1958.

Joan Sims (1930–2001); one of her first roles had been opposite Stanley Baxter at the Glasgow Citizens' Theatre in the 1951 pantomime, *The Happy Ha'penny*.

'Lots of old pals. It was all delightful': KW, diary, 5 November 1958.

'We didn't expect to make a series': interview with Peter Rogers, by phone, 15 April 2008, from his office at Pinewood Studio. Right up to his death, aged ninety-five, Rogers continued to work daily at the studios, arriving at about 11 a.m. and returning home after lunch. He never lost hope of producing one more *Carry On*, and during this interview talked with enthusiasm about the latest script — *Carry On London*.

Patrick Cargill (1918–96) spoke with a sternly cultivated accent, which Ray Galton and Alan Simpson believed was the model Williams used for his 'professional types' — solicitors, doctors and so forth. Among Cargill's best-known roles is the doctor who requests a full pint from Tony Hancock in *The Blood Donor*.

Jill Ireland (1936–90) was married to David McCallum; she later remarried, to Charles Bronson. After her diagnosis with breast cancer, aged forty-eight, she became a spokeswoman for the American Cancer Society.

'Kenneth baulked at the idea': Norman Hudis, phone interview, 4 May 2009.

122 the Rodgers and Hammerstein version of *Cinderella*: written the previous year as a television vehicle for Julie Andrews. The original American broadcast was watched by an estimated 107 million people. The panto was enhanced by three numbers from the Rodgers and Hammerstein musical, *Me and Juliet*.

123 'took me aside and apologised': KW, diary, 13 December 1958.

'I thought you were really fabulous': letter undated, but evidently written on the opening night, 18 December 1958. Jackson's handwriting, a precise copperplate in close lines of black ink, was unmistakable.

'Children loved the slapstick': KW, diary, 20 December 1958.

'He said, "You were wonderful"': KW, diary, 29 December 1958.

Tommy Steele (b.1930) played Buttons; the part had been written into the show for him. Yana was the stage name of Pamela Guard (1932–89), a singer best known for her hit, 'Climb Up The Wall'.

124 Ted Ray, born Charles Olden (1905–77), was the father of the child star Andrew Ray, who became a friend and correspondent of Williams in the sixties and seventies.

Harold Fielding (1914–2003) handled Tommy Steele's career, and later commissioned the musical *Half a Sixpence* for him.

'Peter Eade telephoned to say . . . 2 performances': KW, diary, 20 January 1959.

'Ted Durante was most hurtful': KW, diary, 28 February 1959.

125 Leslie Phillips met Williams at the Salisbury Arts Theatre, where he was a repertory regular, though the two did not share a stage there. His comments are taken from his autobiography, *Hello, Leslie Phillips: The Autobiography* (Orion, 2006).

'permanently attention-seeking', and 'colossally irritating': Leslie Phillips, *Hello*, p. 205.

Each episode opened with a sketch: for instance, Episode 8, Series 2, opens with a sculptor who must mutilate his *Venus de Milo* to get her out of the workshop door: 'That,' announces Williams, 'was an excerpt from *A Farewell to Arms*.'

CHAPTER 8
APRIL 1959–DECEMBER 1960

127 'Throwing temperaments in sapphire mink': KW, diary, 17 December 1960.

He resisted spending money on possessions: for Peter Sellers, who was Williams's only equal as a vocal comedian, all symbols of status were impossible to resist, and he bought and exchanged cars every few weeks; Ray Galton and Alan Simpson recalled that Sellers was able to leap any waiting list for the latest model – 'The salesmen always knew they'd get the cars back inside the month.' (Interview, 1 December 2008, at Ray Galton's home.)

with a friend called Terry: Duff was the partner of Stan Walker, a former army colleague of Williams.

128 'a fabulously lovely day': KW, diary, 24 April 1959.

Codron had 'found some v. good material': KW, diary, 13 June 1959.

The designer would be Tony Walton: Walton, who was then married to Julie Andrews, had designed *Valmouth*, the Sandy Wilson musical starring Fenella Fielding at the Lyric Hammersmith and the Saville, Shaftesbury Avenue, as well as a Codron production titled *Fool's Paradise*, which opened at the Royal Lyceum in Edinburgh. 'Peter of course wanted to star in it': interview with Tony Walton by phone, from his home in New York, 5 May 2009. Walton designed the posters for both *Pieces of Eight* and its sequel, *One Over the Eight*, featuring pen-and-ink drawings of Williams and Fielding, skipping about with balloons and holding hands, and Williams clutching a glass of champagne.

'Wrote long letter to Codron': KW, diary, 2 July 1959.

'I started to realise': interview with Michael Codron at the Aldwych, 21 October 2009.

129 'asking what is the point of life': KW, diary, 29 June 1959.

'There is no real answer': KW, diary, 31 July 1959.

filming, at Elstree with Tommy Steele: Williams played the vice-consul in *Tommy the Toreador*. 'My bit was horrid and the whole thing stank. It was really ghastly' (KW, diary, 27 December 1959).

'Common as muck + a sycophant to boot': KW, diary, 4 August 1959.

'It was very hard for Peter to sit down': interview with Tony Walton by phone, 5 May 2009.

'I didn't really see': interview with Fenella Fielding at the Russell Hotel, 5 May 2008.

130 'Infuriated by cuts on my sketches': KW, diary, 28 August 1959.
'unadulterated agony': KW, diary, 30 August 1959.
'I cut my leg coming down on the wire': KW, diary, 1 September 1959.
'I was incensed': 2 September 1959.
'It's a disgraceful insult': KW, diary, 8 September 1959.
'Wrote rude letter to Codron': KW, diary, 10 September 1959.

131 'He did something awful before we opened': interview with Fenella Fielding at the Russell Hotel, 5 May 2008.
'After the performance': KW, diary, 30 September 1959.

132 'I've got a viper in this box': three years later, Williams was surprised when, at Drury Lane Theatre to see Margot Fonteyn and Rudolf Nureyev, he met Judy Garland and she asked, 'How is your asp?'
sketch called 'Balance of Trade': this sketch and others from both *Eight* revues are reprinted in *Tragically I Was an Only Twin*, ed. William Cook (Century, 2002).
Peter Cook (1937–95), like Williams, dazzled in so many comic spheres, from revue to television and writing to radio, and possessed talents so ephemeral, that the public could comprehend him only when he was shrunken, as a waywardly hilarious guest on TV chat shows.

133 'Woke feeling awful': KW, diary, 8 October 1959.

134 Williams was fêted by admirers including Julie Andrews: he rehearsed and recorded a television special with Andrews from 3 to 8 November.
'I hate getting up at 6.30': KW, diary, 30 November 1959.
Peter Rogers remembered: quoted in his biography, *Mr Carry On*, by Morris Bright and Robert Ross (BBC Worldwide, 2000).
'On the set it seemed to me': Victor Maddern (1928–93), quoted in *The Carry On Companion* by Robert Ross (Batsford, 1996).

135 'Surely Eric is not so bitter': *Round Mr Horne: The Life of Kenneth Horne*, by Barry Johnston (Aurum, 2006) maps the rift between Merriman and Took in fascinating detail, and includes a long letter from Horne to his producer and BBC department heads, which reveals how difficult it had been to nurse the feuding scriptwriters through the 1959 broadcasts: 'B.O.K. has the reputation of being the happiest show on the air. For one reason and one reason only [i.e., Merriman's temperament] I had my job cut out to keep it so during the last series!'

the backers, including Williams: Williams invested capital in the production, though it is not clear how substantial a sum – his first share of the profits, in February, was £25. Other backers for *Pieces of Eight* included George Borwick (1922–94) who would become one of Williams's closest friends.

'Noise above atrocious': KW, diary, 9 January 1960.

'unfortunately *no* bathroom': KW, diary, 11 January 1960.

136 'To Eade to ask him to speak to Codron': KW, diary, 28 January 1960.

137 'Walked with folks in Hyde Pk': KW, diary, 28 February 1960.

138 'Long letter from Ralph Hallett': KW, diary, 26 January 1960.

'Spencer Tracy was exceedingly good': KW, diary, 28 June 1960.

Pinter's *The Caretaker* 'marvellously well done': KW, diary, 23 June 1960.

Robert Bolt's *A Man for All Seasons*: Noel Willman, who would also become a close friend and regular correspondent, directed *A Man for All Seasons*.

'Some nights it could be rather like a gentleman's club': interview by phone, June 2009, with Richard Caswell, who was a twenty-one-year-old actor when he worked on Sundays at the Spartan, and who became a successful lighting designer.

139 Patric Walker (1931–95) was later the astrologer for *Harpers and Queen*; his *Mail on Sunday* stars column was syndicated to 20 million readers.

140 *Kenneth Williams Reads the Phonebook*: Cf. Peter Sellers reading the lyrics of 'She Loves You (Yeah Yeah Yeah)' in the style of Sigmund Freud counselling Adolf Hitler (recorded 1965, released 1981).

'murder' . . . 'lousy': KW, diary, 1 May 1960.

this time he 'rang Stanley B. who helped me': KW, diary, 14 May 1960.

'Peter Eade arranged fr. me to talk': KW, diary, 8 August 1960.

'I wrote [to] Took to tell him': KW, diary, 25 August 1960.

Michael Codron 'returned from America': KW, diary, 25 August 1960.

his friend Michael Hitchman had been found dead: the cause of death was later discovered to be a brain haemorrhage; presumably the police had initially suspected suicide. Hitchman, a poet as well as an actor, had suffered from serious depressions, and Williams had spent several days with him in 1960, at the seaside or on picnics, trying to brighten his mood.

'I really loved M': KW, diary, 29 October 1960.

141 'Val was here for hours!': KW, diary, 8 November 1960.

a ragbag stitched together in a hurry: Fenella Fielding made her first appearance in the series: her sequence was twelve pages long, but 'it was all shot in a day. We worked very fast. Twelve pages in an ordinary kind of movie would probably take about three days, but I got the feeling as the day went on that if we didn't get to the end they wouldn't bother with it, they'd just leave it.' Interview with Fenella Fielding, 5 May 2008.

'Because Gerry [Thomas] started on me late': KW, diary, 29 November 1960.

Amanda Barrie took the title role in *Carry On Cleo* four years later.

'throwing temperaments in sapphire mink': KW, diary, 17 December 1960.

CHAPTER 9
SEPTEMBER 1960–DECEMBER 1962

142 'I have been taught the severest lesson': KW, diary, 6 December 1961.

'I am not happy': KW, diary, 30 September 1960.

La Notte Brava, also known as *Night Heat* and *Bad Girls Don't Cry*, was a tale of three petty criminals in Rome, written by Pier Paolo Pasolini. One the same bill, Williams saw a film about 'Swedish lesbians', which impressed him less.

'*One Over the Eight* might have come': interview with Michael Codron, 21 October 2009.

inviting him to read plays by David Perry: David Perry's television play *The Trouble with Our Ivy*, a comedy of suburban rivalries, was broadcast with Gretchen Franklin and Dandy Nichols in ITV's *Armchair Theatre* slot in November 1961; the playwright followed it with others for the series.

'I am amazed and naturally disappointed': letter from Michael Codron, 10 October 1960. It begins, 'Thank you for your sheaf of letters which I received this morning.'

143 'Michael dislikes doing a sacking': KW, diary, 5 January 1961.

'Sheila came back to flat': KW, diary, 27 January 1961.

projected from slides . . . a curved background screen: the lighting and the slides were designed by Richard Pilbrow and Tony Walton, who hid two 5,000-watt projectors on towers behind a false proscenium arch.

John Mortimer (1923–2009), playwright, autobiographer and novelist, and creator of *Rumpole of The Bailey*. Williams's understudy on *One Over the Eight* was Ken Loach, the future film-maker who was to direct *Kes*.

144 'Michael Codron said to me': KW, diary, 1 February 1961.

'Dear Michael, I've written you loads of letters': unsent letters, headed Albion/Friday – that is, his hotel in Brighton, on 17 February 1961.

145 'I am typing this': unsent letter, dated 26 February 1961.

146 Susan Sontag defined it in her 1964 essay, *Notes on Camp*: published in *Partisan Review*, republished in *Against Interpretation* (Vintage, 2001). Sontag's *Notes* were partly an extension of another definitive essay, *Avant-Garde and Kitsch*, by Clement Greenberg, published in 1939.

147 'The sceptic finds refuge in irony': letter to Rae Hammond, 10 March 1975.

'I mentioned the bad reviews': KW, diary, 1 May 1961.

Desert Island Discs: On 30 March 1987 Williams returned to the desert island, this time to be interviewed by Michael Parkinson: the only piece of music which he took on both occasions was Jayme Ovalle's *Azulao*, sung by Gerald Souzay. His luxury the second time was a bottle of his favourite cologne, Les Plus Belles Lavandes.

Alexander Cohen (1920–2000) had produced Flanders and Swann on Broadway in *At the Drop of a Hat*, and staged *Beyond the Fringe* there from 1962 to 1964.

'I like Alex more every time I see him': KW, diary, 8 April 1961.

'I have decided not to go to America': KW, diary, 10 May 1961.

148 *Raising the Wind*, directed by Gerald Thomas, was in effect a remake of *Doctor in the House* with music students; it co-starred James Robertson Justice and Paul Massie.

'She said to me when I asked': KW, diary, 9 May 1961.

'I must try to keep up this correspondence': KW, diary, 29 July 1961.

149 'You are a good person to have about': letter from Jo Bolt, 13 September 1961.

'The Police used filthy methods': KW, diary, 17 September 1961.

'When you talk about love, I think you mean idealised love': interview with Melvyn Bragg, Baron of Wigton, at the House of Lords, Monday 14 July 2008.

150 'I think that people who manifest their love': KW, 4 January 1953.

Kerr replied: 'My dear no': KW, diary, 11 January 1953.

'Annette Kerr arrived at 4 o'clock': KW, diary, 7 October 1962.

151 'I told her we ought to go through with it': KW, diary, 16 July 1962.
'I went round backstage': interview with Thelma Ruby by phone, 23 May 2008.
'Lovely sunny day': KW, diary, 31 August 1962.
John Gielgud's arrest a decade earlier: John Gielgud (1904–2000), a leading Shakespearean actor who had also enjoyed Hollywood fame, was convicted in 1953 of 'persistently importuning for immoral purposes' in a public lavatory in Chelsea. He was mocked in the press, and was so deeply embarrassed that he considered suicide, but he returned to the stage after a crisis conference with friends including Binkie Beaumont, Laurence Olivier, Vivien Leigh and Ralph Richardson. When he appeared on the opening night of *A Day at the Sea*, by N.C. Hunter, in the West End, the production was brought to a halt by a standing ovation.

152 'He was a sort of Virgin Queen': interview with Trevor Baxter at his home in Blackheath, London, 18 March 2009.
'Lovely letter from Paul': KW, diary, 18 March 1966.

153 'Lunched with Celia Johnson at the Ivy': KW, diary, 25 January 1960.
'Robin Tutt . . . he's just one of those': KW, diary, 1 April 1960.
'Met Bent Ore Petersen', 'Took her round the city': KW, diary, 3–4 July 1960.

154 'Artistically it has been complete stagnation': KW, diary, 27 October 1961.
'The kindest headline we got': quoted in *The Carry On Story*, by Robert Ross.
'This week will see me into December': KW, diary, 26 December 1961.
Peter Shaffer was already renowned for *Five Finger Exercise*; he went on to write *The Royal Hunt of the Sun*, *Equus* and *Amadeus*. *The Public Eye* was filmed by Carol Reed as *Follow Me!* in 1971, with Topol as Cristoforou and Mia Farrow as Belinda.

155 'I am asking: 1) 6 month release': KW, diary, 15 December 1961.
'v. funny, and I laughed more than I've laughed': KW, diary, 20 January 1962.

156 *Carry On Sherlock*, with Williams as Holmes: 'More than a glimmer of how Ken might have played it,' Hudis added, 'was the way Jeremy Brett played it for real in the television series. He was outrageous, he just went too far and then a step further.'

157 'My dear Ken, to say that we've had our difficulties': letter from Kenneth Horne, 15 February 1962.

Bill Pertwee asked, in a handwritten note brimming with charm, to be excused from contributing to this biography.

'I *feel* I ought to go to Malaga': KW, diary, 28 January 1962.

'I did a terrible load of rubbish ad lib': KW, diary, 15 February 1962.

'full of awful English and dirty Spaniards': KW, diary, 19 February 1962.

'He was mobbed and [. . .] before we had been': Hugh Paddick is quoted in Michael Freedland's *Kenneth Williams: A Biography* (Weidenfeld & Nicolson, 1990), p. 177. He took a cine camera with him; perhaps, in some junk shop, there is a reel of Julian and Sandy's Bona Vacationette.

'full of drears . . . stuck together with stamp paper': KW, diary, 23 February 1962.

'I'd be on the beach sunbathing': Hugh Paddick, quoted in Michael Freedland, *Kenneth Williams*, p. 177.

158 'The south of Spain,' Williams remembered later: interview with David Bruxner, *Topic* magazine, 1 September 1962.

'P. Wood is asking one to do the reverse': KW, diary, 20 March 1962.

'One fluff from me': KW, diary, 11 April 1962.

'somehow this theatre nullifies one's acting': KW, diary, 19 April 1962.

the Globe: now the Gielgud Theatre, in Shaftesbury Avenue.

159 Noël Coward, who was 'full of praise for me': KW, diary, 16 May 1962.

'Harold Hobson prints a fabulous notice': KW, diary, 13 May 1962.

'What a superb performance': letter from Kenneth Horne, 19 July 1962.

'The brilliance of your playing': undated letter from Peter Shaffer.

James Roose-Evans, later acclaimed as the West End director of *84 Charing Cross Road*, which he adapted for the stage.

'Everyone keeps on at me to buy property!': KW, diary, 26 June 1962.

160 'Lunched folks. Pat was there': KW, diary, 25 March 1962.

'the face was askew on the shoulders': KW, diary, 5 June 1962.

161 'He has caused a lot of trouble in the ward': KW, diary, 28 July 1962.

'He is now demanding money from her': KW, diary, 1 October 1962.

162 'Show went OK. Audience good': KW, diary, 15 October 1962.

'I shall be so glad when this wretched inquest': KW, diary, 17 October 1962.

The court records no longer exist: 90 per cent of the coroner's files from that period were discarded during a reorganisation. There is also no record of a police inquiry in the Metropolitan Police Archives or in the National Archives at Kew.

163 'I ordered champagne': KW, diary, 19 October 1962.

'I told her she was NOT': KW, diary, 21 October 1962.

The service was held that Tuesday: catering was provided by the café proprietor and ex-army chum Stan Walker, who was hoping to persuade Williams to finance another business venture, a kennels.

164 Suicide was no longer illegal: the Suicide Act 1961 made it legal for anyone to take his (or her) own life, but illegal for any other person to assist.

'So all in all, she's not done too badly': KW, diary, 28 November 1962.

'It was a good year really': KW, diary, endnote 1962.

CHAPTER 10
JANUARY 1963–APRIL 1964

165 'God has given me the opportunity': KW, diary, 19 November 1963.

'It would be very odd': letter from Robert Bolt, 9 January 1963.

166 she was 'shaking all over': KW, diary, 18 December 1962.

'she puts on an emotional heave': KW, diary, 31 December 1962.

'I think she is the sort of girl': KW, diary, 16 January 1963.

Stott was 'converging on me': KW, diary, 26 January 1963.

'I just walked out': KW, diary, 28 January 1963.

'Told Judith Stott I was not seeing her socially': KW, diary, 30 January 1963. Judith Stott met the comedian Dave Allen the following year and, within six weeks, they were married. They had two children.

167 'Went over to Louie': KW, diary, 15 March 1963.

he kept a ledger: Williams would have loved computer spreadsheets.

'It's driving me round the bend': KW, diary, 23 November 1962.

'I laughed like an idiot': letter from Dirk Bogarde, on Connaught Hotel notepaper, 31 October 1962.

'they can stick their awards': KW, diary, 14 January 1963.

'I said certainly not': KW, diary, 7 February 1963.

168 'I rather wilted a bit': KW, diary, 27 February 1963.

George Rose (1920–88), an actor whose first major success was in Bolt's *A Man for All Seasons*. *Variety* named him best supporting actor, as the Common Man, when the play transferred to Broadway in 1961. He was also acclaimed on Broadway as Truscott in *Loot* and as Henry in *My Fat Friend*. Having echoed Kenneth Williams's career for much of his life, he died within a month of him, on 5 May 1988.

'We had supper at the G+C': KW, diary, 10 December 1962.

Richard Pasco, a Shakespearean actor who became well known on television in the mid-sixties as Cardinal Richelieu in *The Three Musketeers*.

On . . . *Monitor*, he read five poems: the poems, chosen by Williams with the assistance of the director Patrick Garland, and with the interference of Sir Huw Wheldon, who was head of Music and Documentary at the BBC, were: 'Englishmen' by Daniel Defoe; 'Oxford Voice' by D.H. Lawrence; '1805' by Robert Graves; 'The Vicar', part of a series of poetic letters titled *The Borough*, by George Crabbe ('Habit with him was all the test of truth / It must be right: I've done it from my youth'); and 'It' by Ezra Pound. He read a further poem, 'The Great War Major' by Alan Ross, which was recorded but not broadcast because the show overran.

'We enjoyed it enormously': letter from Humphrey Burton, [16 April 1963].

169 'It opens a world of loveliness': KW, diary, 14 May 1963.

'I was pretty hard on him': Richard Williams, interview by phone, 26 January 2009. *Love Me Love Me* was recorded at the end of Williams's run in *One Over the Eight*; it climaxed with a chant that he thought delightfully comic: 'When it comes to love, no one really has it good.' The cartoon told of a man who takes a correspondence course in being lovable: 'After seeing you in *Twice Around the Daffodils*,' Richard told Kenneth, 'I figured you must be about the loneliest guy in town.'

the piece is almost nauseating: this adaptation of *Diary of a Madman* was based on the censored version of Gogol's story that first appeared in the collection *Arabesques* in 1835. Censorship was responsible for the extraordinary, surreal quality of the last line Williams reads: 'Oh, and by the way, did you know? The caliph of Baghdad has a wart, right on the end of his nose.' Gogol had originally written, 'The king of France'.

he was 'strangely nervy + upset': KW, diary, 23 May 1963.

170 'a pan – a symbol of the Animal': KW, diary, 23 December 1962.

'I am . . . quite helplessly writing it': undated letter from Robert Bolt, February 1963.

I'm not at all sure': KW, diary, 27 April 1963.

'The whole thing is so "surprise"': KW, diary, 27 May 1963.

171 Beverley Cross (1931–98), author of the West End hit *Half a Sixpence*: 'What an extraordinary spell Tommy Steele casts over the auditorium! They were hanging on him! It has a delightfully innocent air the whole show and smells of success' (KW, diary, 25 June 1963).

'I said to Mags I don't think': KW, diary, 17 May 1963.

'all v. peasant and quite revolting': KW, diary, 6 June 1963.

'like a ruined graveyard': KW, diary, 12 June 1963.

172 'Sorry to be a nuisance': letter from Peter Rogers, 18 June 1963. The changes would have been for Rogers's own rewrites of the Rothwell script.

'We never wrote a script for anybody': interview with Peter Rogers, by phone, 15 April 2008.

Carry On Cabby: though it starred Sid James, Hattie Jacques and Charles Hawtrey, it was not conceived as a *Carry On*, and went into production as *Call Me a Cab*. Williams always held that he appeared in every *Carry On* until *Up the Jungle* in 1969.

now renamed *Carry On Jack*: after spells of being *Carry On Mate* and *Carry On Venus*.

'fundamental feeling of gloom': KW, diary, 23 August 1963.

'I've spent all my life': KW, diary, 22 August 1963.

173 'My little electric clock': KW, diary, 23 August 1963.

Farley Court: 'I think I will settle on No. 62. This number often re-echoes for me. I was 62 MRS in Ceylon' (KW, diary, 24 August 1963). Both he and his father were sixty-two when they died.

'I suddenly don't want to know': KW, diary, 19 August 1963.

trip to Stratford to see three plays: Peter Hall staged the War of the Roses plays at the Royal Shakespeare Theatre in 1963, with Ian Holm and Peggy Ashcroft.

Jim Dale as a cut-rate sedan cabman: Jim Dale's sedan chair had no bottom; passengers had to walk.

'He used to chat with the crew a lot'; 'People probably think': Alan Hume, interview by phone, 8 December 2008.

174 'it all got v. hot under the collar': KW, diary, 10 October 1963.

'I want to shout, "Do it yourselves"': KW, diary, 22 October 1963.

Louie being 'a doll': KW, diary, 11 October 1963.

Juliet Mills, the sister of Hayley and the daughter of John Mills, was married at that time to Russell Alquist.

'lovely, lovely [. . .] quite adorable': KW, diary, 5 October 1963.

175 'The sky is all pearly grey': KW, diary, 17 October 1963.

The cast of *Gentle Jack* were intimidatingly good: they included Michael Bryant, in the role intended for Burton, and Timothy West, Siân Phillips and Gretchen Franklin.

'What a daft thing to say': KW, diary, 6 November 1963.

a favourite anecdote: this story (which continued in a rambling description of a late supper with Dame Edith, where the night porter farted forcibly as he bent to fetch a bottle of brown ale from a sideboard) is regarded by Michael Parkinson as one of the outstanding highlights of all his chat shows (first broadcast 2 December 1972).

176 'I have waited a long time for this': KW, diary, 19 November 1963.

praising '[your] conscious artistry' and 'your application': letter from Robert Bolt, 19 November 1963.

Ned Sherrin wrote, 'it looks lovely': undated note, received and preserved in his diary by KW, 20 November 1963.

Maggie Smith wielded the fatal sliver of praise: Smith was rehearsing at the National with Olivier in *The Recruiting Officer*, by George Farquhar; Williams and Olivier kept their distance but earnestly admired each other. 'He's got sex appeal,' the National's star told Smith, and of course this compliment was reported. Williams repaid it six months later, when he wrote an adoring letter to Olivier after seeing his Othello: 'I was hoping so much to please you,' returned Olivier, 'as I hope you know, I have such a very deep admiration for you and your work' (letter, 24 June 1964).

'It is a lonely part': KW, diary, 6 December 1963.

177 'disastrous. Not only was it a bad play': Jeremy Rundall's retrospective view was published in *Plays and Players*, January 1966. This periodical had slaughtered the play on its launch: '[Bolt] sends great waves of boredom sluicing through my bloodstream. He juggles pint-sized ideas as if they were ten-ton weights,' wrote Charles Marowitz in the January 1964 edition, which had Edith Evans and Kenneth Williams on its cover.

'Shaffer's brother came round': KW, diary, 24 December 1963. This was Anthony Shaffer (1926–2001), later the writer of *Sleuth* and *The Wicker Man*.

'I am sad that in spite of the cast': letter from Binkie Beaumont, undated but received 23 January 1964.

'I will now confess that the chorus': letter from Robert Bolt, 7 February 1964.

Richard Wattis (1912–75), who had appeared on television with him in *Hancock's Half Hour*, received just £150 for his contribution, compared to Williams's £5,000.

Billy Cotton (1899–1969), dance-band leader, racing-car driver, and radio and TV personality.

178 'I haven't been to one of these': KW, diary, 14 March 1964.

'a soulless waste of time': KW, 3 March 1964.

The worst days left him feeling physically injured: Peter Rogers, when he was encouraging Williams to take the film, wrote a note dated 25 November 1963, which began, 'My dear Kenneth, I can assure you there will be no pain. I would very much like you to play the part . . .' In pencil, initialled and dated 15 May 1964, Williams added the annotation, 'Carry On Spying. There was pain.'

'they hung us upside down': KW, diary, 11 March 1964.

'I was crazy about the theatre . . . Don't you yell at me': interview by phone with Barbara Windsor, 17 January 2010.

'I really love you, Bar': quoted in *All of Me: My Extraordinary Life*, by Barbara Windsor (Headline, 2002).

179 a bad omen for a marriage: for instance, Robert Taylor took his mother on his honeymoon with Barbara Stanwyck, after studio heads decreed their wedding, and John Barrymore Jnr and Cara Williams were accompanied by her mother, who apparently pushed the groom through a window during a row.

'It sounds so romantic': Barbara Windsor, talking to Melvyn Bragg on *The South Bank Show*, September 1994.

'dreary decor, arum lilies': KW, diary, 3 April 1964.

180 'He was an absolute pain on holiday': phone interview with Barbara Windsor, 17 January 2010.

CHAPTER 11
JULY 1964–DECEMBER 1965

181 'It was Felicity's twenty-first!': interview with Michael Codron, 21 October 2009.

'Nobody can teach me anything': interview with Fenella Fielding, 5 May 2008.

'Still looking for IT': letter from Michael Codron, 29 July 1964.

'I introduced him to Joe Orton': interview with Michael Codron, Aldwych, 21 October 2009.

Entertaining Mr Sloane transferred from the New Arts Theatre to Wyndham's on 29 June 1964; the cast included Peter Vaughan, aka Captain Olm from Singapore, which might explain why Williams condemned the 'mediocre acting' in this 'fascinating play' (KW, diary, 6 July 1964).

182 'The story of my life': KW, diary, 13 July 1964.

'It's all SUCH A JOKE': KW, diary, 1 July 1964.

Jean Anouilh's *La Foire d'Empoigne*: it was staged as *Catch as Catch Can*, and broadcast on 30 September at 9.45 p.m. on BBC1. *Poor Bitos* was also an Anouilh play. It opened at the New Arts, at the same time as *Gentle Jack*, to awestruck reviews.

'I said I didn't give a damn': KW, diary, 28 June 1964.

183 'I must be a v. good study': KW, diary, 25 June 1964.

Beyond Our Ken had already parodied: the opening episode of the seventh and final series, recorded 24 November 1963.

The best line was borrowed from Frank Muir and Denis Norden: but who remembers Jimmy Edwards saying the line in *Take It from Here*?

'and expose my cock and everything': KW, diary, 4 August 1964.

'He was in a white rage': Amanda Barrie, in *It's Not a Rehearsal: The Autobiography* (Headline, 2002), confesses she had been struggling with an eating disorder, intermittent drug abuse and the discovery of her bisexuality. In this fragile state, a vindictive Kenneth Williams must have seemed a creature from nightmares.

184 'A lot hit the back of my cloak': KW, diary, 19 August 1964.

'All very malicious and pleasant': KW, diary, 19 September 1964.

a Noël Coward compilation: Coward's lyrics, he boasted in his autobiography, *Just Williams*, were 'too difficult for the average instrumentalist; you need a technical virtuoso' (p. 147).

'He did suddenly get fired': John Lahr, quoting Williams in *Prick Up Your Ears* (Methuen, 1978), p. 234.

'Orton had seen me play': from an interview in the *Guardian* with Tom Sutcliffe, 13 September 1980.

'When the play arrived, I could not see': Michael Codron, quoted in Lahr, *Prick Up Your Ears*, p. 235.

'an embarrassment of choices': KW, diary, 14 October 1964.

185 Binkie Beaumont's proposal of a Victorian farce: 'I am wildly keen that we do another play together and I keep searching,' Beaumont wrote on 6 October 1964. *The Private Secretary*, by Sir Charles Hawtrey, was a three-act farce first staged in 1883 and based on a novel in German by Gustav von Moser. The playwright was so well known in the early twentieth century that one young actor (born George Hartree) adopted his name in the hope of reflected glory.

Harold Challenor (1922–2008) was awarded the Military Medal after a seven-month sabotage operation behind enemy lines in Italy in 1943. He first started to beat up prisoners when he was detailed to guard former Gestapo officers. 'One of them made the mistake of smiling at me,' he explained.

'Orton was obsessed with Challenor': Lahr, *Prick Up Your Ears*, p. 236. Orton and Halliwell had also been arrested: photographs of the doctored books and of all the collages on the walls of the flat at 25 Noel Road can be seen in the reading room at Islington Library.

186 'I should probably have been birched': Joe Orton, interview with Giles Gordon, *Transatlantic Review*, no. 24, 1967. Orton expressed a similar lack of contrition to Eamonn Andrews the same year, on a chat show with Eva Gabor and Bernard Braden.

Sloane's arrival on Broadway: *Entertaining Mr Sloane* ran for thirteen performances at the Lyceum in New York, starring Sheila Hancock as Kath.

'Moira and I had invited Ken': interview with Stanley Baxter, 18 December 2008. Stanley Baxter later played Dr Prentice in the first production of Orton's *What the Butler Saw*, at the Queen's Theatre, in March 1969.

187 'for the length of a normal pregnancy': letter from Michael Codron, undated.

'We did it in black and white': Lahr, *Prick Up Your Ears*, p. 241; Richard Pilbrow, who collaborated with Tony Walton on the innovative revue sets, did the lighting.

188 'If much more of this goes on': KW, diary, 20 January 1965.

'dangerously entertaining': profile by Eric Shorter, *Plays and Players*, April 1965.

Ian McShane, son of the Manchester United footballer Harry McShane, went on to television stardom as the eponymous antiques dealer and detective Lovejoy, and the gunslinger Al Swearengen in *Deadwood*.

'If you'd read the script properly' and 'One continually forgets': KW, diary, 27 January 1964.

Duncan Macrae (1906–67) was, like Stanley Baxter, a graduate of the Citizens' Theatre in Glasgow. One of his last roles was as Rene Mathis in the James Bond spoof, *Casino Royale*.

'I've never heard such an absurd idea': KW, diary, 28 January 1965.

189 'I suddenly realised that the first scene': KW, diary, 31 January 1965.

Geraldine McEwan, much later, played Miss Marple on television as well as Lucia in E.F. Benson's *Mapp and Lucia*, broadcast on Channel 4 in 1985 and 1986.

'The play is a disaster': letter from Joe Orton to Kenneth Halliwell, 9 February 1965.

'It was a mistake not to have plumped': Lahr, *Prick Up Your Ears*, p. 241.

'Near us in the dining room': KW, diary, 8 February 1965.

190 'You haven't got a play here': KW, diary, 11 February 1965.

'It was the most painful period of my life': Lahr, *Prick Up Your Ears*, p. 244.

'They always looked like two delinquent schoolboys': Peter Wood, speaking on *Desperately Funny/Seriously Outrageous* (BBC, 1998).

'P.W. came out of it rather splendidly': KW, diary, 14 February 1965.

'She had to be taken home . . . Everyone on the verge': letter from Joe Orton to Kenneth Halliwell, 19 February 1965.

Donald Albery (1914–88) was the Don of the Donmar Warehouse (Margot Fonteyn was reputedly the Mar). He staged the first London production of Samuel Beckett's *Waiting for Godot* and, with William Donaldson, produced *Beyond the Fringe* in 1960.

'*Loot* was bad': interview with Fenella Fielding, 8 May 2008.

191 'unnecessarily filthy': Joe Orton, interview with Giles Gordon, *Transatlantic Review*, no. 24, 1967.

lines that had been forbidden: the watch committee was prepared to tolerate sexual innuendo, but not references to illegitimate children. The following exchange was shortened:

TRUSCOTT: Where does he engender these unwanted children? There are no open spaces. The police patrol regularly. It should be next to impossible to commit the smallest act of indecency, let alone beget a child. Where does he do it?

HAL: On crowded dance floors during the rhumba.

386

Benedict Nightingale reported that this was performed as:

TRUSCOTT: Where does he engender?
HAL: On crowded dance floors doing the rhumba.

'He would pretend that': Michael Codron, interview at the Aldwych, 21 October 2009.

'It was Felicity's twenty-first!': interview with Michael Codron, 21 October 2009.

192 'The end of *Loot* started my decline': Michael Codron, interview at the Aldwych, 21 October 2009.

a play directed by John Osborne: this was *Meals on Wheels* by Charles Wood, one of the screenwriters on the Beatles movie *Help!*.

'He still wants to die': KW, diary, 20 May 1965.

'I thought tonight, "There is no point"': KW, diary, 29 May 1965.

193 'cascades of salmon pink blossoms': KW, diary, 11 June 1965.

Gordon Jackson was shooting *Cast a Giant Shadow* with Kirk Douglas and Yul Brynner: 'Kirk charming, Yul hasn't appeared (probably having a haircut in Jerusalem).' Postcard from Jackson, Tel Aviv, 16 June 1965. John Wayne and Frank Sinatra also starred.

'We drove to Fedhele': KW, diary, 25 June 1965.

194 'The voice took a bit of getting used to': KW, diary, 23 July 1965.

Dave Freeman would write some of the last *Carry On*s, including *Behind* and *Columbus*.

John Hurt had made his stage debut in 1962, in a play at the Arts produced by Michael Codron, *Infanticide in the House of Fred Ginger*. In 1965 he was on the West End in *Inadmissible Evidence*. He had been considered for the role of Dennis in *Loot*.

Peter Wood 'a shit + a fraud': KW, diary, 14 September 1965.

Roger Longrigg (1929–2000) became a prolific novelist under a variety of pseudonyms, as well as writing histories of horse-racing and fox-hunting. *The Platinum Cat* was his first play, produced by David Conville, who ran the Open Air Shakespearean theatre in Regent's Park.

Caroline Mortimer was the daughter of Penelope, author of *The Pumpkin Eater*, and the stepdaughter of John Mortimer, Williams's one-time sketch-writer; she was also the lover of the former *Carry On* player, Leslie Phillips.

195 'I only had the meat + some beans': KW, diary, 26 September 1965.

'If not, we're all going to be sunk': KW, diary, 27 September 1965.

'Played the Bach Double Violin': KW, diary, 17 October 1965.

196 double the salary: £200 a week plus 7.5 per cent of the gross takings above £2,000.

'My point is – there are two ways': KW, diary, 31 October 1965.

197 'Henry had a cold there': KW, diary, 4 December 1965.

'Frankly, I'm amazed you stuck it'; 'No longer the fear': KW, diary, 10 December 1965.

198 His oldest friend was in Australia: Stanley Baxter was touring with a production of *Chase Me Comrade*, by Ray Cooney.

'Made me change all my arrangements': Stanley Baxter, interview, 18 December 2008.

CHAPTER 12
FEBRUARY 1965–AUGUST 1967

199 'You always talk to the one you *don't* like': KW, diary, 19 February 1965.

'long and boring, all about modern theatre': this and the subsequent quotes are from an interview with Tom Waine and Clive Dennis at their home, 28 April 2009.

201 the published version of Joe Orton's diaries: *The Orton Diaries*, edited by John Lahr, published by Methuen in 1986.

Waine kept all his handwritten notes and letters: I am immensely indebted to Tom and Clive for making available not only their archive of letters, but also their diaries for the years of their friendship with Williams, and for sharing their photograph albums, and their innumerable memories and insights.

202 'I could always take you along if you liked': letter to Tom Waine, 7 April 1965.

203 'she was swirled round': Stanley Baxter, interview, 18 December 2008.

'Replied saying I didn't want to do anything': KW, diary, 1 January 1966.

'Suddenly I was plunged back': KW, diary, 15 January 1966.

204 'more swollen-headed and difficult': letter from Kenneth Horne to Mollie Millest, 24 April 1962.

he took the cast for coffee and cakes: before the pastries, the cast were photographed at Houston Rogers's studio for the sleeve of the latest *Beyond Our Ken* LP; the producer, George Martin, was also there.

205 in the penultimate *Beyond Our Ken*: 'He's in a bad way, he's getting blue.' 'That's nothing, you should hear him at rehearsal.' From the *Forever Amber* episode, broadcast 9 February 1964.

Marty Feldman (1934–82) had been writing with Took since 1954. He became a TV star in the late sixties, in series called progressively *Marty*, *Marty Amok*, *Marty Abroad* and so on; his biggest film role was as Igor with Gene Wilder in *Young Frankenstein*. Feldman chain-smoked up to six packets of cigarettes a day; he died of a heart attack.

a reading from *Lady Chatterley's Lover*: readers who don't understand why this is so risqué will just have to find a copy.

Sir Cyril Black (1902–91) was Tory MP for Wimbledon, 1950–70, and a leading Baptist churchman.

'within reasonable bounds ... to clean this show up': quotes from internal BBC memos in April and May 1965, sent by the Director of Sound Broadcasting, Frank Gillard, and the Chief of the Light Programme, Denis Morris; quoted in *Round Mr Horne* by Barry Johnston (Aurum, 2006).

207 'I'm sick of the self-important posturing': KW, diary, 30 June 1966.

The writers of *Steptoe and Son* were Alan Simpson and Ray Galton, who had achieved even greater success after parting from Hancock.

208 'Jim Dale I like, and Peter Butterworth': KW, diary, 26 January 1966.

Talbot Rothwell (1916–81) began his career writing entertainments as a prisoner of war in Stalag Luft 3: the shows helped to drown the sound of excavation as escape tunnels were dug. He went on to write twenty *Carry On* films, the stage show and three Christmas TV specials.

Alan Hume's Hammer horror movies include *The Kiss of the Vampire* (1962) and *Dr Terror's House of Horrors* (1965). He modestly deflected praise of his work on *Carry On Screaming*, saying, 'I was pretty aware of the type of photography you needed. If the actors are well costumed, lighting can be very helpful and creative.' Interview, 8 December 2008.

'She was v. pleasant': KW, diary, 17 January 1966.

'I must start accepting myself': KW, diary, 11 January 1966.

209 'Peter E. sends me a script for a film': KW, diary, 27 May 1966.

'a raving and rather posh poof': Nicholas Parsons eventually played the part.

Peter Bridge (1925–82), though he discovered Alan Ayckbourn, believed a successful production relied on its stars, not its writer, and so he favoured revivals of Shaw, Wilde and Priestley. 'Few other managers could so serenely allow the so-called new wave of British drama to pass them by,' wrote Eric Shorter in the *Oxford Dictionary of National Biography*.

'Walked to the Old Bailey': KW, diary, 26 April 1966.

210 'I've attended the Old Bailey very regularly': *Just a Minute*, broadcast 11 April 1981.

a letter from Edna Welthorpe (Mrs): Edna Welthorpe's prim, verbose criticisms, sent to figures of authority from hotel managers to business leaders, were always composed in the distinctively irregular lettering of Joe Orton's typewriter.

211 Richard Williams worked on *The Thief and the Cobbler* from 1964 to 1991, before losing the rights to it. The film was finally released, in a mangled form, as *The Princess and the Cobbler*, and recut as *Arabian Knight*. Kenneth Williams returned to the project on several occasions to record voices, including one session with Stanley Baxter: they played four courtiers – Gopher, Goblet, Slap and Tickle.

Wendy Toye (1917–2010), who continued to teach dance into her nineties, was a many-talented actress, director and producer.

'I think that could be done': KW, diary, 9 May 1966.

'fantasies about sexual licence in Morocco': KW, diary, 17 April 1966.

Orton wrote from Tangier at the end of May 1966: 'Dear Ken, excuse the writing and paper – you're lucky not to receive a note written on toilet paper and then only a very outrageous mind would venture to fathom what I'd use for a pen!' Handwritten letter from Joe Orton at Marina Residence in Tangier, with a postscript from Edna Welthorpe, 31 May 1966.

212 'He didn't want advice': KW, diary, 13 June 1966.

Tom Sloan (1920–1970), a man with a stuffy military manner, was the BBC executive who capitalised on Tony Hancock's split from Galton and Simpson, by inviting them to write the *Comedy Playhouse* series that led to *Steptoe and Son*.

'I think it's high time I had a shot': KW, diary, 27 June 1966.

'into completely strange waters . . . I wouldn't throw you': Williams recounted the conversation in his address at Peter Eade's memorial service, on 25 April 1979.

John Law (1930–71) met Williams as a writer on *One Over the Eight*; his most celebrated sketch, co-written with Marty Feldman, starred John Cleese (at six foot five), Ronnie Barker (at five foot eight) and Ronnie Corbett (at five foot one), as examples of the upper, middle and working classes. It was first shown on *The Frost Report* in 1966.

213 a BBC radio discussion programme: *Would You, Should You, Could You?* with Margaret Powell and Lord Cromarty, presented by Derek Walker. An interview on *Late Night Line-Up* followed a week later.

'The despair inside': KW, diary, 7 July 1966.

'A lousy first night': KW, diary, 8 July 1966.

214 'I shot in to that John Law': *International Cabaret*, broadcast 5 December 1966.

'When you're standing on a stage': KW, diary, 30 July 1966.

215 'Ken introduced me to everyone': interview with Tom Waine and Clive Dennis at their home, 14 January 2009.

his job at *The Times*: Tom Waine was a junior executive at *The Times*, before moving to Ulster Television.

Loot opened . . . in the West End: *Loot* opened at the Jeanetta Cochrane Theatre on 29 September 1966, with Michael Bates as Truscott; the director was Charles Marowitz. It transferred to the Criterion in the West End on 1 November.

'LOOT has had the most wonderful notices': letter from Joe Orton, signed 'Joe', headed Flat 4, 25 Noel Rd, London N1, and dated Sunday 16 October 1966.

'Mr Joe Horton must have taken some handling': letter from Edna Welthorpe (Mrs), dated 25 February 1967, who lived, according to the address head, at Halliwell's West Hampstead apartment where he and Orton first lodged together: Flat 3, 161 West End Lane, London NW6.

216 Williams chose to dress in a 'dust-coloured mac': *The Orton Diaries*, pp. 110–13, entry dated Sunday 11 March 1967.

'Sexually he really is a horrible mess': Joe Orton, *Diaries*, 11 March 1967.

Both men loved to talk about sex: cross-referencing Orton's diaries with the full, unpublished text of Williams's journals is revealing: one of the KW anecdotes that JO (13 April 1967) partly remembers, for instance, makes much more sense when it becomes clear that the 'dismal drag queen' in Tangier who wrote a job application that concluded 'keep your legs and your cheques crossed' was Barri Chatt.

217 'When I re-read some of them': letter to Tom Waine, 15 August 1970.

'All sexual depravity': KW, diary, 30 August 1967.

218 'I certainly DID NOT like yr. latest "offering"': letter to Tom Waine, 15 June 1967.

'Listen ducky, if you're going to come straight from work': letter to Clive Dennis, 12 April 1967.

'Joe Orton rang and said how delightful': letter to Tom Waine, 27 April 1967.

219 'I said that all this promiscuity': KW, diary, 7 August 1967.

CHAPTER 13
AUGUST 1967–AUGUST 1968

221 'You can't be childish at 42': KW, diary, 22 February 1968.

Lionel Bart (1930–99) never learned to read or write music, but composed, in addition to his hit musicals *Oliver!* and *Maggie May*, chart-toppers including Cliff Richard's 'Living Doll' and Matt Monro's 'From Russia with Love'. The weekly rental of York Castle was £150 – at a time, as Tom Waine points out, when a first-class upgrade on a flight cost £10. Bart's earnings at his height were estimated to be £150,000. a week; notorious for parties where tumblers full of cocaine and banknotes for his guests were scattered through the rooms, he went bankrupt in 1972.

'Lionelli told me that after remonstration': KW, diary, 4 April 1967.

their flight was diverted: the forty-six-mile hop from island to coast-line was the world's shortest intercontinental scheduled flight. From 1967, Spain refused to allow British planes to fly through its airspace en route to Gibraltar, forcing pilots to make a 90-degree turn when approaching or leaving the runway. Crosswinds sometimes made the manoeuvre too dangerous, and flights were cancelled; at least three of Williams's holidays to Morocco were affected.

Robert Eliot and David Herbert: David Alexander Reginald Herbert (1908–95), whose father was both 15th Earl of Pembroke and 12th Earl of Montgomery; his ancestral home was Wilton House near Salisbury. Montague Robert Vere Eliot (1923–94), younger son of the 8th Earl of St Germans; the family seat was Port Eliot, St Germans, Cornwall.

222 Phil Silvers (1911–85) starred in 143 episodes of *Bilko*. His biggest cinema success was in *It's a Mad Mad Mad Mad World*.

'[He] started another monologue': KW, diary, 6 May 1967.

223 from Sean Connery to Zsa Zsa Gabor: Jule and Sand explain the value

of mystique: 'If you're going to be made into a celebrity, people have got to be intrigued by you, they got to wonder about you, like, take Sean Connery, we all wonder about Sean Connery, don't we, Sand?' 'Yes, we all wonder about him, all right!' From the second series, 29 May 1966.

a five-year ban on the most popular comedian in Britain: Max Miller was barred from broadcasting on the BBC in 1945 after joking that he'd once met a naked woman on a narrow mountain path above a gorge, and hadn't known whether to block her passage or toss himself off.

224 'There's no question but what': KW, diary, 5 May 1967.
'If there is one thing to learn from this': 9 May 1967.

225 Myles Rudge (1926–2007) was a former Bristol Grammar schoolmate of Peter Nichols. He worked with composer Ted Dicks; Bernard Cribbins had big hits with their songs 'Hole in the Road' and 'Right Said Fred'. They had also supplied the theme song for *Carry On Screaming*.

226 telegrams, promising that Howerd would be dropped: Howerd was not dropped; he played Francis Bigger, a conman who puts his back out while exhorting an audience to banish illness with positive thinking.
'When I said goodbye to him': KW, diary, 27 September 1967.
'ommelette': names aside, Williams's spelling was generally excellent. 'Ommelette' was one word he always got wrong, even in the forties, when the double M was unlikely to be a Polari pun.
'All criticism is a form of vanity': KW, diary, 29 October 1967.
a new model, 'fr. £15.19.6!!': KW, diary, 9 June 1967.

227 Williams wrote for nothing: he even refused payment for the cabaret scripts, which enabled a grateful John Law to increase his own fee by 50 per cent.
'cacoethes scribendi', the all-consuming urge: John Coldstream applies this phrase to Dirk Bogarde, in the edited edition of his letters (Weidenfeld & Nicolson, 2008). Despite his numerous novels and volumes of memoirs, and taking into account the years of diaries that he burned, even Bogarde's vast output does not approach the scale of Kenneth Williams's.
'Mon cher Noel': letter to Noel Willman, 2 December 1967.
'Alec Guiness': Williams almost never got names right, unless he particularly liked a person.

'the show at Wyndham's last night': Guinness and Jackson were appearing in *Wise Child* by Simon Gray, with Simon Ward and Cleo Sylvestre. The play was an Ortonesque farce: at one early perform-ance, a theatregoer led his family out, calling, 'I thought you were above this sort of thing, Sir Alec!'

'that awful Redgrave and Sadoff': Sir Michael Redgrave (1908–85) was acclaimed both as a Shakespearean actor and a Hollywood star. Fred Sadoff (1926–94) was Redgrave's personal assistant and later his business partner.

228 'This play about Rosearse and Goldbum': *Rosencrantz and Guildenstern are Dead*, by Tom Stoppard.

230 'Tops tonight [was] the Loathsome Sandy Shore': KW, diary, 24 December 1967.

'I hate figures, but ironically': KW, diary, 19 October 1967.

'If I earn £1,000 I tend to think': *Evening Standard*, 10 August 1968.

without Marty Feldman, Bill Pertwee or the Fraser Hayes Four: Feldman had become a television star, Pertwee was a victim of cost-cutting, and close harmony quartets were antiquated; instead, the cast performed medleys of music-hall hits, which was slightly more up to date. The new writers were Donald Webster, and Johnnie Mortimer and Brian Cooke, who went on to script *Man About the House* and *George and Mildred*.

231 'Williams was the worst (or best)': Brian Cooke, quoted by Barry Johnston in *Round Mr Horne*.

232 'On the set today Gerald said': KW, diary, 14 May 1968.

233 he had guested . . . on *The Eamonn Andrews Show*: the other guests were Carol Channing ('bore'), Topol ('bore') and Matt Busby ('crashing bore'): KW, diary, 2 June 1968.

'I'm off again + not sorry': letter to Tom Waine, 5 June 1968.

234 'I told Tom in the car': KW, diary, 14 August 1968.

CHAPTER 14
SEPTEMBER 1968–DECEMBER 1969

235 'It's all whoops and bonnet': letter from Kenneth Williams to Tom Waine, 3 July 1969.

Nora Stapleton . . . working as a stage manager: Nora had just finished working on a musical, *Mr and Mrs*, based on Noël Coward's *Brief*

Encounter, by John Taylor and starring Honor Blackman, at the Palace Theatre, Manchester.

'We've both of us wasted our lives': KW, diary, 3 October 1968.

'All my dearest love . . . Having come to terms': letters from Nora Stapleton, 31 August 1968, and undated, probably 1968.

'I LOVE YOU KENNETH WILLIAMS': telegram, 30 May 1969. Nora Stapleton (1931–88) died from alcohol-related diseases, four months after Williams.

'Kenneth Heart – Tried to 'phone': letter from Nora Stapleton, 1 June 1969.

236 Richard Williams saw how attractive the actor: phone interview, 26 January 2010.

On the second day . . . he tested it: *Just Williams*, pp. 238–9.

'This voyage is curious': KW, diary, 13 February 1969.

Kenneth Horne . . . had suffered a heart attack: three months earlier, Horne had followed the advice of a faith healer and stopped taking the anticoagulants that his doctor prescribed.

237 Horne's 'particular brand of humour': Forces Radio, recorded 18 February 1969 and broadcast the following day. Williams also sat in for Horne on six editions of *Call My Bluff* that spring.

'You were sensational': letter from Michael Codron, undated.

238 'Done by you, it will be extremely funny': letter from Anna Home, 30 October 1968. Anna Home, producer of *Jackanory*, became BBC Head of Children's Programmes and retired in 1997.

The serial ran in fifteen-minute segments: *Jackanory* was a staple of BBC Children's output from 1965 to 1996.

Ian Messiter (1920–99). *Twenty Questions* was hosted from 1960 to 1967 by Kenneth Horne.

Clement Freud (1924–2009) was a racing enthusiast, nightclub owner, celebrity chef and, between 1973 and 1987, a Liberal MP. Derek Nimmo (1930–99) was an actor famous for playing monks and chaplains in sitcoms such as *Oh, Brother!* and *All Gas and Gaiters*; he was also the founder of Intercontinental Entertainment, whose productions toured all over the world.

David Hatch (1939–2007), was variously head of BBC light entertainment (Radio), controller of Radio 2 and Radio 4, and chairman of both the National Consumer Council and the Parole Board. He was knighted in 2003.

239 'Once he'd found his feet': interview with Nicholas Parsons, Jurys Hotel, Bristol, 20 January 2008.

'I must just write and say': letter from David Hatch, 21 January 1969.

240 'You are here to work until 5.20': KW, diary, 7 October 1968.

What the Butler Saw: the posthumous debut of Orton's last play was at the Queen's Theatre on 5 March 1969.

Sir Ralph 'Face Like A Bumhole' Richardson: KW, diary, 3 November 1968.

241 a two-hander opposite Joan Greenwood: Joan Greenwood (1921–87). The play was *The Au Pair Man* by Hugh Leonard, also starring Donal McCann, at the Duchess Theatre.

The Two Ronnies: the show ran for twelve series between 1971 and 1987, and starred Ronnie Barker (1929–2005), who was a client of Peter Eade, and Ronnie Corbett, later a sitcom star in *Sorry* and now regarded as a national treasure. Bill Cotton noticed their double act at an awards evening and was instrumental in launching their Saturday-night series.

'I'd like you to break out': KW, diary, 15 October 1968.

'I think he's a good man': KW, diary, 15 October 1968.

'He said, "What's the point"': KW, diary, 27 October 1968.

Stop Messin' About: the first title proposed was *It's Bold*, which did stem from *Round the Horne* – unlike 'Stop messin' about', a catch-phrase coined in *Hancock's Half Hour*.

242 John Simmonds had produced the last two series of *Beyond Our Ken*, and all of *Around the Horne*.

'A little of you is a very rich diet': KW, diary, 12 May 1969.

a one-off *Comedy Playhouse* sitcom: *Master and Man* by Myles Rudge.

'I could not attempt this script': letter to Michael Mills, 25 June 1969.

'I quite understand your worries': letter from Michael Mills, 26 June 1969.

'I told you in my letter': letter to Michael Mills, 3 July 1969.

a talk on his life in the theatre, at the '84 Club' in Margaret Street: on 5 March 1969.

243 *Carry On Jungle Boy*: released as *Carry On Up the Jungle*.

a bantering note, with an invitation to lunch: letter from Gerald Thomas, 24 June 1969.

'I am sorry you have apparently . . . I feel this is probably the parting of the ways': letters from Gerald Thomas, 30 June and 3 July 1969.

'Pesaro was Ken's idea': email from Tom Waine, 22 May 2009.

244 'This was only intended to be a little note': letter to Tom Waine, 3 July 1969.

'he said of Barry Took': letter to Tom Waine, 9 July 1969.

'Living with someone always means a denial': letter to Tom Waine, 3 July 1969.

245 'John M[aynard] is coming round at 7.30': letter to Tom Waine, on Rembrandt Hotel notepaper, 20 August 1969.

'brown and white limbs locked': letter to Tom Waine, 28 August 1969.

'He was prone to elaborate': email from Tom Waine, 9 June 2009.

'instead of going home at 1.30': KW, diary, 29 August 1969.

he had recorded another *Jackanory*: 'The Founding of Evil Hold School' by Nikolai Tolstoy. 'We had one rude letter before it even went out,' wrote Anna Home (16 September 1969). 'Some lady saying how dare we frighten children about to start school for the first time!'

246 'I hope you have a lot of new and loving friends': letter from Juliet Mills, 7 October 1969.

'I longed just to stop and break down': KW, diary, 6 October 1969.

'People for whom you have been working': letter from Peter Eade, 7 October 1969.

John Law was now in hospital . . . and was taken into intensive care: at the Royal Brompton Hospital in Chelsea.

'What Blake called the "mental fight"': letter to *The Spectator*, 18 October 1969. It was a response to Christopher Hollis's column, 'Swinging Together'. The magazine did not publish a second letter from Williams.

247 actress and director Shelah Richards: Shelah, or Sheelah, or Shelagh Richards (1903–85); her productions for RTE included Shaw's *Man of Destiny* and Hugh Leonard's adaptation of *The Darling* by Chekhov.

'Easily the loveliest and most talented actress': letter to Ian Little, 23 October 1969.

Simon Brett went on to produce *The Hitchhiker's Guide to the Galaxy* on Radio 4, and is now president of the Crime Writers' Detection Club.

'I am grateful not only for': letter from Simon Brett, 25 November 1969.

'in the bar with the sailors, I was shouting': KW, diary, 27 November 1969.

248 'Of course Ken knew it was a ship': interview with Tom and Clive at their home, 14 January 2010.

'schoolboy cuddles . . . His answer to all the normal urges': email from Tom Waine, 7 May 2009.

249 The noise . . . was 'getting beyond sanity': KW, diary, 16 December 1969.

the first day of run-throughs: rehearsals started at St Mary Abbot's church hall off Kensington High Street, 16 December 1969.

'Oh what's the point?': KW, letter to Robert Eliot, 15 January 1970.

CHAPTER 15
FEBRUARY 1970–JUNE 1973

250 'I adore this woman': KW, diary, 24 February 1971.

the first broadcast [of *The Kenneth Williams Show*]: on BBC1, at 9.10 p.m., 9 February 1970.

the *Mail* review: by Virginia Ironside, later agony aunt of the *Independent*.

'a load of shit': KW, diary, 10 February 1970.

Australia was a byword among British comics for washed-up talent: it was not a coincidence that Tony Hancock was in Sydney when he took his own life in 1968.

251 'fundamental bleakness . . . I wouldn't put it as strongly': email from Tom Waine, 22 May 2009.

'There is no doubt about it': letter to Tom Waine, 23 February 1970.

'the tradeola, 20D[inar] all in': letter to Tom Waine, 24 February 1970.

'Much funnier . . . Clever boy': letter from Peter Rogers, 2 April 1970.

252 'Who . . . is to silence Connor': letter from Charles Hawtrey, 3 October 1969.

'I have to decline because these grand functions': KW, diary, 28 March 1970.

'When offered something which obviously isn't': unpublished letter to the editor, 28 October 1969.

a thirteen-part series: scripted by Myles Rudge, David Cumming and Derek Collyer.

Lord Snowdon, born Antony Armstrong-Jones, portrait photographer, married to Princess Margaret at the time. He photographed Williams in both *Hotel Paradiso* and *Pieces of Eight*.

'Let's face it, we all know it's YOUR show': KW, diary, 10 April 1970.

253 'T+C arrived at 60c': KW, diary, 5 June 1970.

'A dreadful looking woman moving': letter to Tom Waine, 15 July 1970.

254 'having the drinks': letter to Beverley and Gayden Cross, 17 August 1970.

No Sex Please – We're British, by Alistair Foot and Anthony Marriott, opened at the Strand Theatre in 1971, starring Michael Crawford, and ran for eight years.

'There is no gaiety on a cruise': letter to Paul Florance, 28 September 1970.

255 'Mon cher Tom, your letter sounded': letter to Tom Waine, 30 September 1970.

'Ken was like a child': interview with Tom Waine, 28 April 2009.

'Spiritual malaise my arse!': letter to George Borwick, 15 October 1970 (the first of two that day). The ontological creed, a theological conundrum first propounded in the Middle Ages by Avicenna, had preoccupied Williams since Erich Heller explained it to him in the early fifties: it is the circular argument that, since we exist and can conceive of a perfect God, it is inconceivable that God might not exist.

Ingrid Bergman (1915–82) had starred in the 1948 film version of *Joan of Arc*, as well as *Casablanca*, *Spellbound*, *Notorious* and *Gaslight*. Frith Banbury (1912–2008) had been a favourite director for H.M. Tennent since the early fifties.

256 'it rather fizzles out': letter to Beverley Cross, 20 November 1970.

an excuse for avoiding jury service: 'I quite fancy myself in the role,' he wrote to the summoning officer (3 December 1970), 'but I start rehearsals very shortly for a play [. . .] and the management will naturally bill me on the posters.' Ten years later, in February 1980, he ducked out of jury service again, despite his fascination with criminal cases at the Old Bailey; he claimed his habit of impersonating a judge on *Just a Minute* made him an unsuitable candidate. 'I agree with the reasons you give,' the summoning officer replied: 'your presence might liven up proceedings a little too much!' (Letter of excusal, 4 March 1980.)

'spectre at the feast bit': letter to George Borwick, 7 January 1971.

257 The reviews were mixed: Arthur Thirkell was critic at the *Mirror*, Felix Barker at the *Evening News*. Dan Leno, born George Galvin (1861–1904), the best-known comic actor of the music halls (and a

champion clog-dancer), was born in a row of slums where King's Cross station now stands, among the streets in which Williams grew up.

'Another piece of odd casting': *Plays and Players*, Helen Dawson, April 1971.

258 'To them, all wit is really unacceptable': KW, diary, 9 March 1971.

'I ADORE this woman': KW, diary, 24 February 1971.

The broadcaster Humphrey Burton was one of the founders of London Weekend Television. The programme was filmed on Friday 12 February 1971, and screened on Saturday 20 February. Williams wrote in his diary: 'I looked absolutely frightful in it. The eyes like slits and looking every bit of sixty-five.'

259 'I actually don't LIKE Rudge': KW, diary, 23 February 1971.

The actor Hilary Minster became well known as General Erich von Klinkerhoffen in the sitcom *'Allo 'Allo*.

the old mix of stars, has-beens and novelty acts: the Danish singing duo Nina and Frederick, for instance, were the guests on 23 May 1971.

a series written by Rodney Wingfield: R.D. Wingfield (1928–2007) was the creator of Detective Inspector Jack Frost, played on television by David Jason.

260 a desolate evening at 'a lousy restaurant': KW, diary, 22 August 1973.

Kenny had once wooed Joanie with the promise: as told, in a pair of perfect impressions, by Nicholas Parsons, phone conversation, 1 January 2008.

'He said to me one day – we were walking along': interview with Barbara Windsor, 17 January 2010.

261 Williams had been taking Sims to lunch since 1958: 'Lunched at the Vega – I took Joan Sims, she is a good and forthright girl' (KW, diary, 23 July 1958).

'The truth was that friendship with Ken': email from Tom Waine, 8 May 2009.

262 'Your daughter and Ken': letter to George Borwick, 22 December 1970.

'Ah! Gracious sir, your kind remarks': letter to Tom Waine, 17 December 1971.

263 a three-page telegram from Richard Burton: 'HELP ME CELEBRATE MY BIG 40 [. . .] DRESS SLACKS FOR SATURDAY NIGHT IN SOME DARK CELLAR AND SOMETHING GAY AND PRETTY FOR SUNDAY NIGHT DARK GLASSES

FOR HANGOVERS IN BETWEEN LOTS OF LOVE ELIZABETH AND RICHARD',
telegram, 18 February 1972.

'Do you not like to be recognised?': KW, diary, 21 February 1972.

264 *The Betty Witherspoon Show*, also starring Miriam Margolyes, written
by Michael Wale and Joe Steeples, produced by Simon Brett, music
by Neil Innes.

'The whole thing started in such high hopes': interview with Michael
Codron, Aldwych Theatre, 21 October 2009.

Eric Thompson (1929–82) was an actor, part of the Old Vic company
of 1952 with Peter Finch and Robert Donat, who was best-known as
the narrator of *The Magic Roundabout*.

265 'reppy, uninspired pedestrian muck': KW, diary, 24 August 1972.

'The play is light enough': letter, unsent, to Michael Codron, 29
October 1972.

'On the third day, I was subjected to this': letter, unsent, to Michael
Codron, 29 October 1972.

266 'Sticking your bum out': KW, 19 November 1972.

his dentist: John Akester at the Royal Free Hospital.

'It feels WONDERFUL!' and 'He is a darling boy': KW, diary, 6 December
1972.

267 'Everything's Coming Up Roses': this Ethel Merman number from
Steven Sondheim's *Gypsy* – 'Curtain up, light the lights!' – was a
favourite of Williams, who once kicked up his legs so high as he
performed it on set at Pinewood that he fell flat on his back and ripped
his suit.

The reviewers lauded him: the critics were Arthur Thirkell (*Mirror*),
Garry O'Connor (*Financial Times*), Frank Marcus (*Sunday Telegraph*),
Peter Buckley (*Plays and Players*) and Felix Barker (*Evening News*).

268 The landlady . . . was played by Jennie Linden: best known for *Women
in Love*, opposite Glenda Jackson, directed by Ken Russell.

'It represents an appalling betrayal': letter to Michael Codron, 7
January 1973.

'I'm afraid I can't read my own writing': KW, diary, 8 January 1973.

'listing all the idiot tricks' and 'mad drawing out': KW, letter to
Michael Codron, 10 April 1973.

269 Maggie Smith was . . . next door in *Private Lives*: 'What with both he
and his nearest counterpart Maggie Smith currently dominating the
upper reaches of Shaftesbury Avenue with cascading vocals, fluttering
eyelashes and swirling wrists, the area was in danger of taking on the

aspects of high and low camp masquerading as theatre,' wrote Peter Buckley in *Plays and Players*, February 1973.

'She said, "It must have been PLANNED"': KW, diary, 9 January 1973.

'I think they drilled a hole': Michael Codron, interview, Aldwych Theatre, 21 October 2009.

'I had to go on and get laughs!': KW, diary, 2 February 1973.

'MAGGIE came in at 70c': KW, diary, 6 March 1973.

270 Paul was a 'dreary philistine': KW, diary, 30 March 1973.

Toby Rowland (1916–94), joint managing director of Stoll Moss Theatres (with Louis Benjamin), was an impresario who first presented Alan Bennett's play *Forty Years On*, with John Gielgud, and helped Peter Hall make his name as a director.

271 the pyjamas she brought from Selfridges 'felt like cardboard': KW, diary, 9 June 1973.

'The letters pour in with every quack's idea': KW, diary, 21 June 1973.

the waiter's jokes: 'I used to be in the timber trade . . . sold matches outside Woolworth's!' (KW, diary, 25 June 1973).

'We were crawling along': interview with Tom Waine and Clive Dennis, 28 April 2009.

CHAPTER 16
DECEMBER 1972–AUGUST 1977

273 'Critics will say "tired, laboured, unfunny"': KW, Diary, 13 July 1977.

a 'North Country nit': KW, diary, 10 December 1971.

Frank Muir (1920–98) and Patrick Campbell (1913–80), the 3rd Baron Glenavy, were humorists, raconteurs, and team captains on *Call My Bluff*.

'If you are on stage': KW, diary, 2 February 1972.

one critic claimed his stories 'touched greatness': 'Jay's Say' in the *Birmingham Evening Mail*, 4 December 1972. Ivor Jay (1917–2006) was a television critic and the creator and script editor of *Crossroads*.

274 'They all get worked up': Kenneth Williams on *Parkinson*, 17 February 1973.

'Ken went into some tirade': phone interview with Michael Parkinson, 14 September 2009.

Jimmy Reid, shop steward of the Upper Clyde Shipbuilders, a Communist Party member at that time, and now a Scottish Nationalist.

275 'the illiterate mind with a grudge': KW, diary, 10 March 1973.

'I hated that interview': phone interview with Barbara Windsor, 17 January 2010.

'I behaved atrociously': KW, diary, 21 February 1974.

277 *What's My Line* had been a popular panel game in the sixties (and in the US from 1950). Celebrity teams had to guess the occupations of the guests. It was revived on BBC2 from 1973 to 1974, with David Jacobs as chairman. William Franklyn, Lady Isobel Barnett and Nanette Newman were other regulars.

'Tim Rice was altogether charming': KW, diary, 17 September 1973.

'I said it was disgraceful': KW, diary, 6 October 1973.

Pomagne cider: Williams preferred a sweet and cheap German wine called Black Tower.

Chris Serle, a presenter on *That's Life!*, had also been a straight man on *The Dave Allen Show*.

Frederick Russell Harty (1934–88) was a ex-presenter of ITV's arts programme *Aquarius* who launched his own chat show in 1973, as a rival to *Parkinson*. Williams recorded his appearance on 31 October 1973.

'The Crystal Spirit': 'No bomb that ever burst / Shatters the crystal spirit,' from George Orwell, 'Looking Back at the Spanish War', 1942.

a review in *The Times*: by David Wade, 11 May 1974. Though he pasted the review in his diary and refuted its arguments with angry annotations, Williams was also flattered that his anthology had merited comment, and he reprinted the column in his autobiography.

278 'When I said, "The spirit is inviolate"': KW, diary, 30 November 1974.

'Professor' Stanley Unwin (1911–2002) spoke a fluent gobbledegook called Unwinese, which first gained an audience on *The Spice of Life* with Ted Ray.

Mrs Craik's 'Oh, the comfort, the inexpressible comfort': Dinah Maria Mulock Craik (1826–87) wrote as Miss Mulock, Mrs Craik, and Dinah Craik. The quote, from 'A Life for a Life', published in 1859, was made popular when it appeared, set as blank verse, in *The Best Loved Poems of the American People* in 1936. Williams always attributed it to George Eliot.

279 He quoted Mrs Craik to Mavis Nicholson: *Good Afternoon with Mavis Nicholson*, recorded on his forty-eighth birthday, 22 February 1974, and broadcast on Thames TV on 1 August 1974.

280 Fanny Cradock, born Phyllis Nan Sortain Pechey (1909–94), was television's first celebrity chef, a domineering woman whose partner, Johnny Cradock, provided obedient help in the kitchen and also his name (they did not marry until 1977). She was lampooned as Fanny Haddock on *Beyond Our Ken*.

'all so barmy you begin to doubt your sanity': KW, diary, 8 February 1974.

'certainly better than anything I've ever eaten': KW, diary, 11 February 1974.

the WRVS: the Women's Royal Voluntary Service was founded in 1938, and originally gave help to evacuees and families made homeless during the Blitz. Louisa Williams was awarded the WRVS long-service medal, which she wore on her eightieth birthday (20 December 1981) for a portrait photograph with her son.

'Gawd help us! She must want a job!': 'At 1.30 we went out for a walk – first to the Trafalgar Square post office, and then to St James's park. The afternoon was bright and sunny. As we walked thro' the park we saw a middle-aged woman sitting on a man's lap and he was fondling her breasts and she was kissing him rapturously. They were both large and the position (on the park bench) was ungainly ... the whole effect at once clumsy, obscene and pathetic ... his spectacles had misted over and one of his shoelaces was undone. Louie said "gawd help us! She must want a job!" and I said "it must be quite a strain on that elderly man's legs cos she's a weighty looking creature."' (KW, diary, 2 February 1974).

David Hatch ... joined the pair of them for dinner: at Romano Santi, 50 Greek Street, another favourite Italian restaurant.

'I foolishly shouted to some people': KW, diary, 24 October 1974.

281 'One thing I have learned': KW, diary, 11 February 1974.

'There is no way to show this lady': KW, diary, 23 April 1974.

Paul Richardson retired in 2008 as technical director at Sadler's Wells. 'She was a great character'; 'He used to spend a lot of time': interview with Paul Richardson, 29 February 2008, in the café at Sadler's Wells Theatre, Islington.

282 'Williams is the funniest man I have ever met': Simon Brett, quoted by Wilfred De'Ath in the 'Reputations' column of *The Listener*, 24 June 1976.

Cold Comfort Farm by Stella Gibbons (published in 1932) was a send-up of the rural Gothic romance, as though the Marx Brothers were cast in *Wuthering Heights*.

283 he must once have seen something very like it himself: possibly in Tangier.

'heavenly' . . . 'You're better than Mummy': KW, diary, 12 September 1974.

the BBC's *Read All About It*: also featuring the writers Julian Symons (1912–94) and Lady Antonia Fraser.

'I think . . . he'd expected to be able': interview with Melvyn Bragg, Baron of Wigton, at the House of Lords, 14 July 2008. The novels Williams most admired of Bragg's were *For Want of a Nail* (Secker & Warburg, 1965) and *The Second Inheritance* (Secker & Warburg, 1966).

on his way to the Paris Studios: to record *The Year in Question* with Sheridan Morley, Terry Wogan and Lady Isobel Barnett.

he received a postcard: the postcard Codron chose was of Brueghel's *Peasants Collecting Faggots*.

'"That was spooky . . . keep well, M"': KW, diary, 21 March 1975.

284 'the moron's wink and the cretin's nudge': a favourite Williams phrase, which recurs in letters, diaries and elsewhere: e.g. the 'Letter from Kenneth Williams' in the 1970 Durham University rag mag.

'He would be very dismissive of fans': interview with Stanley Baxter, 18 December 2008.

a hotel lounge with 'the worst staff': KW, diary, 21 June 1975.

285 He turned down a detective series on TV: Williams did not record any details, except that the concept was suggested by Ernest Maxin. He was a great fan of police shows, from *Softly Softly* to *Kojak*. Unorthodox, compassionate, lonely, a genius of disguise: all the components of a classic detective series were already present in Kenneth Williams's life.

Christopher Hampton later won Oscars for his screenplays of *Dangerous Liaisons* and *Atonement*.

Helen Montagu (1928–2004). She had just had a critical and commercial success with *The Bed Before Yesterday* by Ben Travers at the Lyric, with Helen Mirren and Joan Plowright.

'"We don't need names"': KW, diary, 16 September 1975.

'I would have adored to have been': letter, dated 'Monday', possibly Monday 27 October 1975: Hattie phoned him the next day to invite him to dinner. He refused and sat alone in Louie's flat, watching *The Benny Hill Show* instead.

Margaret Rose 'Peggy' Mount (1915–2001) made a speciality of roles such as Mrs Malaprop in *The Rivals*, Angelique Boniface in *Hotel Paradiso*, and Emma Hornett in *Sailor Beware!* – all daunting personages. Bryan Pringle (1935–2002) appeared on television for decades in soaps and dramas. Jane Carr was one of Maggie Smith's pupils in *The Prime of Miss Jean Brodie*.

Patrick Garland had first met Williams in 1963, when he directed his poetry readings on *Monitor*.

286 '[Patrick] said, "They didn't understand"': KW, diary, 10 May 1976.

'It has been like a Siberian exile'; 'It's a question': letters to Tom Waine and Clive Dennis, 7 and 9 June 1976.

'Everything depends on a couple of hours': *The Times*, arts pages, 23 June 1976.

287 'I said "it will get SLATED by the press"': KW, diary, 23 June 1976.

'We get large doses of "Carry On Barillon"': *The Times,* review, 24 June 1976, by Ned Chaillet.

John Bratby (1928–92), a vehemently expressionist painter. The curators of the National Portrait Gallery have expressed an interest in hanging the painting; sadly, it cannot be found.

'Financially I'm aware that I SHOULD': KW, diary, 2 May 1977.

288 'like a new-found old key': KW, diary, 6 January 1975.

'We adored Louie': interview with Tom Waine, 28 April 2009.

289 'Sorry about the outburst': letter to Tom Waine, 2 May 1977.

'only in the cause of social harmony': KW, diary, 2 May 1977.

Sid was dead: Sid James, born Solomon Joel Cohen (1913–76), died from a heart attack at the Sunderland Empire Theatre.

290 support to a Richard Harris thriller: *The Golden Rendezvous*, from the Alistair Maclean novel.

strong supporting casts: Beryl Reid and Henry McGee are two of the least painful elements of *Emmanuelle*.

'All my life . . . I am conscious': letter to Gerald Thomas, 16 March 1978.

Paul Morrissey began his career as a director in collaboration with Andy Warhol. He discovered and signed the Velvet Underground.

291 'Critics will say "tired, laboured, unfunny"': KW, diary, 13 July 1977.

'My conversation is endlessly repetitive': KW, diary, 24 September 1977.

'It's being played for absolute reality': *Evening Standard*, Friday 29 July 1977. The 'absolutely real' film included a version of the 'One-Legged Tarzan' sketch that Williams had performed in *Pieces of Eight*.

'Edith Sitwell became an enormous CULT': KW, diary, 2 August 1977.

'I wield my mighty sway': *Just a Minute*, 23 January 1982. Clement Freud challenged: 'Repetition of cult.'

CHAPTER 17
OCTOBER 1969–DECEMBER 1983

292 'The tide is receding and leaving': KW, diary, 26 October 1980.

he had been writing 'just as I speak': KW, diary, 24 September 1965.

'I feel like Lytton Strachey today': KW, diary, 11 October 1969.

293 'I remember the shock': Leicester University rag mag, written 4 November 1970.

'Sonya came + made about six phone calls': KW, diary, 7 June 1974.

'It is the capacity for taking pains': *Radio Times*, p. 5, 22 June 1974.

'Tried doing the rest of the PREVIEW article': KW, diary, 9 September 1975.

294 'Little Jim' by Edward Farmer; 'Billy's Rose' and 'In the Workhouse' by George R. Sims. *Parlour Poetry* was released on the Saydisc label.

Benazir Bhutto (1953–2007) was twice elected prime minister of Pakistan.

Peter Jones (1920-2000) had written, and was about to star in, the sitcom *Mr Big* with Prunella Scales, Ian Lavender and Carol Hawkins.

'analytical and perceptive and entertaining and anecdotal': KW, diary, 26 October 1976.

'If you ever thought of doing a sort of': letter from Anne Powys-Lybbe, 25 October 1975.

'Obviously the burglar was a man': letter from Gordon Jackson, 23 April 1975.

295 its figureheads were well-known actors: they included Vanessa Redgrave and her brother, Corin.

296 'I found it all appallingly depressing': letter to a potential publisher, identified only as 'Stephen', 3 March 1979.

'Every time I turn to it': KW, diary, 2 May 1979.

'I had a play by an old and dear friend': interview with Bill Kenwright, 18 March 2009.

Trevor Baxter had written one other play, *Lies*, which was staged at the Albery with Wendy Hiller and Michael Aldridge. As a television actor, he appeared in *Dr Who* and *George and Mildred*.

297 Gerald Flood (1927–89) had appeared in *Steptoe and Son*, and *The Galton and Simpson Playhouse*. John Barron (1920–2004) was the boss, C.J., in *The Fall and Rise of Reginald Perrin*. Miriam Karlin starred in both runs of *The Rag Trade*, in the early sixties and the late seventies. Barron and Karlin were both leading lights in Equity. Lorraine Chase's line in the Campari ad, in reply to an admirer who wondered whether she had wafted in from paradise, was, 'Nah . . . Luton Airport.'

298 Donald MacKechnie (1938–2003) was the founding artistic director of New York's GeVa Theater, and the author of *Advice to a Player*, which analysed techniques for speaking forty Shakespearean monologues.
'I was getting really quite unhappy': phone interview with Lorraine Chase, 27 February 2010.

299 'I didn't understand much of that play': KW, diary, 30 August 1979.
the critics tried to help them find it: Mick Brown in the *Guardian*, 31 August 1979; the *Express*, 5 September 1979; Francis King in the *Sunday Telegraph*, 2 September 1979.
'Bill rang me . . . and said': interview with Trevor Baxter, at the playwright's home in Blackheath, south London, 18 March 2009.

300 'John Barron used to whisper': letter to Isabel Dean, a fellow Equity councillor, 18 March 1980.
Monkey, from the sixteenth-century novel *Journey to the West* by Wu Cheng'en, had been translated into English by Arthur Waley and published in 1942. A Japanese version of the tale, dubbed into English, was originally broadcast in thirty-nine episodes on BBC1 in 1979–80.
Count Alexander Labinsky, alias Numa Labin (1923–94), a baritone whose professional singing name was Shura Gehrman. Brought up in Birmingham by his Franco-Russian family, he founded Nimbus records in 1957, and pioneered 'surround sound' recording techniques.

301 Roald Dahl (1916–90) had enjoyed a film success in 1971 with Gene Wilder in *Willy Wonka and the Chocolate Factory*.
The Rose and the Ring: by W.M. Thackeray, broadcast from 6 January 1975.

302 'the French soldier crying out': *Just a Minute*, 21 July 1984.
'He would go into a sulk': interview with Nicholas Parsons, 20 January 2008.

'PARSONS was death': KW, diary, 27 October 1980.

303 he listed calligraphy as his primary recreation in *Who's Who*: his first entry in *Who's Who* appeared in 1980, and he barely edited it over the years, except to cite his later work. His other recreations were given as reading, music and walking.

304 His theme was 'the cruel bon mot': KW, *Acid Drops*.

Acid Drops topped the best-seller lists: his royalties were negligible, though – 2.8125 per cent, a figure that was both ridiculously precise and exceptionally low. In the first six months, he sold 126, 000 copies for which he received less than £4,000.

305 'I remember walking along Albemarle Street': Michael Anderson, phone interview, 5 November 2009.

Margaret 'Peggy' Ramsay (1908–91) was also the agent for Robert Bolt, Alan Ayckbourn, Eugene Ionesco, J.B. Priestley and Stephen Poliakoff.

'When I first approached her': David Porter, interview by phone, 3 March 2010.

He turned for advice to Michael Codron: Williams wrote occasional notes to Codron, and gradually their friendship was re-established. In November 1987, Williams visited the producer's home and, gazing at the surroundings, declared, 'Well . . . you've certainly landed with your arse in the marmalade.'

306 David Ryall, a veteran character actor; Grandad in the BBC1 sitcom *Outnumbered*, and Elphias Doge in the Harry Potter series. John Malcolm (1936–2008) was the founder of the Theatre, Chipping Norton, and Edinburgh's Traverse Theatre.

'Your world is entirely *real* to you': KW, diary, 18 August 1980.

Joan Blackham has enjoyed a successful career as a supporting actress on television, in series such as *Judge John Deed*.

'I asked Philip Martin Brown': KW, diary, 22 August 1980. Philip Martin Brown played Dennis.

'His cheek is breath-taking': KW, diary, 1 September 1980.

a 'prize bore': KW, diary, 10 September 1980.

an 'unctuous creep': KW, diary, 15 September 1980.

307 the notices were excellent: all reviews are dated 16 September 1980, and it was not Billington who was the 'prize bore'.

308 'He was a smashing director': interview with Bill Kenwright, 18 March 2009.

Hattie Jacques (1922–80) was just fifty-eight when she died, her health ruined by obesity and heavy smoking.

'All the chums have died': KW, diary, 26 October 1980.

'a juddering mess': KW, diary, 10 November 1980.

309 'He said to me, "Joe's been moaning"': interview with Barbara Windsor, 17 January 2010.

Dave King, born David Kingshott (1929–2002), was a stand-up comic, balladeer and film actor, best remembered now for his role in *The Long Good Friday*, as the policeman, Parky. Williams saw the movie: 'It was all v. glossy and pretentious but the story? I couldn't find it . . . must have been buried somewhere in all the technical cleverness' (KW, diary, 8 March 1981). He liked it well enough to go and see what he thought was the sequel; it turned out to be a horror film, *Friday the Thirteenth*.

'Just slow down and make a point': KW, diary, 16 March 1981.

'I don't seem to have anything else': KW, diary, 18 May 1981.

310 'He didn't travel well': interview with Michael Parkinson, 14 September 2009.

'I said, "My God, I hope"': interview with Bill Kerr, 14 May 2008.

'I asked the steward for an osteopath': KW, diary, 29 June 1981.

311 'He didn't like anyone using his loo': email from Tom Waine, 7 May 2009.

'Washed and shaved and waited': KW, diary, 10 July 1981.

Temik pesticides: Williams, Arthur Mullard and Pat Coombs were insects.

his reading of a poem: Tennyson's 'The Old Order Changeth', from 'The Passing of Arthur' in *The Idylls of the King*.

312 a pantomime satire on the Chinese opium wars: *Poppy*, with music by Monty Norman. Lady Dodo, the widowed mother of Dick Whittington, was played by Geoffrey Hutchings when the play opened at the Barbican Centre; it transferred to the Adelphi and ran for eighteen months.

'noting with dismay that it's a DRAG role': KW, diary, 29 July 1982.

'I said it could be left till the last minute': KW, diary, 22 November 1982.

old friends convulsed with laughter: they included Joan Sims, Nanette Newman, Gordon Jackson, Gyles Brandreth, Peter Nichols, Ted Moult, Ian Lavender, Henry Kelly and Matthew Kelly.

313 'They were all very encouraging': KW, diary, 1 December 1982.

'A brilliant and sustained performance': Mary Kenny, *Daily Mail*, 27 December, 1983. This was one of the first 'Audiences With': previous episodes had featured Jasper Carrott, Dame Edna Everage and Dudley Moore. The format remains popular: *An Audience with Donny and Marie Osmond* was broadcast in November 2009.

CHAPTER 18
JANUARY 1984–APRIL 1988

314 'Nobody should live': telephone interview with Michael Whittaker, 2 July 2009.
'Caught in a shower of light rain': KW, diary, 17 October 1984.

316 There were friends on the teams: Michael Parkinson, Ernie Wise and Shirley Eaton, who had co-starred in *Carry On Sergeant*.
'BOOKS!! Which weigh a ton': KW, diary, 7 June 1984.
'not so much impaired as SLOWED': KW, diary, 10 June 1984.
'fighting the shadows that are closing in': KW, diary, 14 June 1984.
'God! I'd like to be miles away': KW, diary, 6 October 1984.

317 she said, 'Yes, as long as it isn't somewhere posh': KW, diary, 25 February 1986.

318 'In the week, we would often go': telephone interview with Michael Whittaker, 2 July 2009.

319 'When I phoned Kenneth, there was no code': interview with Michael Anderson, 5 November 2009.

320 Orton's biographer offered loyal praise: John Lahr in the *Times Literary Supplement*, 25 October 1985.

321 George Melly was less equivocal: *Sunday Times*, 13 October 1985.
'It is not flattering': KW, diary, 13 October 1985.
It was titled *I Only Have to Close My Eyes*: 'I only have to close my eyes / And I can quickly see – / A castle reaching to the skies / That no one knows but me.'

322 *So You Want Your Shop to be a Success*: co-starring Rodney Bewes and Nerys Hughes, directed by James Cellan-Jones.
three other veteran comics: Tommy Trinder (1909–89), who was the first host of television's *Sunday Night at the London Palladium*; Jimmy Edwards (1920–88), star of *Take it from Here* and *Whack-O*; and Michael Bentine (1922–96). Henry Kelly was the host. A few weeks later Williams appeared again, with Bernard Manning (1930–2007).
a show that 'went like a bomb': KW, diary, 27 October 1984.
farting during *The Public Eye*: Lorraine Chase remembers that this

incident occurred during *The Undertaking*; Williams might have felt that the story was better if he was scolded by Smith instead of Annette Crosbie, but it is likely the anecdote applied to both plays and others besides – farting on stage had always been one of his favourite ploys to torment other actors.

The Mike Walsh Show: Mike Walsh is now a producer and theatre owner.

323 'I keep thinking about this job in Australia': KW, diary, 12 October 1984.
'Michael Anderson phoned': KW, diary, 3 April 1986.
'Everyone there was v. nice': KW, diary, 4 April 1986.

324 'Derek was sweet': KW, diary, 21 April 1986.
Stephen Fry was as nervous as he was: 'I could remember that my Christian name began with an "S" and that I used to be younger, but that was about it,' Fry wrote in the *Literary Review*, June 1986.
'Got home + told Lou I was dissatisfied': KW, diary, 23 April 1986.
The Friday show featured Nicholas Parsons: the other guests were the jazz singer Bertice Reading (1933–91), who had been performing since she was three; Fay Masterson, a child actress, who went on to feature in numerous TV series; Denise Coffey, who had co-starred with Stanley Baxter on his shows, and helped to write them, in the sixties and seventies.
'He went on, and he was absolutely perfect': interview with Paul Richardson, 29 February 2008.
'Must say, if anyone had told me': KW, diary, 26 April 1986.

325 'I think this is all going to be a bit HAIRY': KW, diary, 22 November 1987.
Barbara Kelly (1924–2007) was the former star of *What's My Line*, married to another broadcaster, Bernard Braden.

326 Dr Carlos Bertram Clarke (1918–93) was also a broadcaster who played for the BBC First XI until he was seventy. He was awarded the OBE in 1983 for his work with London's Caribbean community.

327 'load of blacks': KW, diary, 12 June 1987.
'He always used to sit behind me': interview with Dennis Parkinson, 4 March 2010.
'Nobody should live past sixty-five': telephone interview with Michael Whittaker, 2 July 2009.

328 it is not unusual for the son to commit suicide: Robert E. Howard, the author of the Conan tales, shot himself on learning that his terminally ill mother had lapsed into a coma; the comedian Jimmy Clitheroe

took an overdose of sleeping pills on the day of his mother's funeral; the designer Alexander McQueen hanged himself the day before his mother was buried.

329 'Woke conscious of secum': KW, diary, 15 August 1987.

'churning + gurgling': KW, diary, 3 October 1987.

his last television appearance on *Did You See?*: with Ludovic Kennedy and Janet Street-Porter.

'It was rather dreary': KW, diary, 19 December 1987.

'the girl made me go back on it': KW, diary, 25 February 1988.

He appeared before a BBC radio audience: on *The Spinners' Show* for Radio 2, from the BBC's Paris Cinema studio.

'Oh! it was a delight to see him again': KW, diary, 7 March 1988.

330 Fox wrote, pleading that he 'would love you': letter from Robert Fox, 4 November 1987. The play ran for two years and won Maggie Smith a Tony Award when it transferred to New York.

the revival of *South Pacific*: the Rodgers and Hammerstein musical, at the Prince of Wales Theatre, which ran for a year from January 1988.

'Awake since six': KW, diary, 16 March 1988.

an autopsy . . . could discover the cause of his pain: Dr Christopher Pease, who performed the autopsy at the London Hospital, Whitechapel, in April 1988, discovered 'a very large (35mm), deeply penetrating posterior (at the back of the stomach) gastric ulcer, and this was adherent to his pancreas. The stomach wall was intensely congested and inflamed.' The ulcer was not cancerous, and there were no signs that it had been exacerbated by drinking or smoking. Quoted in Wes Butters and Russell Davies, *Kenneth Williams Unseen* (HarperCollins, 2008), p. 33.

331 'It was the last time I saw him': interview with Stanley Baxter at his home, 18 December 2008.

'It was LOVELY being with actors again': KW, diary, 24 March 1988.

'I remember thinking it must be something': interview with Nicholas Parsons, 20 January 2008. Kenneth Williams's last appearances on *Just a Minute* showed him at his funniest and most cruel. One caustic jibe followed Derek Nimmo's remark that Mrs Beeton, author of the Victorian cookbook, was just twenty-eight when she died. 'Oh,' snapped Williams, 'poor bitch!' (*Just a Minute*, recorded 11 January 1988; broadcast 5 May 1988).

332 '18th day of NO SMOKING': KW, diary, 12 April 1988.

His last words were to remind her: after Williams's death, Michael

Whittaker bought a flat for Louie, upstairs from her daughter Pat's apartment in Camden, and provided her with an annuity. Louie died in July 1991, aged eighty-nine; Pat died in September 1996, aged seventy-three.

333 His pathologist: Dr Christopher Pease.
'Oh! what the hell, what's the good?': KW, diary, 3 April 1948.
His final actions, though reckless, were not clear-cut: the coroner, Dr John Elliott, recorded an open verdict.

334 'I thought I actually saw him': interview with Paul Richardson, 29 February 2008.

AFTERWORD

335 'It's fascinating, it's a little defeat of death': interview with Robert Hardy, 14 April 2008.

337 The playwright Trevor Baxter recalled a dinner in Whitehall: interview, 18 March 2009.

338 'Stanley started on about America': KW, diary, 3 November 1967.

339 'You've got such rich veins': interview with Robert Hardy, 14 April 2008.

Bibliography

Barrie, Amanda, *It's Not a Rehearsal: The Autobiography*, Headline, London 2002

Bennett, Alan, *Writing Home*, Faber & Faber, London 1994

Bolt, Robert, *Gentle Jack*, Heinemann, London 1965

Bright, Morris, and Robert Ross, *Mr Carry On: The Life and Work of Peter Rogers*, BBC Worldwide Ltd, London 2000

Butters, Wes, and Russell Davies, *Kenneth Williams Unseen*, HarperCollins, London 2008

Challenor, Harold, and Alfred Draper, *Sas and the Met*, Pen and Sword Books, London 1990

Coldstream, John, *Dirk Bogarde: The Authorised Biography*, London 2004

Coldstream, John (ed.), *Ever, Dirk: The Bogarde Letters*, Weidenfeld & Nicolson, London 2008

Cook, William (ed.), *Tragically I Was an Only Twin: The Complete Peter Cook*, Century, London 2002

Craik, Dinah, *A Life for a Life,* Bernhard Tauchnitz, Leipzig 1859

Davies, Russell (ed.), *The Kenneth Williams Diaries*, HarperCollins, London 1993

Davies, Russell (ed.), *The Kenneth Williams Letters*, HarperCollins, London 1994

Dear, I.C.B. (general ed.), *The Oxford Companion to the Second World War*, consultant editor M.R.D. Foot, Oxford University Press, 1995

English, Christopher (trans.), *Nikolai Gogol: Plays and Petersburg Tales*, World's Classics, Oxford University Press 1995

Fisher, John, *Tony Hancock: The Definitive Biography*, HarperCollins, London 2008

Freedland, Michael, *Kenneth Williams*, Weidenfeld and Nicolson, London 1990

Gammond, Peter, *The Oxford Companion to Popular Music*, Oxford University Press 1991

Green, Jonathon, *Dictionary of Slang*, Cassell, London 1998

Hancock, Freddie, and David Nathan, *Hancock,* Ariel BBC, London 1969

Herbert, Ian, with Christine Baxter and Robert Finley (eds), *Who's Who in the Theatre*, sixteenth edn, Pitman Publishing and Gale Research, London and Detroit, Michigan 1977

Hudis, Norman, *No Laughing Matter: How I Carried On*, Apex, Clacton-on-Sea 2008

Johnston, Barry, *Round Mr Horne: The Life of Kenneth Horne*, Aurum, London 2006

Lahr, John, *Prick Up Your Ears: The Biography of Joe Orton*, Allen Lane, London 1978

Lahr, John (ed.), *The Orton Diaries*, Eyre Methuen Ltd, London 1986

Lewis, Roger, *Charles Hawtrey: The Man Who Was Private Widdle*, Faber & Faber, London 2001

McCann, Graham, *Spike & Co.*, Hodder & Stoughton, London 2006

Mercer, Derrik (ed.), *Chronicle of the Second World War,* Longman Group UK Ltd and Chronicle Communications Ltd, London, 1990

Merriman, Andy, *Margaret Rutherford: Dreadnought with Good Manners*, Aurum, London 2009

Muir, Frank, *The Oxford Book of Humorous Prose: A Conducted Tour*, OUP, Oxford 1990

Nichols, Peter, *Privates on Parade: A Play with Songs*, Samuel French, London, 1977

Nichols, Peter, *Feeling You're Behind: An Autobiography*, Weidenfeld & Nicolson Ltd, London, 1984

Nichols, Peter, *Diaries 1969–1977*, Nick Hern Books, London 2000

Orton, Joe, *Orton: The Complete Plays*, Eyre Methuen Ltd, London 1976

Orwell, George, *Nineteen Eighty-Four*, Secker & Warburg, London 1949

Percy, Edward, *The Shop at Sly Corner*, Warner Chappell Plays Ltd, London 1946

Phillips, Leslie, with Peter Burden, *Hello, Leslie Phillips: The Autobiography*, Orion, London 2006

Plowright, Joan, *And That's Not All*, Weidenfeld & Nicolson Ltd, London, 2001

Ross, Robert, *The Carry On Companion*, B.T. Batsford Ltd, London 1996

Ross, Robert, *The Carry On Story*, Reynolds & Hearn Ltd, London 2005

Ruby, Thelma and Peter Frye, *Double or Nothing: Two Lives in the Theatre*, Janus, 1997

Sallis, Peter, *Fading into the Limelight*, Orion, London 2006

Shaffer, Peter, *The Private Ear/The Public Eye*, Hamish Hamilton, London 1962

Shaw, Chris, and Arthur Oates (compiled and eds), *A Pictorial History of the Art of Female Impersonation*, King-Shaw Productions Co. Ltd, London, 1966

Sherrin, Ned, *Theatrical Anecdotes*, Virgin, London 1991

Silvester, Christopher (ed.), *The Penguin Book of Interviews*, Viking, London 1993

Sims, Joan, *High Spirits*, Partridge, London 2000

Sontag, Susan, *Against Interpretation*, Vintage, London 2001

Tynan, Kenneth, *Curtains*, Longmans, London 1961

Tynan, Kenneth, *Tynan Right and Left*, Longmans, London 1967

Tynan, Kenneth, *Profiles*, Nick Hern Books, London 1989

Webber, Richard, *Fifty Years of Hancock's Half Hour*, Century, London 2004

Williams, Kenneth, *Acid Drops*, J.M. Dent, London 1981

Williams, Kenneth, *Back Drops: Pages from a Private Diary*, J.M. Dent, London 1983

Williams, Kenneth, *Just Williams: An Autobiography*, J.M. Dent, London 1985

Wilmut, Roger, *Tony Hancock, 'Artiste'*, Eyre Methuen Ltd, London 1978

Windsor, Barbara, *All of Me: My Extraordinary Life*, Headline, London 2000

Yorke, Malcolm, *Mervyn Peake: A Life, My Eyes Mint Gold*, John Murray, London 2000

ONLINE

A selection of useful websites:

The Oxford Dictionary of National Biography, at www.oxforddnb.com/index.jsp

Archives, listings and programmes at www.bbc.co.uk

The catalogue of *Beyond Our Ken*, *Round the Horne* and other Williams radio shows, at www.britishcomedy.org.uk

Obituaries at www.guardian.co.uk, www.telegraph.co.uk, www.times.co.uk, www.nytimes.com

Births, marriages, censuses and deaths, at www.findmypast.com and www.ancestry.com

Actors' biographies and movie casts at www.imdb.com

Television, film and radio clips at www.youtube.com and video.google.com

Also: the British Library at www.bl.uk, the Bristol Library at www.bristol.gov.uk, the Joe Orton Collection at www.le.ac.uk, www.joeorton.org, library.kent.ac.uk, www.musical-theatre.net, www.tv.com, www.offth-etelly.co.uk, just-a-minute.info, www.bfi.org.uk, www.amazon.co.uk, www.historylearningsite.co.uk, scotlandonsunday.scotsman.com, www.workhouses.org.uk

Index

Kenneth Williams is referred to as KW.

Theatre, film, TV and radio productions in which KW was involved are shown under his name, with the exception of *Beyond Our Ken*, *Hancock's Half Hour*, *Just a Minute* and *Round the Horne*, which are indexed under their own main headings. Details of the *Carry On* films may be found under the main heading of '*Carry On* film series'.

Annette; Moray, Sonia; Sims,
Joan; Smith, Maggie; Stapleton,
Nora; Waine, Tom; Williams,
Alice Patricia (sister); Williams,
Charles George (father);
Williams, Louisa (mother);
Windsor, Barbara
SEXUALITY: infatuation with
'James', 18; early homosexual
experiences, 18, 25; infatuation with 'Ted', 25; avoidance
of male physical intimacy, 43,
150, 203; hides sexuality from
parents, 43, 48–9; has brief affair
with Oliver Ford, 50–2, 56;
short-lived affair with Laurie
Sellstrom, 56; avoidance of
close relationships, 56; romantic illusion of Rachel Roberts,
60; confesses homosexuality
to father, 62; writes of sexual
frustration to Annette Kerr, 63;
masochistic fantasies, 63, 110,
187, 217; boasts of relationship
with Zsa Zsa Gabor, 106; on
sexual encounter with 'David',
110; has crush on Scott Hylands,
128; frequents the Spartan Club,
138–9; avoidance of sexual
element in friendships, 150; failed
opportunities for marriage, 150,
151, 235; mildness of homosexual encounters, 151–2; seeks
sexual anonymity in Amsterdam,
182; takes vicarious pleasure from
sexual experiences of others,
216–18, 244, 248
WRITINGS: 'Dejection' (poem),
27; 'Regrets' (poem), 27;
'Obbligato Nostalgia' (poem),
27; 'Catastrophic Man' (poem),

27; writes lyrics for 'The
Stranger' (song), 31; poem to
Oliver Ford, 51–2; writes labour
exchange vignette, 65; experi-
ments with one-act playlet, 68;
Observer rejects letter on Craig
trial, 68; *Just Williams* (autobiog-
raphy), 87, 320, 335; *The Kenneth
Williams Diaries*, 92; articles for
Film (magazine), 194, 292; *Acid
Drops*, 303–4, 331–2; *Back Drops*,
304, 335; *I Only Have to Close
My Eyes*, 321

PROFESSIONAL:
FILM: *Trent's Last Case* (1952),
65; *Innocents in Paris* (1953), 67;
The Beggar's Opera (1953), 67,
156; *The Seekers* (1954), 71, 73;
Raising the Wind (1961), 148;
Twice Around the Daffodils (1962),
154, 156, 188; *The Hound of the
Baskervilles* (1978), 290–1; *So You
Want Your Shop to be a Success*
(training video), 322; *see also
Carry On* film series
RADIO AND RECORDINGS:
makes first radio broadcast
(for CSE), 34; *Gordon Grantley
KC*, 52; *The Immortal Lady*, 63;
Twelfth Night, 66–7; *Happy-
Go-Lucky*, 77; *Variety Bandbox*,
81; *Henry IV Part Two*, 104;
Follow the Stars, 117; commer-
cial voice-overs, 117, 254, 277,
287, 311, 316, 321, 329, 331;
Woman's Hour, 140, 270, 293;
One Over the Eight (Decca LP),
143; *Desert Island Discs*, 147;
Diary of a Madman (animation
voice-over), 168–9; *Love Me
Love Me* (animation